✳ INSIGHT GUIDES

Las Vegas
& THE DESERT

APA PUBLICATIONS L

Part of the Langenscheidt Publishing Group

INSIGHT GUIDE
Las Vegas & THE DESERT

Editorial
Project Editor
Martha Ellen Zenfell
Editorial Director
Brian Bell

Distribution

UK & Ireland
GeoCenter International Ltd
The Viables Centre, Harrow Way
Basingstoke, Hants RG22 4BJ
Fax: (44) 1256 817988

United States
Langenscheidt Publishers, Inc.
46–35 54th Road, Maspeth, NY 11378
Fax: 1 (718) 784 0640

Canada
Thomas Allen & Son Ltd
390 Steelcase Road East
Markham, Ontario L3R 1G2
Fax: (1) 905 475 6747

Australia
Universal Press
1 Waterloo Road
Macquarie Park, NSW 2113
Fax: (61) 2 9888 9074

New Zealand
Hema Maps New Zealand Ltd (HNZ)
Unit D, 24 Ra ORA Drive
East Tamaki, Auckland
Fax: (64) 9 273 6479

Worldwide
Apa Publications GmbH & Co.
Verlag KG (Singapore branch)
38 Joo Koon Road, Singapore 628990
Tel: (65) 6865 1600. Fax: (65) 6861 6438

Printing

Insight Print Services (Pte) Ltd
38 Joo Koon Road, Singapore 628990
Tel: (65) 6865 1600. Fax: (65) 6861 6438

©2003 Apa Publications GmbH & Co.
Verlag KG (Singapore branch)
All Rights Reserved

First Edition 2003
Reprinted 2003

ABOUT THIS BOOK

This guidebook combines the interests and enthusiasms of two of the world's best-known information providers: Insight Guides, whose titles have set the standard for visual travel guides since 1970, and Discovery Channel, the world's premier source of nonfiction television programming.

The editors of Insight Guides provide both practical advice and a general understanding about a place's history, culture, institutions and people. Discovery Channel and its website, www.discovery.com, help millions of viewers explore their world from the comfort of their own home and also encourage them to explore a destination firsthand.

Insight Guide: Las Vegas & the Desert is carefully structured to help convey an understanding of Las Vegas, the surrounding area and its people, as well as to guide readers through all the fantastic sights and activities Sin City and the desert can offer:

◆ The **Features** section, indicated by a yellow bar at the top of each page, covers the natural and cultural history of the region in a series of informative essays.

◆ The main **Places** section, indicated by a blue bar, is a complete guide to all the sights and areas worth visiting. Places of special interest are coordinated by number with the maps.

◆ The **Travel Tips** listings section, with an orange bar, provides a handy point of reference for details on travel, hotels, car rental, shops, restaurants, outdoor sports and much more.

The contributors

The guiding hand behind this book was that of **Martha Ellen Zenfell**, who has been the project editor of most of Insight Guides' North American titles. Zenfell's first task was to recruit **Catherine Karnow**, her favorite photographer and visual collaborator on several books, certain that Karnow's distinctive eye was perfect for capturing the glitz, the glitter and the sheer hard work that goes into organizing and running America's best-known playground for grown-ups.

Zenfell and Karnow ran around the Las Vegas Strip in 110° temperature like a pair of dervishes, and got busted for jay-walking when Karnow spied the perfect shot in front of the Monte Carlo Hotel *(see page 139 for the result.)* Karnow

was also given unique access to take pictures in the gaming rooms of Bellagio, the Venetian, Caesars Palace, Paris Las Vegas and the Aladdin; these images are published here for the first time. When the desert was too hot to handle, **Richard Cummins** and **Glyn Genin** filled in the visual gaps.

Meanwhile, **Gina Cunningham** of the Las Vegas Convention and Visitors Authority, with the able assistance of **Karen Silveroli** and **Erika Brandvik**, smoothed the way for Zenfell to go through what seemed like hundreds of boxes of archive pictures to illustrate the history section, selecting images that for the most part have rarely been published.

At the same time, principal writer **John Wilcock**, who has worked on many Insight projects, including the *Insight Guide to Los Angeles* and the *Insight Compact Guide to Las Vega*s, was pounding away on the keyboard. Little of city life escaped his scrutiny, from showgirls and food to the gaming habits of men versus women.

Other articles were penned by **Mike** and **Linda Donahue**, writers who currently operate Little Meadows horse farm outside the Valley of Fire State Park. For more than 25 years, the Donahues have lived in and written about all aspects of Southern Nevada, including desert wildlife and Las Vegas wild life (nightlife).

We are grateful to all the casino public relations directors who allowed us to document such a fascinating city. Many thanks, too, to **David Whelan**, a dab hand at the typewriter who is in the process of perfecting his technique at the tables.

Map Legend

—— - -	International Boundary
----	State Boundary
—•—	National Park/Reserve
----	Ferry Route
✈ ✈	Airport: International/Regional
🚌	Bus Station
❶	Tourist Information
✉	Post Office
✝ ✝	Church/Ruins
✝	Monastery
☾	Mosque
✡	Synagogue
🏰	Castle/Ruins
🏠	Mansion/Stately home
∴	Archeological Site
∩	Cave
1	Statue/Monument
★	Place of Interest

The main places of interest in the Places section are coordinated by number with a full-color map (e.g. ❶), and a symbol at the top of every right-hand page tells you where to find the map.

INSIGHT GUIDE
Las Vegas & THE DESERT

CONTENTS

The eye-popping architectural illusions of the Las Vegas Strip at night

A DELIRIOUS DESERT CITY

Chancers, dreamers, gangsters and entrepreneurs –
all have been lured across the desert to test their luck

D esert springs watered Las Vegas, and the hot-house canopy of arid isolation nourished the town's primary business, which was best conducted away from the prying eyes of the outside world. Since 1920, when Mayme Stocker opened the first casino, chancers, dreamers, gangsters and entrepreneurs have been lured across the desert to try their luck at games of chance.

The lights, the shows, the fortunes turning on the roll of a die – Las Vegas is a world of neon fantasy and eye-popping architectural illusion. Enticements include an indoor parody of the ancient wonders of Egypt, hourly sea-battles, roadside volcano eruptions and surreal reincarnations of Venice, Paris, Luxor and New York. Lush and lavish pools, surrounded by Italian gardens, museums and art galleries with treasures from the ancient and modern world provide, among other things, a breeding colony for a rare human sub-species – the Elvi, otherwise known as the scores of people earning a decent living impersonating the Mississippi rock 'n' roller.

Novelist David Thomson said, "Some believe that Nevada is nothing but that unique international city, not just the fastest-growing metropolis in the United States, but an abiding El Dorado or Hell for the rest of the world. But Nevada is much more and there is no getting to Vegas without crossing the desert first." The city is still spreading itself out and slowly, incrementally, but inexorably conquering the surrounding arid landscape.

The character of modern Las Vegas has been most obviously shaped by three groups of extraordinary individuals: the casino visionaries, a handful of world-class singers and the arcane masters of magic and illusion. All of them brought innovations that shaped the way Vegas has evolved, by drawing their own crowds of devotees from across the States and beyond.

The gaming entrepreneur who reinvented Vegas hospitality was Jay Sarno. His Caesars Palace was the first of the casinos designed and built as an integrated, themed fantasy. The Luxor, Treasure Island, Bellagio, Paris Las Vegas and the Venetian all took their cue from Caesars. From this starting point the city re-branded itself in the 1980s and 1990s as a child-friendly vacation destination, perfect for families. Lately, though, the casino moguls seem to be wearying of the squeal of younger voices, and are swinging their marketing sights back towards adults.

PRECEDING PAGES: at home at the Liberace Museum located just off the Strip; showgirls limbering up for the big time; everybody dreams of leaving Las Vegas richer than when they arrived.
LEFT: neon fantasy in the desert.

Although 90 percent of visitors claim to be attracted to Sin City by something other than gambling, somehow 90 percent of people do find time to play the tables or the slots during their stay, contributing an average of $655 each to the casinos' coffers.

From the world of entertainment, Frank Sinatra set the tempo. Ol' Blue Eyes sang songs for swinging lovers in Las Vegas lounges, and the aristocracy of Hollywood came out to play. The fabled Rat Pack soon followed. When Elvis began his residency at the International (now the Las Vegas Hilton), it was Sinatra who introduced him, a little like passing on the baton. Until the King arrived, the Regent of Rhinestone was the piano player Liberace, extravagant in every way and, like Elvis, commemorated by the town with a museum.

Tom Jones has drawn a steady stream of admirers since the 1970s, and Wayne Newton's personal style of greeting his audience almost individually has made him a perennial favorite. Less well-known but certainly influential are the choreographers and set designers of the Cirque du Soleil. The phenomenon from Montreal has revived the almost lost circus arts to such an extent that visitors come from all over the world especially to see their *O* show at Bellagio.

And then there's magic. Magic is such an integral part of Vegas that no fewer than four museums here are dedicated to the art. The whole city is itself a vast showcase of sleight-of-hand, and it's no coincidence that the magicians' most basic, intimate illusions often involve the manipulation of playing cards, only the throw of a die away from the gaming tables. Every kind of magic is on show here, from the spectacle of Siegfried & Roy's white tigers and the magician's magician, Lance Burton at the Monte Carlo, all the way to the inevitable topless trio of female magicians in the Hotel San Remo's *Showgirls of Magic.*

In all of this evolution and revolution, the downtown area has struggled to play catch-up. Downtown casinos, losing out heavily to the fantasies of the Strip, fought back with the Fremont Street Experience, a six-block overhead light show, and Neonopolis, a recently completed shopping complex. Although respectable numbers of visitors are tempted, not enough of them have stayed to play. A monorail link is projected, but its completion all the way Downtown is a long way off. Still offering many of the best deals for serious gamblers, the slots and tables need company, fast.

Las Vegas' tourist bureau's vice-president of marketing, Rossi Ralenkotter, said "What makes it possible for us to attract 36 million people a year is the fact that we have something for everybody. We found that people are increasingly considering travel as a way to escape and take a break from the current weight of the world." ❏

RIGHT: the *Folies Bergère* embody everything that is glamorous, naughty, nightly and over-the-top in Las Vegas.

BIRDSEYE VIEW, LAS VEGAS, NEVADA

Decisive Dates

300 BC The Anasazi tribe are thought to have inhabited the territory about 60 miles (96 km) north of present-day Las Vegas.

1829 Mexican trader Antonio Armijo's party discovers the area and calls it Las Vegas; *las vegas* is Spanish for "the meadows," or fertile valley.

1830 Caravans of traders begin trekking along the Old Spanish Trail through Paiute Indian land, camping without permission.

1844 Noted explorer John C. Fremont, leading an overland expedition, camps at a site that later

becomes Fremont Street, in downtown Vegas.

1848 The United States acquires the region by treaty after winning the Mexican War.

1855 Mormon settlers build an adobe fort in what is today the Downtown area of Las Vegas to protect the mail route from Los Angeles, California, to Salt Lake City, Utah. They abandon it three years later.

1859 Discovery of the gold- and silver-rich Comstock Lode makes millionaires out of William Randolph Hearst and others. Three white men are killed by Paiutes. An expedition from Fort Tejon, California, kills five Paiutes and leaves their bodies hung from the gallows "as a warning."

1864 Nevada is admitted into the Union during the American Civil War.

1866 – 68 US troops suppress the Paiutes in the "Snake Wars." In the end, 1,000 Indians are force-marched across the desert to Fort Tejon.

1905 The San Pedro, Los Angeles and Salt Lake Railroad (later known as the Union Pacific) makes an inaugural run, and lots are auctioned locally.

1908 Phone lines and water lines are established.

1910 In the first of many policy changes, gambling is outlawed throughout the state of Nevada.

1911 The city of Las Vegas is incorporated. Noted ranch owner Mrs Helen Stewart deeds 10 acres (4 hectares) "for the use of Paiute Indians."

1920 Mayme Stocker opens the first Las Vegas gaming hall, the Northern Club, in Downtown's Fremont Street.

1922 Westside School is built in Mission style for the children of Old Town, the original town site on Washington Avenue along the railroad tracks.

1923 The Hitching Post wedding chapel is built at 228 Las Vegas Boulevard South.

1926 Western Airlines lands its first commercial flight in Las Vegas.

1928 Herbert Hoover, as Secretary of Commerce, steers enactment of the Boulder Canyon Project Act, making way for the Hoover Dam.

1931 The Legislature passes a gambling bill by rancher Phil Tobin to raise taxes for public schools. Construction begins on Hoover Dam.

1935 President Franklin Roosevelt dedicates Hoover Dam.

1941 Tommy Hull builds El Rancho Vegas on land opposite today's Sahara Hotel. El Cortez Hotel opens Downtown.

1942 The Last Frontier Hotel opens, later to be called the Frontier. The Basic Magnesium plant, employing 3,000 workers, opens at Basic, a community south of today's town of Henderson.

1946 The state levies gaming taxes for the first time. The mobster Benjamin "Bugsy" Siegel, a member of the Meyer Lansky crime organization, opens the Flamingo Hotel. He is murdered six months later, allegedly for "skimming the take."

1949 The *Las Vegas Review-Journal*, incorporating earlier papers, is born, followed the next year by the *Las Vegas Sun*.

1950 Las Vegas' population reaches 24,624.

1951 Vegas Vic, the huge Downtown neon icon, is erected on Fremont Street.

1955 The 9-story Riviera Hotel is the city's first high rise. Former heavyweight champion Joe Louis is co-owner of the Moulin Rouge, but black entertainers have to live off the premises. Nevada legislature creates the Gaming Control Board.

1959 In an attempt to control gambling practices in Las Vegas, the state legislature creates the Nevada Gaming Commission.
1960 The El Rancho Vegas burns down. Las Vegas' population reaches 64,405.
1966 Howard Hughes arrives to buy casinos and live in a penthouse on top of the Desert Inn.
1967 Nevada's legislature allows publicly traded corporations to obtain gambling licenses.
1970 Las Vegas' population doubles to 125,787.
1975 Nevada gaming revenues exceed $1 billion.
1977 The gaming revenues in Clark County – in which Las Vegas is resident – exceed $1 billion.
1989 The Mirage casino and hotel opens with 3,039 rooms.
1990 Las Vegas' population doubles again in just a decade to reach 258,295. Car saleswoman Jan Jones is elected mayor of Las Vegas. Chinese-American Cheryl Lau becomes the Secretary of State. (Nevada's Asian population is 3 percent.)
1992 The success of Warren Beatty's movie *Bugsy* prompts the Flamingo Hilton to open the Bugsy Celebrity Theater.
1993 The Dunes' owner, Steve Wynn, demolishes Bugsy Siegel's office to make way for a new resort. Treasure Island and the Luxor open. The MGM Grand opens as the world's biggest resort, with 5,005 rooms. Nevada gaming revenues are more than $6 billion.
1994 Fremont Street is closed to traffic as work begins on the Fremont Street Experience. Nonstop regular charter flight services from Europe begin. Pedestrian skywalks are built over the intersection of Tropicana Boulevard and the Strip. Buffalo Bill's, in the town of Stateline, and Boulder Station Casino on Boulder Highway both open.
1995 Clark County population tops one million. Clark County casino gaming revenues are $5.7 billion – 78 percent of the US total. A $25 million monorail between the MGM Grand and Bally's opens on the east side of the Strip. Construction begins on the hotel-casino Bellagio. The Fremont Street Experience opens to woo visitors away from the Strip to Downtown.
1996 The town of Stateline on the California border is renamed Primm, as suggested by its founder Ernest Primm's postman. Wayne Newton celebrates his 25,000th Las Vegas performance.

PRECEDING PAGES: Las Vegas, 1909.
LEFT: Vegas' Old Mormon Fort, established in 1855, is Nevada's oldest building.
RIGHT: the Venetian, built less than 150 years later.

Siegfried & Roy celebrate their 15,000th Las Vegas performance. A tunnel under the Strip is finally completed: the Desert Inn Road arterial. The Monte Carlo and the Stratosphere Tower open on the Strip. The Sands is imploded to clear the way for the Venetian Hotel and Resort with 6,000 suites, the largest hotel to date.
1997 New York-New York opens, initially welcoming 100,000 visitors a day.
1998 The Aladdin Hotel is imploded. Bellagio opens, billed as the most expensive hotel in the world (costing $1.7 billion). A 66-year-old Las Vegas resident wins a $27 million jackpot at the Palace Station Hotel Casino.

1999 Paris Las Vegas resort opens with a replica of the Eiffel Tower. Barbra Streisand is reputedly paid $1 million to open celebrations for the new millennium.
2000 The Venetian opens. Las Vegas now has 19 of the world's 20 biggest hotels and attracts 36 million visitors per year.
2002 Nevada is the fastest-growing state in the US. Meeting with opposition from Nevada (and a veto, subsequently overridden, by Governor Kenny Guinn), the Federal government gets approval to allow shipments of nuclear waste to a permanent burial site in Yucca Mountain, 100 miles (160 km) north of Vegas. The US Energy Authority License application is due in December, 2004. ❑

EARLY YEARS

For centuries, Native Americans lived peacefully in the desert,

but the discovery of water, precious metals and the railroad changed this forever

L as Vegas – Spanish for "the meadows," or fertile valley – grew around an oasis in the desert, but the valley wasn't always so harsh and arid as it is today. In 1993, construction workers in Nevada uncovered the remains of a Columbian woolly mammoth. As well as halting construction, this 8,000–15,000-year-old beast indicated that in prehistoric times the terrain was sympathetic enough to nourish life in relative abundance. Hidden for centuries from all but Native Americans, the Las Vegas Valley oasis was protected from discovery by the surrounding harsh and unforgiving desert.

The Paiute Indians had adapted over the centuries to survive in what seemed to be a barren, inhospitable terrain by careful husbandry in a semi-nomadic existence. They planted corn and squash in the well-watered areas and timed their return to when the crops were ready. Judging by remains discovered at Tule Springs, an archeological site in the northwest of the valley, they hunted caribou, mammoths and bison.

300 BC

There are traces of the so-called Archaic Indians, a foraging culture of hunters who harvested mesquite and cholla fruit. As early as 300 BC the Anasazi who had settled about 60 miles (96 km) north of the present-day city, along the Muddy and Virgin rivers, were known for their basket-making skills. The prehistoric Native Americans were hunter-gatherers who collected seeds and pods from cacti, yucca and agave, and hunted rabbits, coyotes and rodents in the desert, heading into the mountains after deer and Bighorn sheep. Annual expeditions led to still higher elevations to collect pinon nuts.

The first non-Indian person known to have discovered the springs was a young Mexican scout, Rafael Rivera, who came with a party led along the Spanish Trail to Los Angeles by Mexican

trader Antonio Armijo. Rivera was an experienced scout, and in search of water. The exact date of the find is unknown, but he is thought to have left the party around Christmas 1829 and made his momentous discovery sometime in the next few weeks. Over the following 30 years, hundreds of traders, miners, soldiers and pioneers

traveled along the Old Spanish Trail, previously known as the Paiute Trail, between what is now Abiquiu, New Mexico and San Gabriel, California. About 135 miles (217 km) of the trail crosses the state of Nevada.

Although the abundant spring water discovered at Las Vegas eased some of the rigors for Spanish traders – and hastened the rush West for California gold – it didn't make the journey much less arduous. For the preceding hundreds, and maybe thousands of years, the whole region had been covered in marshes with vegetation nurtured by the water, but the marsh receded and gave way to desert. Rivers disappeared beneath the surface, and what had been teeming wetlands

LEFT: trapping a woolly mammoth; in 1993 a prehistoric mammoth was discovered in the desert.
RIGHT: mountainman John Moss and Tercherum, a Paiute chief, at Fort Mohave in the 1860s.

transformed into an unforgiving baked landscape, though underground water surfaced to nourish luxuriant plants and creating welcome oases.

The incursions of the pioneers were, of course, disastrous for the Paiute Indians. By the 1830s, the traders and travelers who camped without permission at Paiute home sites near springs and streams were becoming a menace. Their stock damaged the plant life and they depleted the land's resources by shooting the game, and sometimes the Indians too. The Paiutes were prepared to defend their way of life, and mounted raids on mines, settlements and stagecoaches. When Indians attacked the intruders in 1859 troops from

Fort Tejon, north of modern Los Angeles, mounted a punitive expedition. Federal troops were preoccupied with the American Civil War from 1861 to 1865, but from 1866 to 1868 engaged in what became known as the "Snake Wars," and the Paiutes were ultimately force-marched into a reservation at Fort Tejon.

The United States acquired the region after winning the Mexican War in 1848, and just seven years later the Mormons arrived. Leader William Bringhurst was the man in charge of 30 settlers, despatched by Brigham Young to establish a fort for protection of the mail route between Los Angeles and Salt Lake City. The fruit trees and

MORMONS IN THE MODERN ERA

By the 21st century, when nearly one quarter of local jobs were in casinos, Mormons – prized for their integrity – filed top posts. John Marz, vice president for corporate marketing at Mandalay Resorts, says: "People just wouldn't be here without these jobs. For me it came down to 'can you function in the job and still be a good Church member?'"

In his book *Saints in Babylon: Mormons and Las Vegas* Kenric F. Ward said that, "While Church leaders remain queasy about gambling – regularly denouncing it as a pernicious pastime and fighting its importation into other states – Latter Day Saints in Nevada have played a major role in regulating the business, and in some cases

promoting it." In 1959, Senator Jim Gibson helped create the Nevada Gaming Commission. Don Shaw, who ran the Castaways hotel casino says, "As long as you're ethical and honest in your dealings, that's what counts." His partner Mike Villamor, who converted to the Church when he was 21 and married in the Las Vegas temple, says, "Yes, I've seen people lose their life savings in casinos. I've also seen a man die from overeating in a restaurant."

Still there are hold-outs, including the globally-prominent Marriott Corporation which operates seven local hotels – all free of slot machines or spinning wheels, but with a Book of Mormon sitting in most guest rooms.

vegetables that they cultivated failed to thrive in the alkaline soil, and a mining venture at nearby Mount Potosi was also unsuccessful. The lack of water for processing the ore meant that the metal was flaky. Some of the silver-laced lead bullets from the era have turned up in recent years.

Mormon settlement

The adobe brick fort with stone foundations established by the Mormons had thick walls 14 feet (4 meters) high and 150 feet (46 meters) long. Rawhide thongs and wooden pegs secured planks to beams because nails were scarce. Three years later the settlement was abandoned by the Mormons, partly because of Indian raids, but more to pre-empt a rising threat from the Federal government to march on Salt Lake City. Buildings which were added to the site and used by successive ranchers have been removed, but the portion of the Mormon Fort that survived, with some added reconstruction, is still maintained as a historic site in downtown Las Vegas *(see pages 228–9)*.

Scientists began an archeological dig on the site in the early 1990s, to see what was below. In the year 2000 a group dressed as 1850s Mormons re-enacted the Mormon pioneers' 600-mile (965-km) route in covered wagons.

Members of the Church of Jesus Christ of Latter-Day Saints (the Mormons) currently make up about 12 percent of the Southern Nevada population and in December 1989 a Mormon temple was dedicated in Las Vegas. The temple spires are visible in the foothills of Sunrise Mountain to the east of the city. Although LDS leaders originally were opposed to gaming – Joseph Ira Earl thundered, "I deny that gambling can be made safe and honorable by any means" – they eventually came to an accommodation with it.

On May 13, 1844, America's well-known explorer, John C. Fremont, leading an overland expedition West, chose to camp at Las Vegas Springs and subsequently thousands of copies of the map he drew were freely distributed. His name is remembered today not only in museums and history books but glowingly in neon. The Fremont Hotel-Casino in downtown Las Vegas bears his name, as does Fremont Street – the main casino-lined thoroughfare.

LEFT: Mormons preaching in the wilderness, 1853.
RIGHT: explorer John C. Fremont, after whom Las Vegas' Fremont Street is named.

Lawless times

The 19th century was a lawless time. An early historian, Hubert Bancroft, wrote in an 1890 book that between 1864 and 1890 there were 400 murders in Nevada, a very high number when one considers the sparseness of the population.

But by this time – the final decade of the 19th century – railroad developers had determined the water-rich Las Vegas Valley would be a prime location for trains to stop. The town, along with the ranch and vineyard on the old Mormon site, was eventually acquired by Senator William Clark's railroad. Half a dozen different railroad companies tried to build a

track from Salt Lake City to Los Angeles along the old Mormon Trail. Clark's San Pedro Los Angeles Salt Lake Railroad (later to become known as the Union Pacific) advertised for workers in *The Searchlight* newspaper. The company offered $2 per 10-hour day for white men, $1.75 for Mexicans and Indians with teamsters (union members) promised $40 a month, including board.

Sub-contractors lined up 1,200 workers who were accommodated in groups of 50 to 100 in canvas tents for which they each paid 75¢ per day. Each shelter, which could be as small as 7 by 9 feet (2 meters by 3 meters), housed several workers and their cots.

Food and drink

In the railroad workers' kitchens and dining halls, canned fruits and vegetables, syrup, bacon, locally grown potatoes and onions were served. Archeologists have found dome-shaped ovens for bread baking, and blasting powder tins reshaped into cooking pans and sieves. Water was first brought in by wagons. Later the railroad, which merged with E.H. Harriman's Oregon Short Line in the early part of the 20th century, installed a pipeline.

Helen Stewart, the biggest landowner of the time, owned 1,800 acres (728 hectares) which included the site of the old Mormon Fort on

had been paid for her property lining the tracks. On January 20, 1905, trains made their inaugural run from California to points east.

The railroad yards were located at the birthplace of a partially paved, dusty Fremont Street. Today, Jackie Gaughan's Plaza Hotel, located at Main and Fremont streets in downtown Las Vegas, stands on the site of the original Union Pacific Railroad depot. Freight and passenger trains still use the depot site at the hotel as a terminal – the only railroad station in the world located inside a hotel casino. In 1905, the Las Vegas Land & Water Co installed redwood pipes to bring water from the main line at Clark and

which her ranch stood. Her husband was killed in a dispute with a former ranch hand, but she continued to operate the ranch for another 20 years or so afterwards. Mrs Stewart sold land the railroad needed to Senator William Clark for $55,000. She later deeded 10 acres (4 hectares) "for the use of Pauite Indians."

From a collection of tented shacks with saloons, stores and boarding houses, the town grew to a population of 1,500 by early 1905 when the railroad was completed. The railroad offered free rides to town for the big auction at which 175 lots were sold almost immediately for $450 each. Eventually the land brought in a sum of $265,000, five times as much as Helen Stewart

Main streets but there were constant leaks and bursts which on one occasion left the town without water for several days. Artesian wells later solved some of the water problems.

Even after the turn of the 20th century, mining was still viable in the region. A mining camp at Searchlight – on what became the main Las Vegas to Los Angeles highway – established by George Colton in 1907, produced $7 million in gold, silver and other precious metals. It was an era when personal disputes were settled with guns and duels were commonplace.

"The most pernicious of all habits," a local paper editorialized, "is that of packing an unnecessary gun or knife. The habit stamps the man as a moral coward; one who does not dare to meet his fellow man on equal terms... but the worst feature of the habit is someday, acting on the impulse of the moment, the gun will be used. Then rests the curse of Cain upon him."

Not all crimes involved guns. Mugging was common in Searchlight, and embezzlement was not unknown. For weeks in 1906, the front pages of the newspapers followed the case of W.B. Atwell, the town postmaster, who admitted stealing $5,730 in government funds.

Atwell was finally jailed for four years, but there were lesser crimes, the most common being "high-grading," the term used to describe smug-

Mining town

The work of a miner is very different today since most mining is done with heavy machinery in above-ground open pits. Nevada is still the nation's leading producer of silver, and the state's mines yielded more than 8 million ounces (227,000 kg) of gold in 2001. But most of the Searchlight mines were worked out long ago, and the town declined.

It continued to service travelers on the Arrowhead Highway until 1927 when what is now Interstate 15 bypassed it. Edith Head, the Hollywood costume designer, and World War II aviator William Nellis, after whom Nellis Airforce

gling rich ore out of the mine in clothes, hair or a lunchbox. With a double canvas shirt, ore could be secreted between the layers. A hat with a double crown could hold five pounds of ore, as could an extra canvas pocket that had been sewed into a trouser leg.

When miners were working high-grade ore, owners would require them to shower and change clothes after coming off shift, but men constantly found new, and more ingenious ways to smuggle and steal, like using hollowed-out ax handles.

Base is named, both hailed from Searchlight. Today it is little more than a stop on US 95 for drivers traveling from Needles to Las Vegas, or visiting Lake Mojave.

Only a few years into the 20th century, Nevada followed the lead of other western states and outlawed gambling. "Stilled forever is the click of the roulette wheel, the rattle of dice and the swish of cards," was the rueful but innaccurate comment of the *Nevada State Journal*. As anybody might have predicted, the activities simply went underground, and for the next two decades anybody who knew somebody who knew the right door to knock on and a password had no trouble joining any one of a hundred games. ❑

LEFT: railroad depot, waiting room and ticket office, situated in 1905 on a Las Vegas sidetrack.
ABOVE: Nevada silver-mining camp, 1894.

Sept. 17 '30

BOULDER JUNC

THE GROWTH OF GAMBLING

The building of the Hoover Dam brought men and money.
All that was needed to part them from each other were a few gambling dens

When the city of Las Vegas was incorporated on March 16, 1911, it was hardly a pretty sight. "Anyone who lives here is out of his mind," said newcomer Mayme Stocker from Reading, Pennsylvania. Her husband Oscar had come for work as an engine foreman at the railroad yards. In her recollections many years later, Mayme said, "There were no streets or sidewalks and there were no flowers, lawns or trees." Nevertheless, Mayme stayed, and in 1920 opened the Northern Club on Fremont Street, for which she was granted Las Vegas' first casino license.

Five games were then legal: stud, draw and lowball poker, "500" and bridge. The club served no straight liquor, only mixed drinks, because of the lengthy, expensive analysis the Feds would have had to make to prove the cocktails contained alcohol. Much of the liquor was moonshine, illegally distilled in out-of-town caves. In 1945, Mayme leased the Northern Club to Wilbur Clark who changed its name to the Monte Carlo Club.

Mr Las Vegas

The first man to be known as "Mr Las Vegas" was Robert Griffith. Griffith helped his father build a home at the southwest corner of 2nd and Fremont streets, where the Golden Nugget now stands. At the age of 26 he was appointed postmaster and instructed to prepare for an airport. He leveled a site in the desert, near today's Sahara and Paradise roads, where the first flight landed on April 17, 1925, taking several hundred letters which he had specially hand stamped to mark the occasion on the 2 1/2 hour flight back to Los Angeles. The following year, Western Airlines inaugurated commercial passenger flights into Las Vegas.

The next few years saw a lot of artesian wells drilled for water, but after an initial boom the

PRECEDING PAGES: opening ceremonies for the building of the Hoover Dam, 1930.
LEFT AND RIGHT: the Flamingo Hotel was both a desert fantasy and the downfall of mobster Bugsy Siegel.

town remained more or less isolated until the early 1930s, when it was revived with the building of the Boulder Dam.

There were hopes even in those early days that Las Vegas could be turned into a tourist resort, and entrepreneur David Lorenzi dug two lakes in the northwest part of town. His planned

"high-class resort" came to nothing, but the lakes are still there in appropriately-named Lorenzi Park. Frank Garside, a publisher who had operated papers in Tonopah and other boom towns, had seen an opportunity in Las Vegas, buying a struggling weekly, the *Clark County Review*, and hiring Reno-born Al Cahlan to run it. Between 1930 and 1970, Cahlan wrote a column for what became the *Las Vegas Review-Journal*. His busiest time as editor was during the building of Boulder Dam, 34 miles (55 km) away in Black Canyon on the Colorado River.

This enormous project employed 5,300 workers with a monthly payroll of half a million dollars, and by the time it was finished, the population of Las Vegas was up to 5,000. In the decade between 1930 and 1939, the Federal government pumped $70 million into the area, much of it going towards the Boulder Dam. When it was completed, Garside still thought the town would "blow away" like so many of the other boom towns with which he had been associated in the past.

Cahlan married Missouri-born Florence Lee Jones in 1940. She covered the story of a truck driver's suit brought against the Six Companies, the contractors who had won the construction contract with a bid of $48,890,955.

food and drink, and the lack of safety precautions. The "muckers," who did the most dangerous job of shoveling up dynamite-loosened rock to be hauled away, got the lowest pay.

Great Depression

Legalized gambling returned to Nevada in 1931 during the Great Depression, legitimizing a small but lucrative industry. Phil Tobin, a Northern Nevada rancher who had never visited Las Vegas, persuaded the Nevada Legislature to pass a gambling bill whose proceeds would raise taxes for public schools, an idea so durable that today nearly one-third of Nevada's

The driver claimed he'd lost his sexual powers from exposure to the carbon monoxide fumes in the tunnels, but his suit failed. Undoubtedly there were fumes. Murl Emery, a river boat operator who took many of the men to work up the river to the dam, said that at one time, "They were hauling men out of those tunnels like cord wood. They had been gassed. I laid them on the bottom of the boat, on the seats and what not... They were real sick from being gassed working in the tunnel along with the running trucks."

In August 1931 the workers went on strike complaining also about heat prostration from working in 130° F (54° C) temperatures, poor

current $1.8 billion annual state budget comes from the 6.25 percent tax on casino winnings. "I had two reasons for introducing that bill," Tobin said later. "First, illegal gambling was prevalent. Everyone had a blanket and a deck of cards and it was getting out of hand. Some of these tinhorn cops were collecting 50 bucks a month for allowing it. Secondly, the state needed revenue. This way we could pick up the money from the license fees for the games."

Local businessmen had been operating most of the original gambling halls, with enforcement handled by the sheriff. The city relied on their lawman to rid the town of undesirables – vagrants, card cheats, suspected thieves, moonshiners, drug dealers and the like – usually by giving them a "floater," meaning they had to leave town and soon, or face incarceration. Later came the realization, born out of the Prohibition era when bootleggers bribed local authorities and politicians, that bribes and payola could be converted into legitimate revenue, and the state legislature set up the Nevada Tax Commission.

Originally Las Vegas had been visualized as a resort city, serving visitors who came to see the Boulder Dam and go boating on Lake Mead, but the nationwide crackdown on illegal gambling unexpectedly benefited the state.

banned. Cars were searched and impounded if liquor was found. Naturally, its off-duty residents flooded into Vegas to enjoy themselves. This created problems with black people in particular, and sometimes pitched battles occurred.

Ernie Cragin, a former insurance salesman, was the mayor. An unashamed racist, his policemen rigidly enforced segregation in a town where most of the casinos and nightclubs refused to serve blacks.

During WWII, when black military officers guarding the dam came to town, there were gun battles with the local police. Matters didn't improve for blacks until two decades later,

when NAACP lawyer Charles Kellar instigated protest marches on the Strip, and civil rights lawyer Ralph Denton helped to get Governor Grant Sawyer elected.

Bootlegger

Tony Cornero, who had been smuggling liquor off the Southern California coast during the Prohibition years, opened the $31,000 Meadows Club at the corner of Fremont Street and Charleston Boulevard as soon as gambling was legalized. "America's most luxurious casino," was the verdict of the *Las Vegas Age*, which called it "potent in its charm and mysterious in its fascination" – all this at a time when most

"Nevada owed its initial good fortune to the moralistic fervor sweeping the nation," said veteran journalist Sergio Lalli. One man in particular, an ex-carnival barker named Harold Smith, spread the message around the world with no less than 2,300 signs advertising his Lake Tahoe Harold's Club in places as far afield as Casablanca and the Antarctic.

Boulder City was a federally-run enclave, created to house the workers in a place where liquor, gambling and prostitution could be banned.

LEFT: conditions during the construction of the Hoover Dam were primitive and damaging to the health.
ABOVE: Las Vegas in the 1930s.

gambling joints were untidy sawdust-floor bars.

By 1941, with the population about 8,000 people, a group of local businessmen invited Tom Hull, owner of a chain of El Rancho motor inns, to town. Hull chose a site just outside town where Highway 91 intersected San Francisco (now Sahara) Avenue for his El Rancho Vegas. Here, with cheap land taxes and water, he built a 65-room motor inn with a swimming pool. The casino was an afterthought. Guests who attended the opening wore evening wear, but

SHALL WE PLAY CARDS?

When Tom Hull, owner of a chain of motor inns, built El Rancho Vegas, he concentrated on the swimming pool. The casino was an afterthought.

ernor, helped to pass a law in 1947 allowing the Highway Patrol to close down the rip-off highway casinos, known locally as zoos. Often here, gambling games involved animals and chickens to decide the outcome. Nor was everybody happy with what they saw as Vegas' lax morals. District attorney Roger D. Foley, who had studied for the priesthood, charged stripper Lili St Cyr with lewd conduct after watching her act at El Rancho Vegas where she bathed in a glass bathtub and exited behind a towel.

Colorado Springs-born Hull showed up in jeans, boots and a cowboy shirt. Later expanded to 125 rooms, El Rancho Vegas became popular for banquets and wedding parties. It was the headquarters of the valley's first radio station, an ABC affiliate named KENO. The station's owner Maxwell Kelch was a major Vegas promoter who sold the town like a product. He never ran for office or invested in a casino on the principle, as he told his son, that "there's two businesses you don't get involved in. One's liquor and the other's gambling." El Rancho Vegas was destroyed by fire in 1960.

It was always easy for the unwary to lose their shirts. Clifford Jones, the Lieutenant Gov-

Bugsy Siegel

The next year, the El Cortez Hotel was built at Fremont and 6th Street. Among its partners were Meyer (real name: *Suchowljansky*) Lansky and Benjamin "Bugsy" Siegel. Lansky invested $60,000 for his 10 percent stake of El Cortez and left it to Siegel to run. In their youth the pair had been allied in a New York protection racket, beating up and killing bootleggers, and Siegel had traveled to Los Angeles to consolidate the rackets there. Later he came to Las Vegas to handle the Mob's lucrative race book wires and gambling business. In Manhattan, Siegel had lived at the Waldorf Astoria and traveled in a bullet-proof limousine accompanied by bodyguards. Out West, he soon made friends with Clark Gable, Jean Harlow and Cary Grant as well as other members of Hollywood's movie colony. He was himself handsome and a movie star-wannabee.

"He was a frustrated actor who secretly wanted a movie career," actor George Raft said, "but he never quite had nerve enough to ask for a part in one of my pictures." Siegel muscled his way into illegal gambling, including Tijuana's Agua Caliente racetrack in Mexico. He also helped

DON'T BUG ME

In Manhattan, Bugsy Siegel traveled in a bullet-proof limousine. Out West, he made friends with Clark Gable, Cary Grant and Jean Harlow.

obsessive gambler, he would charter a plane to fly from Los Angeles to Las Vegas, and soon thought of owning his own hotel in the desert resort, in order to entertain his movie-star friends. That was the genesis of the Flamingo Hotel which – through amply-documented chicanery – came to be known as Siegel's place.

In December 1942, movie chain mogul R.E. Griffith introduced a western motif at the Last Frontier. The casino had Pony Express lanterns hanging from wagon wheels, Texas cattle horns, leather bar

to import narcotics from Mexico, and took a cut from a huge prostitution ring.

His big break in Vegas came soon after, with the arrival of a colorful Hollywood entrepreneur named W.R. Wilkerson. Wilkerson had begun betting on the World Series and at the track while he was at college. He founded the influential *Hollywood Reporter* in 1930, and played regularly with $20,000 chips at movie mogul Sam Goldwyn's weekly poker game. An

LEFT: Betty Grable and Harry James opening at El Rancho, one of the first of Vegas' casinos.
ABOVE: ex-president Ronald Reagan at the Last Frontier, another early club.

stools in the shape of saddles and a bullet-riddled mahogany bar. The hotel, later renamed the Frontier, offered horseback and stage coach rides into the desert terrain. Frontier Village was established with ancient buildings rehabilitated from old Nevada ghost towns. The Last Frontier also started the idea of "the junket," gaming tours arranged by the operator of a small airline called Kirk Kerkorian.

The next casino on the Strip was the Thunderbird. The Mills Brothers, Ziegfeld Follies and Scandals on Ice performed there, with nude skaters. It became a hangout for hip locals. Resort owners held their meetings at the Thunderbird and Governor McCarran stayed there on his visits to town. Soon the Strip was dotted with small motels, the last demolished in 1995.

In his book, *The Kandy Kolored Tangerine Flake Streamlined Baby*, Tom Wolfe said, "The war created money, it made massive infusions of money into every level of society. Suddenly classes of people whose lives had been practically invisible had the money to build monuments to their own styles. Las Vegas was created out of the war (among) gangsters."

The late 1940s and early 1950s saw the growth of the Fremont Street area with a whole clutch of clubs springing up. The Golden Nugget was built, then the Monte Carlo Club.

Then came Benny Binion, a colorful Texas gambler who sported a western style with big, white cowboy hats and a buffalo hide overcoat. In his early career Binion had been twice convicted for bootlegging and once, after getting a jailor drunk and using a key, stole a truckload of liquor right out of the jail. In the late 1930s in Dallas he operated craps games out of hotel rooms by taking the tables in and out disguised as beds. In 1947, with his partner, Binion opened the Las Vegas Club on Fremont Street. Four years later, he opened the Horseshoe and set the town on its ear by offering a $500 limit on craps games – ten times the other casinos' limit. A cherished principle of Benny Binion's

was "giving a lot of gamble for the money."

In 1946, "Bugsy" Siegel took over the part-completed Flamingo Hotel when the *Hollywood Reporter* publisher's initial investment of $1.5 million ran out. By the time the Flamingo opened, Siegel was heavily in debt. Costs escalated massively because Siegel took his eye off the business. "We never had a complete set of plans," said Robert Johnson of the Del Webb company that worked on the Flamingo. "We would build what he (Siegel) wanted, and then the architect would draw what we had built."

Skimming the take

Expensive construction materials hiked the costs, though maybe not as much as the freight that was driven in through the front gates and out the back gates over and over again without ever being unloaded. Palm trees kept appearing, disappearing and then reappearing again. By the opening night on December 26, 1946, the still-unfinished Flamingo had already cost $6 million, and because the hotel rooms weren't ready, the few celebrities that braved the dreadful weather to attend, went across the street to El Rancho Vegas or the Last Frontier to stay and bet their money.

Siegel closed the place to get it finished, reopening in early 1947, but the Mob was displeased with the money that had been sunk into the venture. Meyer Lansky discovered that Siegel had been skimming the Flamingo building fund and sending his girlfriend Virginia Hill to deposit large sums in a private Swiss bank account. On June 20, 1947, as the hoodlum sat reading in the window of Miss Hill's Beverly Hills home, a single shot blasted through the glass. Bugsy Siegel was dead.

"In death he became a legend taller than any Las Vegas resort," said *Review-Journal* columnist John L. Smith. Virginia "Flamingo" Hill was in Europe at the time of the murder, probably on the advice of her killers.

A few years later, Hill appeared before a commission on organized crime. Asked why she had associated with mobsters like Frank Costello and Joseph Epstein, an Al Capone underboss, Flamingo replied, "Senator, I'm the best god-dammed cocksucker in the world." ❑

LEFT: the "Dancing Dice" of the El Rancho, 1948.
RIGHT: assembling "Vegas Vic," the lucky icon of the Fremont Street area.

PLAYERS AND DESERT PALACES

Mobsters and mincing showgirls, wire-taps and wild publicity stunts –

in 1950s Vegas, this was all in a day's take

On a New York spring morning in 1957, Frank Costello, the "Prime Minister of the Mob," was cut down by a volley of gunshots in the paneled lobby of his apartment building in Central Park West. The injured mobster was rushed to the hospital and in the ensuing bustle, a quick-thinking cop checked the pockets of Costello's beautifully cut suit. A hand-written note was among the contents. It read, "Gross Casino Win as of 4-26-57… $651,284," which tallied the first 24 days' takings from the Las Vegas gaming house, the Tropicana Hotel.

Memo from the Mob

The Costello memo was the first solid evidence of Mob ties to Vegas casinos since a series of ground-breaking hearings into organized crime headed by Tennessee senator Estes Kefauver in 1950 and 1951. This was also the year that Alan Dorfman, son of one of Al Capone's soldiers, first started to get loans to finance casino construction from the Teamsters Union's western states pension fund.

During the proceedings, Nevada's Lieutenant Governor Cliff Jones was asked about "undesirable characters with bad police records" who had earlier been engaged in gambling in the state. He conceded that there had, indeed, been such occasions. But Jones – himself a part owner of the Thunderbird casino – elaborated further, "…people who came here when the state started to grow – they weren't particularly Sunday school teachers or anything like that. They were gamblers."

Nevadans of that time, wrote Sergio Lalli in the book *The Players: The Men Who Made Las Vegas*, judged men "by the way they had always judged people on the frontier, not on their backgrounds but on the way they conducted themselves at present." In the early days, casinos "were the pariahs of the business world," with

only Nevada granting them license to operate.

After Kefauver concluded his hearings into Mob connections, he proposed a 10 percent federal gaming tax which was averted only through persistent efforts by Nevada senator Pat McCarran. A defense lawyer and later district attorney, McCarran had lost many races before being

elected senator in 1932, and had served for 20 years when he halted a move to tax gaming. "It isn't a very laudable position for one to have to defend gambling," he conceded. "One doesn't feel very lofty when his feet are resting on the argument that gambling must prevail in the state that he represents. The rest of the world looks upon him with disdain."

McCarran, a popular politician in his native state, had fought for the retention of silver in US coins – Nevada is "the silver state." He also wrote much civil aviation legislation, and McCarran airport was named for him, but his reputation was marred by a friendship with the Communist-baiting senator Joseph McCarthy.

PRECEDING PAGES: inside the Desert Inn, 1956.
LEFT: showgirl and friend at the opening of the Dunes.
RIGHT: Frank Costello, "Prime Minister of the Mob," during an investigation into his casino activities.

On this he had faced considerable opposition from Hank Greenspun, until his death in 1989 the publisher of the *Las Vegas Sun* newspaper, the only rival to the dominant *Review-Journal*. Greenspun arrived in Vegas in 1946, acted as publicity manager for Bugsy Siegel's Flamingo, and founded KLAS-TV, a CBS outlet, which he sold to Howard Hughes in the 1960s.

Four years after Estes Kefauver's exposures about Vegas' involvement with the Mob, a Gaming Control Board was established in an effort to regulate and legitimize the industry. Gambling, by that time, had already become the state's greatest source of income.

The whole southern Nevada region was on a roll by the early 1950s, largely due to the efforts of publicity man Steve Hannagan, who had promoted the Indianapolis Raceway and Miami Beach before he was hired to promote the city of Las Vegas.

"Hannagan made it clear that he would ignore the obvious glamour of gaming, divorce and marriage chapels, and would instead publicize Las Vegas as the hub of a surrounding scenic wonderland," Perry Kaufman said in *City Boosters, Las Vegas Style*. "He felt that the coverage by outside writers, on the land of Sodom and Gomorrah, made Las Vegas known as a gambling resort and wanted to diversify the other images in order to entice wives and families."

It was a bright Hannagan protegeé, Harvey Diederich, who gained massive coverage from a stunt in the 1956 US presidential election. He posed a scantily-clad showgirl holding a campaign poster for Dwight D. Eisenhower in her right hand and one for Adlai Stevenson in her left. She was named "Miss Bea Sure 'N Vote." Another girl posed sitting astride an ice turkey carved by the chef at the Topicana Hotel. "Cold Turkey" was the caption on that one. "Publicity far exceeds the value of advertising," said Diederich. "It's more believable."

Downtown began its rapid growth when Texan Benny Binion opened the legendary Binion's Horseshoe, the first off-the-Strip casino with a carpet, as well as being the first to offer free drinks not just to high rollers but also to slot-machine players. He also arranged for customers to be collected at the airport in limousines. "If you wanna get rich," Binion said, "make little people feel like big people."

Around that time, the Atomic Energy Commission started conducting above-ground nuclear test explosions at test sites about 100 miles (160 km) northwest of Las Vegas. President Harry Truman declared the valley "a critical defense area," which did wonders for Las Vegas' economic well-being. In 1951, the first year of testing, the Commission's construction payroll topped $4 million, much of which was spent locally.

The idea for the Desert Inn, with its lavish golf course, came from a former San Diego bellboy named Wilbur Clark. "It was Wilbur's dream… he worked hard to get the hotel together," his widow Toni said years later. "He always said the bubble would never burst in Las Vegas and he was right. It was all class then. People used to dress every night. It was a very glamorous place, a winner from the day it opened. Everybody loved being there." Frank Sinatra's first singing engagement in Vegas was at the Desert Inn on September 4, 1951, when he was still getting over his break up with actress Ava Gardner.

Moe Dalitz

Along with his Cleveland partners, Moe Dalitz, "a smart, brilliant man," according to some, owned three quarters of the Desert Inn. During prohibition Dalitz had bootlegged liquor with Meyer Lansky across the lake from Canada, and in 1958 kept his chain of Midwestern laundries free from union interference with hoodlum strong-arms. In a dazzling display of business acumen, Dalitz raised $8 million from the Teamsters Union pension fund to finish building the Stardust Hotel.

Government investigations showed that the Teamsters Union investments in Nevada casinos eventually exceeded $238 million. Dalitz got out, but years later the mobsters who still owned it were jailed for skimming the profits, or "conspiracy to defraud the government of taxes through illegal and unreported income," as the rap sheet put it.

THOSE WERE THE DAYS

According to the *New York Times*, in 1953 a first-class hotel in Vegas charged $7.50 a day, while a motel charged $3.

same approach that many other American capitalists did. He donated generously to political causes and wrapped himself in the tailored suit of corporate citizenship."

Dalitz himself told an interviewer in 1975, "I was never a member of any gang. I never considered myself a gangster or a mobster. I was always in a business that threw me into meeting all kinds of people."

When he died in 1989, the foundation that he had set up distributed $1.3 million to charities, and the 300 mourners at his funeral included

A mobster and a gentleman

In his book, *Gamblers' Money*, Wallace Turner wrote, "In Cleveland, Moe Dalitz was a bootlegger but in Las Vegas he stands as an elder statesman of what they call the gaming industry," and *Las Vegas Review-Journal* columnist John L. Smith rhetorically asked, "How did a former bootlegger and illegal casino operator... go about gaining respectability? Dalitz took the

LEFT: Estes Kefauver's investigation into organized crime in 1950–51 exposed Mob connections.
ABOVE: singer Phyllis McGuire, seen here with Desert Inn owner Moe Dalitz, was a girlfriend of Mafia boss Sam Giancana.

politicians, judges and other influential figures.

The Stardust was the first to break from what had already become conventional casino star policy by bringing the *Lido de Paris* stage show from France, which ran for 31 years. The topless revue was produced by legendary showman Donn Arden. Arden, a onetime tap dancer, went on in the 1990s to produce the on-stage sinking of the *Titanic* in one of the current Strip revues, which – by the end of the 20th century – had sunk 15,000 times and looks well on its way to being about to sink indefinitely.

The Dunes had brought topless revues to the Strip with *Minsky's Follies* as early as 1957, but it was Arden who was most associated with the statuesque, bare-breasted showgirl who became such an emblematic Vegas legend.

"There's a certain way a girl can walk, particularly when crossing a stage," he once explained. "By simply twisting the foot it swings the pelvis forward, which is suggestive and sensual. If you twist right and swing that torso, you get a revolve going in there that's just right. It isn't the way a woman should walk necessarily unless she's a hooker. You're selling the pelvis. That's the Arden walk."

THE SHOWGIRL WALK

"If you twist right and swing that torso, you get a revolve going in there that's just right. It isn't the way a woman should walk necessarily – unless she's a hooker." – promoter Donn Arden

Las Vegas Valley from the resort's third-floor Skyroom – cocktail and dancing favorite of visitors, residents and celebrities. Soon after, the Riviera Hotel rose to nine stories and took the towering title to become the city's first high-rise building.

That same year, the Moulin Rouge opened across the city, at a time when blacks were still unwelcome guests at Strip casinos and black entertainers were required to live off-premises while entertaining. The hip, interracial crowd that filled the Moulin

Talent agent Bill Miller, former partner in a dance act, is credited with originating Las Vegas' famous lounge shows. The lounges became major entertainment attractions in their own right, spawning the names of comedians Don Rickles, Buddy Hackett, Shecky Greene and Alan King among others. As entertainment manager of the Sahara in which he had bought a 10 percent stake, Miller hired bandleader Louis Prima and his wife Keely Smith to play the Sahara's Casbah Lounge. In 1955, Miller shifted to the Dunes and introduced the first of what became known as "production shows," a revue called *Smart Affairs*.

Until 1955, the Desert Inn had offered guests the highest unobstructed panoramic view of the

Rouge's club after midnight attracted so many showgirls and performers from other casinos that some threatened to dismiss cast members who were seen there.

Banned from the building

The Moulin Rouge starred former world heavyweight boxing champion Joe Louis as owner-host, and singer Bob Bailey from the Count Basie Orchestra as producer of the stage show. The club had a stormy existence, closing and re-opening many, many times, and when Bailey moved his show onto KLAS-TV, he had to go back to using the service entrance. Bailey himself worked to get Grant Sawyer elected governor in 1958. "He indicated that if he was elected governor, certain changes would be made. He struck me as a man you could believe."

Three years later, the legislature established a commission to examine the subject of discrimination. Joe Louis moved on to become a much loved casino host at Caesars Palace. The Moulin Rouge was declared a national historic site in 1992.

In 1955, casinos were going up right and left, and the city's population was on the verge of a huge increase, from 45,000 to 65,000 residents. But Governor Sawyer abhorred the fact that so much of the industry was under the sway of hoodlums, and helped to set up the Nevada Gaming Commission and the Nevada Gaming Control Board to license and police the scene. At the time, there were hundreds of hidden investors, constantly changing names and faces and holding different percentage points in different operations, an ever-shifting mosaic of fronts and corporations.

The Black Book

Then, and for a decade afterwards, Nevada law required all casino owners to be individually licensed, which made it impossible for public companies with multiple stockholders to be owners. The law was changed in the late 1960s, allowing small investors to own less than 10 percent of a casino's stock without the need for individual licenses. Sawyer also promoted the idea of the board publishing a list of disreputable characters who could be barred from casinos. To his surprise, the US Federal Court upheld the state's right to introduce the List of Excluded Persons, familiarly known ever since as "the Black Book."

Some of the "disreputable characters" were, of course, already established in management *inside* the casinos. The hidden FBI microphones at the Fremont Hotel in 1961 picked up one of the owners, Ed Levinson, discussing what seemed to be a skimming operation involving Meyer Lansky and several casinos. Las Vegas telephone records show that from 1961 to 1963, they had leased 25 lines to the FBI, leading from the local FBI office to concealed listening

devices in various hotels including the Desert Inn, the Stardust, the Fremont, the Sands, the Dunes and the Riviera.

Later, the FBI found evidence of skimming at the Flamingo; apparently the New York office was the beneficiary of gambling debts which had somehow not been entered on the casino's books in Las Vegas. The hotel owners pleaded guilty and admitted skimming $36 million of untaxed income during the decade.

In the late 1950s, city and county community leaders realized the need for a Las Vegas convention facility to help fill the hotel rooms during slack tourist months. Clark County

Commissioner George "Bud" Albright was no fan of gambling, and he lobbied hard for the building of the convention center. He gave his young son this view of how a slot machine works: "Well, with this machine you put $500 into it and get $250 back," and he believed that Vegas should not rely solely on leisure visitors.

A site was chosen one block east of the Strip, and in April 1959 a 6,300-seat, silver-domed rotunda with an adjoining 90,000 square foot (8,360 square meter) exhibition hall opened on the site of the present-day Las Vegas Convention Center. The silver dome was demolished in 1990 to expand the center to become one of the largest single-level facilities in the world. ❑

LEFT: Marlene Dietrich, seen here in 1953, was a frequent guest and performer in Vegas.

RIGHT: the silver-domed convention center opened in April 1959 with the World Congress of Flight.

THE RAT PACK, THE KING AND THE RICHEST MAN IN THE WORLD

The first and second kings of Las Vegas, along with the reclusive lord of the valley, left distinctive impressions on the city

Three men cast such long shimmering visions over Las Vegas that the town will never be quite the same again. Sinatra brought high-society elegance into the lounges. Elvis brought the mass market to the Strip. And Howard Hughes brought the appearance, at least, of respectability to the business of owning and running casinos.

A crooner called Frank

Jack Entratter had been the general manager of New York's Copacabana Club and later brought entertainers like Lena Horne, Danny Thomas and other stars to the Sahara. In 1952, Entratter's attention turned to a crooner named Frank Sinatra, and soon, Frank was on a roll. He won an Oscar for his role in the movie *From Here to Eternity*, and released an album, *Songs For Young Lovers*, that became a best-seller.

Veteran lounge singer Sammy King said, "He was actually the king of Las Vegas because the minute he stepped in town, money was here. He drew all the big-money people. Every celebrity in Hollywood would come to Las Vegas to see him."

Sinatra bought two percent of the Sands for $54,000 and within a decade owned nine percent, by which time the Rat Pack – a loose conglomerate of singers, actors and comedians – was the hottest thing in town. "Now you've got the greatest, cool, hippest entertainers around," Paul Anka said, a singer who was himself playing the Sahara aged only 18.

One night, as a version of the story goes, actress Lauren Bacall was at the Sahara watching Noel Coward perform. Across the table were Humphrey Bogart, Frank Sinatra, Judy Garland, David Niven, Angie Dickenson and agent Swifty Lazar. Glancing across their faces

---

PRECEDING PAGES: comedian Milton Berle, part-time Rat Packer and card spinner at the Sahara.
LEFT AND RIGHT: the Rat Pack were "the greatest, cool, hippest entertainers around."

she said, "You look like a goddam rat pack," and the name was born. In true Vegas style, it was heisted by Sinatra, Dean Martin, Sammy Davis Jr, actor Peter Lawford and comedian Joey Bishop as the moniker for their own gang.

The Pack's era began when Sinatra joined Dean Martin on stage at the Sands in January 1959, and loosely came and went through 1963. Together the group performed two shows a night in the Copa Room, followed by a friendly and less formal gathering in the lounge, getting together in the daytime for filming. When they were scheduled to perform, there wasn't a hotel room to be had anywhere which, according to some estimates, benefited Sin City to the tune of an extra $20 to 30 million a week.

As a group, the Rat Pack never recorded an album or released a single, although some informal live recordings survive. "Together they had chemistry, attitude and charisma,"

Richard Abowitz wrote. "The Rat Pack injected an atmosphere of suave decadence into a fading frontier town famous only for its old-style vices and cheap buffets."

Sinatra and the broads

Tony Badillo, a longtime dealer at the Sands, said, "Back in those days we used to let Frank and Sammy and those guys deal the game. Of course, with the Gaming Control Board you couldn't do that now. Frank was a pretty good gambler (but) sometimes he'd get angry. Like if a woman at the table didn't laugh at his jokes he'd say, 'Tony, get that broad off my table…'"

assemble the entire cast during the five-week shoot. Sinatra turned up, usually late in the afternoon, on only nine days. The others also turned up late, restricting Milestone to a day's shoot of about three hours. "Frank would tear handfuls of pages out of the script and allow (Milestone) only one take," Lawford recalled.

"Some people think Frank is arrogant and overbearing and something of a bully," Milestone said in *The Rat Pack*, a 1998 book written by Lawrence J. Quirk and William Schoell. "Well, he isn't really; he just won't take crap from people." Everybody who could turned up for the star-studded premiere at Las Vegas' Fre-

In 1959, Peter Lawford, Pack member and brother-in-law to John F. Kennedy, discovered a movie script about a group of World War II veterans who rob several Vegas casinos simultaneously. When Jack Warner gave the green light to what was to become *Ocean's 11*, Sinatra said, "We're not setting out to make *Hamlet* or *Gone With the Wind*." Warner himself said, "Let's not make the movie. Let's pull the job."

Filming on *Ocean's 11* was scheduled to coincide with the group's January 1960 "Summit at the Sands," and was as loose as the pack's image. Veteran director Lewis Milestone, an Oscar winner for *All Quiet on the Western Front* (1930), was only once able to

mont Theater on August 3, 1960. In the next day's *New York Times* strait-laced reviewer Bosley Crowther criticized the film's "surprisingly nonchalant and flippant attitudes towards crime." Taking a look back at the movie 41 years later – during the filming of the George Clooney remake – *Las Vegas Life* called it "a time capsule of a Las Vegas that no longer exists," and said that Milestone "would have been better off shooting the Rat Pack's nightly performances."

Ocean's 11 certainly was no *Hamlet*, and was trashed by most critics. But *Variety*'s assessment that it "would rake in the chips," was right on the money. According to the *Hollywood

Reporter, the movie went on to become one of the five biggest box-office attractions in the history of Warner Bros. It spawned two Rat Pack celluloid reunions, *Sergeants 3* and *Robin and the 7 Hoods*.

Sinatra and the Mob

Joseph Kennedy asked Peter Lawford, his actor son-in-law and Rat Pack member, to throw his support behind his son John F. Kennedy's 1960 presidential bid. In the process, Lawford got Sinatra involved in what became a murky political campaign. Two weeks after announcing his race for the presidency JFK picked up a $1 million donation from Sinatra's friend, Mafia boss Sam Giancana, during a trip to the Sands. "(Jack) loved his brief visits to Las Vegas," reported Michael Herr in the book *The Money and the Power: the Making of Las Vegas and Its Hold on America*. "He was the most star-struck of stars... and his Vegas friends arranged everything for him, especially seeing to it that his privacy would be respected."

Some of the million bucks' donation was funneled to Frank's friend Skinny D'Amato, owner of an Atlantic City club where the singer returned to perform faithfully year after year. That money was used to ensure that JFK won the West Virginia Democratic primary.

In the Chicago primary, Kennedy was facing defeat and Giancana again came to the rescue. Exerting the kind of juice available only to high-ranking mobsters, the Chicago primary was fixed – resulting in a 100,000 vote plurality for JFK, the smallest margin in history. Giancana, who boasted to associates that he had elected a president, had been promised by Sinatra that in return for his help he would have Bobby Kennedy's investigation into organized

crime called off. Understandably, Frank felt betrayed when the new Attorney General resumed his attacks, Giancana topping the list.

Worse was to come. Shortly after his election, President Kennedy was scheduled to stay at Sinatra's lavish mansion in Palm Springs, but a few days beforehand the FBI uncovered evidence of a two-year affair JFK had been conducting with a woman named Judith Campbell. Surveillance tapes showed her also to be the mistress of Sam Giancana. FBI director J. Edgar Hoover delivered the tapes to Bobby Kennedy in person, and JFK's Palm Springs vacation was abruptly canceled. The president had been introduced to Campbell by Sinatra.

LEFT: Pack members Frank Sinatra and Peter Lawford with Lawford's brother-in-law, Robert Kennedy.
ABOVE: the Sultan of Swing, with harem, in 1955.

In 1963, two months before President Kennedy was assassinated, Sinatra did battle with the Gaming Control Board. The FBI discovered Sam Giancana's presence at Sinatra's Cal-Neva Lodge in Lake Tahoe. (Cal-Neva was where Marilyn Monroe had spent the week before her suicide, distraught from her affairs with both Kennedy brothers.)

Hoodlum Jimmy Hoffa was suspected by the FBI of providing a loan from the Teamsters Union pension fund for improvements to the lodge. The subsequent investigation showed that Sinatra's loan had, in fact, been turned down by Hoffa. Nevertheless, when the FBI

instead decided to divest himself of his casino interests and let the license go.

Four years later in 1967, intemperate language and tone occurred again after Howard Hughes bought the Sands Hotel. Sinatra had continued to play there since unloading his stock, but there was animosity between the singer and his new boss. Hughes had once invited actress Ava Gardner to a Lake Tahoe cruise, where he made an unsuccessful play for her. Sinatra was furious, as he was wooing Gardner at the time. When the new owner stopped Sinatra's credit at the tables, the singer lost his temper and started rearranging the fur-

reported their findings to the Nevada Gaming Commission, Sinatra's gaming license was suspended. He had been one of the public partners, Giancana a secret partner. A girlfriend of Giancana's, singer Phyllis McGuire, spoke of Sinatra's relationship to the mobster, "He'd been friends with the boys for years, ever since he needed to get out of his contract with (bandleader) Tommy Dorsey."

Gaming Control Board chairman Ed Olsen said that he received a call from Sinatra who had "used vile, intemperate, obscene and indecent language in a tone that was menacing in the extreme and constituted a threat." Sinatra was ordered to appear and defend himself, but

niture in a rage which ended when a burly casino manager knocked out two of "Ol' Blue Eye's" teeth. Sinatra promptly took his show across the street to Caesars Palace.

The boy from Mississippi

Elvis Presley's first Las Vegas gig was in April 1956 at the Frontier. He was 21, billed as "the atomic-powered singer," and opened a show for comic Shecky Greene. *Newsweek* magazine reported that the audience "underwhelmed," and made comparisons to "a jug of corn liquor at a champagne party."

Recalling the date Shecky said, "The presentation was terrible. He wasn't ready. He walked out with three or four guys. It looked like a rehearsal hall." After that, "Colonel" Tom Parker steered Elvis away from live performance and into Hollywood for a 12-year series of low-budget, high-yield movies, most of which the singer loathed. The move did wonders for the Colonel, however, and made some money for the boy from Mississippi.

In 1969, Kirk Kerkorian, owner of the Flamingo, put the finishing touches on the International (now the Las Vegas Hilton) and talent agent Bill Miller contacted Parker about getting Elvis to perform. Elvis had married his child bride Priscilla Beaulieu at the Aladdin two years earlier and been a long-time Vegas fan. "Parker didn't want him to open in that big 2,000-seat theater. He said we'd have to put somebody else in to open and Elvis would follow." Miller booked Barbra Streisand.

Parker is said to have signed Elvis for a four-week engagement at $100,000 a week. Having been a long time off the stage, the singer was nervous. He studied other performers in showrooms and lounges, and took Tom Jones as his model, particularly for the way the Welsh singer aroused a female audience.

Elvis was a sensation on opening night. He delivered a relaxed show, rated by many among the best of his career. He referred to his time in Hollywood as, "ten years with my top lip curled." Colonel Parker sat down with the International's general manager and wrote a contract the following day, according to the late Kenneth Evans, a Nevada newspaper writer and later, media relations manager for the Nevada Tourist Commission. Elvis was to appear at the International for four-week gigs twice a year, and he was to be paid $125,000 a week. By the end of the singer's first four-week stint, the hotel's showroom had generated more than $2 million in revenue.

Evans wrote that Elvis' contract was for a "piddling sum," and speculated that it was due to Parker wanting to settle in Las Vegas, where he became one of the highest rollers in town, often losing $50,000 a night. Evans called Parker a "degenerate gambler," a phrase used by other observers at the time. *(For more on Elvis, see pages 202 and 207.)*

LEFT: Elvis was nervous about playing Vegas, and secretly studied the performances of Tom Jones for tips.
RIGHT: Howard Hughes "changed Las Vegas forever."

Howard Hughes

Early in the morning on or around Thanksgiving Day in 1966, the eccentric tycoon Howard Hughes arrived in the parking lot of the Desert Inn and was carried on a stretcher to the hotel's ninth-floor penthouse. The windows were blacked out with drapes, armed guards were stationed by the elevator and seven Mormon personal aides worked shifts around the clock, catering to his every need. He checked in for 10 days, and, during the four years he was there, never left his far-from lavish bedroom. He took daily codeine injections for spinal injuries he'd sustained in an airplane crash, and subsisted,

THE AUTOBIOGRAPHY THAT WASN'T

In 1972, novelist Clifford Irving made publishing deals with McGraw Hill and *Life* magazine for what he claimed was billionaire Howard Hughes' autobiography. Mike Wallace inteviewed Irving about the book on CBS's show *60 Minutes*. Hughes was so reclusive that it took months for the manuscript to be exposed as a fake, Hughes himself finally giving a telephone press conference. *60 Minutes* called Irving "Con Man of the Year," and he admitted, "I was filled with the success of my fairy tale." He repaid the $765,000 advance to McGraw Hill, was convicted of fraud, and served 14 months in jail. Years later, Irving published the whole story in *The Hoax*.

it's said, on Campbell's chicken soup and banana-nut ice cream. He stored his urine in sealed glass jars and, despite his phobia about germs, the room was never cleaned during the whole of the four years.

Hughes hired Robert Maheu to act as his personal liaison to the outside world. Maheu did not meet Hughes when he was hired, nor during his four-year employment, or ever afterwards, but during his tenure, he was as close as anyone outside would get to Hughes.

When the reclusive tycoon hadn't initially checked out in time to make room for the high rollers booked in for the Christmas season, the

owners of the Desert Inn were furious. So was Hughes. Hughes' man, Maheu, contacted John Rosselli, the Mob's liaison with Vegas. Maheu and Rosselli had known each other allegedly from their having collaborated on an abortive CIA plot to murder Fidel Castro. Maheu also called on Jimmy Hoffa for help as the resort's owner, Moe Dalitz, had been partly financed from the Teamsters Union pension fund which was under Hoffa's control. Dalitz succumbed and agreed to sell the resort to Hughes. After a lot of quibbling Hughes took possession of the Desert Inn on April 1, 1967 for $13.2 million.

"Just by showing up, Hughes changed Las Vegas forever," Kenneth Evans said in *The*

First Hundred, a book about the men and women who shaped Las Vegas. "If one of the richest men in the world, one of the nation's largest defense contractors, was willing to invest in Las Vegas, it must not be such a sordid, evil place after all."

Lord of the valley

Hughes had seen Las Vegas' potential, and was attracted by the fact that it would take only money for him to become lord of the valley. Nevada had no income tax, inheritance tax or state corporate tax. "We can make a really super environmental city of the future here," he wrote. "No smog, no contamination, efficient local government where the taxpayers pay as little as possible and get something for their money." He sold his TWA stock, and went on a buying spree. He acquired the Frontier for $14 million, and the land now occupied by the Mirage and Treasure Island, which he never developed. He also bought the lot now occupied by the Fashion Show Mall, then the Silver Slipper adjoining the Frontier, although he was denied the right to buy the Stardust Hotel. His aim was to own all the property opposite the Desert Inn. Then Hughes bought the Sands. Together with the Landmark, large lots on the Strip, the North Las Vegas airport, a TV station, and a small airline, Hughes spent a total of $300 million. He reportedly bought KLAS-TV just so that he could write their late-night movie schedules to suit his own taste.

Predictably, Hughes declined to emerge from his hideaway to fill out application forms or be fingerprinted, and Governor Paul Laxalt waived all requirements. About him not appearing personally, Control Board chairman Alan Abner stated, "Hughes' life and background are well known to this board and he is highly qualified." Shortly before, Hughes had written to the governor pledging money for a medical school at the University of Nevada.

On November 5, 1970, Howard Hughes was carried from the Desert Inn, still on a stretcher, and put on a plane to the Bahamas. He died five years later, aged 70. ❑

LEFT: Jimmy Hoffa was president of the Teamsters Union and helped friends like Moe Dalitz purchase casinos by embezzling from the union's pension fund.
RIGHT: Elvis Aaron Presley ties the knot with Priscilla Beaulieu at the Aladdin Hotel, May, 1967.

MODERN LAS VEGAS

The opening of Caesars Palace heralded the current era of
fantasy writ large. And larger. And then as large as it could get

Jay Sarno's visions were studies in excess. It's rumored that he once wanted to stock the fountain pool of a restaurant at Caesars Palace with piranhas, which would be fed a baby pig at mealtimes. The Health Department banned the stunt. His deputy at the Circus Circus casino, Don Williams, said, "His insights all came from his own appetites. Get prettier girls. Build bigger buildings, get better restaurants, have bigger gamblers around. All those things came from his loins, not his brain."

Hail Caesar

The opening of Sarno's Caesars Palace in August 1966 heralded the modern Las Vegas era of fantasy writ large. The towering white palace of illusion with Greek and Roman edifices set the tone for the giant spectacles which now line the Strip. Jay Sarno, owner of a chain of theme hotels, was a frequent visitor to Vegas in the 1960s to play craps, at which he was a consistent loser. He later admitted that he lost $1 million gambling over two years. Although Sarno may have been a lousy gambler, he was an imaginative visionary. He felt that the hotel casinos were unattractively commonplace.

His daughter September says, "He was building slick, gorgeous hotels and making a living. Then he saw modest hotels here making money hand over fist. He realized he wasn't building the wrong kind of hotels, he was building them in the wrong place." Former *Nevada Journal* editor A.D. Hopkins said that Sarno's radical philosophy was for casinos to be "an island of fantasy in a mundane world." Sarno traveled to Europe, photographing columns, pilasters, rooftops and flying buttresses.

So was born Caesars Palace, a new kind of gambling resort that shifted the style of the city. Inspired by Italian baroque, its approach dotted with pillars and fountains and its staff

dressed as Roman gladiators, Caesars Palace was a sensation. The main restaurant was called Bacchanal where wine goddesses massaged diners as they ate. "People would travel from faraway places just to get a shoulder and neck massage from these goddesses," September told an interviewer.

Three years later Sarno sold Caesars Palace for $60 million, double what it had cost, and planned an even more ambitious casino, Circus Circus, targeted exclusively at the high-rollers. For Sarno, though, Circus Circus was a bust. Money was wasted trying to fly a pink-painted elephant on an overhead track. Patrons descended by fireman's pole or a waterslide into the casino, but too many drunks were nearly injured. Some concessionaires on the midway operated crooked rackets, and serious gamblers were distracted by the overhead show. There were no hotel rooms to keep customers on the premises, but the fatal flaw was probably the notion of an admission charge.

PRECEDING PAGES: aeriel view of Las Vegas today.
LEFT: the implosion of the Sands Hotel in 1996 marked the beginning of the Venetian Hotel.
RIGHT: Steve Wynn, architect of modern Las Vegas.

After five years of losses, Sarno sold out to new owners, who turned Circus Circus around. It was successfully marketed to a middle-class audience. *Las Vegas Life* writer Greg Blake Miller called Jay Sarno,"The Freud and Ford of Las Vegas. The first in town to fully realize the link between our dreams and our appetites. The central assumption of his career was that we wanted the same things he did."

Howard Hughes' stay from the 1960s to 1970 brought change to the casino business. His acquisition of six casinos, generating about a quarter of Vegas' gaming revenues, marked the shift to corporate ownership, and the influence of the Mob is said to have virtually disappeared. Today, vigilantly monitored by the state gaming authority and tax watchdogs, the gambling business seems financially respectable.

As usual, this paid off. The 1970s and 80s saw Vegas continue in its role as playground to the stars – whether they were appearing on stage, gambling in the casinos or working it off on the golf courses. Everyone who was anyone made a pilgrimage to Sin City: Liz Taylor and Richard Burton, Sonny and Cher, the Beatles.

Steve Wynn became a familiar face to American television viewers when the youthful casino boss appeared in the 1980s in a series

A MODERN TALE OF SEX, DRUGS, DEATH AND BURIED TREASURE

On September 17, 1998, Sandy Murphy, 26, called for an ambulance at Ted Binion's Las Vegas ranch. Paramedics found Binion lifeless in his den, surrounded by drugs and drug paraphernalia. Police quickly concluded that death was by a self-inflicted overdose.

Ted had succeeded his father Benny in running the family businesses, including Binion's Horseshoe, the casino in downtown Vegas. He always kept cash handy, and buried silver worth $6 million in a desert vault. Ted had drug problems and a stormy affair with Sandy, a lap-dancer. Ted's lawyer, James J. Brown, told police of a call from Binion the previous day. "Take Sandy out of the will if

she doesn't kill me tonight," Binion said. "If I'm dead, you'll know what happened." Ted's associates were amazed no cash or items of value were discovered when the ranch was searched. The next night, police found Murphy's "companion," Rick Tabbish, unearthing Binion's silver stash in the desert with a truck and a digger.

Following a lengthy trial, Murphy and Tabbish were found guilty of Binion's murder by "Burking." After sedating him with a cocktail of heroin and Xantax, one of the killers sat on his chest while a pillow was pressed to his face. "Burking" leaves few marks and was named after William Burke, a 19th-century Scottish murderer.

of teasing TV commercials with Frank Sinatra. The world's most famous crooner had signed a three-year contract to appear at the Golden Nugget, of which Wynn was president.

Wynn's winners

In 1989, Wynn bought the Mirage. With a waterfall, an active "volcano" and white tigers, it made a $44 million profit in the first quarter, and profits of 17 or 18 percent in its first year, at a time when Caesars Palace, its next door neighbor, declined by 43 percent. Ever the self-publicizing showman, Wynn conducted a video tour of the hotel in all 3,044 guest rooms. He followed this in 1993 with Treasure Island, and filled the sidewalk with spectators who gawked at its nightly "naval battle."

At the time, Wynn's annual salary of $34.2 millon made him the highest-paid executive in America. In 1992 he paid $75 million for the Dunes, then spent another million blowing it up, accompanied by a huge fireworks display for an audience of 200,000 people on the Strip.

He promised that its replacement, Bellagio, would be "the single most extravagant hotel ever built on earth." With choreographed colored fountains jetting water 160 feet (49 meters) into the air and a lobby dominated by Dale Chiluly's massive glass chandelier *(see page 158)*, it fulfilled his boast.

Wynn sold all of his holdings in March 2000 to Kirk Kerkorian's MGM Grand Inc. for $6.4 billion to plan a new spectacle; Le Reve, "the dream," in French. For a location, Wynn bought and demolished the 50-year-old Desert Inn. Speaking to a convention in 2001, Wynn said, "Le Reve has been the most wonderful experience of my life. It's about our desert and the southwestern United States."

The MGM Grand was the biggest hotel in town, and both incarnations of this casino were owned by Kirk Kerkorian, a former charter airline operator. In 1967, as owner of the Flamingo Hotel, he was able to start work on the International. This was so successful that his $16.6 million investment was soon worth $180 million. After selling the International and the Flamingo to the Hilton hotel group, Kerkorian became a majority stockholder in both

MGM and United Artists Studios. The first MGM Grand was opened in December, 1973 with 2,100 rooms. It suffered a disastrous fire on November 23, 1980, in which 700 people were injured and 83 died. When the hotel was sold to the Bally Corporation in 1985, one fifth of the price – $110 million – was reserved for outstanding settlements arising from the fire.

Kerkorian has always craved privacy. "I think it's better to keep your business private," he told writer Dave Palermo during an interview in which he expressed his admiration for his former rival Howard Hughes. "I liked him. He was a helluva guy. If you take him early in

his career he didn't get the credit he deserves." Of Kerkorian himself, a stock analyst said, "Every shareholder who has participated with him has doubled or tripled his money. That's a record few men have."

In 1994, plans were announced for the 1,500 room hotel-casino New York-New York. When it opened three years later, 100,000 visitors a day came. One very satisfied customer was Sue Henley, a Las Vegas construction inspector who won $12.5 million from a slot machine, the largest jackpot up to that time.

Downtown casinos were regarding their competitors on the Strip with both awe and envy and in 1994 began to fight back by break-

---

LEFT: Jay Sarno was, according to a local writer, the "Freud and Ford of Las Vegas."

RIGHT: Kirk Kerkorian, money-maker *extraordinaire*.

ing ground for the Fremont Street Experience, a six-block section of the main street topped with an elaborate canopy onto which were presented giant animation shows.

Costing millions of dollars both to build and to operate, it drew tourists but ultimately proved to be a financial disappointment and by 2002, there were signs that the whole idea might need to undergo a reappraisal.

The closing years of the century were marked by even greater expansion on the Strip. The first tunnel under the Strip was completed, the Desert Inn Road arterial; the Monte Carlo and the Stratosphere Tower both opened; and in

quick succession came Steve Wynn's Bellagio, the even larger Venetian – on the site of the former Sands Hotel – Paris Las Vegas with its replica of the Eiffel Tower; and the Mandalay Bay Resort, where the owners, Circus Circus Enterprises, went so far as to change their name to the Mandalay Resort Group. MGM Grand's acquisition of Mirage Resorts Inc. from Steve Wynn created the largest corporate buyout in gaming history. By now, Las Vegas had 19 of the world's 20 biggest hotels and was attracting 32 million visitors per year.

But all was not well. Urban growth brought with it all-too-familiar problems. Police reports show an influx of the kind of street gangs seen in almost every other major city. A *Washington Post* story suggested that some citizens actually yearn for the bad old days. "Those punks wouldn't have dared show their faces when Bugsy was around," one old-timer groused.

Trouble in paradise

But not all of this is new. Throughout the last three decades, the Strip has had its share of labor problems. Unions voted for strike action on March 11, 1970, known as locally as Black Wednesday. The Desert Inn, Las Vegas Hilton and Caesars Palace were hit. The strike was said to have cost the casinos $600,000, and the state lost $500,000 tax revenue. The Frontier was hit by a strike for 75 days in 1985, and again on September 21, 1991 in action that lasted six years and four months. The unions vowed they would be out "one day longer than the Elardi family's ownership," and they achieved it. There was talk of strike action again in April 2002, when unions representing staff in 36 casinos complained of lay-offs after a downturn in trade following September 11, 2001, and increased burdens in working conditions. That same year, a bartenders' strike was called in the downtown area.

About one quarter of the visitors to Vegas each year are coming for the first time, and they were the among first block of trade to fall off after the September 11, 2001 debacle. To lure them back, along with as many Vegas veterans as possible, a $13 million eight-week campaign was centered around a rediscovered and never-before-released Sinatra song, *It's Time for You,* which was licensed by Tina Sinatra.

An important part of the city's – and particularly the Strip's – plans for the future is the Las Vegas monorail. Significantly, the monorail is a rare example of a public transportation system substantially funded by the private sector. It is claimed to be the first such project "in the world," but that's just Vegas.

The existing link between the MGM Grand in the south and Bally's/Paris was opened in 1995 at a cost of $25 million. The current system uses two trains which were purchased from Walt Disney World. The project is to extend the route to the Sahara in the north along a 4 mile (6.5 km) route, with stops serving the Flamingo Hilton, Harrah's/Imperial Palace, and the Las Vegas Convention Center. The nine fully automated four-car trains will be capable of carrying up to 5,000 passengers per hour in both directions, and making up to 4.4 million passenger trips annually.

Travel by monorail

The monorail design is built to be upgraded to 20,000 passengers per hour by the addition of further trains, considerably more than any current projections of demand. An automated fare-collection system is also incorporated into the project. While the present monorail is free to travelers, the extended system is intended to collect a fare per journey. The scheme should be completed around 2005, if not sooner.

ground test site in the Nevada desert in 1992, its actions continued to arouse passions in the community when, six years later, it announced that Yucca Mountain, just 90 miles (144 km) northwest of Las Vegas, was to be the site where the entire nation's nuclear waste was to be entombed.

Congress decided, supposedly after a 15-year-long study, that the mountain was the best place to hide 77,000 tons of radioactive rubbish that would theoretically remain deadly for hundreds of thousands of years. The announced plan, furiously opposed by Nevadans, would be for the site to begin storing the nuclear waste

Present estimates are that the railway will reduce traffic around the Strip by 4.4 million journeys per year, cutting annual carbon monoxide emissions by 135 tons. Ultimately, the monorail is hoped to be extended as far as Downtown, although the fortunes of the downtown area may need a fillip in some form well before then.

Although the United States' government stopped exploding nuclear bombs at its under-

in 2010 and continue for the next century, after which the tunnels would be capped. Nevada governor Kenny Guin vetoed the plan, declaring it "based on bad science, bad law and bad public policy." He said that the nuclear industry had spent $120 million in support of the Yucca Mountain proposal and he asked all Nevadans to contribute to a fund to counter the initiative.

The veto was overridden by simple majorities in the House and Senate, but the battle goes on. The license for the US Energy Authority is not due to be presented until December 2004, and between now and then many Nevadans will be looking for ways to prevent the scheme. ❑

LEFT: in the last few decades, Vegas has suffered from a succession of strikes.
ABOVE: the monorail currently being built plays an important role in the future of the city.

VIVA LAS VEGAS

The city is built on illusion and dreams.

In many ways, this is reflected by the people who live here

Las Vegas is truly a 24-hour city. Most modern cities make that claim, but try to get served a decent meal at 4 am. Here, night and day really are almost indistinguishable. At any hour of the day or night you may need to and you can, without difficulty: buy clothes and jewelery, get married, hire an attorney, get divorced, or engage an Elvis impersonator.

Just ordinary stars

But in other ways Vegas is a city just like any other – ordinary folks live here and go about their business, albeit with a larger percentage of people associated with entertainment, nightlife and the *demi monde*. Between them, the casinos and hotels employ a total of 166,000 Las Vegas residents. For many, Vegas is their last stop – a place to work at that final job before retiring. But it's not just the aging butchers, bakers or cabinet makers who will settle in Sin City. For many others it just seems to become a natural home. These include musicians, comics, dancers and other performers who have spent a part of their working lives here and developed an abiding affinity with the place.

Professional athletes – tennis players, golfers, football and baseball stars – may also have earned some of their living here, and for many of them, gambling may not be an unfamiliar pastime. Wild-haired Don King and his fellow-promoter Bob Arum have chosen residence in this city where boxing plays such a large part. The defeated heavyweight and ex-convict Mike Tyson keeps a home here, too.

World champion basketball star Shaquille O'Neal, center for the Los Angeles Lakers, has a home, reputed to be a mere five minutes from the Strip. The multiple Grand Slam winner Andre Agassi, still ranked as a world-class tennis player, enjoys family life here with wife Steffi Graf and their son Jaden Gil.

PRECEDING PAGES: Blue Hawaiian Room of Viva Las Vegas; Sin City allows smoking and encourages eating.
LEFT: Elvis is alive and on almost every Vegas stage.
RIGHT: training for the big time.

Basketball star Greg Anthony, who got his start playing on the Las Vegas campus of the University of Nevada, has played for a number of professional teams during his 11-year career, and is now with the Milwaukee Bucks but still maintains a home locally, as does Las Vegas-born Marty Cordova, currently a left fielder for

the Baltimore Orioles. Former Boston Red Sox second baseman Marty Barrett ended his career with the San Diego Padres in 1991. He has supported local youth baseball players and provided TV commentary for the Las Vegas 51s. Kevin Elster settled here after spending most of his 13-year career with the New York Mets, and former city councilman Frank Hawkins had once been a professional footballer with the Oakland Raiders.

Stage and television stars who have chosen Las Vegas to set up home include the former teen heart throb David Cassidy, actor and artist Tony Curtis, and singers La Toya Jackson, Clint Holmes, Gladys Knight, Steve Lawrence and

Eydie Gorme, Tony Orlando, and Sheena Easton. Comics Marty Allen, David Brenner, Rich Little and Jerry Lewis have settled in the Las Vegas Valley, as have musicians Sam Butera and Carl Fontana.

Performers Debbie Reynolds and Wayne Newton have made businesses here, much like magicians Lance Burton, Penn and Teller and Siegfried & Roy. Celine Dion seems to be following the trend in the opposite direction. Impressed by the Cirque du Soleil's having a theatre custom designed and built around a single show, she wanted one of her own. Now she has it, designed by the same outfit.

"Trying to identify all the celebrities who live here is difficult," said Sonya Padgett, who compiled a list for the *Review-Journal*, "because many prefer to keep a low profile… (and) while we think our hospitality and favorable weather are selling points, it's just as likely celebrities decide to move to Southern Nevada for the tax advantages."

One of the disadvantages, however, might be the commuting problems. After Los Angeles, Las Vegas was named as the worst rush-hour traffic city in the country, offering the fewest ways to avoid it. More than 35 percent of Las Vegans' travel time is spent in traffic jams. Having said that, it's not every town where

Meals on Wheels might be delivered by a nationally known racing car driver in his souped-up speedster, which is what happened the day that NASCAR Busch Series driver Larry Foyt kicked off the casino Harrah's sponsorship of the famous program that feeds needy seniors. Often praised for its community outreach, Harrah's recently donated a refrigerated Meals on Wheels delivery van to the Catholic Charities of Southern Nevada and, through its 25 casinos in 12 states, is a national corporate sponsor of the program.

Like anywhere else, but maybe for different reasons, people arrive in Las Vegas for a visit and then never leave. And some become active in local affairs. One such, media consultant and TV producer Mike Lavine, was active in a successful battle against the local power company to reduce a proposed rate increase. Two of his recent "causes" have been medicine malpractice and the controversy over the Yucca Mountain nuclear waste dump *(see page 61)*.

The rest of his time is devoted to organizing handicapping events, including a World Cup of Video Poker and the World Cup of Football Handicapping. "I am pretty much known around the world as the grandfather of handicapping tournaments," he said. "I started them all." He believes Las Vegas' future lies in conventions and special events. "You can be anywhere in the world and gamble. You don't have to come here and gamble. The convention center just expanded another million square feet, Mandalay Bay is adding 1.5 million square feet. When they finish I think we'll be number one in convention space. Nevada should get on and ride that horse as hard and long as it can."

What's more, the city is a perfect man-trap. After Alaska – which has a ratio of 107 men to every 100 women, Las Vegas has the second highest men-to-women ratio, 103.9 men to 100 women. Nationally there are said to be 143.4 women to every 100 men.

Gambling family

Annie Duke, 36, and her brother Howard Lederer, 38, are professional poker players who have both reached the finals of the World Series of Poker, Annie when she was nine months pregnant. Howard is twice World Champion. Their father, Richard Lederer, has written about linguistics, and their sister, Katy, 29, is author of a book *Poker Face: Growing Up in a Family of Gamblers.* "The household was very competitive," Katy said. "It wasn't just the card games, it was who got to eat the last Oreo, who decided what to watch on TV. Everything was cut-throat in that household."

Howard Lederer was a chess champion at school in New Hampshire and left Columbia to take up poker full time. He now plays non-tournament high-stakes games at Bellagio a couple of times a week and occasionally competes in tournaments as far afield as Mississippi or London.

Annie Duke attended the University of Pennsylvania, but left to get married and live in rus-

and cultural life including two active theater companies, concerts, a winter season by the Las Vegas Philharmonic, and a community center which screens art-house movies and stages both jazz and classical concerts.

Queen of culture

The university's Performing Arts Center hosts ballet, chamber orchestra and jazz concerts, and the city turned over an old Mormon facility which it had been using as a city hall while a new one was built. This old building, renamed the Reed Whipple Center after one of the commissioners who brokered the deal, was desig-

tic Montana with husband and now four kids. She persuaded her brother to teach her poker about ten years ago and frequently finds him an opponent at Bellagio. "We're not brother and sister at the poker table," said Duke. "If my emotions were that ratcheted up I'd be a pretty bad player." Lederer said, "Whenever I do well, I am referred to as the brother of Annie Duke, which is pretty amusing considering I taught her to play."

Although Las Vegas is a city dedicated to tourism, there is a surprisingly rich local social

LEFT: Cirque du Soleil have two permanent shows.
ABOVE: guarding the *gondoliere* is all in a day's work.

nated for recreational and cultural affairs. "It's rare that a municipality seeks out the arts," commented Jody Johnson, who used its stage for productions by the Rainbow Company, a children's theater she started with local playwright Brian Strom.

Almost immediately the troupe won recognition from the Children's Theater Association of America as best in the United States. Many of its graduates, now grown up, have gone on to successful theater careers.

The City Council chose local artist Patricia Marchese to run the town's highly active cultural affairs program. Las Vegas' "Queen of Culture," as one of the local papers called her, takes enormous pleasure in the increasing privatization of the arts. "The arts are not going to make it in this town till the casinos get into the business. And now they have. You have top Broadway shows here. Cézanne here, Russian jewels here, all in casinos.

"I would hope that this would turn into an enlightenment that will lead people to greater support of the local arts. Any time people are exposed to high-level arts, it engenders a desire for more," she said.

> **MAN POWER**
>
> The Las Vegas area has the second-highest man-to-woman ratio in the United States, exceeded only by far-flung Alaska.

plots of Dallas-like magnitude and, yes, people angry and suspicious."

"The architectural madness," she said, "sometimes reminds me of bad opera in which the libretto and the music do not harmonize... try to imagine what this place would be like if only more poets, painters, writers and other artists moved in to create the right atmosphere... It is crying out to be an artist area like Soho or the Village in New York. All it needs are the cafés, bookstores, studios and art galleries." The city has something like

Locals live here, too

A few years ago, Syl Cheney-Coker moved to Las Vegas from Sierra Leone with her husband. At first she was frustrated, trying to find the "city." She wrote in *Las Vegas Life* that the initial impression was surreal.

"I kept asking people, 'Where is it? Show me the center, its soul, its rhythm (besides the awful traffic), the complex social atmosphere of happily interacting souls.' But drive away from the Strip and half a dozen blocks later you are in a different world, less magical – something I believe Fellini would have found absurd; a vast, disconnected suburban sprawl howling of empty hours, loneliness, family-inheritance

this in mind, Anthony Curtis wrote in the *Las Vegas Advisor* – a six-block area on Fremont and Carson streets east of Las Vegas Boulevard, where it aims to create an entertainment area with bars, nightclubs and restaurants. But, he concluded, "nerves are still raw after the city's last land grab (for the Fremont Street Experience) so don't count on such a development any time soon. What we are likely to see for a while is more expansion and renovation as the most profitable casinos grow bigger and the rest do what they have to do to keep pace."

But, significantly, 2002 was the first year in a decade that not a single new casino opened. "Las Vegas has its casino corridor but that's not for its residents," says the architect Bernardo Fort-Brescia. His Miami-based firm is busily developing a 64-acre (26-hectare) residential and technology park in Hong Kong.

"Las Vegas is now large and sophisticated enough that it demands a focal point, a sense of place for its residents," he responds, when the subject of the endless plans for reviving Downtown comes up. Because of the sale in 2001 of 1,900 acres (769 hectares) by the US Bureau of Land Management, a further 5,000 homes are pro-

PEAK POPULATION

A local study concluded that the population of the Las Vegas Valley had increased 194 percent in the last 20 years.

where luxury and exceptional service is a top priority," says vice-president of sales, John Riordan. Another development is Park Towers, where marble fountains, cast iron statues and antiques from Paris adorn the gardens and public spaces. Home prices here range from $720,000 to $3.2 million.

Summerlin

Summerlin is an upscale community development spread over 35 square miles (9,000 hectares) of land once owned by Howard Hughes but undeveloped until recently. Built

jected in North Las Vegas which abuts the downtown area. There has been an increase in upscale development in the city itself. Four 40-story towers comprise Turnberry Place, a luxury high-rise at the corner of Paradise Road across from the Hilton.

Glass balconies offer "unparalleled city views," and there are indoor and outdoor pools centered around a spa in the Stirling Club, and a restaurant complete with wine lockers for individual members. "People want to live in a place

LEFT: the glamorous life of a showgirl.
ABOVE: Oscar Goodman, ebullient mayor of Las Vegas, at the Golden Nugget casino.

to house 160,000 people with one-bedroom apartments starting at $800 per month, five-bedroom homes cost more than $1 million. At the foot of the Spring Mountains, 12 miles (19 km) west of the Strip, Summerlin sits off US 95 at the end of a long ramp built by the Hughes Corporation.

At the time the ramp led into empty desert and was ridiculed as "the road to nowhere," but now leads to the fastest growing planned community in the US. "The Federal Bureau of Land Management considers most of Nevada a wasteland, and it was quite a trick to turn wasteland into an attractive place for people to live," says urban planner Mark Gottdiener, author of *Las Vegas – the Social Production of an All-American City.*

One of the first corporations to build in Summerlin was Del Webb, named after one of Hughes' ancestors. Nearly 8,000 homes were bought as soon as they went on sale. "People see Las Vegas as five miles of hotels and casinos but there's another side to it," says A. Somer Hollingworth, president of the Nevada Development Authority which recruits businesses to come to the area. Additionally, more upscale accommodations were becoming necessary for the top-quality people the bigger Strip resorts were hiring. Summerlin has parks,

golf courses, ball fields, desert trails, a library, and a performing arts center with a "town center" planned for the future comprised of hotels and more shops and offices.

Dissenters in the desert

Former Las Vegas city councilman Steve Miller is critical of the valley's growing sprawl, which he claims has resulted in increased crime, insufficiency of schools and even worse traffic congestion. "As we crowd more and more people into a small space, and crowd each square mile of desert with higher population ratios, our quality of life is suffering," he charges. A national study concluded that the city's population had increased 194 percent in the past 20 years but had increased land area by less than half that in the same period.

"Sprawl is defined in the study as either an increase in population and its effect on existing infrastructure," Miller writes, "or the paving over of rural areas to accommodate the influx of new residents with more shopping centers, neighborhood casinos, sewage treatment facilities, schools, roads, etc. Las Vegas represents the first scenario: more new residents (6,000 per month) taxing existing facilities."

What was once mere horse country had turned into high-density per square mile urban population sprawl and, he said, "our limited public facilities are being strained to capacity. We should be building more and larger parks, schools, roads, libraries, colleges, police and fire stations to maintain even a minimum quality of life, but we are not."

In the last few years, Las Vegas' homeless population has doubled to 12,000, but for many, Las Vegas is the American dream come true – affordable housing, no state income tax and well-paying jobs that don't require much education," said an Associated Press story in 2002. "Only three states have fewer college graduates, but the average household income of $24,177 is the nation's 19th highest. Valet car attendants can easily bring in $50,000. Card dealers on the Strip can make much more than that and don't need a high school diploma."

Between 1990 and 2000 the Las Vegas Valley had the country's biggest metropolitan area increase. "The city has become a glamorous getaway for visitors but also attracts the desperate, people who couldn't make it anywhere else and came here as a last resort."

A stripper in a local bar might make $300 on a good night, and one just off the Strip could more than triple that. Barbara Brent, a sociologist at the University of Nevada Las Vegas said that the city "is built on illusion and dreams. Its whole goal to tourists is to sell fantasy. In some ways that spills over into people who see it as a place where they can fulfill things that they couldn't do elsewhere."

Maybe it's the glamour of the 24-hour twilight zone, in this town with no sense of time. ❑

LEFT: moving walkways keep pedestrians on the move from one casino to the next.
RIGHT: bride, groom and the Venetian.

DICING WITH LADY LUCK

Hope springs eternal in the human breast,
and nowhere is this more evident than on the floor of a gaming hall

Alan Wykes once said in a book on the subject, "Gambling is a way of buying hope on credit." Or, as Alexander Pope said, "hope springs eternal in the human breast." Everybody dreams of leaving this town a lot richer than they arrived.

A couple of years ago, a survey called the Las Vegas Visitor Profile reported that more than 90 percent of the city's tourists claimed the primary purpose for their visit was other than gambling. But a follow-up was more revealing, indicating that almost an equal number had actually had a little flutter. For some it was nothing more than quarters dropped into a slot machine, yet the average number of hours spent gambling was four, and the average spent on gaming $655.

A Godfather speaks

Mario Puzo, author of *The Godfather*, has written from his own gaming experience. "A gambler should never write a check or sign a chit," he said, "gambling only with the money he brought with him, if he wants to stay out of trouble." He discussed what he refers to as the "ruin factor," which is less important when you have nothing to lose, but "now I have too much to lose, and the ruin factor is decisive. Of course, I had to lose a great deal of money and come close to ruin before I could figure this out. Gambling education is not cheap."

Once upon a time in America, government policy was to discourage or even prohibit gambling, but that was another age. Today, more and more states not only allow, but encourage gaming. Politicians seem to have fallen under the spell of easy revenue, almost as much as the casino bosses and the punters.

The most significant change on the green baize map in recent years has been the growth of gambling on Native American reservations. As semi-autonomous regions, Indian nations are able to

run casinos even in states which otherwise prohibit it. Of America's 561 tribes recognized by the Federal government, 108 are in California. Las Vegas casino owners were alarmed by the competition so nearby, and spent $20 million fighting to prevent Indian gambling businesses, until a Californian legal decision allowed it in

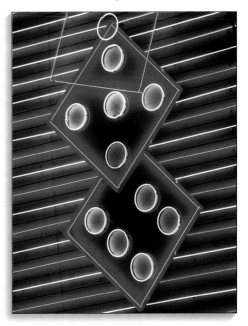

1988. Forty tribes already have bingo parlors and 50 more are demanding recognition from the government and the right to reservations of their own. Las Vegas claims that the Indian casinos in California, from where up to one-third of their 36 million visitors come each year, are taking 10 percent of their business – a whopping $1 billion a year. In what looks like an acceptance of the new reality, however, Harrah's are in partnership with the Rincon Reservation near Escondito in California for a co-managed casino resort.

Nevertheless, with new gambling outlets opening every day, Las Vegas continues to hold sway because, according to *The Wine Spectator* "Nowhere on earth will serious bettors find more

LEFT: more than $1 million in chips at Bellagio.
RIGHT: casino security are very careful about dice: cheats have been known to load them with weights so a die always rolls to the bottom number.

games and fairer odds... more diversions and greater spectacles... a city as wonderfully warped and slick as this incongruously lush outpost in the desert."

From high rollers like radio host Howard Stern, who tried to place a $1 million bet on a black-jack hand, to the nickel-slots players, more than most leisure activities, gambling cuts across social and economic classes.

Gambling as a subject has been studied from just about every angle, and in minute detail, and in almost every way the statistics go up and up. According to the *Las Vegas Review-Journal*, Nevada gaming revenues for 2001 were around

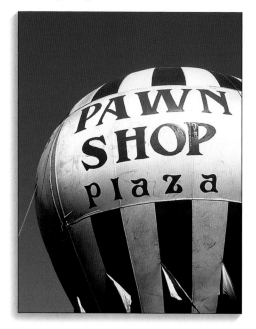

$9.67 billion. The average gambler is in the $48,000 a year income bracket and the troubled ones had gambling debts of $37,000, based on 3,000 recent calls made to New Jersey's Council on Compulsive Gambling. More than 80 percent of the callers were male, white and between the ages of 21 and 55.

The percentage of women gamblers has also soared, as reported by the Connecticut Council on Problem Gambling, with a huge increase in calls to its hotline. Statistically, men and women carry similar gambling debts, about $21,000 according to the council, but men have a greater average lifetime loss: $74,000 against $54,000. Independent studies suggest that compulsive gambling

may be higher among teens than adults. For teenagers, gambling may begin with friendly wagers on sports events, penny-ante card games or the lucky "gift" of a lottery ticket from an adult family member.

To their credit, the casinos do not sweep the problem of compulsive gambling under the rug. Eight gaming companies are represented on the Council on Problem Gambling, which develops treatment resources and displays large posters exhorting, "Know when to stop." The posters also give a 24-hour-a-day help line number to call (tel: 800 522-4700).

Compulsive gambling

Compulsive gambling is described as "an emotional illness that remains hidden until the consequences begin to affect the financial and emotional security of the gambler and his family." Early warning signs, according to the leaflet, include any of these: losing time from work or family, borrowing money to gamble, gambling to escape worry, selling personal possessions to get gambling money, and lying about the time and money spent on gambling.

Harrah's, a member of the council, is more forthcoming than some gaming companies on the subject. The company's director of community relations, Mary Jane Fuller, says that Harrah's has invested $250,000 a year in compulsive gambling programs. "In a gambling addiction," said writer Joseph Epstein, "one tends to bet on anything – from the gestation period of a gerbil to different lengths of two paper clips."

One thing that might help is the Innovative Gaming Corporation of America's technology, which allows gamblers to program their ATM

CITY OF SLOTS

There are a few non-gambling oases in Vegas, but slot machines seem to pop up in more places all the time. In 2000, the Gaming Commission allowed druggists and groceries to install slots if they were walled off from the rest of the store, but they also made specific exceptions: new liquor stores, gas stations, no-booze restaurants, car dealerships, motels, car washes, fast fooderies and sandwich shops. Tourists at McCarran airport find slot machines as much of a lure as the shops. Contrary to the myth that machines outside the casinos seldom pay off, within a two-week period in 2002, there were two million-dollar winners on McCarran's slots.

cards at a casino kiosk with a set limit, and then use them in slot machines which "lock up" when the limit is reached. The gambler is not allowed to use it again for five to 10 days.

The history of blackjack

Also known as "Twenty-One" or *vingt-et-un*, blackjack is a descendant from the French game of *chemin de fer*, as is baccarat. There are stories of the game having been played in casinos in France as far back as the early 1700s. It arrived in the United States in the 1800s, and got its modern name from the frontier practice of paying out extra on a hand of an ace with the jack of spades,

The top hand of an ace and either a 10 or a picture card is called blackjack. The house pays evens (1-1) to a winner, and 3-2 for blackjack.

There are innumerable systems for blackjack which all promise to tip the odds in favor of the player. The system known as "card counting," however, is still treated as cheating by Nevada casinos. Widely regarded as the world's greatest blackjack player, Ken Uston gave up his post as a senior vice-president of the Pacific Stock Exchange in order to organize teams of card counters. He also developed a tiny computer, worn in the user's shoe, which was claimed to predict the fall of the cards with 80 percent accu-

i.e. "blackjack." The natural house edge is 3.5 percent, but a skilled player can reduce it to 1 percent or less, among the best odds in the casino.

Avery Cardoza, a gambling author and publisher said, "Blackjack is a game of skill that can be beat. However, to win, you must learn the game properly." The game is played against the house, the object being to beat the dealer. This can be done by drawing a higher hand than the dealer without going over 21 – called "busting" – or it can be by not busting when the dealer does.

LEFT AND ABOVE: statistically, men and women carry similar gambling debts, but men have a greater average lifetime loss.

racy. When the Atlantic City casinos tried to bar him, he mounted a successful challenge at the Supreme Court.

Body language and "tells"

Regardless of status, motive or method, most people make unconscious revelations through body language. In poker, this can be the difference between winning or losing. Tics, twitches, nervous laughs, trembling hands or facial expressions of an opponent can be crucial giveaways. Andy Bellin discussed these "tells," as they are called, in an article in *Atlantic* magazine:

"Pop psychologists theorize that tells are unintended actions birthed in the subconscious," he writes. "Having a poker tell can be disastrous (although) overcoming a tell is as difficult as changing any other habitual aspect of your personality." Often, he says, a player will react to a called bet, slumping in his chair when he has nothing, jumping to flip the cards over when he has a good hand.

"The more attention you pay to the body language of your opponents, the less money you'll leave on the table when you walk away."

New Yorker reviewer Joseph Epstein says that poker is not a game for delicate souls. "Good players always beat less-good players over the long haul, but in poker the short haul can kill

you." He identifies aggression as the main dividing line between poker players, "the instinct for the jugular."

Newer games such as Let It Ride, Caribbean Stud, Casino War and Spanish 21 are played against the dealer. "The intimidation factor has been diminished a lot," says Barney Vinson, casino floor supervisor at Caesars Palace. "In a poker room, you don't know who you are playing against, and it can be expensive if you turn up against the wrong person."

However, the odds of winning in these specialty games are lower than in standard casino games. The house edge on craps and blackjack can be 1 percent or less, but it's about 3.5 per-

cent in Let It Ride and around 5 percent in Caribbean Stud. The casinos claim that it takes longer for the house to make a profit, and there's some truth in that. The games are popular in part because the hands take longer to play out.

Working the pit

The noisiest, rowdiest places in a casino are usually the craps tables. The play is fast and generates a great deal of excitement. Players crowd around the table – called the "pit" – and the stickman calls the shots like a carnival barker. Working the pit with the stickman are two dealers who handle the bets, and a boxman who supervises the game and settles disputes. The dice move from one player to another, and the game offers players the chance to bet either for or against the "shooter" making his target, or "point."

Dice games date back to the Bible, and craps is traced back to before the 1700s, when it is thought to have been brought to America from Europe. Craps was introduced to casino gaming in Texas by Benny Binion, and he brought it with him to Vegas when he opened Binion's Horseshoe, the Downtown casino.

Kirk Kerkorian, founder of the MGM Grand, was known as the "Perry Como of the craps table" for his style and equanimity in regularly winning – or more often losing – from $50,000 to $80,000 in an evening. Legend has it that he and a buddy were down to their last $5, and the buddy suggested they buy breakfast. Kerkorian snatched up the five dollar bills and took them to the craps table, returning half an hour later with $700. After he established his own casinos, Kerkorian reputedly stopped playing craps.

Granddaddy of all slots

The century-long history of the slot machine began with the original three-reel, Liberty Bell machine which emerged from Charles Frey's San Francisco workshop in 1898. The German-born inventor pioneered many kinds of coin-operated gaming devices, most of which found a place in the gambling clubs of San Francisco's Barbary Coast district.

The basic design of "Liberty Bell," the granddaddy of all modern American slot machines, is still used in mechanical gaming devices today, although the simple trio of reels have evolved into microprocessor-controled machines, with up to five spinning reels holding hundreds of symbols. By the time Bugsy Siegel added slots to his

Flamingo Hotel in the late 1940s they had already spread across America as a way to entertain the wives and girlfriends of high rollers. Soon they were making more revenue than the table games.

Slot machines generate two-thirds of Nevada casinos' take, with the nickel slots producing $1 billion annually. Today, slots take up 60 percent of casino floor space and generate more profits for the casinos than from all table games combined. Currently, casinos average about 3,000 slots apiece. The programming of the machines makes a jackpot rare enough for the big pay off, but still allows for a tidy profit for the casino. Most machines are set to pay out somewhere

the ever-increasing nickel slots. "We're not tightening the slots," he said, "It's the customers who are opting to go for the nickel games."

Phenomenal popularity

The phenomenal popularity of slot machines is doubtless because they require no skill and the pace can be set by the player. Players are driven by the illusion that a machine will be ready to pay off after a certain amount of play. The machines are driven by random generators that make new selections every 1,000th of a second, with no reference to what went before, so in reality the machines are never "ready to hit."

between 83 to 98 percent, but slot payoffs vary from one casino to another.

Payoffs can also vary from one year to the next. Reuters reported that in 2002, casinos on the Strip kept 6.67 percent of the slot receipts, as against 6.3 percent in 2001. The average take for all games on the Strip has also risen from 5.53 percent in 1996 to 6.03 percent in 2002. Nickel slots pay out significantly less than the higher-stake machines, though Gary Thompson, speaking for Harrah's, said this was not the reason for

LEFT AND ABOVE: slot machines were first introduced to entertain the wives and mistresses of high rollers; now they generate more revenue than table games.

These days, some machines don't even pay a jackpot on one single coin, but the three-coin jackpot often pays 150 percent of a two-coin win. Theoretically costing a quarter or a dollar, they only pay out substantial sums if two or three coins are deposited instead of one.

But less than half of slot players play more than one coin at a time, says Crevelt in his book *Video Poker Mania.* He advises, "You should always play the maximum number of coins because there is a bonus when you win (which) can be up to 5 percent of the payback, which doesn't apply if you are not playing to the full extent." Playing only a single coin at a time leaves the casino an extra advantage.

Video poker

Multiple-coin slot machines were soon followed in America by video machines which substituted screens for the old-fashioned reels. This enabled other games like poker, keno, blackjack and craps to be played on them instead of just at the table. William Silas "Si" Redd was the developer of video poker machines when he bought Fortune Coin Co. and started making kits to convert the early Pong machines.

Casinos were quick to capitalize on the explosive growth of video poker, and in a short amount of time, such machines were taking the place of the orignal slots. More than 15 percent of Har-

The 3,000-year-old game

Keno has evolved from a Chinese game which is at least 3,000 years old. Chou Kung, first son of the Kung dynasty, proclaimed the "Canon of Change," in 1120 BC, and with it raised a levy from the game which is said to have financed the Great Wall of China. The modern game makes a slightly inclined bow in Kung's direction in the "Yin-Yang" symbols on most tickets. Keno runners, like many casino workers in Vegas, count on tips for most of their income, so they're usually easy to find and eager to help. The idea is to predict as many numbers as possible of the 20 picked in a random draw. There are about half a

rah's 1,760 slots are now devoted to video poker, and the percentage is increasing, not only in Las Vegas casinos, but in other gambling towns across America. The video poker machines far outrank the table games in popularity, especially among women; almost three quarters of visitors to Las Vegas play slots as opposed to the 29 percent of players who opt for table games such as blackjack or craps.

But playing the slots can also lead to other games. "A lot of people have learned to play poker on the video poker machines," says Alan Abrams of the El Cortez casino. "Now they enjoy the camaraderie of a table game where people interact with each other."

dozen combination tickets, the bets tend to be small, and payouts can be up to $50,000. The probability of winning is too low to make keno a game for serious gamblers, but for those who seek a frivolous flutter, there is a game about every 20 minutes in most casino hotels, often in the bars or coffee shops.

Super Bowl and other sports

Every January, the handful of men known as Las Vegas Sports Consultants meet in a three-story building near McCarran airport to establish the "line," (i.e. set the gaming odds) on America's Super Bowl football game. The Sports Books in Las Vegas, plus some in other casinos around the country, are among the clients who await the official word, the yardstick from which bets can be figured. Betting during Super Bowl weekend is about three times that of an average weekend during the National Football League season and includes not only low-wagering tourists, but the high rollers – who tend to stick around, and the "wise guys" – professional sports gamblers who stay in town only long enough to win or lose big. Georgia-born Billy Baxter, a wise guy and three times winner of the World Series of Poker, wagers about $1 million that weekend, half on college football games on Saturday, the rest on pro football on Sunday.

Cards, chips and cheats

The accoutrements of games – dice, cards and chips – have to be as tamper-proof as human skills can make them. Thousands of years ago, dice were made from the knucklebones of sheep, today those used for craps are crafted to a tolerance of one ten-thousandth of an inch.

Most of the thousands of decks of cards used annually in Las Vegas are supplied by the US Playing Card Company of Cincinatti, Ohio, whose Bicycle brand – and the Bee brand for casinos – are the most widely used cards in the country. The Bee, first introduced a century ago, uses the highest percentage of rag content. This

LVSC has 14 odds-makers for sports, all of whom are licensed by the Nevada Gaming Control Board. After the Super Bowl, the NCAA basketball tournament is the single biggest gambling event. "Blink at the wrong time," says the Stardust's Sports Book manager, "and you can easily lose six figures." In 2001, according to the Nevada Gaming Control Board, casinos pulled in $2 billion in sports wagers but pocketed only $118 million, a winning margin of 6.5 percent.

LEFT: dealer at Caesars Palace of *pai gow*, a form of poker adapted from a Chinese domino game and beginning to grow in popularity.
ABOVE: playing craps at the Venetian.

gives the card a good "memory," the term that describes how well a card snaps back to its original position after being bent. "Dealers especially like the card's elasticity," says Bob LeFevre, senior vice president of USPC, which shares about 85 percent of the market with Gemaco of Independence, Missouri.

Gemaco is number one in that other gambling town, Atlantic City, partly because their cards stand up well to the coastal city's notorious humidity. The company has also patented a special design called Safety Peek Faces which enables a dealer to identify his face card without turning it over entirely. Commemorative chips are always a winning move for casinos because many gamblers take the chips home without redeeming them. Chipco International Ltd of Windham, Maine, specializes in colorful, designer graphics which have what is termed a high "walk factor," meaning that many people do take them home.

Its SmartChip, however, can be tracked by computer and trips a sensor-activated alarm if it is taken from the casino.

Paul-Son is among a small number of highly security-conscious companies manufacturing casino gambling chips which are, after all, as

CHIPS WITH EVERYTHING

When the Rolling Stones came to town, the Hard Rock casino issued a series of commemorative chips featuring the British rockers.

ting circle and angle the chips slightly towards the dealer... an attempt to block the dealer's view of the bottom chip," says George Joseph. Then, "if the cheater gets a good hand he will slide a higher value chip underneath."

The slight of hand evidenced by most magicians are much the same as those employed by casino cheats. "They're magicians, too," says writer Deke Castleman. "They're expert at diverting attention while they pull off their scam. The quickness of the hand deceives the eye."

good as cash. Casino officials are trained to check all chips for an alpha-dot no bigger than a speck of pepper. This is an anti-counterfeiting device which, under magnification, yields encoded symbols. The other big Las Vegas chip manufacturer, the Bud Jones company, makes chips with embedded metals. The latest are three-dimensional and holographic chips which they claim are almost impossible to counterfeit.

Magic skills

Since in one way or another the house nearly always wins, some casino customers are constantly devising new ways to cheat. "Some cheaters will place a stack of $5 chips in the bet-

Because it plays the highest odds (35-1 if betting on a single number), roulette is a popular target for cheats. Sometimes one of a team will blatantly try to place a late bet and, while the dealer is distracted and arguing about it, a confederate will execute the ploy.

Determined cheats surreptitiously slip their own dice into a craps game, which have been "loaded" with tiny gold or platinum weights behind the dots. This causes the dice always to fall with the weight on the bottom. Magnetic dice have been manipulated by players in wheelchairs equipped with hidden but powerful electro-magnets. For table games, cards can be bent, as well as marked with sharp fingernails. "Sanding" is done with a piece of sandpaper glued to the underside of the finger, which can then scratch off some of the print on the card. Oils, waxes and "daub," a substance like eye shadow, are used to mark cards. Inks can change a card's design or markings. Wearing red-tinted sunglasses or deep-red contact lenses enables otherwise-invisible green or violet markings to be read.

Blackjack is the casino game that gives the best odds to the gambler, and some players, like Ken Uston *(see page 77)* have improved the odds still further with a technique known as "card counting." This involves mentally logging the high-value cards (10 or above) and low-value cards (6

sional rings are known to many casinos, and when detected, their pictures are circulated among gaming establishments.

Gambling for Jesus

The late Jesuit minister Joseph R. Fahey was a mathematical genius and a skillful card-counter. Fahey was eventually banned from casinos after winning tens of thousands of dollars, all of which he donated to the church to uphold his vow of poverty. He died in Boston in 2002, aged 65.

Even slots are not proof against illicit intervention. On the old machines, there'd always be one bettor playing around with wire and mag-

or below) as they are dealt, to calculate the probable turn of the cards remaining. When there are a large number of high-value cards left in the deck, the odds are with the player, and he increases his bet. When there are less, the odds are in favor of the house, and he lowers his stake.

Since the margin between the house and the player is close already, this gives a skilled "counter" a strong chance of beating the house over a long sequence of games. The casinos consider this to be "cheating," and are alert to tell-tale signs of those employing the technique. Profes-

nets. Once Bally's introduced electrical slots, a new type of tech wizard appeared. Most electronic slots have a light optic reader which counts the number of coins being paid out. It didn't take long to discover that a "light device" can be inserted into the machine through the same opening and "blind" it so that it keeps paying.

So, do the casinos do their own cheating? Apparently not, at least in the view of Mario Puzo, who said, "after 15 years of watching and trying to figure out how they cheat, I reluctantly came to the conclusion that Vegas has honest casino gambling, and it may be the first time in the history of civilization that gaming houses have been run straight." ❑

LEFT: play moves quickly in almost all circumstances.
ABOVE: a private game in Bellagio's baccarat room.

How to Win

There is one sure-fire way to make money from a casino – buy one. If you play the slots, the tables or the Sports Book in Las Vegas, do it to have fun. You may have Lady Luck at your shoulder and win a fortune at the tables, but then again, you may not. The golden rule for happy gambling is to set yourself a limit beforehand and don't exceed it. Figure out how much money in total you can play and lose, and stick to it absolutely.

If you can manage that, the other motto is "quit while you're ahead."

Serious players pre-calculate a stake range – highest to lowest bet – by multiplying the number of hours that they intend to play by the number of games per hour, and dividing their "bankroll" by the result, in order to set a maximum stake. A low stake is then set around 20 percent of the maximum, or less. Low bets are made until a winning streak is hit, then stakes are progressively raised. This way, losses are kept small and winnings are maximized.

It's a good idea to ride a winning streak. If you strike it lucky, put a profit to one side, then raise your stakes and go for it. If you start to lose, cut back or – better still – walk away. Playing comfortably low stakes offers more fun in the long run.

Betting $5 one hundred times and winning some of the time provides more hours of entertainment than playing $500 once, and possibly losing, once.

Blackjack

Blackjack offers some of the best odds in the casino. The house's natural edge is between 3 and 5 percent, and a skilled player can narrow that to 0.5 percent, using the best betting and playing combinations.

The object of the game is to get a hand of cards closer to 21 than the dealer. Cards take their face value, except for pictures, which count as 10, and aces, which the player can choose to value as 1 or 11. The top hand, an ace with a 10 or a picture, equals 21 – in other words, "blackjack."

Most blackjack deals are from a plastic "shoe" with six or eight decks. Some casinos, like Binion's Horseshoe in downtown Vegas, play with a single deck. This gives the player a much better chance of predicting the cards left to be dealt.

Craps

The game of craps may appear daunting, but is really fairly simple. Craps also offers among the best odds for players; the house edge on a simple "pass line" bet is only 1.4 percent.

Bets are placed for and against a dice roll, which are referred to as "right" or "wrong" bets. Right bets are for the thrower succeeding, and wrong bets are against. The pair of dice pass around the table. No-one has to roll, but the thrower must bet on his own game.

At the first, or "come out" roll, a throw of 2,3 or 12 is known as craps. This is a win for bets on the "don't pass" line, in other words, wrong bets. The numbers 7 or 11 are automatic winners for "pass-line," or right bets. Any other number rolled establishes the shooter's "point," and a series commences. The object then is to roll the point again before hitting a 7.

Keno

Keno is hugely popular because it is so simple to play, and a $50,000 payout is possible on a $1 bet. All the player needs to do is pick some numbers on a ticket and wait. It's easy, and it's fun. It's also among the lowest player odds in the house, with a casino edge of 20 to 30 percent.

Due to a mystery of Nevada gaming regulation, Keno is not, technically, a lottery. Payouts must be collected immediately after each game, and before the next game starts, or they are forfeit. Keno is played at most hotel casinos. Pick a place at the bar or café and call a keno runner over. These tend to be women, usually dressed in a uniform. Mark your lucky numbers and wait for the draw. Any number of tickets can be bought for each game, and there are endless combinations to mark the numbers. The runner will be happy to show you some of the combinations. If she comes back with winnings, it would be polite to offer a tip.

Roulette

The wheel spins, the ball spins against it. The ball drops, and clatters. It bounces once, twice and comes to rest in number 7. The dealer places the white marker next to your chip on the 7, and your $100 bet is joined by $3,500 in chips.

Or not. Pay out can be a dizzying 35 to 1, but the 0 and 00 make the odds 38 to 1 against you predicting the correct number. If the ball falls on 0 or 00, all bets lose, save for those people predicting that exact outcome. This makes the overall house edge 5.26 percent, and about the poorest table odds in town.

The safest bets on the wheel are the outsiders. These are the "dozens" (first 12, second 12, third 12 or one of the three "columns"), which pay out 2 to 1. Otherwise, 1 to 1 payouts are offered by "red or black," "odd or even" or "first or last 18."

Sports Books

In the Sports Book, players back their expertise in predicting different sports events. Odds are offered on football, baseball, Indy Car and championship boxing. But the main event in the book is horseracing, still the largest spectator sport in the United States. A horse's previous performance, or "form," is a good guide, and the simple bets – "win" or "place" – are the most profitable.

The Sports Book is the one place in a casino where you will be guaranteed to find a clock.

Poker

A tip from one professional poker player is this: sit down at the table and spot the sucker. If you haven't made them within five minutes, get up and leave. It's you.

The ability to read other players at the table can be as important in poker as getting the best cards. In the betting rounds, the players who think they

have the strongest hand will try to lure money into the "pot." But players who believe they have weaker cards may also be trying to scare the others out of the game. Poker is the only game in the casino where you play against other gamblers and not against the house. Instead, the house makes its living from a cut – usually around 5 percent – off the top of each pot.

A common form of poker in Las Vegas is "Texas Hold 'em," played with five cards. Each player is dealt two cards, face down. Through progressive betting rounds, five "community cards" are dealt, face up. Each player then makes the highest five-card hand they can from the seven cards available.

Advice from the pros

Be sure to protect your winnings. If you find yourself on a roll, then pocket at least some of the profits before placing another bet. It's tempting to think that while you are ahead, you're playing with the casino's money, but serious and professional players consider whatever is in front of them as their own money – not the house's – and safeguard their chips accordingly.

The house plays most games with what seem like relatively small odds. Over time, though, the odds will most likely eek your bankroll across the table. The main thing you can do with skill is to slow the roll. Every time you get something back, you win. ❑

LEFT: the best way to win is to own a casino.
RIGHT: the surest bet on a roulette wheel is a number on the outside.

BEHIND THE SPECTACLE

Surveillance in the sky, sex that sells, transporting tigers through

rush-hour traffic – keeping Vegas running to schedule is big-time business

Of the apparent paradoxes in quantum physics, Albert Einstein said, "God does not play dice." Maybe he does, maybe he doesn't, but if he did, Las Vegas wouldn't be a bad place to check the table action. Paradox is deeply embedded in every aspect of this most modern of cities, and nowhere more than in the built-up landscape of illusion, facade and *trompe l'oeil*. Indoor rivers, canals and sunsets, erupting volcanoes – nothing here is presented without a giddying sprinkle of star-dust.

The zany architecture, of course, is the first thing visitors tell their friends back home about, but being Las Vegas even something so obvious is hardly ever what it seems. In the words of one commentator, "it's the only place in the world where they try to make buildings look smaller." Writing in *The Atlantic*, Richard Todd said it was hard to believe visitors who visited such casinos really thought they were having a New York or Paris or Venetian experience. "We like this architecture, if we do, for its ingenuity, not its realism. We are gratified that someone has gone to such lengths to entertain us: it's performance architecture."

Illusion by effort

Bellagio, by any standard, is spectacular, but its executive vice president Alan L. Feldman said its theme, unlike, for instance, the theme of the Luxor, is understated.

"The theme we had in mind was just 'romance.' We had thought of classical French styling but we had also thought of something very modern. In fact, we had a design and announced a hotel built in the shape of a great wave. But then Steve Wynn went to Italy and he was sailing on Lake Como and he looked back at the shore and said, 'This is the most romantic place I've ever seen. Let's build this."

What visitors are blissfully unaware of is

LEFT: making pretty a private Pompeian Fantasy Suite in the Forum Tower at Caesars Palace.
RIGHT: it takes thousands of people many days and long, hot hours to maintain the city's illusions.

how much behind-the-scenes activity must be generated to create such "effortless illusion."

Spectators who fill the street to watch Treasure Island's daily battles between a pirate ship and a British Navy frigate have no idea how widely designers Jon Jerde and Roger Thomas scoured the world to find the shutters, window

grilles, cannons and cauldrons to create the 18th-century pirate village's fake authenticity. Craftsmen and designers from Hollywood said they were delighted to create something that wouldn't be destroyed when the film ended.

Craig Dunbar, 50, a former Shakespearian actor, is one of the 10 original cast members, sometimes portraying a pirate and sometimes a British officer. None of the 30 actors knows from one day to the next what part they'll be assigned to. But Dunbar loves it anyway. "It plays to the child in us" he says. "What child didn't want to play buccaneer, pirate, cowboy?" Treasure Island gets hundreds of applications for jobs but there is very little turnover.

New recruits, whether actors or not, start on the British ship working their way through all the parts except captain before transferring for more training to the *Hispaniola*. The pirate ship is more popular because the British sailors get dunked in the water when their ship is sunk – five times every day.

Operations personnel usually come from amusement parks or theaters where they have learned technical skills like pyrotechnics, hydraulics, audio and lighting. Every step is well-rehearsed, with remote switches to stop the action in the hands of both captains and two overhead observers. "We've done everything

humanly possible to make this as safe and exciting a show as possible," Dunbar says. "It looks spectacular and dangerous but it is well orchestrated and safer than it looks. But it is still live, and danger is there."

Horticulturists are taught rappelling and climbing so they can reach plants in the rocks and lagoons of the pirate-village waterfront. Less visible are the scuba-diving plumbers who maintain the waterfalls at the neighboring Mirage, while 17 florists work round the clock shifts pampering the 60-foot (18-meter) palms, banana trees and orchids.

Stars at Mandalay Bay's Shark Reef are the diver-aquarists, most with biology degrees, who plunge into the tank with headsets, which allows them to answer visitors' questions. Sea turtles like to nibble on the divers' ears but sharks usually keep their distance. Brine shrimp are served to the jelly fish, and crocodiles are fed with long poles.

Tigers take a trip

Animals can play a surprisingly large role in everyday Las Vegas life. Rick Thomas is one local who uses tigers in his magic act in the Tropicana's Tiffany Theatre. Thomas and his family live with tawny tigers Zeus, Maximilian, Morpheus, Rocky, and white tigers Samson and Kira on a 2-acre (1-hectare) property north of town, and the trainer has to drive in and out of Las Vegas every day. "People don't see the work that goes into this," he says. "They're animals; they're not potty trained."

Up at 11am for bathing and primping, an air-conditioned trip into town, a nap in the dressing room adjoining the showroom, then two 10-minute afternoon shows are on the agenda before Rick drives all of them home to a dinner of 5 lb (2 kg) of steak tartare. "The cats are not just a prop," said Thomas. "The moment I make a cat appear on stage, I'm no longer a magician. I'm a trainer."

The most extravagant show in Las Vegas may well be the Cirque du Soleil's *O* at Bellagio. Founded in Quebec, Canada in 1984, Cirque du Soleil tour the world with shows combining spectacle with circus art, gymnastics and choreography. With *O* they added water ballet, swimming and diving, made possible only by the theatre which was designed and built around the production. The performers have to combine a dazzling array of skills to bring off the show. A team of 15 divers work every show, 12 of them underwater the whole time, and all the cast are scuba-certified.

Kirsty Powell was a nationally-known American gymnast before auditioning for the company, but she still found the mix of disciplines challenging. Speaking to *Las Vegas Life* she said, "When I'd been an athlete, it felt like, if I was (playing games), it was goofing off. I know that's what they were asking for, but I hadn't much practice and experience."

Fabrice Becker, Cirque du Soleil's acrobatics scout said, "We are looking for three main aspects. A basic evaluation that includes abilities and strength, after that are the technical parts on the different aparatuses and disciplines, and the third part, which is the most important, is the artistic evaluation." Of Kirsty he said, "We know that she is a great gymnast; I had to find out if she was ready to dance and play some acting games." Did she make the cut? You'll have to check the show to find out.

Casino hotels on the Strip naturally employ hotel staff, and being Las Vegas, they employ them in huge numbers. At the MGM Grand, the business of hospitality takes 740 maids and 62 telephone operators singing the corporate mantra, "Thank you for calling the MGM Grand, have a Grand day," thousands of times

creative director for the agency, R&R Partners, was not surprised. Up until a few years ago, no reference could be made to gambling, and even the word "casino" was barred. Snow said, "We used to refer to it as 'Nevada-style action.'"

Stage-door Johnnies

Backstage of certain shows, usually the ones featuring showgirls, have always held a certain attraction for what were once known as "Stage Door Johnnies." John F. Kennedy, both before and during his presidency, loved to watch the girls perform, and Frank Sinatra sometimes courted the leggy beauties by sending flowers

a day. Fifty waiters and waitresses at a time handle room service, and the restaurants serve 30,000 meals every day.

High rollers stay far off the general public's radar. But when a local ad agency was hired to run a campaign for the city's High Roller Fantasy Sweepstakes, the ABC television network wouldn't even allow mention of the term "high roller." CBS also asked for undisclosed revisions before broadcast, and eventually the $8 million promotion campaign ran with heavily modified 30-second commercials. Randy Snow,

LEFT: around 150 staff groom the gardens at Bellagio.
ABOVE: snatching phone calls home between shifts.

backstage with amorous notes. Rich gamblers who made extravagant promises were occasionally hooked into marriage but officially, dancers and showgirls are no longer permitted to fraternize with the audience or in the casino. After more than half a century, however, the mystique of the showgirls remains, and misconceptions abound. To help put them straight, the Tropicana offers a backstage tour of its *Folies Bergères* show *(see page 135)*.

The classic showgirl, tall, stoic, slim and poised, must not be so overly endowed as to offend wives and girl friends, and these days topless shows are usually confined to the late performances. Dancers, who rarely appear topless in production shows, tend to be shorter and originally were "saloon girls," hired to spruce up a casino. Then legendary producer Donn Arden brought in a group of dancers to the Desert Inn's Painted Desert Room which began the tradition of runway models.

First showgirl

One of the first showgirls was Dorothy Dandridge, whose beauty and dancing skills made her a headliner at the famed Club Bingo in the late 1940s. Dandridge won a Best Actress nomination in 1954 for her part in *Carmen Jones*. *Minsky's Follies*, which opened at the Dunes in

to see an important part of it's future in family vacations. Though there are still many entertainments for children and a number of hotel casinos have been themed around family-friendly motifs, the resort is turning back to its earlier market.

The *Las Vegas Review-Journal*'s Dave Berns wrote, "Marketeers of the desert city, *circa* 2000, have made an aggressive push to reposition the town as an adult getaway." He said it is "a hip place Frank Sinatra would have enjoyed, a setting where people can leave their day-to-day lives behind in Des Moines, Iowa, or Des Plaines, Illinois and chase drink, song, money

1957, was the first topless production show. The *Follies* ran for more than four years, and set show attendance records. The Sands never went topless. The "Texas Copa Girls" or "Pony Girls" were a line of 16 beauty queens from Texas brought specifically to entertain the big Texas money-men (and therefore big spenders) in the late 1950s. The women were not trained dancers nor did they have any show experience. The first foreign dancers to appear in Las Vegas arrived with the opening of the Stardust in 1958, and *Lido de Paris* became the longest running show in town.

In the 1980s and 1990s, Las Vegas was marketed as a resort for young families and seemed

and sex." Casino executives are attracted to the demographic of the middle-aged baby boomer because their average age is 49 and up. As the Mandalay Resort's president Glenn Schaeffer clarified, "For the next decade, one American will turn 50 every 11 seconds."

Sex

Sex is a major component in the Las Vegas spectacle, and the part on display is barely the tip of an iceberg. In a city whose very essence is promise and enticement, the sex trade flourishes. Some visitors find themselves victimized by sex-tease clip joints where women hustlers extort huge sums for drinks with the promise of future action later. "Later" never comes. These operators prey mercilessly on the unwary and the mistaken belief that prostitution is legal in Las Vegas. Reputedly they will charge anything up to $6,000 for a bottle of non-alcoholic "champagne," and the "non-alcoholic" part is the giveaway.

Although sex-tease clubs are tolerated, they aren't granted liquor licenses, so if you find yourself, for any reason, in a bar with no beer, you may want to leave smartly.

Prostitution is illegal in the city, but nobody pretends it doesn't happen. Out on the Strip are countless freesheets and flyers, with phone

Legalize the liaison?

Pressure to legalize prostitution dates back almost as far as the city itself. Harold Stocker, a former dealer and bootlegger who went on to become chairman of the state's Republican Party in the 1950s said, "They're trying to lay all this crime we have today on hookers and pimps. Well, if that's the problem, why the hell don't they legalize (prostitution) so they can regulate it? Regulating it is all you can hope to do because they have never succeeded in eliminating it in a thousand years of trying."

Stocker made his remarks in 1982, the year before he died, still advocating the legalization

numbers for women who offer a wide range of exotic services in your hotel room. Probably it's just like any city in the world but Las Vegas style – more overt and out there, with a lot of glitz and show.

Expectations are high because of the apparently large and seemingly endless population of glamorous women, anxious to make a living by any means necessary. This goes for men, too; a growing market in Sin City is the number of full-time male striptease revues.

LEFT: Anthony, Caesar and Cleo take the weight off their sandals.
ABOVE: dinner with the Tropicana's Rick Thomas.

of all "victimless" crimes, especially prostitution, a lesson that he said should have been learned from gambling's history. Nevada state law prohibits a brothel in any county with more than 400,000 inhabitants. The closest legal brothels to Las Vegas are in Nye County, particularly in the desert town of Pahrump about 60 miles (96 km) away.

The very existence of a place tagged as Sin City attracts all kind of people with all kinds of motives. It's not surprising that the euphemistically-styled "adult entertainment" industry holds its annual trade show – the Adult Video News Expo – at the convention center in Las Vegas.

That, in turn, is part of the attraction for Mike Foster and Craig Cross of xxxchurch.com, a Vegas-based crusade against the porn and flesh trade. "If Jesus were walking the earth today," said Cross, 26, "he'd be here, too. After all, he hung out with prostitutes and stuff." They work with a church, whose pastor said, "It is very near to our hearts to help people overcome sexual addiction and to help them have healthy sexual boundaries with other people."

And surely, God would love Las Vegas as much as any of us. Referring to Einstein's quote, Stephen Hawking, the modern cosmologist said, "God plays dice all the time."

part of the customers, although dealers and pit bosses are not above suspicion, and casinos also have to keep an eye on their own security staff.

Review-Journal columnist John L. Smith wrote about the time when the MGM Grand hired a former hotel burglar and jewelry fence, now dead, for its surveillance team. He "made a small fortune turning in people who not long ago would have qualified as his running mates," Smith wrote, reminding readers of the old adage, "set a thief to catch a thief."

Casinos, he explained, "have a long tradition of employing convicted card and slot cheaters to catch those still practicing the racket."

Security and surveillance

Not many gamblers glance upwards as they navigate the aisles but most of them are well aware that their every move is watched through the ubiquitous one-way mirrors and cameras that the casino has mounted along the walls and catwalks and in the ceiling.

The video cameras are programed to zoom in automatically at the earliest sign of unusual activity. They are silent because recording audio contravenes the Federal laws against wiretapping, but surveillance goes on around the clock with particular attention, sometimes with the aid of binoculars, on games where illicit activity is suspected. This is often on the

The plastic bubbles in the casino ceiling house flexible cameras which can rapidly shift to any angle, and zoom in instantly. They are part of a system mandated by the enforcement division of the Nevada Gaming Control Board, whose agents have full access at all times, and the power to demand any videotape they want. Officials are unwilling to give details, but all the videotape of both play and players is said to be collected daily and stored in a warehouse, ready for replaying if necessary. Tapes are usually saved for seven days but in certain areas, the law mandates 30-days' retention.

George Joseph, formerly the director of surveillance at the Dunes, reveals some things about surveillance techniques in his book *Why Shouldn't a Woman Wear Red in a Casino*, subtitled *The 101 Most Asked Questions About Las Vegas and Casino Gambling*. Dyes can be applied to clothes for concealment or camouflage, so surveillance equipment is tuned to detect dyes on clothing. Cheats conceal devices under hairpieces, so the cameras also exaggerate the color tone bet-ween real hair and a wig or toupée – an uncomfortable discovery for rug-wearers.

Surveillance cameras have been known to

TAKE THE STAIRS

Surveillance cameras pick up more than just casino cheats. Apparently, videotapes of people having sex in the elevators are particularly popular.

those that monitor audio in the count rooms, where the sound of money can be as important as the actual sight of it.

Magazine writer Sergio Lalli says that five people are likely to be in the count room at one time, and each of them has to be authorized by the Gaming Control Board. They are not subject to casino authority.

Nevertheless, new methods of skimming keep turning up which manage to bypass all the best-laid plans. An ingenious scheme at the Stardust some time ago involved

pick up almost invisible beams of infra-red light from a hidden miniature video camera. In one instance, it was in the purse of a woman sitting by a blackjack dealer, and it transmitted a picture of his hole card as he peeked at it before taking players' bets.

In the days when microphones were allowed, Joseph says that some customers used to "audition for the lounge shows," by singing into the mics mounted at gaming tables. Today, though, the only microphones allowed in casinos are

a change booth which operated with "surplus" coins from a miscalibrated scale. The bills received by the girls who dispensed change were deposited back into the rogue booth, whose takings never went to the count room.

In his book *Loaded Dice,* self-confessed "casino cheat" John Soares recounts his years working with a team adept at switching the dice in craps games with custom-crafted dice of their own. Soares repeatedly points out the risks inherent in cheating – when failure might have resulted in sudden death and an unmarked burial in the desert – but he claims that he and his canny team ripped off millions without any serious setbacks. ❑

LEFT: sex is a big component in the Sin City spectacle.
ABOVE: in most casinos, someone, somewhere, is always watching.

FAMOUS FOOD

It's common knowledge that Vegas is excellent for inexpensive eating;
what's making the news is how many chefs are dishing up world-class food

When America's best-known chef, Wolfgang Puck, first came to town with his designer and partner Barbara Lazaroff a decade ago, Las Vegas was among the last places anybody would think of as a gourmet capital. The desert town's restaurants were most famous for its $2.99 steak-and-egg breakfasts, and its ubiquitous all-you-can-eat buffets.

One of Puck's first visits was to a local fishmonger. "He couldn't wait to show me his walk-in freezers stocked to the ceiling with fish," the restaurateur said with disdain. Today, as then, he ships fresh fish, meat and produce from Los Angeles to Las Vegas every day of the week.

Celebrity cuisine

Puck had not planned quite as many signature restaurants in the desert town as he currently operates. "I expand if the demand is there, and I have the people. I wouldn't open a restaurant if I didn't know I had the chefs to manage it." Puck is now in charge of five local restaurants, with Spago and Chinois in the Forum Shops at Caesars Palace, the Venetian's Postrio, the Trattoria del Lupo, and a café at the MGM Grand; together they serve more than 2,300 customers a day.

At the turn of the millennium, figures showed there were a dozen celebrity chefs operating in Las Vegas, and the average that visitors were lavishing on food and drink was double what they were spending on shopping. The more upscale the hotel, the more likely that its customers will prefer the fancier table settings.

Restaurant designer Adam Tihany, of the watering holes Aureole and Le Cirque, feels that the city is on its way to becoming one of the great gourmet resorts. "In five years Las Vegas will have the best stores, the best hotels and the best restaurants in America," he predicts. And Tim Zagat, of the widely distributed Zagat restaurant guides, cites restaurant and kitchen size along with the quality and food service of the top-rated Las Vegas restaurants. He predicts that future celebrity chefs are more likely to make their names here than in New York, San Francisco or Los Angeles.

Too many cooks?

Most periodicals with a culinary view have welcomed the foodie revolution in Sin City. An exception is *Esquire*, whose restaurant critic John Mariani said that the newly publicized growth was "already beginning to deflate." His assessment was that, as with a lot of things in Las Vegas, "there's this veneer that something's quite smashing and dazzling, but underneath there's not much depth to it." There are other skeptics, too.

Restaurateur Charlie Trotter kept his $4 million restaurant at the MGM Grand only for a single year, then returned to Chicago following a disagreement over policy. "Las Vegas was

LEFT: Julian Serrano, chef *extraordinaire* at Bellagio's Picasso restaurant.
RIGHT: outside Mandalay's Red Square is a headless statue of Lenin; inside, serious cooking takes place.

very low on my priority list… but my experience was very good, at least for a while. My question is, is this something that can be sustained? These restaurants will draw plenty of interest the first year or two, but what about five years later or ten? Who knows what's going to happen."

Feed the faithful

Others, though, have appreciated the changes. Professor Patti Shock, a restaurant expert from the University of Nevada Las Vegas, was quoted as saying that she visited the Strip more often than ever because of the restaurants.

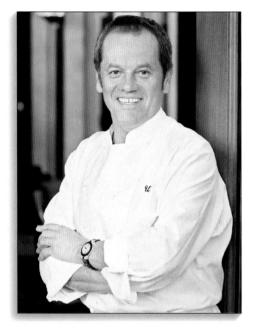

Before the celebrity chefs arrived, she said, "Locals didn't go to the Strip too often." Puck, who estimates that almost 20 percent of his business comes from residents, says he made a special effort to satisfy them. "We always try to attract the local people first – it's really our first priority – because they are here in December or June when it's slow and there are no conventions. It's nice when you own a restaurant to see the same faces coming back." Puck's Las Vegas kitchens generate about $40 million a year – one quarter of all his ventures combined.

Celebrity chefs often have restaurant interests far away and their absence can show on the plate. This was a drawback, restaurant critic Mariani said. "I asked a waitress at Emeril's if (Emeril) ever comes into the restaurant and she told me 'He was in town for the opening of the steak house but he didn't bother to come here.'" She was talking about Emeril Lagasse's New Orleans Fish House in the MGM Grand but she said it could apply to any of the places where famous chefs hired teams to run their show.

Another food critic, Thomas Matthews, takes a different view. He said that he'd enjoyed that very same Fish House even more than the New Orleans original. "The young assistants they have sent to mind the stoves are generally talented, skilled and ambitious," he wrote.

Competition in the kitchen

Lagasse was one of Puck's earliest rivals when he set up shop here in 1994. He followed up a few years later at the Venetian with the Delmonico Steakhouse, dubbed "modern Tuscan" but with "Creole influences."

Lagasse said, "Today, outside of New York, Las Vegas is the culinary mecca of America. The restaurant scene isn't perfect. It hasn't got real depth and I'm not sure if it ever will; there's not enough patience for that. When things go wrong here they just tear it down and start afresh. But now it's so competitive that everyone has to improve. The rest will disappear. And the real winner is the customer who craves great food."

In place of the ubiquitous buffet, the Venetian offers the elegant La Strada Food Court with white pillars, marble and arches between its booths. The resort has almost an embarrassment of celebrity chefs. Among them is Los Angeles' Joachim Splichal and his wife Christine, who opened the Pinot Brasserie. Street markets and salvage yards in Paris and Provence were scoured by the designer. The restaurant was built around antique doors salvaged from a 19th-century hotel located in Monte Carlo, and the floor of a Normandy home was shipped over to become a ceiling in one of the dining rooms. Antique murals and limestone were transplanted from a beautiful but abandoned château.

Splichal said his aim was a restaurant, "where each time you come you get a different experience. A place where each part of the restaurant is appealing and satisfying. I wanted to bring something real to Vegas. Something that's already lasted in Europe for a hundred years and that will live on here." Fishmongers in traditional blue caps, oilskin aprons and rubber boots preside over an oyster bar. Specialities include the scarce periwinkle.

Multilingual linguini

As well as Lagasse and Puck, the MGM Grand has Mark Miller's Coyote Room and Michael Mina's celebrated Nobhill serving Berkeley-inspired cuisine and Bay Area ingredients. Sharing acclaim with Trattoria del Lupo and Aureole at Mandalay Bay is the Mexican-style Border Grill operated by TV chefs Susan Feniger and Sue Milliken. At Caesars Palace,

wisteria-covered bamboo trellis. Tastes not to be missed are provided by Nobuyuki Matsuhisa, who first opened the Matsuhisa restaurant in Beverly Hills, and now presides over Nobu eateries in London, Tokyo and New York, as well as in the Las Vegas Hard Rock Hotel.

André's is the only Downtown restaurant to feature in the critics' Ten Best lists. The French cuisine has been prepared by chef André Rochat for 21 years. *Las Vegas Life* said that, "Puck started the Las Vegas restaurant boom, but André's remains the plinth on which it stands." Rochat also has restaurants in the Monte Carlo and the Palms.

French-born Jean-Marie Josselin ran a chain of island restaurants called A Pacific Café and now presides over "808," offering Asian and European cuisine from organic produce and seafood flown from Hawaii. Caesars Empress Court (chef Pui Kee Hui) was the first restaurant in Nevada to serve live fish.

Hiyakumi, which means "100 tastes," is among the city's most beautiful eating places. Waitresses in *obis* and kimonos glide gracefully between antique Japanese furnishings and a

---

LEFT: Wolfgang Puck, the first celebrity chef in Vegas.
ABOVE: Postrio, Puck's restaurant at the Venetian, is modeled on his original San Francisco eatery.

Fine wine for diners

Another top-tier restaurant is Valentino. Piero Selvaggio said, "What is Valentino famous for? The wine! How are we going to (ensure that) people walk in and know they are in Valentino? We are going to display 6,500 bottles of wine behind the bar at the entrance, just for starters. We are making Valentino a temple to wine. This is the moment of maturity for Las Vegas. Suddenly there are 15 or 20 major restaurants up and down the Strip. This is where things are happening today."

Eighteen Las Vegas restaurants were included in *Wine Spectator* magazine's recent Wine List Awards. Wine is definitely a key attribute of Mandalay Bay's Aureole, with a 42-foot (13-meter) high glass-enclosed wine tower, serviced by "wine angels," two women in black cat suits who climb the 10,000 bottle display. Wine director Steven Geddes, a 25-year veteran of the local scene, said, "I knew we had to open with a great wine program or this would become a laughing stock." Aureole is owned by chef Charlie Palmer who runs a sister restaurant in New York, as well as a celebrated steak house at The Four Seasons hotel. Emeril Lagasse said, "Wine has become the key."

Greg Harrington, wine director for Wolfgang Puck's Las Vegas restaurants, is one of seven

Master Sommeliers in the city, and one of only 38 in the US. Barrie Larvin – who spent $6 million stocking the Rio's wine cellars, and Bellagio's Jay James who estimates he sells $30 million worth of wine each year – also number among the select premier crew.

The gastronomic revolution

A prime mover in the local restaurant revolution has been Steve Wynn. Elizabeth Blau, Mirage Resorts' VP of restaurant development, introduced Wynn to Todd English (Olives and Onda), Jean-George Vongerichten (Prime Steakhouse) and Michael Mina (Aqua). "It took much persuasion to convince such established culinary luminaries to open restaurants here," *Sun* columnist Muriel Stevens said, "but Wynn is a charming and powerful persuader."

"We didn't think the people who care about good food came to Vegas," Wynn said. "They went to Paris or New York. Then Wolfgang Puck opened Spago and proved us wrong… We should have thought of this a long time ago."

Wynn was able to lure Alessandro Stratta from a five-star restaurant in Phoenix, Arizona to run Renoir at the Mirage. People at the hotel were worried that the food was too sophisticated, but Wynn gave him support. Stratta said, "I came here to do what I do. Steve Wynn stood up for me and told them, 'We don't want to tell the painter what color to use.'"

Wynn's instincts, as usual, were right on the money. Bellagio, his masterpiece-du-jour, includes restaurant clones of Manhattan's Le Cirque, run by the charismatic Sirio Maccioni, Osteria del Circo, also operated by famiglia Maccioni, Todd English's Mediterranean-style

Olives from Boston, and Michael Mina's Aqua, situated by the spectacular indoor botanical gardens. Gamal Azis, Bellagio's senior Vice President of Food and Beverage, claims that Bellagio is the only hotel in the world whose food and beverage receipts match the hotel operation revenues.

Gold stars on the refrigerator

Only 18 North American chefs won five stars in a recent Mobil Travel Guide, and two of them cook at Bellagio. One was Stratta, who said, "Five stars means one very simple thing – consistency. A five-star restaurant means that

Alternative eats

Despite the exotic cuisines, the old-style steak houses are holding on. Kerry Simon said, "My instincts told me Las Vegas would be a meat and potatoes town. Lots of gamblers come from the Midwest, where I'm from, and the South. Let's face it, Americans still love meat."

In addition to Aureole, Charlie Palmer operates a relaxed steak house in a corner of the Four Seasons. Most of the major chains – Smith & Wollensky, Ruth's Chris and Morton's – have Las Vegas outlets. They're still mostly male bastions, "dark, clubby and smoky," reported local food critic Max Jacobson, but the times

everything is first class: the service, the food, the wine list, the decor... Food is why most people go to a restaurant, but elegance and decor tip the scale."

The other is Julian Serrano, who left San Francisco's Masa for Bellagio's Picasso restaurant. Diners are served in a room designed by Pablo Picasso's son Claude, who had the salon hung with a collection of paintings, drawings and ceramics of his father's work, etimated to be worth $50 million.

LEFT: see Paris and dine – at Olives in Bellagio.
ABOVE: Picasso: the restaurant's decor is by son Claude, the paintings are by papa.

may be changing. Fleming's Prime Steakhouse and Wine Bar in nearby Summerlin has targeted women, with a softer color scheme, and Nine, "the eccentric steak house in the Palms," has a ceiling with a disco effect. Jacobson's list of 10 best was headed by Smith & Wollensky, but he also noted "the best cheapo steak in town" is served in the coffee shop at Binion's Horseshoe between 11pm and 7am.

Foodies on a budget may find it hard to afford a celebrity restaurant each night, but Vegas is one town where it's easy to save up – every so often, just head for that $8.99 buffet instead. ❑

For a list of restaurants, see Travel Tips.

VEGAS IN THE MOVIES

The fantasy facades of Sin City offer endless opportunities for movie-makers.
The fact that Vegas is just a short hop on a Lear jet from Hollywood doesn't hurt

Las Vegas magic is the magic of illusion, and many of its spectacular displays are the work of designers, set builders and special effects experts from the movie business. The puffy clouds and sunsets inside shopping arcades like the Forum Shops, the millions of mega-watts of artificial light outdoors, the pyramids and volcanoes, and the sea battles of Treasure Island make the town like a Hollywood blockbuster set. The gold and the glitter, the instant flips of fortune, and the fantasy facades also offer endlessly rich plot potential. All this has kept Sin City in the movies and in the business of movies. The fact that Vegas is just a short hop in a Lear jet from Hollywood helps, too.

Made in Vegas

From the days of the silents, Las Vegas had starring roles in movies like *The Hazards of Helen* and John Ford's 1932 film *Airmail*. Edwin L. Mann's 1946 film *Lady Luck* was somewhat of a moral tale about the irresistible lure of gambling. In 1960, both Marilyn Monroe and Clark Gable played their last movie roles in John Huston's *The Misfits*, much of it filmed in the Nevada desert. It was taken from a script by Arthur Miller about a disillusioned divorcée, a role uncannily prophetic of the Monroe-Miller marriage.

Ocean's 11, also made in 1960, was the famous Rat Pack saga, directed by Lewis Milestone when Frank Sinatra, Dean Martin, Sammy Davis Jr and Peter Lawford could spare time from carousing. Though the film wasn't highly rated by critics, it made respectable enough ticket sales for a follow-up, *Robin and the Seven Hoods*. *Ocean's 11* was remade in 2001 with George Clooney, Matt Damon, Andy Garcia and Julia Roberts topping a stellar bill, and featured several interiors that were shot in Bellagio.

Elvis Presley wooed Ann-Margret from the Sahara in the Strip all the way to Lake Mead and

Mount Charleston in *Viva Las Vegas* (1964), a famous pairing rumored to be mirrored off screen, too.

In 1971, Sean Connery went Downtown to Fremont Street as James Bond in *Diamonds Are Forever*, which critic Leonard Maltin described as a "colorful comic book adventure." Dustin

Hoffman won an Oscar for his role in *Rain Man* in 1988, which co-starred fresh-faced Tom Cruise, and featured a scene filmed in the Pompeiian Fantasy Suite of Caesars Palace. Actor Nicolas Cage is a virtual Vegas veteran, having starred in three local movies: the 1992 comedy *Honeymoon in Vegas*; the 1995 dark drama *Leaving Las Vegas*; and two years later, *Con Air*.

Lavish high-roller suites and turns of the tables provided the setting for Adrian Lynn's *Indecent Proposal* (1993), in which Woody Harrelson unwisely encouraged screen wife Demi Moore to spend a night with tycoon Robert Redford for a million dollars, and lived to regret it – until the last reel of the film, of course.

LEFT: Sean Connery as James Bond makes Fremont Street safe for the world in *Diamonds are Forever*.
RIGHT: Sarah Jessica Parker and Nicolas Cage in *Honeymoon in Vegas*, featuring the Flying Elvi.

Sci-Fi on the Strip

In *The Amazing Colossal Man* (1957) Las Vegas came under attack from an Army officer who grew 60 feet (18 meters) tall after surviving an atomic explosion, but the assault came from elsewhere in *Mars Attacks*.

Tim Burton's wild 1996 sci-fi fantasy brought to town a galaxy of stars including Pierce Brosnan, Annette Bening, an extraordinary cameo from Tom Jones and no fewer than two roles for Jack Nicholson. In that film, the Las Vegas Strip was spectacularly demolished by creatures that now have small-screen lives of their own as *Butt Ugly Martians*.

Gangsters and godfathers

In 1972 and 1974, parts 1 and 2 of Francis Ford Coppola's *The Godfather* trilogy were partly filmed and set locally. Between them, the two films won 13 Oscars and 11 Golden Globe awards for their stars and the mercurial director. The saga of the Corleone family includes references to the Mob's attempts at legitimacy in the Nevada gaming business.

The movie also features the now-legendary tale of a Hollywood producer who finds the head of his favorite horse tucked up under his silk sheets, as a timely reminder to employ a certain skinny, Italian-American crooner.

In the same year, the special effects were about the only stars of *Independence Day* to survive with their reputations intact. Some feel that *Independence Day* is easily as funny as *Mars Attacks* but alas, not intentionally. In 1998, Klingons were drawn to Sin City by their dastardly plot to kidnap guests from the Las Vegas Hilton, thankfully foiled by the time-traveling crew of the Starship Enterprise in *Star Trek: The Experience*.

Rick Moranis reprised his goofy scientist role from *Honey I Shrunk the Kids* in *Honey I Blew Up the Kid* (1992) where his two-year-old son becomes 150 feet (46 meters) high and grows even larger when he comes near electricity. In Las Vegas – well, you can imagine.

Warren Beatty played a highly romanticized Benjamin "Bugsy" Siegel while conducting an on-screen romance with his soon-to-be wife Annette Bening in Barry Levinson's *Bugsy* in 1991. Until then, the owners of the Flamingo Hotel had been a little coy about the casino's associations with Mr Siegel, but interest in the movie persuaded them to open the Bugsy Celebrity Theater.

Martin Scorsese's *Casino* (1995), starring Robert de Niro and Sharon Stone, is a brutally comic tale of mobsters elbowing and hustling their way into the casino business, much of it filmed in the Strip's Riviera casino. *Get Carter* was a classic English gangster movie made in

1971, and it reinforced Michael Caine's status as a viable actor. The movie was remade in 2000, set in Vegas and Seattle and starred Sylvester Stallone killing lots of people.

Multimedia money

The 2001 remake of *Ocean's 11*, the caper about casino robberies, unleashed a veritable gusher of television documentaries with Las Vegas as the backdrop. Barely a week goes by without one of the networks shooting in town, a bonanza that brought $135 million in production work in 2001, bringing the total to more than $1 billion since the Nevada Film Office was first set up.

mentaries, corporate and industrial productions all sweeten the pot. Commercials filmed in the state in 1999 generated $16 million; music videos added $37 million or so, and then there was $7.3 million from still photography.

Sometimes movie money gets spread around unexpectedly: a scene in *Rush Hour 2* involved scattering millions of dollars of fake money, some of which was collected by bystanders and allegedly passed off as real currency.

It's not unusual, either, for a group of tourists to discover that their local tour guide, waiter or shop manager had a "starring" role in a movie they have seen *(see photo on page 168)*.

The Nevada Film Office assists hundreds of films, music videos and multimedia productions every day of the week. Mimosa Jones heads the Entertainment Development Corporation, in striving for its share of the $16 billion budget that Hollywood loses annually to "runaway productions." Jones said that the city's 36 million tourists also "provide a steady audience for game shows and audience-based TV shows." Feature films bring between $35,000 and $100,000 a day in goods, services and local talent, while docu-

LEFT: Warren Beatty as a largely fictional but good-looking Bugsy Siegel in 1991's *Bugsy*.
ABOVE: Sharon Stone and Robert de Niro in *Casino*.

TV in town

One of CBS's hit shows, *CSI Crime Scene Investigation*, although shot mostly in studios near LA, is set in Las Vegas. Anthony Zuiker, the 33-year-old creator, is a University of Nevada and Las Vegas graduate and stockbroker who once worked as a tram operator at the Mirage before he started writing scripts.

"I think the town is opening up a little more because the show is a success; a couple of hotels have asked us about cross-promotion," he said. "I want to be sure that we portray the town real, that we don't do anything that jeopardizes its reputation... Besides, I don't want to be pulled over by cops and hassled for no reason." ❑

GOING TO THE CHAPEL

Richard Gere and Cindy Crawford did it; Mickey Rooney did it
eight times in the very same chapel. The neon nirvana is a mecca of matrimony

Las Vegas is a favorite destination not only for gambling and conventions, but it's also a mecca of matrimony, a paradise of promises, a Valhalla for vows. Over 174,000 troths are pledged here every single year.

In 1943 when the Little Church of the West was located at the New Frontier, Betty Grable and trumpeter and band leader Harry James exchanged their vows. The *Las Vegas Review-Journal* reported that more than 100 locals left their beds in the middle of the night to make a trip to the train station, hoping to get a glimpse of Grable as she waited for James to return from Mexico with his divorce papers. The wedding took place not long before dawn and after the ceremony the couple drove right back to Los Angeles.

Here come the brides

Celebrity weddings have always been fashionable in Sin City. Zsa Zsa Gabor married actor George Sanders in 1949 at the Little Church of the West. Zsa Zsa purred through another seven marriages, but she didn't try her luck at love in Vegas again. In 1949, Rita Hayworth married singer Dick Haymes at the Sands. Hayworth had been married to Prince Ali Khan, and to Orson Welles, and her partnership with Haymes lasted only two years. On July 19, 1966 Ol' Blue Eyes married Mia Farrow at the Sands, Sinatra's second home for nearly a decade.

Mickey Rooney married Ava Gardner at the Little Church of the West in January, 1942. Over the next three decades he made seven return trips to the same chapel, concluding with a marriage to January Chamberlin in 1978. Rooney is definitely in line for frequent-matrimony miles.

More recently, on Veterans Day in 1998, basketball star Dennis Rodman married *Baywatch* babe Carmen Electra in the Little Church of the Flowers after an all-night party. Nine days later

Rodman claimed he had been too drunk to know what he was doing, and in April the marriage ended in an annulment. Billy Bob Thornton was married to Angelina Jolie at the Little Church of the West on May 5, 2000.

The Little White Chapel on the Strip was chosen for the happy day for Michael Jordan

and Juanita Vanoy in 1989. Bruce Willis and Demi Moore were married there, and the chapel beams a live wedding over the Web every few minutes via its Wedding Cam onto the Discovery Channel's Internet site. The chapel displays Joan Collins' and Michael Jordan's name in lights. Owner Charlene Richards said, "Joan Collins told me, 'Charlotte, when I leave this place you can tell the world if you like.'"

According to Greg Smith, owner of the Little Church of the West, the oldest wedding chapel in Vegas, and now opposite Mandalay Bay, most big name stars want their weddings quiet and unpublicized. When Richard Gere and Cindy Crawford arranged their nuptials in

---

LEFT: Tom kisses Kelly.
RIGHT: it's cheap to get married – one of the many reasons over 174,000 troths are pledged each year.

1991 he didn't know who the bride and groom were to be until they arrived. "They said it would be a celebrity wedding and if they saw any press hanging around outside they wouldn't come in," said Smith. Both stars were dressed casually and told him they had been having dinner in Los Angeles when they got talking about it.

"Then, they just got on one of Disney's planes and came here and did it." The couple asked that photos be taken but made sure to take the negatives with them when they left.

Las Vegas has hosted 500 celebrity weddings or more, according to Dan Newburn who offi-

Vegas has about 50 wedding chapels which are open daily from 8am to midnight, and stay open 24 hours on legal holidays. The invitation to impulsiveness is taken advantage of by an average of 337 couples every day, with Valentines Day weekend understandably the busiest time of the year, when as many as 2,000 licenses are issued. The chapels issue at least 87,000 marriage licenses per year, each for a $50 license fee. Some form of legal identification like a driver's license, passport or birth certificate is also required, as well as divorce papers if either party has previously wed. Many betrothed couples fly their friends, well-wishers

ciated at the Treasure Island wedding of former boxing champion Ingemar Johansson. Of the public appetite for celebrity splicings, he said, "I think basically people have a latent voyeuristic streak in them and they like to peek in on other people's lives."

Invitation to impulsiveness

In March 2001, Erin Brockovich (who was portrayed by Julia Roberts in a recent movie) renewed her marriage vows with her husband, Eric Ellis, at the Viva Las Vegas Wedding Chapel on the second anniversary of their wedding. They were serenaded by an Elvis impersonator singing *I Can't Help Falling in Love.*

and families out to Vegas for the celebration just as a starting point for the adventure. The inexpensive 32-room motel behind the Viva Las Vegas Wedding Chapel at the northern end of the Strip offers a Blue Hawaiian room named and modeled after the Elvis movie, as well as rooms themed with headstone headboards and a coffin bathtub, and an Al Capone room inside whose closet is an image of a bound-and-gagged bellboy.

The Excalibur provides a medieval-themed ceremony, the MGM Grand offers Merlin to officiate while a fire-breathing dragon attempts to thwart the nuptials. The Las Vegas Hilton provides Intergalactic Federation regalia and hires several of the *Star Trek* characters as witnesses. Betrothals can be made by, with or even to the Phantom of the Opera. Other settings include a beach party, a Wild West wedding on horseback, an ancient Egyptian theme, on a pirate ship, at the Las Vegas Motor Speedway, at the bottom of the Grand Canyon and a wedding under water. Ceremonies can be arranged at the top of Paris Las Vegas' Eiffel Tower.

Drive-thru nuptials

One wedding chapel provides a convenient drive-in window, so the bride and groom don't even need to leave their car. For the more up-

Strip, the Grand Canyon or the Hoover Dam. For more serene mid-air marriages, a hot-air balloon is available with a basket large enough for bride, groom and the assembled company.

For any and all of these imaginative matrimonials, naturally, any number of Elvis impersonators can be engaged to participate, and perhaps even officiate.

The 3-millionth wedding in Las Vegas was celebrated at the Imperial Palace's We've Only Just Begun Wedding Chapel in July 2001, and coincided with the 92nd anniversary of the first recorded wedding in Clark County in 1909. The couple, Alberto and Marian Recio of Miami,

market auto-phile, you can have a limo drive to the scenic backdrop of your choice – and get married right in the back of the stretch. In fact, a few stretch limousines come equipped with whirlpools and hot tubs, so the happy couple can bubble and betroth simultaneously.

Those with a taste for the extreme can marry on a bungee jump, during a roller-coaster ride or, for even whiter knuckles, parachute-jump or sky-dive during a wedding. Ceremonies can be officiated in a helicopter hovering over the

LEFT AND ABOVE: you can choose to be married by a wizard, a medieval minstrel, during a bungee jump or under water. Elvis may participate or even officiate.

Florida, renewed their vows in Spanish and were serenaded by Elton John, Elvis and Wayne Newton look-alikes from the hotel's long-running *Legends in Concert* show.

The Clark County Recorder's office has made marriage records available on the Internet, and certified copies can be bought for around $7 apiece. Requests for duplicate certificates come in from around the world.

If the marriage doesn't go quite as planned, however, a solution is close to hand. About 446 miles (718 km) north of Las Vegas in Reno, Nevada, divorces can be arranged almost as spontaneously as weddings, and in just as many interesting ways. ❑

SPECTACULAR SPORTS

Tennis aces, golf pros, maniacal motorcycle riders,
heavyweight boxers – everybody wants to flaunt their physicality in Vegas

Hundreds of years before the Las Vegas Valley was "discovered" by non-Native Americans, members of the Southern Paiute Indian tribes had been playing and wagering on a game involving several small sticks. The game, which is still played by the Southern Paiutes in the Las Vegas area, takes skill, courage and, of course, luck.

Crowds of spectators gather to watch as the players use finesse and daring to outwit their opponents. Fortunes, relative to the era and values of the time, are won and lost by players and spectators alike.

Although the game, whose exact rules are still closely guarded by the Southern Paiutes, bears little similarity to the games of chance played in the big casinos of today, it could be said that this was the beginning of the history of sports and sports-betting in Las Vegas, which is now a multi-million dollar industry.

In terms of money, Las Vegas is truly a modern-day sports capital, yet surprisingly the city has so far been unable to support a professional sports team of any kind – hockey, basketball, football, soccer or baseball. Attempts have been made to seed professional franchises in Southern Nevada, but no professional team has yet inspired Clark County's 1.5 million inhabitants.

Headline sports

In spite, or perhaps because of this, the city's spectator sports are guaranteed to make headlines. There was, for instance, Evel Knievel's 1967 attempt to jump over the fountains of Caesars Palace, a stunt that landed him in the hospital for 31 days. Or his failed jump over Snake River Canyon in the desert in a souped-up rocket bike called the "Skycycle."

Twenty-two years later, son Robbie Knievel drew equally large crowds when he effortlessly sailed over Caesars' fountains (with no hands

on the handlebars), and later, when he made a successful jump in the Grand Canyon. (Papa Knievel, meanwhile, is rumored to be bored with retirement, and might be opening an Evel Knievel Xperience Cafe in the desert town of Primm.) And who can forget the Flying Elvi, those Elvises in pompadours and white catsuits

who parachute out of airplanes on a regular basis and played a stirring role in the movie *Honeymoon in Vegas*?

Spectacular sports, live-action sports, sports in general and sports betting in particular are prime draws for visitors to Sin City. On Super Bowl weekend (usually late January), Las Vegas swells to capacity when more than 200,000 sports fans converge to join in raucous parties and to bet millions of dollars on their pick for America's football champion. Some resorts host lavish invitation-only bashes to lure gambling "whales," the highest of high-rollers, to the casinos to drink, party and put up as much of their money as they dare.

LEFT: championship NASCAR racing at the Las Vegas Motor Speedway.
RIGHT: golfers rich and famous, unknown and pro, look forward to playing on one of Vegas' 50 courses.

Probably the best known live sport in Las Vegas is boxing. The city hosts many world championship boxing matches, bringing in millions of dollars for both the city and the contenders. The big-ticket ringside seats are coveted by the social, entertainment and sports elite, male fans often in black tie and tuxedoes, their female consorts in long evening gowns and sparkling with jewelry.

Las Vegas was world-renowned as a boxing venue long before defeated and disgraced heavyweight boxing champ Mike Tyson chewed Evander Holyfield's ear (literally) in 1997. Most, if not all, of the great fighters in the modern boxing world have fought in Las Vegas rings, including Sugar Ray Leonard, George Foreman, Oscar de la Hoya, Riddick Bowe, Lennox Lewis and Muhammad Ali. Heavyweight champion Joe Louis became a casino "greeter" at Caesars Palace after his long and illustrious boxing career ended, and he called Las Vegas home for many years.

Mike Tyson currently keeps a multimillion-dollar house in the southern part of the valley. Tyson's 2002 fight with heavyweight champion Lennox Lewis, in which Tyson was knocked out cold by Lewis, was originally scheduled for Las Vegas. The Nevada Athletic Commission,

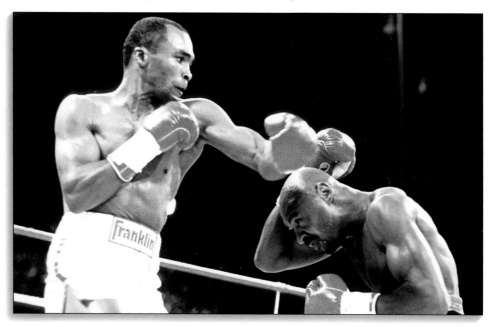

HEAVYWEIGHT CHAMPIONSHIP BOXING

Below are some of the momentous Las Vegas fights in which the world heavyweight title has changed hands:

Sonny Liston vs Floyd Patterson July 22, 1963
Liston landed a knockout punch in the first round.
Cassius Clay vs Floyd Patterson November 22, 1965
Clay won with a technical knockout in 12 rounds.
Muhammad Ali vs Ron Lyles May 16, 1975
Ali (formerly Clay) won, but Lyles held him to 11 rounds.
Muhammad Ali vs Leon Spinks February 15, 1978
Olympic champ Spinks won only his 7th professional bout.
Larry Holmes vs Muhammad Ali October 2, 1980

Muhammad Ali was knocked out in the 11th round.
Larry Holmes vs Tim Weatherspoon May 20, 1983
After 12 long, hard rounds, Holmes won a split decision.
Larry Holmes vs Mike Spinks September 22, 1985
Leon Spinks' brother Mike took Holmes' title.
Michael Moorer vs George Foreman November 5, 1994
Foreman wasn't deemed a suitable opponent due to his advanced years, but knocked out Moorer in the 10th round.
Evander Holyfield vs Mike Tyson November 9, 1996
The fight was stopped in the 11th round, with Holyfield the clear winner. A year later Tyson couldn't win the title back, but took some of Holyfield's ear lobe instead.

however, refused Tyson's license to fight in the state, decreeing that Tyson's image wasn't what Nevada boxing is all about. They had some cause. Before the two ever met in the ring, Tyson bit Lewis on the leg in front of the cameras during a pre-fight news conference in New York City.

Singers and swingers

Golf is another sport long associated with Las Vegas. In the early years – the 1940s, 50s and 60s – the casino builders saw golf as an aspirational game, a sport for those a cut above the common man. Nearly every casino on the Strip

were amateur golfers who enjoyed clearing their heads of cobwebs with a stylish daily round on a Las Vegas Strip course.

The roster of legendary drivers and putters included Dean Martin, Bob Hope, Bing Crosby, Debbie Reynolds, the McGuire Sisters, Willie Nelson, Joe DiMaggio, Burt Bacharach, and others too numerous to mention.

In the early 1990s, however, the landscape began to change for Las Vegas golfers. Strip resort entrepreneurs realized that the land around their casinos covered by grass and sandtraps for golf would be far more valuable covered by a casino, a parking lot or an amusement

sported acres of posh green fairways, kept vibrant with wells dug deep into the Las Vegas Valley aquifer, below the Mojave Desert.

The Tropicana, the Dunes, the Sahara and the Desert Inn all maintained lavish courses, often with their fairways right outside the doors of the casinos. Many of the legendary performers who played Las Vegas showrooms at night

LEFT: Sugar Ray Leonard in the act of defeating Marvin Hagler during their World Middleweight title fight, April 6, 1987.
ABOVE: Floyd Patterson nearly connects with a right on Cassius Clay's chin during their World Heavyweight fight, November 22, 1965.

arcade. Their fate was sealed, and the first of many courses began to sink beneath the creeping spread of concrete.

The Tropicana hotel's golf course, which was on the northeast corner of Tropicana Avenue and Las Vegas Boulevard South, was purchased by Kirk Kerkorian and annexed into a major part of the MGM Grand Hotel, Casino and Theme Park.

The same year the MGM opened, Steve Wynn purchased and blew up the Dunes Hotel. Out of the Dunes' lush green fairways rose Bellagio, with its massive dancing fountains – fountains supplied with the water from wells that had formerly watered the Dunes Golf and

Country Club. In June 2002, Wynn closed the Desert Inn golf course, the last course on the Strip. The opulent course had been a household name in golfing circles, and has been greatly missed. To pacify them, Wynn has promised a new course with his most recent hotel, Le Reve, which is currently being built on the site of the old Desert Inn.

Despite the loss of the Strip courses, golf remains a huge business in Las Vegas for everyday golfers as well as for the rich and famous. There are more than 50 courses nearby *(check the discerning list in Travel Tips in the back of this book)*, including Steve Wynn's Shadow

play Southern Highlands Golf Club when it opened in April 2000.

At least a dozen PGA Tour players live in Las Vegas or have close ties to the city, and often seen on local courses are such stars of the green as Jeff Gallagher, Craig Barlow, Chad Campbell, Bob May, Edward Fryatt, Robert Gamez, Skip Kendall, Stephanie Keever, John Riegger, Chris Riley and Eric Meeks.

Entertainers still flock enthusiastically to Las Vegas courses and are regularly spotted by fans. Celine Dion, George Clooney, Eddie Van Halen, Smokey Robinson, Will Smith, Lou Rawls, and Joe Pesci are all regulars on the links.

Creek Course, rated by many to be among the best in the world. And private trips to private golf clubs – usually in a private limo or helicopter – are a regular perk offered by casinos to high rollers.

Las Vegas courses are still celebrity packed, and it's not unusual to run into the world's elite from the world of sports, politics or entertainment. Golfing phenomenon Tiger Woods won his first major tournament in Las Vegas in 1996, and he still works out on local courses with long-time coach Butch Harmon, who has a home in Southern Nevada. Former president Bill Clinton was known to play golf every time he visited Las Vegas, and was one of the first to

Tennis aces among the dice

Tennis is another sport with Southern Nevada connections. Andre Agassi, the tennis phenomenon of the 1980s and 1990s, was born and raised in Las Vegas. Agassi is one of only a handful of players ever to have won each Grand Slam tournament at least once. For years, Las Vegas has hosted tournaments showcasing great names of the game like Arthur Ashe, Rod Laver, Chris Evert and Martina Navratilova.

One of the fastest growing spectator sports in the US is NASCAR Winston Cup car racing. About 10 miles (16 km) north of the city, Las Vegas has one of America's largest and best racing tracks. Every year the city plays host to the Sam's Town 300 and the UAW-Daimler Chrysler 400 NASCAR race at the Las Vegas Motor Speedway. Tens of thousands of supporters flock to the track to cheer – and place bets on – their favorite drivers.

NASCAR action

In 2002, 137,500 fans turned out for a 3-hour, 400 mile (640 km) NASCAR race, the largest single crowd for a sporting event in Nevada. All kinds of people from all over the USA, and some from around the world attend NASCAR races, paying ticket prices of about $75 a seat. More than 5,000 people who came to the track

Downtown. The Mint 400 is one of the longest-running off-road vehicle races in the country, offering valuable purses to the racing teams, both winners and losers.

Desert driving enthusiasts race anything with wheels and an engine. From big-wheeled motorcycles to huge custom-built trucks that can cost hundreds of thousands of dollars, the vehicles scream, scramble and slide around a track of 50 miles (80 km) in length. Modern racers who compete in the SCORE Henderson's Terrible 250 have five laps of a desert course to complete, starting and ending at the base of Black Mountain.

in recreational vehicles established a virtual city in one of the speedway's massive parking lots.

Since the early 1970s, Southern Nevada has also become the home of an off-road vehicle race sponsored by the Los Angeles-based SCORE International. America's oldest-established major desert racing organization, SCORE's roots in Las Vegas go back to the heyday of the Mint Hotel and Casino located

LEFT: Rachael Sproul rides in the demanding barrel-racing competition of the National Finals Rodeo, December 16, 2001.
ABOVE: Evel Knievel's "Skycycle," used in a failed attempt to jump over Snake River Canyon in 1974.

Cowboy get-together

Every December, Las Vegas shows its western roots by hosting the National Finals Rodeo (NFR). The NFR is the final event on the Pro-Rodeo Cowboy's Association rodeo season, and awards the hotly contested cowboy title, World Champ All-Around Cowboy. Only the top 15 cowboys in each event from the national rankings are invited to compete at the NFR.

The Nevada desert has served as a sports ground for as long as man has inhabited here. From the stick games of the Native American inhabitants to the roar and scream of the NASCAR vehicles, its popularity shows no sign of declining. ❑

THE DESERT

Las Vegas is an oasis near the middle of the Mojave Desert,
terrain that is inhospitable, unforgiving and utterly fascinating

Though it more resembles a mirage, Las Vegas is literally an oasis. The green lawns, colorful gardens, towering luxuriant palms and cottonwood trees – the city's abundant vegetation, as well as the ubiquitous swimming pools, fountains and man-made lakes flaunted by massive Strip resorts – belie the fact that the fast-growing megalopolis is located in one of the harshest, driest environments in the world, the Mojave Desert. Scalding hot in summer, often frigid in winter and bone dry nearly all the time, the Mojave is a beautiful and compelling place.

The uniqueness of the desert, the amazing diversity of plant life and wildlife, and the breathtaking landscape makes a trip out of the city an incomparable treat that many Southern Nevada visitors miss.

Once a sea

Las Vegas lies north of the center of the 25,000-square-mile (6.5-million-hectare) Mojave, which begins at the base of the Sierra Nevada mountains in the west and ranges east to its eastern boundary, the Colorado River. More than 275 million years ago, an immense inland sea covered most of this Southwest corner of North America, but over ages of evolution the sea dwindled and eventually dried up, leaving behind the vast bowls that we now know as the Mojave, Great Basin and Sonoran deserts.

A high water mark on the mountains around Las Vegas is evidence of this vast body of water. Gray limestone that is prominent in the Spring Mountains to the west of the city, the Sheep Range to the north, and Sunrise and Frenchman mountains to the east is a further reminder of the former sea. The limestone was formed on the sea bottom, and it still bears the fossilized remains of invertebrates that inhabited the water eons ago, including worms, corals and trilobites.

Thick deposits of sediment, shale and sand-

stone were left behind when the water dried up, and modern travelers need only take short excursions out of the city to see the remarkable remains. Sandstone was formed when massive mounds of sand, piled up to 2 miles (3 km) deep by ferocious winds, were cemented solid by a natural mixture of water and minerals. As centuries passed, the mountains of sandstone were sculpted by water erosion, blowing winds and furious storms. Some of these vividly colored and beautifully carved sandstone hills and valleys can be seen at Red Rock Canyon, which is about 17 miles (27 km) west of Las Vegas, or in Valley of Fire State Park, 35 miles (56 km) north of the city. Much of the rock in these areas is fiery red, caused by the oxidation of iron in the sandstone.

According to naturalist and author Anne Haymond Zwinger, some two million years ago, the Mojave uplifted, turned and became a transitional desert, meaning it was intermediate in climate and elevation. As nature altered

---

LEFT: Black Mountain Desert near Las Vegas.
RIGHT: flowering Joshua tree.

the Mojave, it grew distinct from the Sonoran Desert by excluding warm-climate species of plant life (mostly succulents) and became more hospitable to the northerly species of plants that are found in the Great Basin Desert.

Both the Mojave and Great Basin deserts are part of the Great Basin province, an area of more than 200,000 square miles (52 million hectares). No internal creek, river or stream that starts in the Great Basin drains to either the Gulf of Mexico or the Pacific Ocean. The Great Basin Desert is more temperate and cooler than the Mojave, which contains some of the most severe climatic areas in the world. More than

20,000 years ago, the arid landscape around Las Vegas was moist and fertile. Although it is difficult to imagine now, Southern Nevada was once a land of meandering rivers and small lakes. It hosted a wealth of lush vegetation and animal life that was dependent on water for survival. Fossils reveal that it was once inhabited by many species of animals that are now extinct, including sloths, camels and herds of three-toed horses. Archeologists have even uncovered the remains of giant mammoths in the Las Vegas Valley.

As the climate changed, the water that had been present in the Mojave Desert gradually disappeared, leaving the land mostly unpro-

ductive, save for a few species of plants that managed to adapt, or that migrated into the area. Current vegetation patterns are less than 10,000 years old, says Zwinger.

Dryness is a characteristic shared by deserts all over the world and the Mojave is no exception. Although many longer-established residents of the present-day Las Vegas Valley tell of winter snow storms that have swept the area in years past, valley snow has become rare in Las Vegas. Nevada is now the driest state in the US, with many areas in the southern portion of the state receiving just 1.5 to 5 inches (3.5 to 12.5 cm) of rain annually.

The plants and animals that make their home in the Mojave Desert are well adapted to the climate. One of the more extraordinary plants in the Mojave is the Joshua tree (*Yucca brevifolia*) and its cousin, *Yucca brevifolia jaegerina*. Both have long, bayonet-like leaves 18 to 24 inches (46 to 61 cm) long. Where the Joshua flourishes, it is usually the tallest vegetation around, and scores of birds and small animals use the tops and the strange, arm-like branches of the trees as a vantage platform to scan the desert. Edmund C. Jaeger in his book, *The North American Deserts*, explains that a line drawn around the outer limits of this strange tree's distribution more or less marks the boundaries of the Mojave Desert region.

A tree that is not a tree

Joshua trees, which are not really trees at all because they have no wood, are rarely seen below about 2,500 feet (762 meters) above sea level. This is simply because the Yucca moth, the insect that fertilizes all yuccas including Joshuas, does not survive at lower elevations. The symbiotic relationship between the moth and the yucca has evolved over time, so that each species of yucca has its own species of moth, as Zwinger explains. The relationship between the Joshua trees and the Joshua moth admirably demonstrates how the fragile balance of life has become perfectly adapted to the harsh desert environment.

Joshua Tree National Forest is located in California along Interstate 15 southwest of Las Vegas. For several miles along the highway between Los Angeles and Las Vegas, travelers drive through a virtual jungle of these strange looking plants.

Other desert plants that thrive in the Mojave

include true greasewood, sagebrush, salt bush, mesquite and creosote, the latter probably the most prevalent plant in the Southern Nevada desert. Creosote has small, dark green waxy leaves that grow abundantly on spindly, tough wooden stems. The sticky waxy substance on the leaves helps prevent moisture loss. After a desert storm, or when the leaves are crushed, the plant emits an aroma as fresh and undeniable as any cultivated flower.

Cacti are the plants best suited to life in the Mojave Desert. Their spines help protect the

JOSHUA TREES

Joshua trees, a common sight on the drive from Las Vegas to Los Angeles, more or less define the boundaries of the Mojave Desert.

tail jackrabbits, desert cottontails, kangaroo rats, antelope ground squirrels, and several different species of skunks.

One of the best known desert animal – which is also the Mojave's largest native animal, and Nevada's emblematic state animal – is the Desert Bighorn Sheep. Often weighing more than 260 lb (113 kg), the male, or ram, has unmistakable massive spiraled horns. The horns of the ewes are much smaller. These remarkable sheep conserve water, and may go two or three days drinking only once.

plant from gnawing animals, and provide shade for the stem, which has evolved to perform the food-making function of leaves. Additionally, the fat stems store moisture. Some of the more common Mojave cacti include the cholla, prickly pear, hedgehog and barrel, which is probably the most recognized species around Las Vegas, and whose spongy interior stores moisture for long periods.

Many species of animals have also adapted to the dryness and heat, including coyotes, black-

They are often to be seen grazing or traversing incredibly steep and mountainous desert terrain, putting any other animal to shame.

Untamed horses

Southern Nevada also has herds of "wild" burros and horses. Although referred to as wild animals by the general public, they are more specifically 'feral' – non-native domesticated species, introduced by man and now breeding in the wild.

The Mojave is home to an amazing array of birds including some endangered species, such as the phainopepla, a 7-inch (18-cm) shiny black bird with a crest like a blue jay. The rare

LEFT: blacktail jackrabbit browsing in the desert shade; coyotes and kangaroo rats also live here.
ABOVE: Valley of Fire State Park.

phainopepla is generally seen atop desert trees such as desert willow and mesquite. The bird's primary food source is a leafless mistletoe, which grows in heavy clumps in mesquite trees.

A more common bird is the greater roadrunner, which seldom flies but can often be seen running with neck and long tail outstretched as he hunts for prey including snakes, lizards and even other birds.

Although much of the arid land of the desert is from 2,000 to 5,000 feet (610 to 1500 meters) above sea level, the desert also encompasses portions of Death Valley, of which 550 square miles (142,450 hectares), is actually below sea

level. At 282 feet (86 meters) below sea level, Badwater, west of Natural Bridge Canyon, is the lowest elevation on dry land in the US.

Death Valley National Monument was established in eastern California and western Nevada in 1933. Fifty-two years later, the area was recognized by the United Nations and was designated part of the Mojave and Colorado Deserts Biosphere Reserve. Death Valley, approximately 115 miles (185 km) northwest of Las Vegas at its closest point, is the epitome of how one would expect a desert to appear.

For the most part, the harsh and barren lands of Death Valley spread in alluvial fans beneath craggy, sharp-faced mountains. Brassy natural

colors ignite the landscape, especially in the valley's Sand Dunes area where huge piles of undulating sand create a barren landscape, devoid of life, save for animals passing on their way through to a more hospitable place.

More than 200 square miles (52,000 hectares) of Death Valley contains an accumulation of natural salts that prevent any plant from growing. At the Devils Golf Course, salt is 3 to 5 feet (1 to 1.5 meters) deep.

Death Valley is the hottest spot in North America. Although tourists visit the year around, the ideal time to view Death Valley's wonders is from November through March, when more moderate temperatures are the rule.

Improbable ski resort

A more hospitable environment and much closer to Las Vegas is Mount Charleston in the Spring Mountains, a scant 30 miles (48 km) northwest of the city. While it is also part of the Mojave Desert, the mountain hovers a majestic 11,918 feet (3,650 meters) above sea level and sports a snow cap during the winter. Skiers and snowboarders enjoy a small Mount Charleston resort that is generally open from late November to late March or early April every year *(see page 245)*.

Herds of mule deer and elk can be found on the mountain, as well as many other species of animals and birds that prefer an alpine climate. The mountain may be as much as 50° F (10° C) cooler than the Las Vegas Valley over which it towers. Surprisingly, Nevada is the nation's most mountainous state, with more than 150 mountain ranges. Many of these ranges often appear as a single craggy mound that arises from the Mojave Desert floor like the back of a huge whale in the sea.

The Southern Paiutes, one of five Native American tribes in Nevada, believe Mount Charleston is the birthplace of their tribe. Other original Native American inhabitants of Nevada included the Northern Paiute, who historically lived in the northwest part of the state; the Western Shoshones who occupy the northeast; the Washoes, a tribe who ranged over the Sierra Nevada, and the Mojaves, who occupied the extreme southern area of Nevada along the Colorado River.

Modern archeologists believe Native Americans inhabited Southern Nevada for at least 12,000 years. Raoul M. Dixon in *Way of the*

Hunters: An Illustrated Commentary and Prehistoric Record, says that simply by walking through likely desert areas around Las Vegas he collected lithic tools and implements (flint and chert knives and arrowheads) that prove man was inhabiting Southern Nevada thousands of years ago.

The Lost City

About 50 miles (80 km) northeast of Las Vegas in Moapa Valley at the end of man-made Lake Mead is the "Lost City," officially known as Pueblo Grande de Nevada, a series of Anasazi Indian ruins situated along the Muddy and Vir-

and an above-ground pueblo (house) made of sticks and adobe. Museum officials say more than 50,000 visitors a year are attracted to learn about the ancient cultures that previously occupied this corner of the Mojave Desert.

From 1933 to 1938, many areas of the Lost City were excavated by New York archeologist M.R. Harrington. He supervised members of the Civilian Conservation Corps who helped in the excavations, and who built the small museum. The museum's walls are lined with artifacts recovered from the Lost City, including woven yucca sandals, lithic tools and knives, and ceremonial objects.

gin river valleys. First noted by explorer Jedediah Smith when he traveled through the area in 1826–27, the Lost City was occupied by the Virgin river Branch of the Anasazi (basket makers) sometime after the 1st Century AD. Puebloans later moved in from California in AD 700 to 1150, and Southern Paiutes moved in after AD 1000.

The state-operated Lost City Museum of Archeology in the small town of Overton was built on the actual site of Indian ruins. These ruins include a recreated subterranean pit house

LEFT: Indian paintbrush, common in Southern Nevada.
ABOVE: Kelso Sand Dunes, Mojave Desert.

"Archeological research continues to be an important aspect of the museum's operations," says Kathryne Olson, director of the museum. "Staff members can often be found one step in front of bulldozers as the ancient sites are removed to make way for housing tracts."

Evidence of ancient peoples' habitation can be found throughout the Mojave Desert in the form of petroglyphs, pictures that were painstakingly chipped and carved into rocks. As well as Red Rock Canyon, another view of this work can be found in the Valley of Fire State Park. Prehistoric artists found the red sandstone an ideal canvas – as do their modern counterparts. ❑

PLACES

A detailed guide to the city and the region, with principal sites cross-referenced by number to the maps

Las Vegas is a twinkling, flashing, glittering, lop-sided crown, jutting irregularly out of the desert. It soars and scrambles upwards, stranded in an arid, red dust-bowl. When approached at night from the air, it beckons like a seafront arcade from the wilder edges of science fiction. Arriving after dark on the road, it pulsates and looms ever larger, defying belief. Closer up, the giant neon glare evolves into shapes, signs and pictures, and the spectacle of the world's most lavish playground unfurls in the windshield.

Disembarking at McCarran airport, passengers are greeted by the Las Vegas theme tune – the continuous, pattering, tuneless chord of the slot machines, with percussion from jangling coins. Travelers pass through several aisles of gaming machines before reaching the luggage carousels, so there's no need to be bored if the bags are late. In any of the hotel casinos on the Strip, the carpet, the decor and the dress of the staff, all expensively woven into the theme of the resort, tell you instantly where you are. Paris Las Vegas is all blue, European classic. The Luxor is, well, ancient Egyptian. But close your eyes, and the burbling electronic music of the slots is identical everywhere – except perhaps the frequency of the jackpots. Contrary to expectation, however, million-dollar jackpots have actually occurred in McCarran airport. But in case you're disenchanted with coins, there's a small aviation museum on the upper level of McCarran.

The spectacles on the Strip are almost impossible fantasies made flesh; the volcano in front of the Mirage, the breathtaking, choreographed fountains of Bellagio, the campanile and canals of the Venetian; the town is a realization of innumerable show-business dreams. Inside, these pleasure domes take Kubla Khan's invention about as far as technology and invention will go. Expense has clearly been no object. The food and the entertainment are world class. That is to say, world class offerings are plentiful. For those who prefer simpler, earthier distractions, these too are only a short step away.

Downtown works hard to lure the Strip-bound gamblers away. The Fremont Street Experience is a spectacular technological marvel, still drawing long, spontaneous applause at every show. And Downtown competes with the Strip by giving the crowds something that they really want – better odds at the slots and tables.

Whatever your taste in post-millennial recreation, roll up, roll up, ladies and gentlemen, it's all here waiting for you. Step right in. ❑

PRECEDING PAGES: Bellagio's nightly fountain display is choreographed to music; the designer of the Luxor said his aim was to replicate "the essence of Egyptian architecture;" champagne and slots at Paris Las Vegas.
LEFT: a little bit of Italy under the desert sun, the Venetian.

Las Vegas

CROSSROADS OF THE WORLD

*All kinds of visitors from all over the globe
converge on this busy intersection, and its collection of
"performance architecture" reflects a surreal multi-culturalism*

Map
on page
132

The busiest junction in Las Vegas is where Tropicana Avenue crosses the Strip, connecting casino-hotels on all four corners. Everyday, thousands of pedestrians ride up and down the elevators and escalators, and across the elevated pedestrian crossways. CBS Television calls this the "Crossroads of the World," and recruits audiences to test out pilot shows at the junction. As David Poltrack, CBS vice president for research and planning says, the location is perfect because, "It is the one place in the country where you can get a socio-economic cross section of America, with great geographic diversion." In other words, you can find all kinds of people from all over America – and lots of other countries, too – right here. The themes of the adjacent casinos are also – at least outwardly – multi-cultural. In the short stretch of the Strip covered in the next two chapters, the hotels evoke France, olde England, Egypt, the Far East, the Caribbean and the East Coast of the United States.

LEFT AND BELOW:
New York-New
York's towers
include replicas of
famous landmarks.

I love New York

Opened in January 1997, the 47-story **New York-New York ❶** (3790 Las Vegas Boulevard South, tel: 740-6969 or 800/693-6763 was Nevada's tallest casino at 529 feet (160 meters). Its 2,035 rooms were filled even before it opened, by previewers excited by the appeal of staying in the Big Apple without having to actually go there. Visitors can admire the world-famous skyline and visit replicas of landmarks such as the Statue of Liberty, a 47-story Empire State Building and the Brooklyn Bridge.

The resort's dozen towers include the 40-story replica **Chrysler building** and the 41-story Century building. The large gaming area is surrounded by Park Avenue and Central Park, and adjoins **Times Square**, which offers perhaps the city's best selection of fast-food outlets, including Broadway Burger and Pizza. Visitors can cross the 300-foot (90-meter) Brooklyn Bridge, ride the Manhattan Express or a Coney Island-style roller coaster, and stroll along a prettily graffitied Lower East Side street of shops and eateries. Thousands of coins are thrown into the "lagoon." The coins are fished out later and donated to the charitable Make a Wish Foundation.

"The interesting thing to me about New York-New York," says University of Nevada professor Dave Hickey, "is that visually, externally it really is a successful building. It solves the facade problem by multiplying facades, which also solves the scale problem." The facade problem Hickey refers to is the difficult trick of providing thousands of rooms in one complex, but giving all of them a desirable view. This is the reason that so many hotels on the Strip are built in

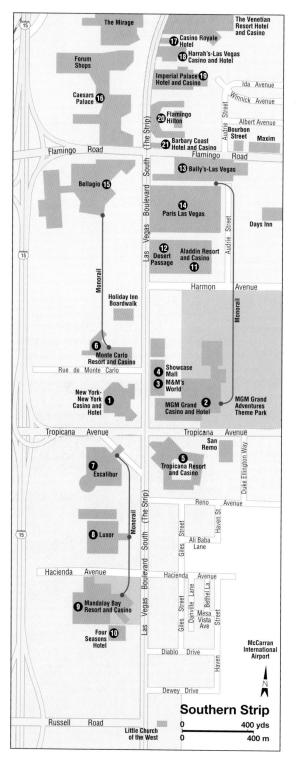

The Mirage

The Venetian Resort Hotel and Casino

⑰ Casino Royale Hotel

⑱ Harrah's-Las Vegas Casino and Hotel

Forum Shops

Imperial Palace ⑲ Hotel and Casino

Ida Avenue

Caesars Palace ⑯

Winnick Avenue

⑳ Flamingo Hilton

Albert Avenue

Bourbon Street   Maxim

㉑ Barbary Coast Hotel and Casino

Flamingo   Road   (The Strip)

Flamingo   Road

⑬ Bally's-Las Vegas

Bellagio ⑮

⑭ Paris Las Vegas

Days Inn

⑫ Desert Passage

Aladdin Resort and Casino

⑪

Harmon   Avenue

Holiday Inn Boardwalk

Monorail

⑥ Monte Carlo Resort and Casino

Rue de Monte Carlo

④ Showcase Mall

③ M&M's World

New York-New York Casino and Hotel ①

MGM Grand ② Casino and Hotel

MGM Grand Adventures Theme Park

Tropicana   Avenue

Tropicana   Avenue

San Remo

⑤ Tropicana Resort and Casino

Duke Ellington Way

⑦ Excalibur

Reno   Avenue

Haven St

Giles   Street

Ali Baba Lane

⑧ Luxor

Monorail   South   (The Strip)

Hacienda   Avenue

Hacienda   Avenue

Giles   Street

Danville Lane

Bethel La

Mesa Vista Ave

Street

⑨ Mandalay Bay Resort and Casino

Four Seasons Hotel ⑩

Diablo   Drive

McCarran International Airport

N

Dewey   Drive

Southern Strip

Russell   Road

Little Church of the West

0   400 yds

0   400 m

an "X" or a "Y" shape. The "scale problem" is that visitors could easily be overwhelmed by the vastness of the buildings in Vegas. Bellagio's architect addressed this by making each "window" actually cover four rooms, making the hotel appear only one quarter of its size.

The exterior of New York-New York is aesthetically better than the interior, but there's a Nathan's Coney Island hot dog outlet and the ESPN Sports Bar with 12-foot (3-meter) screens and 160 TV monitors, of which a dozen are located in the washrooms (designated *Guys* and *Dolls*) so you need never lose track of the track, so to speak. The Disney Company operates New York-New York along with six other casinos around the country. A Las Vegas construction inspector named Sue Henley won $12.5 million on a New York- New York slot machine in 1997, at the time the biggest jackpot ever.

MGM Grand

Currently, Las Vegas' biggest hotel is the 5,005-room **MGM Grand ❷** (3799 Las Vegas Boulevard South, tel: 891-1111 or 800/929-1111). Guests are greeted at 38 reception-desk windows and entertained as they wait by panoramic images of desert scenes, baseball stadiums and advertisements on an 80-panel video screen. Opened in late 1993, the MGM Grand has enough rooms and suites to offer a restless guest a different room every day for almost 14 years.

As the world's biggest gambling operator, the MGM-Mirage company's assets include New York-New York across the street, Bellagio, Treasure Island and the Mirage, as well as the Golden Nugget and the very exclusive Shadow Creek golfing facility. The company is headed by Kirk Kerkorian. A high-school dropout who is now over 80, Kerkorian began his Las Vegas career as a tour operator. He went on to build a series of hotels which were always the biggest in town. "He doesn't do it for the money, he has more money than he'll need in five lifetimes," said one of his friends "He does it because he gets bug-eyed like a little kid when he goes through the place."

The MGM Grand's entrance is flanked by a 45-foot (14-meter) high lion, which is claimed to be the largest bronze statue in the United States. This is the second lion on door duty here, the first was thought by Asian gamblers (of whom there are many) to bring bad luck, as guests' entry to the casino was through the lion's open mouth. The doorway was promptly removed. At the entrance on the Strip, a walkway from the Tropicana leads onto MGM's balcony over the casino floor. At the far side, live musicians and trailers from forthcoming movies are projected onto a giant screen.

In the amusing Rainforest Café, simulated thunderstorms and animated monkeys and crocodiles distract diners as they toy with their food surrounded by imitation birds, animals and butterflies.

Lions sleep here, too

On the casino floor to the right, visitors walking through the glass entrance to the **Lion Habitat** find lions sleeping over their heads or beneath their feet. The 450-lb (204-kg) beasts frolic with their trainer among waterfalls in a rocky African Savannah enclosure. Metro, Goldie and Louis B., three of the resident pride, are said to be descendants of the MGM signature lion whose yawn-like roar was the company's movie logo.

MGM's casino is the biggest in town at 171,500 square feet (16,000 square meters) and significantly has 3,500 slots, 1,000 more than its nearest rival. Slot-machine betting, the fastest growing game of the last decade, increased at the rate of about 12 percent every year, producing $1 billion a year for casinos from nickel slots alone. MGM-Mirage's patent on coinless slot machines using paper currency, preprinted coupons or "cash-out slips," has been licensed to

Map on page 132

Las Vegas welcomes up to 36 million visitors a year.

BELOW: moonrise over the MGM Grand.

Reno's International Game Technology, the world's largest manufacturer of slot machines with an 85 percent share of the market.

The special events area seats 17,157 and has a reputation as a world-class venue for superstar concerts and world championship sports events. A 15-minute walk from the hotel entrance leads to what used to be the 33-acre (13-hectare) **MGM Grand Adventures** theme park, now used only for special events. Behind the time-share Polo Club, a monorail curves around connecting the MGM Grand with Bally's and Paris Las Vegas. The long-time ambition of Las Vegas authorities is to connect the Strip, Downtown and McCarran airport by monorail. Investors have divvied up $600 million for the next phase of the extension, which will run from the MGM to the Sahara.

Outside the MGM Grand is where visitors are recruited to attend the free screenings of CBS pilot TV shows, to give their opinions and help shape the coming schedules. In return they are offered $10 discount certificates that can be used in the adjoining Television City gift shop. Tests are conducted all day, and shows last about one hour, including the time to gather reactions. There is rarely a wait of longer than a few minutes. Previewed shows sometimes offer good entertainment, and the venue has become CBS's most important test-market. "People come here for the night life and try to figure out what to do during the day," said one participant. "This is a place where people have time to spare."

M&Ms play here

Adjoining the MGM Grand are **M&M's World** ❸ (3785 Las Vegas Boulevard South 2, tel: 736-7611) whose candy stores, Racing Cafe and interactive exhibits are especially attractive to children, and the **Showcase Mall** ❹, with

Gameworks, by the Showcase Mall, is jointly run by Sega and Universal Studios. It offers over 200 state-of-the-art arcade games.

BELOW: the Showcase Mall has M&Ms galore, plus a gigantic Coca-Cola bottle you can ascend.

a theme loosely based around the Grand Canyon, with the aid of 60 tons of textured "rock," rope bridges and a hovering helicopter. Climbers with harnesses can ascend the 75-foot (23-meter) studded concrete "tree" to the amusement of the crowd below, and lighting storms and flash floods feature in the hourly show. An elevator takes visitors up the 100-foot (31-meter) high Coca-Cola bottle so they can enjoy the view of the Strip from above.

Map on page 132

The Tropicana

The **Tropicana** ❺ (3801 Las Vegas Boulevard South, tel: 739-2222 or 800/634-4000) is themed as "the island of Las Vegas." The concept began in 1986 when a 22-story tower opened on a 5-acre (2-hectare) landscaped island among flamingos, parrots and cockatoos and swans. Over the years more wildlife, more towers and a walkway link were added, and the pool area expanded. Another island fronts the hotel. Home to two 35-foot (11-meter) tall sculptures of Aku Aku gods and a Polynesian house nestling in tropical landscaping, it gives nightly laser shows that are highly regarded.

The hotel's main attraction is the long-running *Folies Bergère* show. With its origins in Paris in 1869, the show was brought to the Tropicana in 1959 by Lou Walters, father of ABC-TV's Barbara Walters, and has now given more than 25,000 performances. On many nights there are two shows: the "classic" show is at 10pm, while a show "suitable for children," i.e. no nudity and no drinks, begins at 7pm. A Folies performance with no bare breasts seems a strange concept, since nudity is what the show was founded on originally.

Highlights of the show form a part of the afternoon tour, which goes backstage through dressing rooms strewn with sequined costumes, wigs and feathered

BELOW:
the *Folies Bergère* first took to the stage in 1959.

fans. Personal items, flowers and photographs adorn the dressing tables. Each dancer has half a dozen pairs of $150 shoes. Along with their entertainment abilities, performers must have minimum height qualifications to work here – 5 feet 3 inches (1.6 meters) for acrobats, 5 feet 6 inches (1.7 meters) for dancers, 5 feet 10 inches (1.8 meters) for showgirls – and the cast range in age from 18 to about 40. These glamorous girls make around $45,000 a year, but they also have plenty of opportunities for pay-per-hour jobs at conventions.

Topless showgirls first arrived on the Strip in 1957 at the Dunes Hotel show, *Minsky's Follies*. Early shows included a dance group produced by Donn Arden, the man credited with setting the style for modern showgirls, at the Desert Inn. At that time, the hiring practice was for girls 5 feet 8 inches (1.75 meters) tall or above, and today the classic showgirl is still very tall, ultra-thin and perfectly poised. Dancers can be shorter and sometimes perform clothed. The showgirl style was followed successfully at the Stardust Hotel, where the *Lido de Paris* show was imported from France for a run that lasted 31 years.

The birdman

The Tropicana sports a kind of funky, old-fashioned charm, promoting its Caribbean theme with flamingos, macaws and toucans. A wooden bridge overlooking a waterfall offers a romantic backdrop to weddings conducted here. Labyrinths of corridors lead from the flower-filled garden to the casino, in whose **Tropics Lounge** is the "Birdman," animal trainer Joe Krathwohl. His show features eagles, parrots and macaws which he juggles upside down. Tiki the macaw swings from his beak, and Lolita, an Amazon parrot, sings operatic selections. It's a free show (three times daily, except Thursday) during which the

BELOW: Trop tattoo.

Map on page 132

birds perform unlikely tricks like riding scooters and flying through hoops. Krathwohl gives us a glimpse of the trick, saying, "It's a matter of knowing how their brains work."

Star of the show is a rare Andean condor with a huge wingspan which lives with Krathwohl along with 250 other birds and animals, on the trainer and falconer's estate south of the city. He also keeps a black leopard, white tigers and birds from Europe, Asia, Egypt and Africa. Krathwohl, who has appeared with his rare birds on NBC-TV's *Tonight Show,* calls his performance "a little bit of everything." He is also kept busy providing trained birds for Hollywood movies and TV commercials.

Legends live here

The Tropicana's **Casino Legends Hall of Fame** is one of the most interesting museums in town, a museum of casinos and gaming. Colorful and mostly defunct gambling chips, autographed boxing gloves, hotel security uniform patches, ancient slot machines and porcelain decanters shaped like slot machines, packets of Desert Inn cigarettes, record album covers and glittering costumes worn by performers are among the 15,000 items in the three crowded rooms. The walls are lined with historical documents and photographs. Exhibits are drawn from 738 casinos, of which 550 have passed into history themselves, and chart 70 years of Las Vegas gambling history.

A videotape showing the implosions of the Aladdin, Hacienda and Sands hotels runs continually, near to a glass case of memorabilia from El Rancho Vegas, one of the very first casinos *(see page 32)*, and a catalogue from the Sands' auction held in July, 1996. Other screens run scenes of the Sinatra-led Rat

BELOW: never let an opportunity go by at the Tropicana.

Map on page 132

Lance Burton, Monte Carlo magician.

BELOW: Aku, Aku gods at the Trop. **RIGHT:** kids outside the Monte Carlo.

Pack antics, and inductees of a Hall of Fame. These range from Las Vegas veterans like Phil Tobin, who first arranged for gambling to be legalized, to stars like Sophie Tucker and Sinatra himself. There is an admission charge to the museum (open daily 7am–9pm) but free tickets are often handed out – along with a free slot machine pull – in the hotel's parking lot. One intriguing exhibit is a sample page from the secret "Black Book," which gives a glimpse of pictures and background notes on gamblers of "notorious or unsavory reputation" who are banned from the casinos. Between 1960 and 1995, 38 people were listed in the Black Book.

Adjoining the museum is the **Legends Deli** where customers enjoy their favorite stars in the form of sadwiches; the Joey Bishop (pastrami on rye with a pickle), the Liberace (grilled prime rib sandwich on a french roll), Jerry Lewis (baked ham on whole wheat) or, of course, "the King" (grilled banana, peanut butter and grape jelly on white toast).

Monte Carlo

The **Monte Carlo** ❻ (3770 Las Vegas Boulevard South, tel: 730-7777 or 800/311-8999) with arched domes, marble floors, ornate fountains and gaslit promenades, is modeled after Monaco's Place du Casino and is operated by the Mandalay Resorts Group, which runs almost a mile of Strip casinos to the south. The Monte Carlo's marble registration area overlooks the pool, which can produce 30-inch (75-cm) waves.

The hotel also has its own brewery, producing 8,000 gallons (250 barrels) of beer each month. Varieties of ale include Winner's Wheat, High Roller Red and Jackpot Pale, the last checking in at 5.2 percent of alcohol by volume. Beer is brewed here every two or three days and aged from 14 to 60 days. Because it is not pasteurized and no artificial preservatives are used, the beer is best when kept refrigerated.

The giant copper tanks, each holding 620 gallons (2,350 liters), are visible through huge glass windows from the Medici Cigar Club. Stogies run from as little as $3.50 to as much as $25 each. Smokers can lounge around the brewery's main floor where there is nightly entertainment, or on overstuffed couches to view the scene from the floor above.

Outside, sharing space on the **Street of Dreams**, lit by old-fashioned gas lamps, is a Beer on Tap counter for those who want to drink standing up and then scoot. From a tram station at the end of the street, visitors can take the (free) one-minute ride to Bellagio. Both Bellagio and the Street of Dreams are the work of interior designer Terry Dougall, who was responsible for the much-lauded Forum Shops, and who also contributed to both the Venetian and Mandalay Bay hotel casinos.

Lance Burton is a longtime Vegas headliner, who has been starring in his eponymously-named theater at Monte Carlo since 1996. As a kid, Burton spent his money at the magic shop, getting some of it back by doing shows and charging 5¢ admission. The amiable Burton's act includes ducks, Elvis the parakeet, and a seemingly endless flight of white doves. ❑

EXCALIBUR TO MANDALAY BAY

Merry Old England competes with tropical Eastern luxury, while the Sphinx next door shoots laser beams from its eyes. Where else could you be but Las Vegas?

Map on page 132

The multi-colored spires of the **Excalibur** ❼ (3850 Las Vegas Boulevard South, tel: 597-7777 or 800/937-7777) look just like a DisneyWorld castle. Alighting from the monorail, visitors are greeted by a sign setting the tone: "Welcome to the medieval time of your life." Across the moat and drawbridge, the resort itself is filled with heraldic motifs, plastic knights bearing battle-axes, Sir Galahad's Prime Rib House, and couples with their heads in sets of stocks, being photographed. Through the endless, heavily carpeted corridors populated only by huge lamps, the first thing to reach is the Sherwood Forest Café, and then the casino itself. Few visitors look up to notice the colored glass windows and intricate cornices decorated with statues. Inside, it really is as impressive as its startling exterior, assuming you like *faux* England.

Owned by the Mandalay Resort Group, which also owns the Luxor and Circus Circus casinos, this family-style resort was opened in 1990, covering 57 acres (23 hectares). With twin 28-story towers holding more than 4,000 rooms, it was, at the time, the world's largest hotel-casino. Some floors are given over to family-friendly non-gambling entertainment. Excalibur nevertheless serves 1.2 million alcoholic drinks every month.

Jousting and rounds of medieval sport to test agility, strength and endurance are the entertainment at the dinner show, *King Arthur's Tournament of Kings*. Eight rival monarchs each recruit a cheering section of diners. The restaurant seats 1,400 people but somehow – as in most casinos – there's always a waiting line to enter, which in this case is along the path lit by massive iron chandeliers and glittering sconces.

PRECEDING PAGES: pretty as a picture. **LEFT AND BELOW:** Excalibur

Medieval Village

The medieval fantasy continues in the second floor **Renaissance Faire**. Performers garbed in medieval costume play period arrangements on mandolin, flute, and harp, to accompany puppets, mimes, magicians and jugglers. Performances are from 10am on the Court Jester's Stage at **Medieval Village**. Costumed figures and strolling minstrels roam the area to provide entertainment. Of those who choose one of Excalibur's two wedding chapels for their nuptials, about one-quarter opt to do so in medieval attire.

Fantasy Faire holds two motion simulator theaters. The Magic Motion Machines lure visitors into hydraulically activated seats for a rolling ride in either a runaway train or an outer-space demolition derby directed by Hollywood's George Lucas. Kitchen Table Poker, which is a series of free educational poker games, are conducted every morning for half an hour,

after which participants put up $10 in real money and test their newfound skills.

A **Dragon Battle** takes place in the moat at the castle's entrance each evening, where a fire-breathing dragon tussles with the wizard Merlin every hour from dusk to midnight. Excalibur's designer, Weldon Simpson, was also responsible for the Luxor and the MGM Grand. Simpson believes that, "Las Vegas is better than virtual reality, because in virtual reality you have to trick your mind into thinking that you are someplace else – many other places."

Eventually, he believes, slot players will be enclosed in private virtual-reality environments, allowing 3D interaction in a game based on the hotel theme. The more the gambler plays, the further he advances in the virtual reality game. "It will be like playing Nintendo. When you get enough points you will become one of the virtual reality characters yourself."

Charles L. Silverman, a designer of casino interiors for three decades, says that the customer base is not just the gambler any longer, "It is anyone who walks through our doors. If enough people come in, enough of them will gamble, so we are creating lavish palaces to attract them."

The Luxor

The huge atrium of the **Luxor** (3900 Las Vegas Boulevard South, tel: 262-4000 or 800/288-1000) is lined with reproductions from the Luxor and Karnak temples in Egypt, including portraits of Tutankhamen and Nefertiti. The 30-story, glass-paneled pyramid's atrium is said to be spacious enough to park nine Boeing 747s, and the beam of light from its summit shines 10 miles (16 km) into the sky, running up an electricity bill of $1 million per year. It's said the beam can be seen from outer space, but it's more likely to be just Vegas talk.

BELOW:
double jackpot:
in your dreams.

Local architect Dan Juba said that his aim was to replicate in the pyramid "the essence of Egyptian architecture," as faithfully as possible. "Using simple shapes and strict geometric organization about a central axis, the twin towers complement the dynamic pyramid, and they were designed to offer unimpeded views from most hotel rooms."

Map on page 132

After two smaller pyramids, and low-rise villas with courtyards and terraces were added, the Luxor linked the pyramid to its sister property, the adjoining Excalibur, by a moving walkway (there's also a free monorail). The 100-foot (30-meter) Sphinx dominating the entrance can project a 55-ft-high (17-meter) hologram of King Tut's head onto a water screen using laser beams from its eyes, but the Federal Aviation Administration requested the lasers be switched off after complaints from airline pilots. In Egypt, the Sphinx, carved in the form of a lion with the head of a king, is seven storys tall, and a pyramid would typically take thousands of slaves 20 years to build.

The Luxor has real and reproduction treasures from Egypt.

Cairo Bazaar

Many of the Luxor's 4,008 guest rooms are accessed by elevators called "inclinators" which turn sideways and run horizontally along rollers at 39° at the upper floors, but only guests of the hotel are allowed to ride the inclinators. There are views down to the fourth floor. Here, in a thickly-carpeted area reached by elevators from the lobby, are video arcades, a 3D IMAX theater, and video Karaoke machines where you can make your own music video from a choice of 700 music tapes.

BELOW: the beam from the Luxor travels 10 miles (16 km) into the sky.

Elegant stone walkways lead to the **Giza Galleria** where, in the Cairo Bazaar, artisans and vendors offer themed wares. Also for sale are perfume bottles,

papyrus art, carved statuary and small leather items imported from Egypt.

The sight of beautiful, or at least very bold women, is more or less guaranteed in the luxurious nightclub Ra, thanks to its policy of giving free entrance all night to "female adult entertainers." The Luxor's lavish Sports Book area has individual television monitors for each seat, making it easy to bet in comfort. The Sports Books date back to Bugsy Siegel's innovation of the Trans-America Wire Service, which had a monopoly on relaying all horse-race information in the US direct from the race track. No bookie could operate without this information, and so Siegel could charge pretty much what he liked. Today, the rates are set by a state commission.

Mandalay Bay

Elegant **Mandalay Bay** ❾ (3950 Las Vegas Boulevard South, tel: 632-7777 or 877/632-7000) is a luxurious, tropically themed resort on a lagoon, with its own rum distillery and a pool with a sandy beach. The beach is swept by waves from a machine that can generate 6-foot (2-meter) breakers for body surfing. Visitors can see the pool through windows near the entrance to Shark Reef, but only guests are allowed to swim. In its evaluations of Strip pools, *Where Las Vegas* magazine gave top marks to the waves on Mandalay Bay's sandy shore. The Luxor and the MGM Grand, each with five pools, received favorable mentions, and *Where* also sited Caesars' Garden of the Gods, which claims inspiration from Rome's Baths of Caracalla.

BELOW: Mandalay Bay's "beach with surf" has won several awards.

Shark Reef, an open 90,000 square feet (8,350 square meter) aquarium holds 2,000 marine animals. It was installed after the hotel opened and has proved very popular. One and a half million gallons (5,670,000 liters) of water around

ancient temples, statues, old stone stairways and a sunken ship are home to fish of all shapes and sizes. The exhibit contains a dozen species of shark, ranging from a baby Port Jackson shark, only 10-inches (25 cm) long to a 12-foot (4-meter) long nurse shark which, in its coral reef habitat, sucks its prey out of holes in the rocks. The exhibit points out that despite their fearsome reputation, millions of sharks are killed every year for every human killed by a shark.

Another exhibit is **Snakes & Dragons**, the former being pythons, and the latter fish. Visitors carry "narration wands" that describe the golden crocodiles from Thailand and the green-tree pythons. At the touch pool they can put their hands in the water to stroke the horseshoe crabs and baby stingrays.

Map on page 132

Underwater god at Mandalay Bay's Shark Reef.

Huge ferris wheel

Mandalay Resorts Group manages a total of 19,000 rooms, including the Excalibur and the Monte Carlo, and controls all the land on this side of the Strip for about one mile further south. They are constructing a three-level convention center on 17 adjoining acres (7 hectares), which the company hopes will tap into the $4.3 billion of business that conventions bring to the city each year.

It is scheduled to open in January 2003, and with the city's own center now expanded to 3.2 million square feet and a third center under construction by the Sahara, Las Vegas will have three of the country's seven largest convention centers. The widely-read local columnist John Smith said that Las Vegans believe "if it's worth doing, it's worth overdoing."

There are also plans to build the world's second largest Ferris Wheel, a 518-foot (158-meter) high behemoth (the tallest will still be the London Eye in England, at 1,392 feet/424 meters), which will have 35 air-conditioned observation

BELOW: Shark Reef has over 2,000 marine animals.

Map on page 132

booths that will take half an hour to complete a circuit. Of course, the views will be spectacular, not only of the Strip but of the surrounding desert landscape.

Dominating the classy dining area is a 20-foot (6-meter) tall headless statue of Lenin, a reproduction of a Russian statue. He stands outside the very capitalist **Red Square** restaurant, where the cheapest item on the menu is the Chicken Kiev at around $20. Neighbors of this restaurant and entertainment area are the tropical Rumjungle Bar and restaurant, and the **House of Blues**, where the gospel brunch is legendary, and worth getting up for on Sunday (be sure to book before a late Saturday night, though). Mandalay is known for its restaurants, which also include Trattoria del Lupo and Aureole *(see page 95)*. The hotel's showroom offers state-of-the-art ShowTrans headsets providing plot developments in Spanish, German, Italian, Japanese and Mandarin.

Mandalay Bay also has an extremely good giftshop, selling crafts and clothes from around the world with a vaguely tropical theme. One timely buy is a parasol from Thailand, which comes in very useful when trawling the Strip during the 100°-plus (37° C) days in June, July and August.

A Lazy River runs for ¾ mile (1 km) around the resort which comes third in casino size, after MGM and Bellagio. Like Harrah's, Mandalay Bay is experimenting with customer tracking, and awarding points for betting on their tables or buying from its shops and eating in its restaurants.

The Four Seasons

Occupying the top five floors (36–39) of Mandalay Bay is the **Four Seasons** **⓾** (3960 Las Vegas Boulevard South, tel: 632-5000 or 877/632-5000), an opulent hideaway which is the only major hotel on the Strip not to offer gambling. In similar luxurious style to others in the chain, it is a peaceful sanctuary in shades of gold, green, amber and purple. Furnished with antiques and a Renaissance painting, it has its own private driveway, three private elevators and a separate lobby so that guests can avoid the casino in the Mandalay Bay altogether if they wish, a luxury many will pay for if only to avoid the ear-jangling, nerve-shattering and ever-present sound of the slot machines.

Excellent service is guaranteed by a ratio of two staff members to each guest, and there are special little touches like Evian water in the bathrooms, and iced grapes served at the poolside. Traditional Balinese and Javanese body rituals are a feature of the spa, where cucumber slices are dispensed to cover the eyes. The concierge desk stands ready to book guests into any of the 50 golf courses in the area, trips into the Nevada wilderness or, in winter, skiing at the Lee Canyon Ski Resort, only 45 minutes away.

Crossing the street from Mandalay Bay is a journey from the sublime to the ridiculous, the destination being a half-century old bar that for the past few years has been called the **Laughing Jackalope**. Popular with locals, it offers free evening snacks and $1 drinks during its Friday happy hour. For just a little bit more, customers can dig around in a lobster tank with one of those arcade-type crane arms, trying to catch their own crustacean main course. ❑

BELOW: the luxurious Four Seasons is one of the few Strip hotels without a casino.
RIGHT: preparing for one of Vegas' legendary buffets.

ALADDIN TO BELLAGIO

*Sensual, sumptuous, lavish and outlandish,
the resort casinos along this section of the Strip
cater for the discerning sybarite*

Map
on page
132

The 2,567-room **Aladdin** ⓫ (3667 Las Vegas Boulevard South, tel: 785-5555 or 800/582-2228) reopened in August 2000 on the site of its namesake, which was imploded in 1998. Aladdin's greatest asset is its location, right in the middle of the Strip between casinos that clock in 200,000 visitors a week. Entry from the Strip was designed for convenience, past the 50-foot (15-meter) waterfall which cascades over sandstone cliffs. Unusually, the entrance leads directly into a shopping center, not the casino.

Once inside, the Arabian Nights theme is evoked between the minarets by genies in bottles, and magic lanterns. Around the huge Aladdin's lamp centerpiece in the casino, cocktail waitresses waft between the tables in gauzy harem costumes. Among the good restaurants is Josef's Brasserie, serving traditional country French cuisine, in a setting of murals and opulent mirrors. The Oyster Bar serves seafood flown in fresh every day, and is highly rated by reviewers. The 7,000-seat **Aladdin Theater for the Performing Arts** hosts headliner concerts and Broadway shows, and an Arabian Nights production runs every night in the smaller 1,000-seat theater.

Jewel in the crown

Planned as a music-themed hotel before the bankruptcy of Planet Hollywood, one of the original partners, Aladdin was financed by a New York developer and London Clubs International, a gaming entity seeking a foothold in the US market.

Owners of The London Club, a private enclave with its own five-star restaurant inside the Aladdin, touted it as "the jewel in the crown" of their chain of clubs which included branches in England, the Bahamas, Egypt and South Africa. It was fittingly flagged as "a cool oasis in a 100-plus degree desert," in a city visited by more Brits (254,000 in a recent year) than any other European nationals.

Aladdin has had a very checkered history. It began life as the Tally-Ho casino in 1963, and was once owned by organized crime. To some, though, the site is still best known as the venue of Elvis Presley's marriage to Priscilla in 1967, in the private suite of the then-owner, Milton Prell.

Even with good restaurants, a spacious theater and an attractive sixth-floor pool, there have been questions about the quality of management. The 116,000 square-foot (10,775 square-meter) casino was planned to contain 2,800 slots, but the owners gave in to pressure to cut out almost one quarter of them, ending up with 2,270, because the room was thought too cluttered. The average daily revenue from individual slot machines dropped to $80, more than 25 percent below

PRECEDING PAGES:
Paris Las Vegas.
LEFT AND BELOW:
Aladdin is built on
the site of its
namesake.

the industry average of $108 per machine. At its reopening, the 17-story hotel received a very unmusical welcome from the *Los Angeles Times* which slammed it for "miscalculations" like the lack of a grand, sweeping entrance and the need to climb stairs to reach the "underwhelming" doors. Having said that, guests seem to enjoy staying there, and single out the spaciousness of both their bedrooms and, especially, the bathrooms as real treats.

Exotic opulence plus shops

The adjoining **Desert Passage ⓬** (open 10am to midnight daily) is an exotic complex of 135 opulent stores and restaurants. The publicity that described it as "extraordinary" was not exaggerated. Beneath a flawless blue-and-white sky are tiled benches and immense pottery jars. Occasional wall fountains line the smooth cobbled hallways plied by tricycle rickshaws (generous tips expected) for those too tired or too lazy to walk. Street merchants in Moroccan attire display their wares in stylish kiosks, and wedding parties accompanied by musicians and belly dancers thread their processions amid the throngs. The Endangered Species chain has a store, its entrance here guarded by life-size stone elephants. An indoor tropical "storm" with thunder and lightning rains down from time to time, but of course nobody ever gets wet.

A complaint from retailers has been that Desert Passage isn't making money fast enough. Despite annual sales well above the national average, it is far short of other casino shopping complexes. Its usually successful developers, TrizecHahn, were rumored to be planning to sell. Retailers say that it has become such a tourist attraction that many visitors are content to regard it as merely a spectacle and pass right through, with their wallets undisturbed.

BELOW: an elephant prowls the Desert Passage; indoor tropical "storms" take place here, too.

Bally's

What is now **Bally's** (3645 Las Vegas Boulevard South, tel: 739-4111 or 800/634-3434) began life as Kirk Kerkorian's MGM Grand. The approach to Bally's is dramatic, via 200-foot (60-meter) long escalators flanked by cascading water, lighted pylons, and giant palm trees. Every 20 minutes the entry area erupts with a sound-and-water show involving a wave machine and blow-hole fountains. Water is very much in favor here, in the multi-million dollar show *Jubilee*, where the *Titanic* sinks every night on stage.

Bally's has doubled the size of its baccarat room to target players willing to wager hundreds of thousands of dollars on a single hand, "whales" in gaming parlance. Liberal odds and high-bet limits make baccarat a favorite with high rollers, and in one recent year, the Strip's 55 baccarat tables generated $594 million, compared with the $482 million yielded by almost 900 blackjack tables. Bally's was one of six casinos, along with the MGM Grand, New York-New York, Monte Carlo, the Las Vegas Hilton and the Riviera, which voted collectively against representation by the Transport Workers Union, by 1,564 to 554. Since most dealers are paid only $6 per hour, they rely heavily on tips or "tokes" to supplement their income.

About half of a typical casino's revenue is generated through gambling and half of that comes from the tables run by dealers, from $2 roulette wheels to $100,000 baccarat games. Tropicana dealers voted in favor of unionizing by 112 to 51, the Stratosphere by 116 to 48.

Shannon Bybee, a casino industry expert at the University of Nevada Las Vegas, said that most dealers probably didn't want to change the status quo, despite pressure from colleagues to organize and unionize: "They make good

Map on page 132

TIP

Unless otherwise stated, all telephone numbers in this book are preceded by the code 702.

BELOW: backstage at Bally's.

This replica of the Montgolfier balloon glows with night-time neon, and is a significant Strip landmark.

BELOW: Paris' Arc de Triomphe is two-thirds the size of the original.

money in tips and they don't want to risk losing that in contract negotiations."

When the old MGM Grand opened in 1973, it was the world's largest hotel, following a precedent Kerkorian had set in 1969 with his International Hotel. "We opened that hotel with Barbra Streisand in the main showroom," he said. "The rock musical *Hair* was in the other showroom and the opening lounge act was Ike and Tina Turner." But the Grand was the scene of a disastrous fire on November 21, 1980 that killed 84 people and injured 700. In 1993, Kerkorian opened the present MGM Grand further up the Strip.

Gay Paree

The monorail and **Le Boulevard**, a street of shops and French restaurants, connect Bally's to the $800 million **Paris Las Vegas** ⓮ (3655 Las Vegas Boulevard South, tel: 946-7000 or 888/266-5687). Both are owned by Park Place Entertainment, whose empire includes 16 other gaming properties throughout the US, and in Australia and Uruguay. The hotel casino is modeled on the 800-year-old Parisian Hotel de Ville, the Paris City Hall. It is distinguished by one of the city's more prominent landmarks, a 50-story replica of the **Eiffel Tower**, thrusting through the roof of the casino and rising 540 feet (165 meters) in the air, accompanied by a neon copy of the Montgolfier balloon.

A half-size scale model of the original, the Eiffel Tower offers panoramic views of the city from the 11th-story piano bar, one of eight restaurants at the casino specializing in regional French cuisine from Alsace, Burgundy and Loraine. Bastille Day (July 14) is celebrated at the ⅔ scale **Arc de Triomphe** in solidarity with ceremonies at the Parisian Arc. No special celebration is needed to indulge at Napoleon's Champagne Bar, where a collection of featured quo-

Map
on page
132

tations includes one from the blind French monk Dom Perignon who first con-cocted champagne, "Brothers, come quick! I am tasting stars!"

The colossal legs of the Paris's Eiffel Tower are solidly planted inside the 85,000-square-foot (7,900-square-meter) casino which houses an attractive fountain and a plethora of cute signs saying things like "Le Salon des Tables," "Les Toilettes," "La Réception," "Le Bell Captain" and "Les Artistes Steak House." A romantic, lamp-lit bridge straddles the casino high above the room but access is available only to those with a ticket to climb the tower.

Mon Ami

You may prefer to linger and watch passing crowds from Mon Ami Gabi, a raised café just above the sidewalk and backed by a facade of the world's most famous museum, the Louvre. The Paris especially touts its classy spa: "Long ago the French recognized the healing benefits of massage, spa treatment and aroma-therapy," offering "luxurious facilities and amenities," which include many styles of massage and body treatments. The larger suites – ranging from 1,000 to 4,180 square feet (93 to 388 square meters), go under names like Napoleon, St Tropez and Charlemagne.

Aware that many visitors will be familiar with Paris itself, the architects here aimed to duplicate its landmarks "with pinpoint accuracy," studying Gustav Eiffel's original 1889 drawings and covering interior facades with murals rep-resenting Parisian districts before "aging" the buildings appropriately. Fronted at the Strip by the massive Academie National de Musique, Paris Las Vegas' other replicas include the Champs Elysées, the Louvre, the Paris Opéra, and the Palace of Versailles.

BELOW: this bread-seller/opera singer will serenade you in one of five different languages.

The *Notre Dame de Paris* show at the **Theater Paris Las Vegas** plays most days. Among the shops along a typical "Parisian" street is JJ's Boulangerie, where you might encounter "the singing breadman," a local opera singer named Lance Taubold who serenades visitors in any of five languages.

Shops offer ultra-chic Parisian fashion, and the casino has 2,200 slot machines. A knowledgeable but rather stingy local suggests that lunch patrons of the excellent Paris buffet time their visits just before it switches to dinner (at 5:30pm), when more expensive dinner items such as king crab legs are added to the menu. This is a canny strategy at other buffets around town, although some have a break before introducing the more expensive dinner menu.

Bellagio

Superstar entrepreneur Steve Wynn's **Bellagio** ⓑ (3600 Las Vegas Boulevard South, tel: 693-7111 or 888/987-6667), now owned by MGM-Mirage, was admired from the outset for raising the level of local sumptuousness. It is said to have cost $1.8 billion to build, requires $2.5 million a day to break even and has almost 9,000 employees. But by the spring of 2001, Bellagio was posting an annual profit of $323.5 million, making it the world's most profitable casino.

Approaching from Bally's on the bridge over the Strip, visitors are greeted by operatic arias soaring over the lake, where hundreds of fountains dance to music (ranging from Pavarotti to Gene Kelly), all perfectly programed to coordinate with jets as high as 240 feet (73 meters), fading to clouds of mist in quieter interludes. The water, all 1.5 million gallons (5.5 million liters) of it, emanates from a tainted aquifer via the resort's own treatment plant, which also fills the lagoons in front of the Mirage and Treasure Island.

BELOW: Via Bellagio is one of Vegas' most elegant shopping arcades.

DALE CHILULY: MAN OF GLASS

Dale Chiluly, whose spectacular, glass-flower chandelier dominates Bellagio's lobby *(see photo on page 161)*, was the first American to be accepted by Venice's Murano community and his work truly merits the often-overworked adjective "gorgeous." When the Las Vegas Art Museum exhibited hundreds of his pieces in 2001, the show was described by *Where* magazine as "a vibrantly colored veil of glass," and by the museum's director, James Mann, as "abstract expressionism in a transparent medium." The sculptor's works can be found in 190 museums around the world, as well as his native Tacoma, Washington state, where a Museum of Glass is under construction to which he is contributing a pedestrian walkway with soaring crystal towers, the Chiluly Bridge of Glass.

Chiluly himself, blinded in one eye years ago by a studio accident, says "Glass inspires me. As I work it becomes magical… the only material you can blow human breath down. Sun and light come through it. Glass can't be carbon-dated so you can't tell how old it is, how hard it is – there are so many mysterious things about it. It has its own category: it's not a solid, and it's not a liquid. They don't even know quite what it is except that it's the cheapest material in the world."

The lake's design was conceived by Los Angeles' Universal City-based company Wet Dreams. Their staff of 90 designers, engineers and support staff also created the glass caldron which cradled the Olympic flame at the 2001 Winter Olympics in Salt Lake City, as well as the sidewalk fountains in which kids douse themselves at LA's Universal City's CityWalk. "We work expressively with the water itself," notes Mark Fuller, the company's founder. "We don't do a traditional structure or something and then gush water over it."

Map on page 132

Fountains and flowers

In desert climates, fountains are highly prized, and the stunningly lovely water feature in the **Conservatory** was imported from Italy. Fountains also had a religious significance for many ancients, especially the Greeks and Romans. Brides who bathed in water from a *calirrhoe*, a fountain with nine pipes, would anticipate a long and prosperous life.

Bathing at birth, upon marriage and after death was preparation for the journey to the afterlife. In Middle Eastern lore, wells with square enclosures can represent paradise. Fountains and water are the theme of the spectacular, and spectacularly expensive, *O*, the show by **Cirque du Soleil**. It takes 74 performers to mount this unique melange of acrobatics, theatrical effects, diving and swimming which takes place on, in and under an indoor lake. Tickets for the show are scarce since it gets booked as much as three or even six months ahead. If you want to see it, think as far in advance as you can. It's worth it.

From the Bellagio bridge, entrance to the resort is along a retail arcade, the **Via Bellagio**, which includes Tiffany, Chanel, Gucci, Armani, Moschino, Prada and Hermes. By the bank of reception desks inside is a wonderfully refreshing

BELOW: Bellagio was modeled after a town on Italy's Lake Como.

Map on page 132

garden below an original, iridescent work of glass by the famed sculptor Dale Chiluly *(see page 158)*. Living plants and flowers, roses, anemones, peonies, birds of paradise and cherry blossom, to name just a few, are distributed lavishly throughout the Bellagio's Italianate decor and what seem like miles of marble floors. Nowhere is the floral display more abundant than just beyond the lobby under a 50-foot (15-meter) high glass ceiling of the attractive conservatory and botanical garden which changes with the seasons, its displays planned a full year in advance. The hotel employs 150 gardening and greenhouse staff alone.

Pathways lead to Café Bellagio, a 24-hour dining room, and to the **Aqua** restaurant, with Rauschenberg paintings. To one side of the lounge a pianist plays at the Petrossian café. This is only one of 17 different eating places, including a sister to New York's **Le Cirque**, and **Picasso** *(see page 99)* with furniture and carpet designed by Claude Picasso, son of Pablo, and papa's paintings on the walls.

Lake Como

Bellagio was inspired for Wynn by the charming village on the shores of Italy's Lake Como, and the promotional staff pulled out all the stops, lavishing the resort with phrases like "a place of special elegance, quality and distinction... (which) captures the romantic symbolism and classical imagery of Italian architecture. It represents the softer side of the human soul."

The **Gallery of Fine Art** was Wynn's inspiration, and he bought back three of the pictures for his personal collection when he sold the hotel. The gallery's multi-million dollar collection featured works by Renoir, Monet, Van Gogh, Rembrandt, Picasso, Roy Lichtenstein and David Hockney. It welcomed one million visitors from the time it opened in October 1998 to when it closed for renovations in May 2000, despite a $12 admission fee for all, which some guests of the hotel described as "rather cheesy" behavior.

The gallery reopened with a policy of exhibiting high-quality touring exhibitions from both domestic and foreign museums. Director Kathy Clewell says that they plan to bring in two exhibitions per year, "I think that art is here for the long haul."

The 2001 remake of *Ocean's 11*, based the earlier caper movie with the original Rat Pack, was filmed partly on Bellagio's casino floor. "I was able to build a quarter of a million dollar set," says designer Philip Messina. "We cleared out slot machines and gaming machines and built a casino cage set. It was built and painted in LA, trucked out to Vegas and assembled on location."

After the MGM Grand, Bellagio has the second largest casino in Vegas, but *The Wine Spectator* magazine rated it as "positively demure, the kind of place where a gent can feel comfortable in a dinner jacket." Bellagio's **Shadow Creek** golf course, lined with 21,000 pine trees from California and Arizona, is frequented by high rollers who don't mind the $1,000 greens fee (limo transportation, golf cart and caddie included). The course, known for the natural beauty of its rolling terrain, ponds and waterfalls, was designed by architect Tom Fazio. ❑

BELOW: Circo's is one of 17 eating places in Bellagio. **RIGHT:** Chiluly check-in desk.

CAESARS PALACE TO CASINO ROYALE

Map on page 132

The Garden of the Gods, Marilyn Monroe's convertible, Bugsy Siegel's hotel and live penguins in a tropical garden are just a few of the attractions here

Caesars Palace ⓰ (3570 Las Vegas Boulevard South, tel: 731-7110 or 800/634-6661) has been the setting for more than a dozen movies and 80 television shows. The fabulous and venerable facade dominates the western side of this portion of the Strip with 50-foot (15-meter) cypresses imported from Italy, and a trio of eye-catching fountains spraying columns of water 35 feet (10.5 meters) into the air. It is claimed that due to ingenious recycling, water usage is about the same as that used on an average-sized lawn. Beside the reflecting pool into which pours 10,000 gallons (38,000 liters) of water, is a copy of Giovanni's 16th-century sculpture *The Rape of the Sabine Women* while nearer to the street is another famous statue, a replica of the *Winged Victory* (300 BC) from Samothrace in the Louvre.

The approach is dominated by four gold leaf horses and a charioteer, the Quadriga statue. The casino's entrance doors are flanked by more replicas of classical statues, including a lovely Venus de Milo. Most famous of all, an 18-foot (6-meter) high David dominates the **Appian Way** inside the casino. Carved from the same Carrara marble as the Michelangelo original but at twice the height, the replica weighs 9 tons.

Caesars Palace has had several owners since Jay Sarno completed it in 1966. It cost him $24 million, and he sold it three years later for $60 million. By the time ITT purchased the casino in 1995, the price was $1.7 billion. They spent almost another billion dollars increasing its rooms to 2,471. In 1998 it was acquired by Starwood Hotels and Resorts and sold again for $3 billion to Park Place Entertainment Corporation the following year.

Garden of the Gods

The look of the casino owes much to Sarno's belief in the magically relaxing properties of the oval. Jo Harris, the designer who later worked with him on Circus Circus, attributes the casino's success to it's being laid out as a spoked wheel with the gambling area as the hub, so whichever direction you walk, it is in view.

The lush 5-acre (2-hectare) **Garden of the Gods**, named after the Baths of Caracalla frequented by ancient Rome's elite, has three swimming pools and two whirlpool spas, the whole complex landscaped with sweeping lawns, graceful fountains and classically inspired statuary. Even the lifeguard stands are designed to resemble imperial thrones. A sign at the entrance reads, "European-style topless bathing is permitted at Caesars' pools. We prefer that this is restricted to the Venus pool area." As with most of

PRECEDING PAGES:
Caesar swam here.
LEFT AND BELOW:
Caesars Palace.

the hotel casinos, the pool is for the hotel guests only, and admission is allowed only upon the production of a room key.

Caesars 4,000-seat showroom is designed to recall the ancient Coliseum, and built specifically to showcase Canadian singer Celine Dion. The singer has signed a $45 million contract to give five shows a week for three years. Dion said that what convinced her was seeing the spectacular Cirque du Soleil *O* show at Bellagio. "I knew that I wanted to have a show like this and have, like, 60 performers on stage with me, making every song a visual appearance," she says. "It's kind of impossible to travel with a show like this; the effects and the decor and the whole thing make it technically impossible without a base. We found that in Las Vegas."

Artists off the road

This may be the wave of the future for pop singers and other performers. "Artists are looking to get off the road and do something that's more interesting, both for the audience and themselves," says Tom Gallagher, CEO of Caesars' owners, Park Place Entertainment. Gary Bongiovanni, who edits a trade magazine devoted to the concert business, said, "It may be the best of all worlds for the artist. In a way Celine Dion may be pioneering that in the pop world and what better place for it than Las Vegas?"

True to her wishes, the 22,000 square-foot (2,000 square-meter) stage built for Dion's performance is designed by Franco Dragone, who is also responsible for the Cirque du Soleil productions.

The most desirable hotel rooms at Caesars are those in the towers. The 29-story **Palace Tower** has more than 1,100 deluxe guest rooms and suites, all with huge whirlpool bathtubs and great views. The 24-story **Forum Tower** is made up of two-story, four-bedroom apartments known as Fantasy Suites, themed in Roman or Egyptian style and designed for special guests who travel with families or retinues. Fantasy Suites are available only to the resort's invited guests, with one exception; honeymoon couples who marry at the hotel may rent them for around $3,000 per night.

The motto of **Caesars Magical Empire** is "what you believe is real, is real." The experience is a two- to three-hour gourmet repast in what seem to be sub-terranean catacombs. The "descent" is apparently a clever illusion since the exit is on the same floor as you arrived. Do the "walls" go up instead of the floor going down? Before, during and after the meal, diners are entertained by (good) magicians.

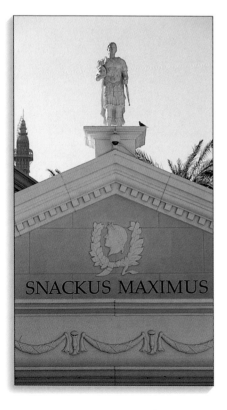

SNACKUS MAXIMUS

Caesar salads

Rumored to be on the verge of closing almost every year, the Magical Empire happily survives in this series of themed rooms, each named after a Roman god, where dinner is accompanied by mysterious and baffling surprises. Try to guess how they correctly serve your order, after apparently jumbling the cards which you have torn to indicate your preference. Speaking of food, 21 tons (19,000 kg) of smoked salmon and 2,700 ounces (76 kg) of caviar are con-sumed in the hotel's various restaurants every year, as well as 336,000 of the aptly chosen Caesar salads. The salad, incidentally, hails from the 1924 recipe of an Italian immigrant chef, Caesar Cardini. The magic-spiced meal is followed by more wizardry at the Spirit Bar, a robed sorcerer in the Secret Pagoda, and a pyrotechnic show in the huge rotunda.

Map on page 132

Sports gods

Caesars has a long association with sporting events, having been the first hotel in Las Vegas with satellite equipment to relay events. They employed former world heavyweight champion Joe Louis as their greeter up to his death in 1981. Frank Sinatra and the Reverend Jesse Jackson delivered eulogies at his memorial service, and the former champ is remembered with a 7-foot (2-meter) marble statue standing at the entrance to the Race & Sports Book, inside which are 90 video screens, hundreds of electronic panels and reader boards, and larger-than-life murals of famous performers.

More than 160 major boxing contests, starting with the bout with Larry Holmes which ended Muhammad Ali's ring career in 1980, and other championship events have been staged in the hotel's spacious grounds. Among the events which drew heavy betting were Wayne Gretzy playing for the Los Angeles Kings against the New York Rangers in a National Hockey League game on an unseasonably hot day in 1991 (300 tons of refrigeration equipment was installed to make the ice); tennis champions Jimmy Connors and Martina Navratilova battling on the Palace courts in 1992; and soccer star Pelé in a World Cup game the following year. Oscar de la Hoya, Julio Cesar Chavez, Evander Holyfield, Riddick Bowe, Marvin Hagler and Sugar Ray Leonard have all fought championship contests on the premises.

BELOW:
Caesars is known for its high-profile sports events.

Forum Shops

The classy arcade known as the **Forum Shops** features Dior, Versace, Gucci, Bulgari, Ferragamo and others, and is always crowded. Revenue per square foot is said to be the highest in North America. Stores range from a clock shop called Roman Times to "Warnerius Fraternius Studius Storius" (Warner Bros Studio Store). Customers are welcomed to Magnet Maximus by a perpetually flying pig. A domed ceiling emulates a changing sky over the arches, columns, fountains and central piazza, where Wolfgang Puck's **Spago** restaurant adjoins a replica of the Trevi Fountain. The liveliest place at night is the floating cocktail lounge known as **Cleopatra's Barge** with furled sails, ostrich-feather fans and waitresses dodging between the dancers, bringing drinks across the gangplank to spectators in the tiered seats.

At one end of the arcade, beneath a pale blue ceiling with puffy white clouds, is an enormous statue of Minerva. Bacchus presides over another piazza, on an elevated throne. Now and again the throne revolves, the god raises a beaker to his lips and speaks, as laser-driven planets, stars and constellations race through the sky above.

BELOW: this person in the Forum Shops is really a movie star; go see his Stone-sharing scene in the film *Casino*.

Plutus controls the music and dancing waters, and Apollo strums a modern fiber-optic lyre. A major attraction just off the magnificent **Great Hall** is the world's first IMAX 3D simulator adventure rider. *Race for Atlantis* is a convincingly scary ride, amazing even without the 3D glasses. Approaching the entrance from the **rotunda** with circular aquarium, the arcade is filled with Aqua Massage tanks, while Japanese slot machines allow you to box and dance with partners on screen, and a photo booth will place you in front of scenes from around the world, or show you what your future child might look like.

Exiting the Forum Shops at the Cyber Station end of Caesars, you can see the bright blue-and-violet windows of the **Casino Royale** ⑰ just across the Strip. You have to take the moving walkway all the way back through the casino to exit, though. Inside the Casino Royale, which has a 25¢ roulette table, for a fee you can don a Victorian costume and be photographed against an appropriate background at Madame Bloomer's Old Time Photo.

Map on page 132

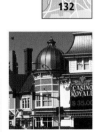

If times are tight, Casino Royale has a 25¢ roulette wheel.

Harrah's

William Harrah was building casinos in the town of Reno and at Lake Tahoe as early as the 1930s, but **Harrah's** ⑱ (3475 Las Vegas Boulevard South, tel: 369-5000 or 800/427-7247) on the Las Vegas Strip dates back only to 1992, having opened 20 years earlier as the Holiday Casino. Its famous riverboat facade was replaced – and lamented by some regulars – by a glitzy exterior with gold-trimmed harlequins, and celebrated its $200 million new look with a high-wire walk 100 feet (30 meters) above the Strip by Tino Wallenda. The company owns 18 other properties throughout the United States, including the Rio, west of the Strip; a free shuttle runs between the two.

Harrah's La Playa Lounge, with multicolored palm trees, illuminated rocks and three-dimensional mural, evokes "a day at the beach," the fantasy enhanced by tropical drinks in exotic glasses. There's an outdoor swimming pool and an entertainment plaza, **Carnaval Court**, with added blackjack tables and stage performers. There is also a bar where bartenders are selected for their skills in singing, dancing, juggling glassware and breathing fire. Other entertainment includes Budd Friedman's **Improv Comedy Club** in a 350-seat showroom. Among the shops are the Jackpot store selling magazines, newspapers and

BELOW: Harrah's famous riverboat facade has had a $200 million new look.

books as well as fresh flowers and Harrah's logo merchandise, and the Old Fashioned Chocolate Shop and Soda Fountain from San Francisco's famous Ghirardelli Chocolate Co. The casino's happily named **Fresh Market Square Buffet** offers a lavish champagne brunch from 10am to 4pm on weekends.

Harrah's is an exuberant place, where the nickel video-poker machines are just inside the door. The Bally Pro Slot machines at Harrah's are advertised as having a noisy stainless steel tray, to make the payoffs even more exciting. The trays are even designed to prevent coin cups being placed in them, in an attempt to modestly deaden the sound.

Phil Sartre, CEO of Promus, Harrah's Memphis-based holding company, says that Bill Harrah was the first casino operator to emphasize slot machines over table games. He began the chain with a bingo parlor in Reno in 1937. The popularity of slot machines has almost doubled since the 1970s, and they now typically account for 62 percent of a casino's winnings. The stakes are much higher, too. "Most casinos are getting on the slot band wagon," says Sartre. "They recognize that it's the most stable customer base. They are not trying to win real big, it's people who are there for fun. They'll be back if they have fun."

Magic sign

The charming Magic & Movie Hall of Fame in **O'Shea's Casino** run by British ventriloquist Valentine Vox until 1999 is now, sadly, permanently closed, but a neon sign still advertises it outside. The sign remains because it is itself deemed to be historic, and so has to be maintained until an appropriate new location can be found for it. Although the museum is closed, live magic continues next door at Harrah's where MacKing claims his performance to be unique. "My head dis-

BELOW: O'Shea's Magic & Movie sign cannot be taken down even though the museum has closed because it's considered to be of historic significance.

appears inside a paper bag. I put on a yellow rain poncho and become invisible. I catch live goldfish out of the air above the heads of the audience," he boasts. Now there's something you don't see every day.

Map
on page
132

Imperial Palace

Owner Ralph Engelstad of the **Imperial Palace** (3535 Las Vegas Boulevard South, tel: 731-3311 or 800/634-6441) is the only sole proprietor of a major casino in this city, and his $400-million fortune usually earns him a place in the Forbes 500 list of America's richest people. Opened in 1979 with an oriental theme, the roof was covered in blue tile from Japan. Inside are carved dragons, giant wind-chime chandeliers and bars called Geisha, Ginza and Mai-Tai. Engelstad has been acclaimed for his friendly policies towards disabled people, who form 13 percent of the 2,600 employees here.

John Stuart's *Legends in Concert* show, which has been running for 12 years, features impersonations (of varying verisimilitude) of luminaries like Liberace, Michael Jackson, Madonna and, of course, Elvis Presley. Stuart rotates a cast of about 100 celebrity lookalikes, most of whom obsessively study videos of their models. "I loved everything about the way he wore his clothes, his hair, the way he sang. I would study myself doing his smile in a mirror," said Graham Patrick who plays Elvis, his upper lip curling.

Impersonators in Vegas are almost as common as high rollers. Another "Elvis," Jim LeBoeuf at the Riviera, owns a dozen costumes, worth up to $4,000 each. He buys teddy bears which he tosses into the audience. "Everybody understands a free teddy bear. (It's) a portion of Elvis' generosity that everybody remembers him for." Doug Sparks, who portrayed Sammy Davis Jr in the

BELOW: "Tina Turner" belts it out in the Imperial's *Legends in Concert.*

Sahara's *The Rat Pack is Back*, recalls the night when Davis' widow watched the show. "It was a weird feeling (but) she said she enjoyed it, that I had the mannerisms down" but told him that Sammy wouldn't have worn "that suit." Sparks was quick to accommodate. "That suit has not been back on stage," he says. Imitating Madonna, Coty Alexander explains: "Right before I go on stage I feel like Madonna. When you're impersonating, you're acting. Sometimes you're really into it and the character overcomes you. When you impersonate somebody every night, your facial expressions actually change."

The Oriental-style, 2,700-room hotel has all the usual amenities including an Olympic-sized swimming pool, 24-hour wedding chapel for those impulsive proposals and an independent on-site medical center.

Gamblers should be on the alert for the sometimes short-lived promotions like the Imperial Palace's "New Member Mania." Under this plan, enrollees could qualify for a variety of freebies ranging from room vouchers to car rental days, concert tickets, spa passes, free meals and even airline credit vouchers. The only drawback was that there seemed to be a requirement for around six hours of straight gambling to qualify.

Imperial autos

BELOW: Marilyn Monroe's 1955 Lincoln in the Imperial Palace Auto Collection.

The Imperial's owner, Ralph Engelstad, is renowned for his antique cars, which are now on show as the **Imperial Palace Auto Collection**. An animated figure of John Wayne stands beside the Duke's silver 1931 Bentley, welcoming guests to the impressive 200-car collection. Priceless motors include a $50 million array of 1930s Duesenbergs; Liberace's 1981 Zimmer with a candelabra hood ornament; Howard Hughes' baby blue Chrysler; a 1929 Isotta Fraschini of the

type seen in *Sunset Boulevard*; and a replica of Karl Benz's 1886 three-wheeler said to have reached speeds of 8 mph (13 kph). Also on show are cars formerly owned by Hitler, Kruschev and many US presidents. The blue-and-white 1976 Cadillac for which Elvis Presley paid $14,409 – including extras like brass hubcaps – and Marilyn Monroe's 1955 Lincoln Capri convertible, in which the screen goddess clocked up only 26,000 miles (42,000 km), are cars that have motor-mad fans eating their room vouchers with envy.

The Flamingo

The **Flamingo** ⓴ (3555 Las Vegas Boulevard South, tel: 733-3111 or 800/732-2111) of today is a far cry from the "carpet joint" of Bugsy Siegel's day; the hotel is now a member of the Hilton group. Almost the last traces of the mobster disappeared in 1995 when his bullet-proof casino office with its elaborate escape routes was bulldozed. This was all part of a master plan which included razing the outmoded, motel-style buildings at the rear of the property and constructing a $104 million tower addition. The hoodlum might well have been forgotten by now but for the success of Warren Beatty's 1991 movie *Bugsy*. Though the movie was more fantasy than fact, it did kindle enough popular interest for the hotel to open the **Bugsy Celebrity Theater**.

Historians like to recount that, tough as he was, Benjamin Siegel did not faze everybody. Since paying tax was not one of his top priorities, he was once challenged by Robbins Cahill from the Nevada Tax Commission, who sent an employee to collect $5,000 owed in gaming taxes. "What'll you do if I don't pay?" the mobster asked. He was told that his license would be revoked, and replied, "You wouldn't dare." The employee reported back to Cahill who told

Map on page 132

In the 1950s, great motels on the Strip were commonplace, but now most of the originals have been pulled down.

BELOW: mobster Bugsy Siegel slept here.

Map on page 132

the hoodlum, "Maybe you'd better try us." Siegel backed down and wrote a check. Six months later, in June of 1946, Siegel was murdered by a shotgun blast at the Beverly Hills mansion of his girlfriend, Virginia "Flamingo" Hill. A plaque near the Flamingo's garden buffet wryly commemorates Bugsy's demise, announcing that his "preoccupation with safety proved to be geographically misplaced." Las Vegas historian Frank Wright mused that, "In a sense, Siegel's death was a great advertisement for the city of Las Vegas. It certainly brought attention, and created a sort of sense of illicit excitement."

The 15-acre (6-hectare) garden, with more plastic flamingos and real penguins, is quite charming at night, which, even though only steps away from the bright-heat roar of the Strip, is filled with the sound of crickets. There are pools, waterfalls, a lagoon and a turtle observation bridge, plus an entire wildlife habitat, with koi, swans, ducks and – of course – Chilean flamingos. The garden is open to the public in the daytime.

Barbary Coast

BELOW LEFT AND RIGHT: the Barbary Coast has what it claims is the largest "Tiffany-style" stained-glass mural in the world.

Down the block, the **Barbary Coast** ㉑ (3595 Las Vegas Boulevard South, tel: 737-7111 or 888/227-2279) stresses "Victorian charm and elegance," more or less sustained by chandeliers with big white globes, Art-Deco glass signs, and waitresses who wear red garters over black-net stockings. Along with its decorative windows in the Victorian Room is what it claims is the world's largest "Tiffany style" stained-glass mural. Some tables are set aside for *pai gow*, a form of poker adapted from an Asian domino game, and there is a poker machine played with gold coins which pays $250,000 for a royal flush, or a free drink for two pairs. ❑

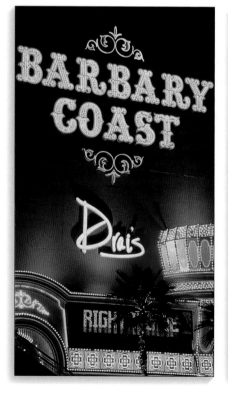

What Price Power?

In 2001, natural gas prices rose and many casinos began to impose small "per room per day" energy surcharges. Since the turn of the millennium, electricity charges to business have risen by 65 percent, more for residential customers. A hotel-casino on the Strip can use up as much energy as 10,000 private homes, and rising electricity bills have come as a shock to the neon-happy resorts.

At the MGM Grand and other hotels, the 750 watts of light in many rooms has been reduced to 500. Motion sensors turn off the lights in empty offices. The current generation of slot machines are designed to consume 25 percent less electricity than their predecessors. Intelligent thermostats are reducing the air conditioning in empty convention rooms.

Seeing power bills rise so steeply, Bally's, Paris Las Vegas and Caesars Palace adopted more energy-efficient lighting, and Fitzgerald's casino now shuts off exterior spotlights at 2am. The Las Vegas Hilton also cut back its hours of floodlighting. At Caesars Palace – whose monthly electricity bill is more than $3.7 million – "smart thermostat" systems have been installed, in order to cut the output in empty rooms.

The city's convention center was luckily between shows in July 2001, when Nevada Power asked customers to "shed load." Lights in the building are now being steadily replaced with low-wattage fluorescent bulbs. To take advantage of off-peak rates, the Cashman Center delayed the start of home baseball games, so that they now begin (more cheaply) at 7:15pm.

Nevada Power is one of the state's oldest companies, and has made itself one of the most unpopular. The state's Public Utilities Commission rejected almost half the $922 million the company sought in increased charges. Local politicians blame much of the utility's troubles on bad public relations.

As of the last decade, there were 15,000 miles (24,000 km) of neon on the Strip. The Rio's 125-foot (38-meter) high marquee, voted the city's best neon sign, uses 12,930 feet (4,000 meters) of neon tubing and over 5,000 light bulbs; the Stardust's 18-foot (6-meter) sign, with 40,000 bulbs, uses enough electricity to light a town of 30,000 people.

Nevertheless, the glare and glitter of the Strip is sacred to the casinos. John Marz of the Mandalay Group said, "Las Vegas has an image and a certain *cachet* that it has to live up to, and that includes the exterior lighting, the neon and the marquee. It's what people come here to see, and reducing those would be the last thing we do."

Some thoughts may at last be turning to "new" energy sources. Wind power, without coal's pollution or nuclear power's risks, is the fastest growing energy industry in the US. In 2001, wind farms came on line with the capacity of six coal-fired plants. The Union of Concerned Scientists estimates that around 100 square miles (25,900 hectares) of the Nevada desert could produce enough solar electricity to power the entire US. Wind and solar plants can generate and store hydrogen, which can then produce heat, electricity and automobile power. ❑

RIGHT: midnight cowboy.

MIRAGE TO THE STARDUST

*Pirate battles, erupting volcanos, white tigers,
leaping dolphins, one-armed bandits, and the hotel where
Elvis played his first Vegas gig. Need we say more?*

Map
on page
180

n 1989, when he was about to open the **Mirage ❶** (3400 Las Vegas Boulevard South, tel: 791-7111 or 800/627-6667), entrepreneur Steve Wynn said that there had been "a terrible sameness" to earlier Vegas casinos. "I wanted to take it to a new level. We presented this place as an alternative for people. I always knew others would follow, as they have, but it happened much faster than even I expected."

The Mirage certainly was different. From the erupting volcano just off the sidewalk to the tigers'glass-enclosed habitat in the arcade of smart shops underground, it drew huge crowds of curious spectators right from the beginning. Within three years, the casino was the biggest money-maker on the Strip. Even though the hotel needed to take more than a million dollars a day to break even, it never seemed to be a problem. The spectacular appeal of the Royal white tigers and their magician owners, Siegfried & Roy, was enough to fill the 1,500-seat show room 480 times a year. Despite tickets costing $100 or more, the shows were usually sold out weeks – if not months – in advance, and even now are still very popular.

Rare species

A **Secret Garden of Siegfried & Roy** (admission fee) displays even more wild animals, this time set in semi-tropical splendor. Past azure blue pools where dolphins swim are 40 rare or endangered species, including the Royal white tigers and white lions. Siegfried & Roy have an admirable commitment to conservation, and participate in schemes around the world. Recording sticks are available offering an anodyne narration.

Sharks and exotic sea life swim in a 20,000-gallon (75,700-liter) tank behind the Mirage's registration desk, inside a glass-enclosed atrium 90 feet (27 meters) high filled with lush gardens, palm trees and tropical foliage. The fine **Dolphin Habitat**, which houses 10 Atlantic bottle-nose dolphins in 2.5-million gallon (9.5-million liter) saltwater tanks, has been visited by half-a-million schoolchildren since it opened in 1990. "Everyone loves dolphins," says the resort's PR manager Tanya Flannagan, "and it's a great way to get an aquatic experience in the desert."

As for **the Volcano**, it erupts 128,000 recirculated gallons (480,000 liters) of water a minute down its sides, a phenomenon powered by a natural-gas pipeline; the sulfuric odor of the burning gas is masked by a piña colada scent released into the air.

The Mirage promoted itself aggressively across America in the Wynn era, with a traveling show which clearly helped to make it one of the state's biggest

PRECEDING PAGES:
sweet, sweet
Mystère of life.
LEFT: the Strip,
looking north.
BELOW: pirate battle
at Treasure Island.

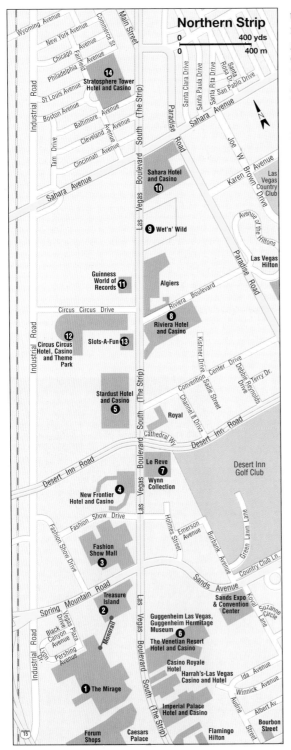

Northern Strip

tourist attractions. The hotel's elegant rooms are nearly always filled, and the guests spend more than $700,000 a day on non-gambling pursuits. Revenue from the casino is what makes the extravagances possible. Less than 5 percent of the Mirage's 4 million square feet (372,000 square meters) are devoted to gaming, but that's still where the big bucks are made.

Kenneth Feld, owner of Ringling Brothers Barnum & Bailey Circus, is a fan, "(Wynn) may call this the hotel business," Feld says, "but he's in the entertainment business, and he stands up there with Michael Eisner and Steve Spielberg for their combination of vision and their ability to make it happen." Wynn may be just "up there" on ability, but he leaves them behind them in cash flow.

Treasure Island

At least as interesting as the Mirage is its neighbor, **Treasure Island ❷** (3300 Las Vegas Boulevard South, tel: 894-7111 or 800/944-7444), which shares the 100-acre (40-hectare) site and is connected to it by a free monorail. Treasure Island's showroom hosts **Cirque du Soleil**'s *Mystère*, where over 70 singers, dancers, jugglers and acrobats deliver a metaphorical journey through life. Be sure to book ahead.

Outside a vast lagoon is the spectacular scene of the **Buccaneer Bay Sea Battle** – a stand-off between two full-sized ships – which occurs several times a day. After numerous fiery explosions, a pirate ship, the *Hispaniola*, sinks the frigate *HMS Britannia*. This spectacle predictably causes traffic jams and stops pedestrian traffic on the Strip every time it happens. The show has a cast of 30 stunt men and actors, and there is an extra 11:30pm show on Friday and Saturday nights.

Treasure Island has waitresses in tiny pirate costumes and croupiers in brocaded vests. Overhead are treasure chests overflowing with fake jewelry. Some slot machines are labeled "Swashbucklers," and the popular Treasure Island Store sells stuffed parrots as well as boxes of individually wrapped truffles.

Mutiny Bay is an amusing arcade with

mostly video games, and at the entrance are two animated skeletons in pirate costume who cackle and wave their bony arms. In the casino is a 13th-century Indian column of carved limestone bought for $2,000 in Morocco, and eight fiberglass copies of the column stand in Captain Morgan's Lounge. The aluminum chandeliers are made from bone molds taken from skeletons. A 200-foot (61-meter) long pedestrian bridge crosses the Strip to connect Treasure Island with the Venetian.

Although the overwhelming majority of the city's 36 million visitors each year do some gambling while they're here, most of them claim that it's not their main reason for visiting. More than half of them, however, do some shopping, spending an average of $183 each ($252 for foreign tourists), according to a recent survey. "Given the quality and depth of the luxury and consumer goods available," says retail analyst George Connor, "we now have one of the heaviest concentrations of retail in the world."

Shop till you drop

One of the major beneficiaries of this heavy spending is the conveniently-located **Fashion Show Mall** ❸ (tel: 369-0704), whose recent $350 million expansion, which doubled its size, has added Nordstrom's to such famous American retail giants as Neiman Marcus, Saks Fifth Avenue and Macy's – more than 120 stores altogether.

Opening sometime in 2003 is a moveable stage with retractable runways, state-of-the art video, lighting and sound equipment to enhance runway fashion shows. A covered canopy area known as The Cloud, onto which images will be projected after dark, will stretch along a major part of its Strip frontage. The

Map on page 180

For retail therapy, the Fashion Show Mall is now better than ever.

BELOW: an Atlantic dolphin, one of the stars at the Mirage.

new-look mall houses several bistros and sidewalk cafés. Open weekdays from 10am to 9pm (till 7pm Saturday, noon–6pm Sunday), the mall is easily accessed via a (free) underground garage. Try to park in the Blue Zone, near the escalator leading up to Macy's. A free shuttle bus from outside Dillard's runs across to the Hard Rock Hotel.

"Stripping" was a term used a few years ago to describe the activity of frolicking from one Strip casino to the next to check out the showbiz lounge acts.

The New Frontier

The **New Frontier** ❹ (3120 Las Vegas Boulevard South, tel: 794-8200 or 800/634-6966) attracts a younger crowd, partly perhaps because of its low prices. The atrium is an indoor garden with fountains, pools and waterfalls. It is also the longest established hotel on the Strip, and has a venerable history. Not only was it the place where Kirk Kerkorian – the city's richest man – began his Las Vegas career with junkets on his fledgling airline, but it was also the venue where Liberace and later, Elvis Presley, first played in Vegas.

Kerkorian had made a fortune selling surplus military aircraft, and began gambling in Las Vegas in the 1940s and 1950s, sometimes losing $50,00 a night. In 1962 he bought 80 acres (32 hectares) across the Strip from the Flamingo for less than $1 million, and acquired the narrow piece of land that separated it from the Strip. He then made a deal with Jay Sarno, who was building Caesars Palace, and sold him the property for $5 million. Later, the Frontier narrowly escaped closure by an employee strike that ran from September 1991 to February 1998.

BELOW:
Siegfried, Roy and young magician in the making.

Old-fashioned one-armed bandit slot machines with pistol-arms you can pull stand as a greeting in the doorway, and Micky Gilly's clone of his now-defunct Texas nightclub, scaled-down but with a bucking mechanical bull, packs in the

MAGIC AND MAGICIANS

In leaps and bounds, Las Vegas has become a world headquarters of magic, with at least a dozen lounge and stage acts running at any given time. As well as Siegfried & Roy, there's Steve Wyrick working an eight-year contract at the Sahara, and Penn and Teller, local residents, who pop up in the Rio's Samba Theater. Some feel that *numero uno* is Lance Burton at the Monte Carlo. Both Burton and Siegfried & Roy began their magical careers as featured acts in the Tropicana's *Folies Bergère* show. The Hotel San Remo's *Showgirls of Magic* are a topless trio who perform sleight-of-hand tricks in seductive, feathered costumes. The Venetian is the site of the tiny Houdini Museum exhibiting tricks, artifacts and memorabilia of the magician and escapologist who drew gasps worldwide until his death in 1926. David Copperfield, who played Caesars Palace before moving to the MGM Grand, warehouses his enormous sets in Las Vegas and most magicians aspire to play here. "These are jaw-dropping spectacles that can't go on tour," says MGM-Mirage Vice President Alan Feldman, "because they have to be presented in theaters designed for the purpose. Anyway, Las Vegas is in its own way an illusion where people come to escape, with a mindset to be wowed."

Map on page 180

punters every evening. Thursday is always Ladies' Night, offering cheap drinks and free bull rides. The huge site on which the New Frontier stands, across from Wynn's soon-to-be completed Le Reve project, is due for a major development as the site for Phil Ruffin's projected City by the Bay. A San Francisco-themed resort is planned with attractions based on Coit Tower, Lombard Street and an Alcatraz restaurant, as well as an as-yet unnamed 1,500-room hotel-casino where the former Silver Slipper once stood. Ruffin and New Yorker Donald Trump also have plans for Trump Tower, a luxurious condominium project similar to the one the developer and Atlantic City casino mogul currently owns in Manhattan. "Now that I'm in Las Vegas," said the entrepreneur modestly, "a lot of things can happen."

The Stardust

The **Stardust** ❺ (3000 Las Vegas Boulevard South, tel: 732-6111 or 800/634-6757) has 2,300 rooms, a highly rated Track and Sports Book, a much loved low-stake poker room, the Wayne Newton Theater, and a very Las Vegas history. The casino was begun in 1955 by Tony Cornero, in his time a bootlegger, hijacker, rum-runner and operator of offshore gambling boats before he started work on the 1,000-room Stardust. It was nearly three-quarters finished when he died of a heart attack after gambling at the Desert Inn.

The Stardust has an exterior bathed in lines of purple light with colored fountains beside the entrance. It was also owned for 10 years by former bootlegger and racketeer Moe Dalitz *(see pages 40–41)*, who had operated small gambling parlors in Cleveland and other parts of the eastern United States before moving out West. Dalitz met future Teamsters boss Jimmy Hoffa through his laundry business and was able to use Teamster funds to finance the purchase of the Stardust, and possibly the Desert Inn, in which he had a 13.2 percent stake when it opened in 1950.

Moe Dalitz once said "How was I to know those gambling joints were illegal? There were so many judges and politicians in them I figured they had to be all right." In his later years, through generous charitable donations and the friendship of Nevada senator Pat McCarran, Dalitz was able to achieve a measure of respectability, even popularity.

He was honored as a humanitarian by the American Cancer Research Center and given an award by B'nai B'rith. Stardust executive Herb Tobman said that Dalitz never neglected a chance to contribute to charity, both national and local, and was legendary for it around town, "There has never been a greater influence on this city," he said. Ovid Dermaris and Ed Reid, authors of *The Green Felt Jungle*, took a more crisp view: "He was a sanctimonious little mobster from Cleveland," they concluded.

Wayne Newton was once listed in a Guinness Book of Records as the world's highest-paid entertainer with earnings of around $325,000 weekly. The singer is now fulfilling a lifetime engagement at the Stardust's **Wayne Newton Theater**, where his show, with lots of hand-shaking, is perennially popular. He is also one of the growing number of celebrity residents. ❑

BELOW: Wayne Newton has played here more times than anyone can remember.

VENETIAN TO THE STRATOSPHERE TOWER

Glide in a gondola past great shops, enjoy world-class art, scare yourself silly on top of the tallest tower in the West, and see the tattooed stripper from Seattle

Map on page 180

PRECEDING PAGES: view of Vegas from the Strat Tower. **LEFT AND BELOW:** the Venetian.

The **Venetian** ❻ (3355 Las Vegas Boulevard South, tel: 414-1000 or 888/283-6423) was conceived by maverick Sheldon Adelson, founder of the massive annual computer convention Comdex. Adelson, the son of a Boston cabbie, financed the Venetian partly from the $900 million proceeds of the sale of Comdex. After their marriage in 1991, Adelson and his wife Miriam, an Israeli doctor, spent their honeymoon in Venice and subsequently set a pair of historians to work compiling a photographic catalogue of original Venetian artwork and architectural details.

Built at a cost of $1.5 billion on the site of the former 44-year-old Sands Hotel, the Venetian was designed to be the world's largest hotel and convention complex under one roof. The rooms are almost twice as large as the average, and the bathrooms have data ports. The restaurants are served by chefs on the critics' Top 10 lists, the luxurious 65,000-square-foot (6,000-square-meter) spa and fitness club is operated by the renowned **Canyon Ranch**, and the complex has enough marble-and-stone flooring to cover a dozen football fields. It adjoins a huge pool deck modeled after a Venetian garden.

"We anticipate seeing a new brand of tourist," says Robert Goldstein, the Venetian's president. He's betting a great deal on this assessment with the hotel's acquisition of a museum that easily fits into the world-class category. The Guggenheim Hermitage is a partnership with Russia's renowned Hermitage Museum in St Petersburg, and for Las Vegas property, 63,700 square feet (5,850 square meters) of exhibition space was built and fine tuned. This could be the start of something big. Jim Mann, curator of the Las Vegas Art Museum on West Sahara, predicts that other museums will follow the Guggenheim and Venetian partnership because of the huge potential audience.

Campanile Bell Tower

Viewed from the Strip, the lavish Venetian really looks like Venice, from the **Campanile Bell Tower** roaring 300 feet (98 meters) above the **Grand Canal** to the *gondolieri* in striped shirts. Like their Italian counterparts, they serenade their sometimes embarrassed passengers, but at least the gondola rides are cheaper than the originals. Adding to the realism, thousands of pigeons have been trained to fly out and swirl around at least twice a day.

Along with the **Doges Palace** and **Rialto Bridge**, the resort sports a scaled-down **Piazza San Marco** in which jugglers, singers and dancers seem to be continually performing. The square is the culmination of

the **Grand Canal Shoppes** which begins with an awe-inspiring frescoed ceiling and segues into the bluest skies ever seen. Dozens of contemporary celebrities are portrayed in wax at **Madame Tussaud's** near the hotel's entrance. The tiny but fascinating **Houdini Museum** (open 9am–11pm) exhibits memorabilia from the famous magician.

Agent Lou Alexander is showcasing at the Venetian an unauthorized musical called "The Main Event" based on the life of Frank Sinatra "with songs and anecdotes zeroing in on his tempestuous love life, his blustery career and even his alleged Mob ties," according to columnist Liz Smith. British lookalike Stephen Triffit plays Sinatra, and impersonator Bob Anderson plays other male members of the Rat Pack and narrates the show. The producer, Jeff Kutash, is from the *Splash* show at the Riviera. "This unauthorized biography has never been done before," says Alexander. "The information is all in the public domain from books, newspapers and TV. We are staying away from his immediate family, so we don't expect any problems there."

Guggenheim Hermitage

The most casual art lover will recognize the names: Camille Pisarro (1830–1903), Vincent Van Gogh (1853–90), Paul Gauguin (1848–1903), Henri Rousseau (1844–1910), Paul Cézanne (1839–1906), Pierre Auguste Renoir (1841–1919) and Pierre Bonnard (1867–1947). Works of these 19th- and 20th-century artists are exhibited in just the *first* room of the impressive and highly regarded **Guggenheim Hermitage** museum (daily 9am–11pm, tel: 414-2440). In subsequent rooms of the museum are famous works by other familiar names: *Green Violinist* by Marc Chagall (1847–1985), *Nymph and Satyr* by Henri

BELOW: guarding just one of the treasures at the Guggenheim Hermitage.

Matisse (1869–1954), *Woman in Armchair* by Pablo Picasso (1881–1973), *Woman Holding Vase* by Fernand Léger (1881–1955), as well as pieces by Robert Delauney (1885–1941), Amedeo Modigliani (1884–1920), and Vasily Kandinsky (1866–1944). It's a staggering collection which has drawn a continous crowd since opening in the fall of 2001.

The state-of-the-art gallery space was designed by architect Rem Koolhaas. Its exterior and interior walls are covered with panels of Cor-Ten steel, never used before as the structure of a museum gallery. The streamlined, textured metal is meant to evoke the velvet walls of the St Petersburg Hermitage while providing a contrast with the over-the-top architecture of the Venetian.

In an even larger gallery at the Venetian was the Guggenheim Las Vegas museum. Its premiere exhibition, "The Art of the Motorcycle," brought from the Guggenheim in New York City, captivated casual visitors and afficionados alike with its comprehensive history of the motorbike, but at the end of a long run, the Guggenheim Las Vegas closed after this first and only show.

Adios Desert Inn

On the 200-acre (80-hectare) site of the old Desert Inn, north of the Venetian, Steve Wynn's $1.6 billion **Le Reve** ❼ is rising, and due to open in 2004.

The resort, accessible via a new walkway crossing above the Strip, will have a glassed-in 48-story tower with 2,611 rooms, a 120,000-square-foot (11,000-square-meter) casino and two showrooms, a huge pool and a 3-acre (1 hectare) lake. Water has always played a key role in Wynn's creations. For a while he even contemplated flooding two Downtown streets and turning Fremont Street into a canal to create a Venice-like environment. It remains a fantasy unful-

Map on page 180

Most Las Vegans believe "if it's worth doing it's worth overdoing."

– JOHN SMITH

BELOW: glide in a gondola past glorious clothes at the Grand Canal Shoppes.

filled. Although man-made lakes are prohibited in Clark County, he alone probably had the political muscle to pull it off.

Wynn may be the best known person in Las Vegas, and there has been endless speculation about his new project, just as there was preceding his Mirage and Bellagio ventures. He is incurably drawn to the spectacular, and to showmanship. After he appeared with Frank Sinatra in jokey commercials on US TV a few years ago, his face became familiar to millions of Americans.

The impressive lobby of the old Desert Inn currently still stands, and serves as a suitable approach to the **Wynn Collection** (3145 Las Vegas Boulevard South, tel: 733-4100), an art exhibition including paintings by Picasso, Modigliani, Matisse, Cézanne, Monet and Van Gogh. It's open every day of the year from 10am to 5pm. Wynn and the Venetian's Sheldon Adelson have recently been granted licenses to open casinos in Macau, and each is expected to invest $500 million in the venture.

The Riviera

Breaking new ground in the 1980s, the **Riviera ❽** (2901 Las Vegas Boulevard South, tel: 734-5110 or 800/634-6753) shifted from headliners to more broad-based stage shows. The first one was *Splash,* which featured performers and specialty acts centered around a huge aquarium. Nine drag artistes perform, led by Frank Marino impersonating Joan Rivers. Following this was *An Evening at La Cage,* and the latest version is a rather tawdry skin show called *Crazy Girls*, which opened in 1987 and begins with the audience being mooned by eight pairs of bare buttocks. Seven bronze Crazy Girls, their rears shiny from being caressed by thousands of hands, flank the casino's sidewalk entrance.

BELOW: *rasul* is an exotic treatment available at the spa in the Venetian.

The fast-food court just off the sidewalk is a convenient and inexpensive place to eat with a choice of hot dogs, yoghurt, burgers, Chinese, sushi, pizza, espresso and pastries. There are half-a-dozen other restaurants including a hot-dog counter in **Nickel Town**. Among the stores is one selling pearls right from the oyster; a magic shop; and one representing Pahrump Valley Vineyards, the state's only commercial winery. The hotel, with its Olympic-sized swimming pool, exercise rooms, spa, tennis courts and a video arcade, was the setting for Martin Scorsese's 1995 film *Casino*. Its casino is slightly bigger than that of Circus Circus, although with fewer slot machines. When the Riviera opened in 1955, it had only 116 of them.

Vegas veterans

Liberace was a Las Vegas veteran with 10 years of performances behind him when he opened the Riviera in April 1955. He was backed by his 23-piece orchestra, and Joan Crawford acted as official hostess. Wearing a white tuxedo by *avant garde* designer Christian Dior, the camp pianist was drawing $50,000 a week, an astonishing fee at a time when a house could be bought for less than a fifth of that figure. The first high-rise hotel in Vegas had been planned to make an impact, and it quickly became entertainment central.

The Clover Room was headlined by 1950s stars Marlene Dietrich, Milton Berle, Harry Belafonte, Orson Welles, Dinah Shore, Red Skelton, Ginger Rogers, Mickey Rooney and Zsa Zsa Gabor. For the next three decades the hotel built more towers – up to the present five – and the stars kept coming. Carol Channing, Louis Armstrong, Cyd Charisse, George Burns, Eddie Fisher, Tony Bennett and Dean Martin all played in the Riviera's **Versailles Theater**.

Map on page 180

The Riviera's bronze "Crazy Girls" have rear ends shined to perfection by an eager public.

BELOW: the Riviera has a very Vegas history.

How are you going to cool off when the temperature hits 110 degrees, which it often does in this desert oasis? Well, one way is to take the 76-foot (23-meter) plunge or just catch the waves at **Wet 'n' Wild** ❾ (2601 Las Vegas Boulevard South, tel: 871-7811, daily till dark, fee) which packs rides, slides, chutes, shoots and floats into its watery 15 acres (6 hectares).

The Sahara

When the **Sahara** ❿ (2535 Las Vegas Boulevard South, tel: 737-2111) opened in 1952, it featured real camels and a North African theme. Marlene Dietrich and Tony Bennett made their Las Vegas debuts in the Congo Room, where Mae West and later George Burns appeared. Don Rickles debuted in the Casbar Lounge in 1959. In 1963, Elvis Presley and Ann-Margret filmed segments of *Viva Las Vegas* in the hotel. The hotel-casino was originally built by the Del Webb Corp. which also later owned The Mint, the Thunderbird and the Lucky Club, but when owner Milton Prell wanted to extend the Sahara, he received the first Bank of Las Vegas casino loan.

The Sahara is entered via a dramatic, neon-lit rotunda with a motif of neon camels and a NASCAR **Café** that features racing on giant projection screens with surround sound. A score of authentic stock cars are displayed, including the world's largest, Carzilla, a Pontiac Grand-Prix that weights three tons. It has an extensive NASCAR **Cyber Speedway** at the rear where visitors can choose a type of car and course to take on a virtual reality adventure, sitting in the life-size racing cars which shake and sway up and down and side to side as a fast-moving racetrack is projected on an enveloping screen. "Speed-The-Ride" lasts only 45 seconds, but riders are propelled from zero to 35 mph (56 kph) in two

BELOW: try your hand at virtual reality NASCAR racing at the Sahara's Cyber Speedway.

seconds, in what a local writer described as "an adrenaline junkie's crack pipe." A loop skywards and then back down. The Sahara was one of the first casinos to display the video poker machines on which a pair of phantom hands on screen "deal" the cards, and there are new gimmicks all the time. Recent machines have featured Elvis Presley singing when you hit the right combination, plus Sinatra and two talk-show hosts from US television, Regis Philbin and Alan Trebek. Today's state-of-the art slot machines are controlled by microchips which constantly generate a series of random numbers whether the machine is being played or not. The precise fraction of a second at which you pull the handle or press the button determines which numbers (represented on the reels by symbols) show up.

"The Rat Pack is Back," a sign proclaims, promoting a show which captured some of the ambiance of the old days when Sinatra, Dean Martin and Sammy Davis Jr hung out here. In the main showroom, magician Steve Wyrick is on an eight-year contract.

Map on page 180

World records

For unfathomable reasons, a local Las Vegas man, Brad Rodgers, has collected more than 8,400 shot glasses and a couple of hundred of them are displayed in the **Guinness World of Records** ⓫ (2780 Las Vegas Boulevard, tel: 792-3766, daily 9am–5pm). Then there's Nick Vermeulen who, even more mysteriously, has gathered more than 2,000 air-sickness bags from 470 airlines. "Somebody has to do it," he explains, though he doesn't say why.

Most of the other exhibits are equally bizarre; a stripper from Seattle, every inch of whose body is covered with tattoos, a wax figure of the late Shigechiyo Izumi who claimed to be 120 years old when he died in 1986 (he was born in 1866, the year Abraham Lincoln was assassinated). Then there's a picture of Ken Edwards, a British man who ate 36 medium-size cockroaches in one minute; videotape of other champion eaters include a guzzler downing 250 oysters in three minutes. The museum includes dozens of astounding facts and figures: did you know that the loudest measured snore clocked in at 90 decibels while a pneumatic drill tops only 70 to 80?

BELOW: see the tattooed stripper and the oldest man at the Guinness World of Records.

Circus Circus

Before he dreamed up **Circus Circus** ⓬ (2880 Las Vegas Boulevard South, tel: 734-0410 or 800/444-2472), Jay Sarno had the vision for Caesars Palace, and everything since has progressed from there. The title of "Mr Las Vegas" has been casually awarded to many people in the town's history and several seem like worthy candidates, but most would agree that the kind of spectacle that Las Vegas displays today owes more to Sarno than to any other individual. How proud he would be if he were able to see how his vision for palaces of fantasy, crafted around single themes, have grown. "Sarno was ahead of his time," said Bob Stoldal, a local TV writer. "People said, 'Circus Circus just doesn't work. It's not Las Vegas.' Clearly that wasn't true." With free circus acts and a midway lined by carnival concessions, ample opor-

Jugglers, trapeze artists and clowns perform here above the gaming hall from 11am until midnight.

BELOW:
this family-oriented resort packs in the punters.

tunities for inexpensive food, a vast family amusement park, bargain deals for hotel rooms and 5,100 parking spaces, 399 of them making up an RV park called **Circusland** with its own pool, laundromat and general store, Circus Circus always seems crowded.

"On the Strip," wrote Aaron Betsky, curator of architecture and design at San Francisco's Museum of Modern Art, "you are part of the most elaborate urban theater ever assembled. After four decades of trying, Las Vegas has finally managed to turn Hollywood into reality, and what we can learn from today's Vegas is that streets can also be theaters, buildings can become their own signs."

Preoccupied with the gaming, Circus Circus gamblers rarely look up to where another world above is populated by crowds jamming the midway attractions as acrobats, jugglers, aerialists, trapeze artists and clowns perform in the world's largest permanent circus from 11am till midnight. Miniature camels race along plastic tracks, children's faces are painted by a yellow-haired clown and an endless line of hopefuls try to win prizes by bringing a big rubber mallet down heavily enough to propel a rubber chicken into a cooking pot.

Gambling fever

Every day for over 20 years it has packed in the crowds, but sadly this kind of success eluded Sarno himself. An inveterate gambler – he once won $10,000 betting that he could sink a long shot on a basketball toss – his instincts failed with Circus Circus, which took a long time to recover from opening with no hotel rooms. It was only after William G. Bennett and his partner Bill Pennington took over and concentrated on the family market that it became a money machine. One explanation for the turnaround comes from Mel Larson, a onetime

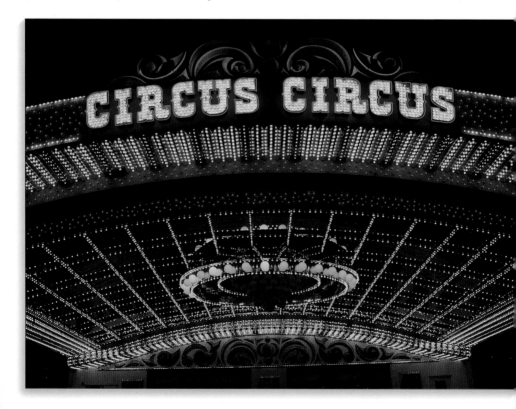

VP of the casino. "I found out that half the people coming to town did not have reservations and more than half were driving," he recalled. "So we just hammered on the radio on the stations that reached people on the freeway. We captured all this walk-in business, which was unheard of at the time. Everybody else was after the upper-income people but we just wanted a lot of folks."

Map on page 180

Now this aggressively successful downmarket, family-oriented resort is owned by the Mandalay Resorts Group which also operates the Luxor, Monte Carlo, Excalibur and the Mandalay Bay, controlling more hotels in the city than any of its competitors.

Next door, **Slots-A-Fun** ⓭ (2800 Las Vegas Boulevard South, tel: 734-0410) offers free beer to all players and has penny slot machines, but as they only take dollar bills you get to play 100 pennies at a time. There's a glass case near the door exhibiting Polaroid photos of earlier winners and usually somebody handing out free ticket booklets and offering a free pull. In some casinos high rollers can find machines that take $500 tokens, but not in Slots-A-Fun, which is distinctly downmarket.

Making money

Satellite casinos like this one are heavy on slot machines, which have become by far the biggest money-making sector in the gaming industry. The old one-armed bandits, now historical relics, have been replaced by electronic machines with TV screens instead of reels. Collectively clearing $17 million in daily profits, the casinos use any gimmick they can think of to keep the money rolling in. One of the most successful is the slot club, where members are given key cards which both operate the machines and keep a tally of their wins and losses.

BELOW: outdoors at night on the northern stretch of the Strip.

Players are also rewarded with a variety of items from key rings to free meal tickets – all part of the $2 million the casinos spend every day in comps ("complimentaries," which are freebies given to gamblers as rewards or inducements) of one kind or another, with high rollers, of course, more likely to receive free rooms, limos or seats in the showroom.

Almost all machines now operate on multiple coins, often feeding into a master jackpot which any machine in the group can win. These jackpots grow into an astronomical amount. The groupings can be a number of machines in one casino, or can be tied to all of the same machines in the entire state. Progressive machines can be identified by flashing electronic payoff signs displayed either on top of the machine or above a grouping of them.

Stratospheric

The **Stratosphere Tower** ⑭ (2000 Las Vegas Boulevard South, tel: 380-7777 or 800/998-6937) is the tallest building in the American West and the tallest freestanding observation tower in the country. It is now owned by wheeler-dealer Carl Icahn, one of the world's richest men. Speedy elevators whisk visitors to a height of 1,149 feet (345 meters) in an ear-popping 30 seconds, where on a clear day California and Arizona are visible. The deck is also a favorite nightspot for visitors, who relish the finest view of the world's best display of neon. The casino offers some of the Strip's more competitive odds.

The 1,500-room resort is topped by a revolving restaurant and offers thrilling rides hundreds of feet above ground on the **High Roller Roller Coaster**. The thrilling **Big Shot** is a kind of reversed bungee jump that shoots riders high into the air. A recent rider said, "I didn't want to do it, my kids made me. It was

Anyone who completes a ride on the Stratosphere Tower's Big Shot and manages to stay alive becomes a member of the "Scream Team," to whom discounts are offered.

BELOW:
thrill-seeking
with a view.

the most terrifying thing I ever did. I couldn't wait to do it again." (Plans for a new thrill ride aiming to shoot across the Strip have been opposed by residents.) The resort also features a showroom, a pool and spa, and a choice of restaurants including the **Around the World** buffet and a 1950s diner. Romantically inclined visitors can get married near the top of the tower.

The best-known denizens of the Stratosphere Tower are the team of Steve Lieberman and Officer Dex, who have garnered press around the country and appeared on NBC TV's *Nightly News*. Officer Dex – a two-year-old German shepherd trained to sniff out explosives – is greeted with big smiles as he cuts through the crowd. Together with his partner he underwent a three-week training course as a K9 security unit in Indiana, and they have been patroling the casino together ever since. "They have been great publicity for us," says PR manager Michael Gilmartin.

Dream weaver

Bob Stupak, who originally dreamed up the tower, was described by local newspaper columnist John L. Smith as "perhaps the greatest huckster in Las Vegas history," something of an accolade given the competition. Stupak ran illegal card games right after leaving school, almost killed himself racing motorcycles and had a brief career as a nightclub singer. In 1974 he acquired what Smith called "the worst piece of real estate on Las Vegas Boulevard," a former used-car lot, and built Bob Stupak's World Famous Historic Gambling Museum, a grandiose name that Stupak says "was about one foot longer than the casino."

After it burned down, he followed up with the 20-story Vegas World, where the cash flow helped to pay for the $550 million Stratosphere Tower. ❑

Map on page 180

The Big Shot ride on top of the Strat Tower is truly terrifying.

BELOW: the Stratosphere Tower is the tallest in the West.

BEYOND THE STRIP

Elvis and Liberace, bountiful buffets and a spa that offers "fruity body slushes" in piña colada for the skin. Who says it all happens on the Strip?

Map on page 202

L ocated about three blocks east of the Strip, the **Hard Rock Hotel ❶** (4455 Paradise Road, tel: 693-5000 or 800/693-7625) is a magnet to rock fans with its lively vibes, guitar-shaped chandeliers and glass cases filled with the ephemera of rock aristocracy, including a large Rolling Stones display with a couple of Keef's guitars and one of Mick's leopard-skin jackets. It has 657 rooms, luxury suites, a spa and a huge Beach Club. Restaurants include the Pink Taco, a version of the Japanese restaurant Nobu, and a steak house said to be reminiscent of 1950s Las Vegas style. A sad piece of rock history was made here recently. The day before a US tour was to commence, John Entwhistle, bass player of The Who, died in the hotel on June 27, 2002.

If the casino business resembles what marketeers define as the ideal television audience, then the swinging style of the Hard Rock is probably delighted with its clientele who, unsurprisingly, tend to be the right age demographic. Competition is fierce between casinos and it's probably no surprise to learn that the Hard Rock and others use the services of middlemen to entice "whales" (the Vegas term for big spenders). One of them is Steve Cyr, who applies what a recent magazine profile called "a mixture of genial charm and rocket-fueled salesmanship." Cyr says he takes care of people who don't think twice about gambling $100,000 on their visits. "My goal," he says, "is that a guy loses a hundred grand, shakes my hand and says, 'Steve, I had a great time and I'll see you again next month.'"

Topless magicians

Hotel San Remo, 115 East Tropicana Avenue (tel: 739-9000 800/522-7366) is smaller and less frenetic than some of the Strip casinos, with around 700 rooms, many overlooking a pleasant garden pool. It's showroom features a popular presentation called *Showgirls of Magic,* whose late-night show is performed topless.

The **Las Vegas Hilton ❷** (3000 Paradise Road, tel: 732-5111 800/687-6667), is a hotel familiar to high rollers who enjoy its opulent, marble-floored penthouse apartments with chandeliers, fireplaces, gold-plated bathroom fixtures, individual pools, 24-hour butler and room service, and workout facilities. Even a "media center," is turned over free to players who spend in excess of $2 million.

The 3,174-room hotel introduced a million-dollar blackjack tournament, where the $1,000 entry fee includes a three-night stay at the hotel. There are 13 restaurants, a pool, a spa, a spacious casino and *Star Trek: The Experience* in which visitors can assume the identity of a Starfleet or alien crew member and participate in virtual-reality and video adventures. The

PRECEDING PAGES: don't try to sneak past security. **LEFT:** Elvis-a-Rama. **BELOW:** a magnet to music fans.

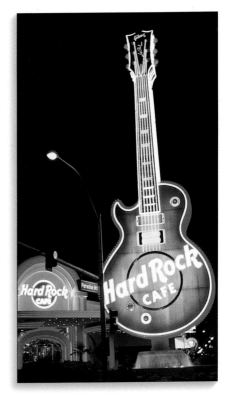

Hilton also has a huge showroom where Elvis Presley famously performed 800 times. The late singer, just about the biggest star to hit this town, was living in one of the Hilton's rooftop suites when Barbra Streisand came calling in August 1974. She had starred in the hotel's showroom when it opened as the International five years previously. She was currently hot from her famous Oscar-winning appearance in *Funny Girl* and her rapturously received concert in Manhattan's Central Park. The singer tried to interest Elvis in her remake of *A Star is Born*. Why it didn't work out is still disputed, but the role was taken by Kris Kristofferson.

Elvis really was here

Since his disastrous debut at the Frontier in 1956, Presley had spent a lot of time in Las Vegas but, until 1969, as a visitor more than a performer. Then Frank Sinatra hosted a "Welcome Home" TV special for Elvis when he left the army in 1960, and they sang each other's songs. "We're working the same way only in different areas," Sinatra told the audience.

On July 31, 1969 Presley made his comeback performance on the Hilton's stage. He had studied for the show by sneaking into the Flamingo showroom after the lights went down, to watch singer Tom Jones, described by Nick Naff as "among the horniest men I ever knew." Elvis couldn't project that sex image, says Naff, an executive at the International, "but he could suggest to females that he was the nicest guy in the world. That's the very reason they love him today. He played on his own projected qualities – the nice guy, the shy guy."

Opening night was packed with celebrities, high-rollers and the press, and any Presley fan who could spring for the price of a hotel room and a ticket for an

BELOW: Elvis and Liberace change jackets and musical instruments, 1956.

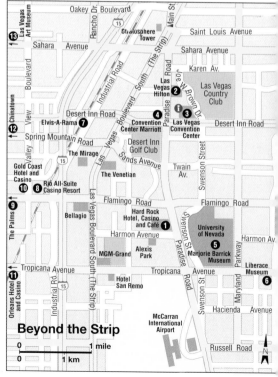

Beyond the Strip

event of this magnitude. "His audience were now ready," said Bill Willard, who was there. "The kids had grown up and had the nostalgia thing going." His gigs at the hotel were a major draw for years and very important to an off-Strip hotel whose showroom was its major draw. Hundreds were turned away for almost every show, and there were two each night, at 8pm and midnight. "The Colonel had him on a brutal schedule," recalled one observer, Lamar Fike. "If somebody did it now they'd die on-stage. I think Vegas contributed as much to his demise as anything else. He literally worked himself to death."

By the mid-1970s, interest was beginning to wane, probably exacerbated by the singer's fading appearance. Not only the grueling work schedule but his drug-enhanced lifestyle and unhealthy diet were taking a toll. "The last two years he still filled the house but it was the diehards at that point," recalls *Las Vegas Sun* columnist Stan Delaney. Elvis Presley played his final Las Vegas engagement from December 2 to 12, 1976. He died eight months later.

Convention central

Las Vegas is the convention capital of the United States, hosting at least 27 corporate jamborees each year. (Chicago is way back in second place with 11.) The **Las Vegas Convention Center** ❸ (3150 Paradise Road, tel: 892-0711) was financed in the 1950s with a hotel/motel room tax which, in 2001, provided $135 million of the $184 million budget. Four million trade-show participants generated $4.8 billion for the city in non-gaming revenue in 2001. With new expansion, the convention center now has 7.5 million square feet (660,000 square meters) of space. Once the Mandalay Bay resort convention center is finished in 2003, the city will have three of the country's seven largest

Map on page 202

Vegas works hard to claim the largest, the tallest and the best of everything.

BELOW: the World Gaming Convention at the Las Vegas Convention Center.

convention centers. Adjoining the Las Vegas center is a **tourist information office** (tel: 892-7573) which supplies free maps, brochures and leaflets. The 278-suite **Convention Center Marriott ❹** (3225 Paradise Road, tel: 796-9300) has meeting rooms of various sizes, a grand ballroom, business services, whirlpool, a health club, an outdoor pool and a restaurant. Set in attractively landscaped grounds, the 496-room **Alexis Park** (375 East Harmon Avenue, tel: 796-3300) is an all-suite hideaway with no gambling.

Mykonos, Vegas-style

If led blindfolded into the **Greek Isles Casino** (305 Convention Center Drive, tel: 952-8000 or 800/633-1777), the interior blue-and-white decor of a typical Greek village would provide instant identification, not to mention the Cyrillic-style signs for the bar and restaurant. This was formerly the financially-troubled Debbie Reynolds casino, then briefly owned by the WWF (World Wrestling Foundation). The show business display has been replaced with an empty lounge, although the showroom itself remains. Check out the electronic roulette machine and admire the long mural on the outside wall depicting a prototypical fishing village.

Located on the campus of the University of Nevada, the informative and interesting **Marjorie Barrick Museum ❺** (4505 South Maryland Parkway, tel: 895-3381, weekdays 8am–4:45pm, Sat 10am–2pm) is best approached from Paradise Road on the east side. Live lizards, gila monsters, a tortoise and a thin, red snake greet visitors from inside glass cases in the lobby, and in the museum are sandy dioramas of Mojave desert life. Stuffed birds from sandpipers to pelicans decorate a desert oasis filled with cholla cactus, desiccated

BELOW: Liberace first performed in Vegas in the 1940s.

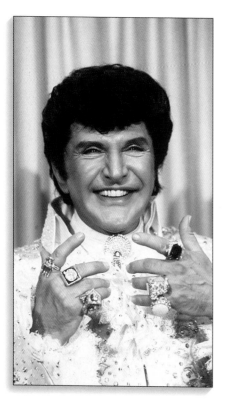

LIBERACE

In 1944, after Walter Liberace debuted at the Frontier casino, he got an offer he didn't know how to refuse. Mobster Bugsy Siegel offered to double his $2,000 weekly salary if the piano player would move to the Flamingo. In the nick of time Bugsy's death occurred to spare him the decision, so Liberace stayed at the Frontier, using in his show the signature candelabra copied from the one he'd seen on Frederic Chopin's piano in the biopic *A Song to Remember*. Liberace's flamboyant manners and costumes went on to make him a Vegas legend and a tremendous draw with the ladies, despite his obvious gay mannerisms.

When he visited England, *Daily Mirror* columnist William Connor called him a " deadly, winking, sniggling, snuggling, chromium-plated, scent-impregnated, luminous, quivering, giggling, fruit-flavored, mincing, ice-covered heap of mother love." Liberace sued, and won $22,400 in damages. Nevertheless, his penchant for young men was widely known, and in the early 1960s his young companion, Scot Thorsen, sued for palimony (but lost) after being ejected from Liberace's home. In 1972, the "ice-covered heap of mother love" opened at the Las Vegas Hilton for $300,000, playing his final show at Caesars Palace in August, 1986.

wood and a tiny kit fox. In another room are three large bears: black, polar and grizzly. There are also exhibits on the Southern Paiute Indians, including turquoise belts, rugs and baskets, Navaho pottery and an explanation of the weaving process with samples of the natural dyes brazilwood and cochineal, alongside Mexican masks, colorful Guatemalan *huipils* and Mayan ceramics whose jars resemble contemporary pottery. Pierced ears were common, one exhibit explains, because it was believed that without them passage to the "other world" would be impossible. There's an explanation of the pictures in a reproduction of the *Codex Barbonicus*, an ancient pictorial manuscript which stretches for several feet, and a display of prewar Vegas slot machines and Hoover Dam exhibits.

Behind the museum is the delightful **Xeric Garden** (from the Greek word *xeros*, meaning dry), with cacti, desert plants and a bird-watching verandah. Ask for the pretty free brochure which identifies and describes all the plants.

Map on page 202

Ostrich feathers and diamond pianos

The glossy brochure for the **Liberace Museum ❻** (1775 East Tropicana Avenue, tel: 384-3466, Mon–Sat 10am–5pm, Sun 1–5pm) says that "though the Strip may sparkle and the neon may shine, nowhere in Las Vegas can be found a more dazzling spectacle than the museum." Even today, the idea of somebody wearing a five-tiered violet cape of ostrich feathers with lavender sequins – as Liberace did for a 1985 television show – is an extravagance that's hard to beat. Here it's just one of a roomful of outrageous items on show.

A black-diamond mink is lined with 40,000 Austrian rhinestones and a separate display exhibits the world's biggest rhinestone, measuring in at 115,000

BELOW: eat, drink and be dumbfounded at the Liberace Musuem.

carats and weighing 50 lb (23 kg). The entertainer was fond of jewelry – like the piano-shaped watch and a piano-shaped 260-diamond ring – antiques, including an inlaid, ormolu desk that belonged to Czar Nicholas II of Russia, as well as cars and musical instruments. A hybrid Rolls Royce Volkswagen (license plate RRVW) is one of the 19 cars on display (he owned more than 30) including a Rolls decorated in brilliant red, white and blue.

There are dozens of pianos, pride of place given to a 1920 Chickering grand on which George Gershwyn composed, plus a hand-painted model which Chopin once played, and Schuman's Bosendorfer. Even rarer is a piano built in 1786 by John Broadwood, credited along with Bartolommeo Christofori as one of the instrument's inventors. Many of the musical artifacts on show – an old English hand-held street organ, for example – appeared in Liberace's television shows, on which there were always candelabras. He even had a candelabra-shaped ring.

Sagamore of the Wabash

Liberace had a Spanish-styled home in Palm Springs, the bedroom of which is recreated here, but during his Vegas career, he bought two adjoining homes on East Tropicana Avenue and had Michelangelo's painting from the Sistine Chapel reproduced over his bed. The houses were turned into a museum after his death on February 4, 1987, but this museum – topped with an enormous symbolic piano – in which visitors now admire his opulent collection is a recent one; it opened in 2002. On a wall near toilet doors painted violet, is a certificate from the state of Indiana granting him the title Sagamore of the Wabash, the highest honor the governor can bestow.

BELOW:
diamonds are
forever – until the
next losing streak.

West of the Strip

Even people who aren't card-carrying fans of "the King" will most likely get a kick out of **Elvis-A-Rama** ➐ (3401 South Industrial Road, tel: 309-7200, daily 10am–7pm) where an embroidered sampler offers his post-mortem message: *Life is fragile; handle it with care.* Elvis imitators pop up everywhere – in wedding chapels, accompanying showgirls, dropping in by parachute or just dispensing handbills, but in this museum is the genuine article, or at least some genuine artifacts. Some exhibits, like a 16-foot (5-meter) boat, a piano and the 1955 Cadillac bought with the $5,000 check he received on signing with RCA, are important enough to stand alone, but many of the museum's displays are categorized in glass cases.

One display devoted to the singer's army career shows his uniform and a collection of letters between him and his fiercely manipulative manager, "Colonel" Tom Parker. Others show a red-trimmed karate robe, rhinestone-speckled jumpsuits worn for performances and a pair of blue suede shoes which were insured for one million dollars. A soundtrack of the familiar, mellifluous voice accompanies the visitor's passage down halls and past walls plastered with movie posters and record album covers, while videos of Elvis performances play all day. An Elvis impersonator performs on the hour from 11am. Access to the museum from the Strip is west via Spring Mountain Road or Desert Inn Road onto Industrial Road, which bisects both of them. Alternatively, call for a ride on the free shuttle.

West of the freeway off Flamingo Avenue is the ostentatiously-lit **Rio** ➑ (3700 West Flamingo Road, tel: 253-7777), an all-suite hotel, the smallest of which are 600 square feet (56 square meters) and the largest, almost three times

Map on page 202

The Rio sign is said to use almost 13,000 feet (4,000 meters) of neon tubing.

BELOW: home of the $10 watch.

that size, featuring wrap-around windows and great views. The hotel promotes a Latin American aura with its Samba Theater, Copacobana Showroom, VooDoo Lounge and Ipanema Bar. Try to catch the panoramic view from the Rio's 52nd floor where the specialty of the VooDoo Lounge is a bubbling, smoking concoction of five rums and three liqueurs which goes by the name of Witch Doctor. The tropical lagoon, complete with waterfalls, has four pools, five whirlpool spas and a sandy beach.

Among the best eating deals in town is the **Carnival World Buffet** in the Ipanema Tower, where the 11 food counters include Chinese, Japanese, Mexican, fish & chips, salads, fruit and pastries. This is separate from the Village Seafood Buffet in the Masquerade Tower. If your stomach can cope with the indigestion potential, you can have a dozen meals for one single price.

Life is a masquerade

The spectacular 12-minute show *Masquerade in the Sky*, which takes place four times every afternoon and evening except Tuesday and Wednesday, is performed above spectators' heads as a procession of gaily decorated floats moves steadily around a 950-foot (290-meter) track. Exotically dressed performers sing and wave from a balloon, and from vehicles decked out as gondolas or riverboats. For a fee, casino guests can join the parade – especially enticing to children – and leave with a photograph. All of this takes place in the lively **Masquerade Village**, complete with eating, shopping and gaming facilities.

The Rio's **Napa** restaurant is French. The chef is Jean-Louis Palladin who came from Washington's Watergate Hotel, nominated by *Gourmet* magazine as the best in town. The grotto-like wine tasting room, which stores 700 wines

BELOW: Vegas' buffet choices are as large as they are legendary.

worth $10 million, is said to be the best collection in the country. It includes a famed Château d'Yquem collection, with bottles from every vintage produced between 1855 and 1990. The cellar is tended by Claudia Tyagi, one of the world's few female master sommeliers. Nearly 300 of the wines are available by the glass. The Rio is one of the properties owned by Harrah's, and a free shuttle runs between the two casinos every 15 minutes until midnight (until 1am on weekends). Guests can also use the **Rio Secco Golf Club**, which is located 15 miles (24 km) from the Resort.

Map on page 202

Oversized beds

Half a mile west of the Strip on Flamingo Road, the opening of **The Palms ❾** (4321 West Flamingo Road, tel: 942-7777) late in 2001 was eagerly awaited because it was the first new hotel for 15 months, a lifetime in this town of non-stop construction. From the beginning it was promoted as the hip new place to be, and fielded an unprecedented 120,000 applications for the 2,500 available jobs. Its owner, George Maloof, owner of the National Basketball Association's Sacramento Kings, planned to cross-promote the two enterprises via the hotel's huge hot-air balloon emblazoned with a 36-foot (11-meter) logo of the Palms. Two dozen of the hotel's 455 rooms are equipped with massively oversized beds. "Our players complain that they stay at hotels and the beds are too small," Maloof said. "We looked into it and there is actually such a thing as an NBA bed." It is 16 inches (40 cm) longer than usual.

Designed by the celebrated architect Jon Jerde with an understated Polynesian theme, the 42-story hotel is decorated in soft color schemes of beige and taupe and has exterior lighting that can be seen from miles away but which, accord-

Gambling is a way of buying hope on credit.

– ALAN WYKES

BELOW:
the swimming pool at the Palms is the "color of sapphires and amethysts."

TIP

Be sure to book Vegas shows months in advance. When in town, call the box-office directly, as there may be one or two seats left on the night that ticket-bookers do not know about. Many theaters are dark on Mondays.

ing to a recent guest, pours too much glare indoors at bedtime. The five bars include the stylish 55th-floor **Ghost Bar**, accessed by high-speed elevators, with extensive views of the city's skyline and an open-air deck in whose floor is inset a plexiglass window. Apparently guests find it exciting to jump up and down on this despite the fact that there is nothing below it but 54 stories of space, then the asphalt of the parking lot.

Fiber-optic lit drink rails rim the bar both here and in the steak house, **Nine**, where it encircles the champagne and caviar bar. The spacious nightclub, called **Rain in the Desert**, has a color-changing wall of water and an elaborate system that produces fog, haze, fireballs and dancing fountains. Near to the swimming pool, "the color of sapphires and amethysts," is a spa offering "fruity body slushes" in a choice of amaretto sour, margarita or piña colada.

Mardi Gras and Dixieland

One of the earliest hotels to open west of the Strip, the **Gold Coast** ➓ (4000 West Flamingo, tel: 367-7111) has recently been renovated with a fitness center overlooking the pool. Dixieland jazz has long been a mainstay in the lounge, and there's a bowling center with its own snackbar. A free shuttle runs over to the company's sister hotels, the Barbary Coast on the Strip and the **Orleans** ⓫ (4500 West Tropicana Avenue, tel: 365-7111), whose New Orleans-type attractions include the French Quarter, Garden District and Mardi Gras. Cajun and Mexican cuisines are available. The buffet is good value, especially at crowded Tuesday lunch times when surplus seafood from the previous night's buffet is carried over for a meal at half price. Regulars at the Orleans, operated by Michael Gaughan, are the Righteous Brothers,

BELOW: going out in gold lamé.

Bobbie Hatfield and Bill Medley. In the 1960s they popularized the song *You've Lost That Loving Feeling*. Bobbie said, "Our songs are the ones people remember from their high school dance. These are the songs you listened to when nobody was in the front seat."

Showroom tickets at the Orleans are inexpensive compared with Strip hotels, a bargain to see acts like Frankie Valli, Frankie Avalon, Bobby Rydell, Peter, Paul and Mary and Neil Sedaka. Other veterans who still pack out Vegas houses include Paul Anka, Chuck Berry, Chubby Checker, Little Richard and the British rock group the Moody Blues.

Chinatown and Marc Chagall

Chinatown (4235 Spring Mountain Road, tel: 221-8448) is easily spotted just west of the Strip by a long row of red pagoda-style roofs. They shelter shops and restaurants with cuisines including Filipino and Vietnamese, culminating in a plaza with a gold-colored statue and an enclosed mall in which is a central restaurant surrounded by shops bearing Chinese signs. There's a souvenir shop for gifts, and Great Wall Books stocks the Chinese edition of *Time*.

The **Las Vegas Art Museum** (9600 West Sahara Avenue, tel: 360-8000, open Tues–Sat 10am–5pm, Sun 1–5pm; fee), about 10 miles (16 km) west of the Strip in the Sahara West Library building, is an affiliate of the Smithsonian Institute. It was founded as the Las Vegas Art League in 1950 by a group of volunteers who believed in the need for a local arts venue. It has since gone on to present a series of major exhibitions, including Marc Chagall, Salvador Dali, Dale Chiluly and Auguste Rodin. With a changing series of programs, it aspires to be one of the country's leading visual arts institutions.   ❑

BELOW:
you can eat Filipino,
Vietnamese and
Chinese food in
Chinatown.

DOWNTOWN

*Downtown is where gaming began and where myths were made.
Gambling odds are good, as is the Fremont Street Experience,
but all is not well on the Street of Dreams*

Map
on page
216

PRECEDING PAGES:
neon nirvana.
LEFT: Vegas Vickie.
BELOW: heading
towards Downtown
from the Strip.

The area between the Stratosphere Tower and Downtown is often over-looked by visitors as they speed down the Strip going from one part of town to another. In fact, its very anonymity contributes to the charm, for this part of the Strip retains a pleasantly funky feel more reminiscent of 1950s Las Vegas than any *faux* re-creation. Popular wedding rooms like the well-known **Little White Chapel** and astonishingly inexpensive motels, like **Viva Las Vegas** with its themed rooms, are a pleasant respite from the crowded hurly-burly that swarms around the rest of the city.

The ultimate destination, of course, is **Downtown**, where gambling started in Las Vegas; the birthplace of the gaming paradise which has migrated to the twinkling glitz of the Strip. Downtown, the neon beats brightly in a dense con-centration of billboards and marquees with the very signs that made Las Vegas famous, like "Vegas Vickie," the high-kicking cowgirl fronting **Glitter Gulch**, and her equally photogenic sweetheart, "Vegas Vic."

But nowadays, Downtown is fighting for a slice of the action that its huge younger brother up the Strip has grabbed for itself. The massive **Neonopolis ❶** complex at the junction of Fremont Street and Las Vegas Boulevard is a recent attempt to revive Las Vegas' moribund downtown area. The three-level mall has 100 retail shops, an art gallery, a food court, a 14-screen theater and underground parking for 600 cars. A bowling alley and other attractions are planned. To ease the pain of being away from the Strip, most casi-nos have parking garages, some charging a small fee which is refunded in the casino itself.

Neon magic

The **Neon Museum** (tel: 229-5366) is not actually a building, but a collective title for the old neon signs that have been hung all around Downtown. Some of the more colorful exhibits hang on an 85-foot (26-meter) tower in Neonopolis's interior plaza *(see photo on page 226.)* These recall the 1920s era of Thomas Young's Electric Sign Company (YESCo) where clients included those of the now-defunct Thunder-bird and Hacienda hotels as well as the Tropicana, the Aladdin and the Sands. "It was a town known for its neon," reminisces Mark Laymon, foreman of what is today the country's largest sign company, still deriv-ing one-third of its income from casinos. Today, how-ever, many of the neon signs are indoors, beckoning gamblers to the banks of slot machines.

Young, who leased his neon signs to smaller busi-nesses to make them affordable, was obliged to deal with mobsters who were behind many of the original casinos. "People would say, 'You're really in a hotbed down there,' but I can honestly say that was never

apparent in our dealings. We had something they needed and we were the only ones who could produce it. And they paid their bills. They were people of honor so far as we knew."

Many of the historic neon signs here have been "curated" from other cities; Hunick's Lounge was an Orange biker bar back in the 1950s, the Hunt's Red Car motel sign came from Compton, California.

Fremont Street throws off enough neon light to read by, but it's all switched off before each performance of the **Fremont Street Experience** (after dark every hour, on the hour), an eye-popping computer-generated light spectacular that spans five city blocks in a frame nearly 100 feet (30 meters) overhead. Two million lights and 208 speakers blast a ten-minute moving picture show across the latticework ceiling, projecting streams of jet fighters, thundering herds of buffalo, a tropical jungle with exotic birds and flora, morphing into a space odyssey, a cartoon orchestra, thunder and lightning and rows of dancing girls kicking to a samba beat. If you happen to be playing a slot machine regu-

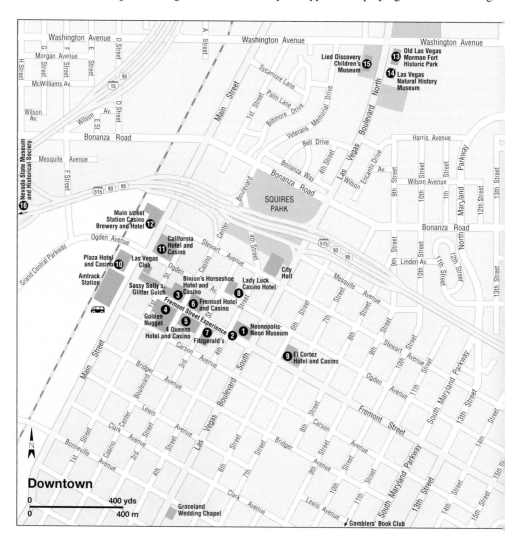

larly, working for a payoff, keep your eye on it as you walk outside to watch the show because there are those who wait for just such a chance to jump on your chair. The balcony at Fitzgerald's (10 seats) or Starbuck's sidewalk cafe (eight tables) are the only places to sit, but you have to get there early. It costs about $6 million a year to operate the show, but it has disappointed its backers. The show is costing them, and not doing enough to reverse the decline in Downtown players. What may well help is the Downtown extension of the monorail, but there is no firm completion date.

In addition to the mall and the casinos, Fremont Street has plenty of liquor stores, strip joints and junk-filled souvenir shops with every kind of useless object from chopped-up dollars-in-a-bottle to T-shirts with slogans like, "If I can't win I don't want to play." The eastern end of the street, one of the most dangerous areas of Downtown, crawls with "feral losers in a city built on the idea that anybody can be a winner," according to the *Los Angeles Times*.

Time to reinvent

Urban downtown areas are in trouble all over America, and Las Vegas is no exception. "When I came here in 1964," says Oscar Goodman, the city's effervescent mayor, "we had a place called Vegas Village, a marketplace where everyone came and did their shopping. The politicians were there, the gangsters, the actors. That's the kind of feel I want to reinvent for Downtown."

While there is consensus on the need for a revival, there is little agreement over how to bring it about. Some think that the big buildings and glitz that pull tourists to the Strip will do the trick. Others see a solution in developing Downtown on a small scale from what's already there, creating, "a neon, desert ver-

Map on page 216

Examples from the Neon Museum can be found on many Downtown streets.

BELOW: take a limo to the Fremont Street Experience.

sion of New Orleans, naughty but eminently livable," as *Las Vegas Life* puts it. The magazine suggested that the light show has maybe been more of a distraction than an attraction, and that the street that was once one of the world's most famous thanks to Hollywood now has, "the emotional drag of an e-mail greeting card. We have taken our (historic) past, wrung it out, sterilized it and put it in a mall."

Urban problems

The city has acquired the 61-acre (25-hectare) site of a former railway switching yard, sandwiched between current Downtown and the two major freeways. Mayor Goodman describes it, with typical Vegas verve, as "the greatest piece of urban real estate in the country. A blank slate on which to create a whole new environment." Proposals include a 2,200-foot (670-meter) Millennium Tower, a minor league baseball stadium, a golf resort, TV and film production studios and an "extreme" sports park with snow skiing and hot springs.

City planners pin their hopes for a Downtown revival not only on flashy buildings but adventurous urban pioneers willing to resettle in refurbished lofts in the currently near-deserted area between Charleston Boulevard and Bonneville Avenue, which a group of younger architects hope to revitalize by redeveloping existing buildings. "In many ways architecture reflects a community's cultural standards and sense of identity," says Goodman. "We deserve to be surrounded by beautiful buildings. We are not content to settle for mediocrity."

Fremont Street ❷, now 100 years old, was where Las Vegas gambling began, the site of the first city traffic signal, the city's first paved street, and the city's first telephone. The first gaming license was issued to the long-defunct

BELOW: Downtown is suffering an identity crisis, and no one can agree on how to solve it.

Northern Club at 13 East Fremont. Tony Cornero's Meadows Club was the place to be when gambling was legalized in 1931, with its 30 hotel rooms providing hot water and electricity, along with the residency requirement for divorce being reduced to six weeks, but it didn't last for long. The next year the Apache Hotel on Fremont Street was the first Las Vegas resort with an elevator, and the Horseshoe was the first to fit carpets, leading to the quaint term "carpet joint," for an up-market gambling establishment.

A local legend

Benny Binion arrived in the 1940s, a colorful Texas gambler with a trademark buffalo-hide overcoat and a big, white cowboy hat. He took over what had been the Eldorado Club, renamed it **Binion's Horseshoe ❸** (128 Fremont Street, tel: 382-1600 or 800/237-6537) and began a 40-year career which endeared him to his customers. He was almost always accessible, sitting at a corner table wearing a cowboy shirt with gold coins for buttons and no tie. His son Jack remembered, "He just liked people more than other people liked people. He worked hard to make them like him." He died in 1989 and his statue on horseback sits at Ogden Avenue and Casino Center Boulevard. "He was a guy you could shake hands with and feel you had met a real American character," says Howard Schwartz, of the Gamblers Book Club.

From the very beginning, Binion welcomed big bets. He established a craps limit of $500, 10 times what other casinos were allowing, and barely blinked on the day in 1980 when a gambler named William Lee Bergstrom asked if he could bet a million. Given the okay, Bergstrom arrived later with a suitcase filled with $770,000, placed his bet on the "Don't Pass" line, won, and was

Map on page 216

BELOW: girls, girls, girls.

Pawn Shops

More than one Las Vegas taxi driver has talked of driving some unfortunate gambler to McCarran airport only to be told that his fare has no money – and been obliged to accept a watch or wedding ring as payment. But for some big losers there is one stop before that taxi ride: the pawn shop. There are seven pages of them listed in the Las Vegas Yellow Pages, some with half a dozen branches or more, and many emphasizing that they are open 24 hours a day. Just what a down-on-his-luck gambler might most want to hear.

Pawnbroker ads invariably include a long list of what they'll loan money on, ranging from rifles and shotguns to tools, camcorders and paintings. A few specialize in automobiles, with one firm promising that you can drive your car away – just so long as you leave them the title.

But jewelry tops the charts at most shops. "Watches, rings, necklaces, you name it,"

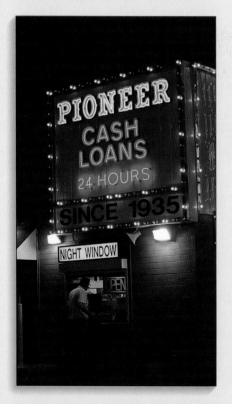

said one dealer. "We had one gent in here along with his girl friend. Made her take off her earrings and then even an ankle bracelet. It was gold. Truth is, I wasn't feeling happy about serving him, but well, you know, that's business."

Surprisingly, between 80 and 90 percent of pawnshop customers subsequently return to redeem their items. By law, shops must keep items for 120 days before disposing of them, allowing redemption by the customer within that grace period. The standard *vigorish*, or interest, is 10 percent, although some places charge more, as much as they can in a few establishments.

As a general rule, pawn shops worldwide have a negative reputation but one local dealer said that he was merely performing a service for his needy clients, making money on somebody else's money "the same way a bank makes interest on a loan."

In most places the shops are to be found in poor neighborhoods because that's where the customers are, but in Las Vegas not only is there at least one pawn shop a mere stone's throw from the Strip, but customers cut across all income levels and social classes. Habitual gamblers are more likely to face ups and downs than ordinary people.

Pawnbroking is a profession so old that it is mentioned in the Bible, which warns Christians against usury, and forbids the taking of the necessities of life as security or any pledge whose loss would severely injure the borrower. "If you take a neighbor's cloak in pawn, you shall return it to him by sunset," admonishes *Exodus* (xxii,25–26), "because... it is the cloak in which he wraps his body; in what else can he sleep?"

No local pawnbroker admits to taking his neighbor's cloak, but fur coats have occasionally turned up (in the desert) as well as hand-tooled leather boots, ivory-topped walking sticks and bicycles.

The world's oldest pawnbroker is undoubtedly Vienna's Dorotheum, founded by Emperor Joseph I in 1707 to provide the poor with easy credit. This venerable institution is still in operation, which only goes to show that where there's a need, someone will always be around to fill it. ❑

LEFT: open 24 hours a day, seven days a week.

escorted out to his car with two filled suitcases by Ted Binion. He subsequently bet other large sums, always winning, and four years later finally brought in one million dollars. Which he bet and lost on one toss of the dice.

Benny once said that the toughest decision to make in a casino was when to extend credit, but he wasn't quite so attentive filing tax returns. He eventually served more than three years of a five-year stretch at Leavenworth prison for evasion. He lost his license as a casino operator but the family took over, and he continued to be paid as a consultant. The year before he died he told an interviewer, "I suppose if I had to do it over again I would almost certainly be a gambler because there's nothing else an ignorant man can do."

From 1964, and for more than 20 years, the casino kept a glass-fronted display of a million dollars in 100 sequentially numbered $10,000 bills, which were eventually sold to an anonymous collector. Five million visitors came to have their pictures taken in front of the display, spending time, and money in the casino while the pictures were developed, which was, of course, the whole point. The Horseshoe, which made $28 million in one year, had originally cost the Binions $3 million, and even 30 years ago was worth almost three times that.

Binion's World Series of Poker

Benny had lost hundreds of thousands of dollars at the poker table in his early Las Vegas days, but nevertheless in 1970 he took over the running of the popular **World Series of Poker**. The game began in Reno, and now fills the 80-room Horseshoe every April through May with 4,000 stony-faced players. For a $10,000 stake anybody can join in, and the match has so far spawned around 25 millionaires. The World Series of Poker soon outgrew the casino (although

Map on page 216

And if you discover that you're not, get outta town reel fast.

BELOW: Binion's Horseshoe is still run by the Binion family.

BELOW:
the Mint was once
the site of the World
Series of Poker.

it later moved back to the Horseshoe), so the Binions bought another corner of the famous Downtown intersection, the 296-room **The Mint**, with a small rooftop swimming pool and a huge illuminated clock face, still the only clock that can be seen Downtown. Gradually the tournament has broadened so that now some competitions cost less than a dime to enter. Would-be world champions beware, though, the value of money is always minimized by gamblers: a "dime" means a thousand dollars, a "nickel" refers to a $5 chip and a "quarter" equals $25. "A dollar straight" is a hundred-dollar bill.

Game of many skills

A frequent tournament player, British writer Al Alvarez says, "Poker is a game of many skills. You need card sense, psychological insight, a good memory, controlled aggression, enough mathematical know-how to work out the odds as each hand develops, and what poker players call a leather ass – patience! Above all, you need the arcane skill called money management, the ability to control your bankroll and understand the long-term implications of each bet so that you don't go broke during a session." Sounds simple enough, doesn't it?

The Horseshoe, whose carpets are patterned with the crossed-T brand used on the Binion family's cattle ranch in Montana, offers late-night gamblers a full New York Steak Dinner for around $3 (10pm–5:45am), which the *Las Vegas Advisor* called "the greatest Las Vegas meal deal of all time." Downtown's older casinos have always had a battle to woo the punters from the glamorous Strip, so they give free food to almost three quarters of them. In contrast, the Strip casinos give nearly half their customers free drinks, which is a slightly better ratio than Downtown.

"Everybody comped big players, but Benny Binion was the first I ever knew who comped little ones," said Leo Lewis, a former Horseshoe executive. Referring to Binion's policy of offering free drinks to slot players, he quoted Binion's dictum that "If you wanna get rich, make little people feel like big people."

The Wine Spectator included Binion's in its top ten list of casinos, right between Bellagio, number one, and Caesars Palace, in third place. "No celebrity chef. No gold leaf. No marble. The denizens of this Downtown institution are resolutely unconcerned with Renaissance art, crystal chandeliers and soothing pastel color schemes," the magazine said. "Binion's Horseshoe is famous for one thing: gambling." Almost everywhere on the planet, casinos charge a 5 percent commission on winning baccarat bank bets, but the Horseshoe charges 4 percent. Also, while the norm is eight-deck blackjack games dealt from a plastic shoe, at the Horseshoe it's mostly a hand-held single deck which gives much better odds to the players.

Generating heat

There are four glittering, pulsating casinos at the main intersection of Fremont Street and Casino Center Boulevard, but the **Golden Nugget** ❹ (129 Fremont Street, tel: 385-7111 800/634-3454) stands out against the neon crassness of its neighbors, with its classy white exterior trimmed with soft gold lights. The Golden Nugget has retained the Victorian style that it displayed when it first opened as a saloon 50 years ago, an era when horses could still be seen on the streets. Crystal chandeliers reflect off polished brass and marble in the lobby.

Brass and granite squares shine from the surrounding sidewalk. Its buffet always has long lines, especially for champagne brunch on Sundays. An outdoor

Map on page 216

BELOW: the 4 Queens is a good place to play the slot machines.

See the world's biggest gold nugget, the Hand of Faith, at the Golden Nugget.

BELOW:
the Boneyard,
where old signs
fade away.

pool sits in landscaped gardens with tall palm trees, the terrace is lined with white alabaster swans and bronze sculptures of fish. In the Spa Suite Tower, the Grand Court is modeled on a room in the Frick Museum of New York. On display in the casino is the **world's biggest gold nugget**, weighing a staggering 59.84 lb (27.2 kg), and called the Hand of Faith. It was discovered in Australia. One of the casino shows features country and western lookalikes.

In 1972, Steve Wynn more or less began his career at the Golden Nugget, becoming the youngest corporate chairman in Las Vegas history at the age of 31. He added hotel rooms and suites of which there are now almost 2,000. *Time* magazine once said that Wynn was on a mission to gentrify gambling in America, cleaning it of its associations with high life and low life while delivering it to a suburb near yours as the innocuous extension of the middle-class weekend. "I am in the recreation business," Wynn claims. "What I do for a living and what keeps me young and happy is creating places where people go 'Wow!' and have fun. It's not that I'm insatiable, it's just that I love the exercise."

Lessons fit for a queen

Three times a day at the **4 Queens ❺** (202 Fremont Street, tel: 385-4011) Jimmy "The Scot" Jordan gives free one-hour lessons on how to win at various games, and the casino claims that some of its slots have a 97.4 percent payback, which is better than the Downtown average of 95.6 percent. Downtown slots, according to *Casino Player*'s Jim Hildebrand, pay back almost 2 percent more than the 25¢ machines on the Strip. Those differences don't look huge from the 95–97 percent end of the telescope, but the 1.8 percent shift (from 95.6 to 97.4) means that the house "take" is reduced by 23 percent.

Map on page 216

The biggest gambling bargain in the downtown casinos like Binion's, El Cortez or the Golden Gate are the 25¢ craps tables, and often the drinks are free. Don't forget to tip the waitress. Whether or not it's justified, the 4 Queens describes itself as "the jackpot capital of the world." The Queens promotes both, "the world's largest blackjack table" and the world's largest slot machine, which can be played by six people at a time. Magnolia's Veranda offers views of the casino as you eat, and Hugo's Cellar has had good reviews from food critics. The Queens is one of the few casinos that invites visitors to take photographs, but not of people, and no video is allowed.

Completing the quadrant of hotels is the **Fremont Hotel & Casino ❻** (200 East Fremont Street, tel: 385-3237 or 800/634-6460) which claims that with 450 seats in its garden buffet, would-be diners don't get stuck in the usual long line-ups. The hotel has three other restaurants, including a Tony Roma's and the 24-hour Lanai Café. If you hit $100 on the slots, there's a free T-shirt.

Next door to the Four Queens is **Fitzgerald's ❼** (301 Fremont Street, tel: 388-2400 or 800/274-5825), which has 200 slot machines in its Nickel Zone. It claims that it has paid out over a billion nickels. Fitzgerald's will give you a free O'Lucky Bucks card to improve your gambling chances and offers trinkets like key chains, beanie animals, autographed sports memorabilia and free meals. Displaying green shamrocks everywhere, Fitzgerald's is so Irish in theme that it has instituted a "Halfway to St Patrick's Day" celebration in mid-September with green beer and Irish stew.

Two blocks away is **Lady Luck ❽** (206 North 3rd Street, tel: 477-3000 or 800/523-9582), which began as a small newsstand with 20 slot machines, but has grown to become a casino hotel with 792 rooms, an outdoor pool and three restaurants. (It was recently bought for $14.5 million by Isle of Capri Casinos, which may change its name to Isle of Capri after spending $35 million.) The casino's Mad Money Slot Players can get complimentary rooms, limo transfers and arena seats in the casino's private box for rodeos, concerts and sports events. The casino's free "funbook" includes a one-night stay and a free long-distance phone call.

Free membership

One of the ways that casinos increase loyalty is to offer free club membership. Members get a card to use in a slot machine which allows them to play for credit. It also tracks how much and how often members gamble. Even small-time players can earn rewards like $10-a-night motel rooms or 1–2 percent of their gambling money returned in gifts. Near the buffet is a red English telephone booth, equipped with a modern phone. A free limousine service runs hourly from McCarran airport.

Beyond Neonopolis is Jackie Gaughan's 308-room **El Cortez Hotel & Casino ❾** (600 East Fremont Street tel: 385-5200 or 800/634-6703), one of the last places with penny slots. A man once won $76,000 playing them. They are undoubtedly a reflection of Gaughan's attention to the less affluent corner of the market. He is an expert on slot machines, especially where to place them to maximize yield. About his

BELOW: sassy salsa chicks.

This Neon Museum exhibit positively glows with health.

BELOW LEFT: Xmas in an X-rated town.
BELOW RIGHT: Neonopolis, with examples from the Neon Museum.

penny slots he says, "You use them to make a place look alive because people stay there longer playing them. They collect the pennies people have in their pockets and want to get rid of, and they make a little money."

Old-time gambler

Bill Boyd calls Jackie Gaughan "one of the few old-time gamblers left in Las Vegas. He grew up in the business and his word is his bond." Gaughan was running a book and illegal games while he was in the Army Air Corps at Tonopah north of Vegas, after getting his start as a bookie in the Midwest. In 1946, he arrived in Vegas and bought 3 percent of the downtown Boulder Club then, a few years later, 3 percent of the Flamingo.

Jackie's son Michael trained at El Cortez, ran a school for dealers, and then opened the Gold Coast Casino on West Flamingo, popular with Las Vegas locals, where he has space for a bowling alley, a dance hall and a movie theater. Beginning with El Cortez in 1963, which he lives above in a five-room penthouse, Gaughan has acquired the Union Plaza, the Gold Spike, the Las Vegas Club, Nevada Club and the Western Hotel & Bingo Parlor. He says, "I don't want to get involved in something that I can't get to every day." He begins his routine at 5am in the El Cortez and ends there 12 or 14 hours later.

Back up towards the glittering intersection of Fremont and Casino Center Boulevard are more old-style casinos. Next to Binion's Horsehoe and pitching itself as the city's only sports-themed casino is the **Las Vegas Club** (18 East Fremont Street, tel: 385-1664 or 800/634-6532), decorated with framed pictures of sports heroes, medals and trophies. Old posters abound near the Sports Book, and even the gift shop is called the Short Stop.

Towering at the top end of Fremont Street, the 1,000-room **Plaza** ⓾ (1 Main Street, tel: 386-2110 or 634-6575) has become the first downtown casino to install cashless slot machines. There are eight daily sessions of bingo upstairs, and free music in the Omaha Lounge. Behind the Plaza are the railroad tracks, currently used only by freight trains, although it is constantly rumored that passenger service to Los Angeles will eventually resume.

One block from the Las Vegas Club is Sam Boyd's **California** ⓫ (Ogden and 1st Street, tel: 385-1222 or 800/634-3484) promoting what it calls, "an aloha spirit," derived from Boyd's five years working in Hawaiian bingo parlors making contacts with travel agents who helped fill the place with visitors from across the Pacific. "Dad worked the Hawaiian market like you couldn't believe," Bill said. "He became something of a god to the people in Hawaii."

Map on page 216

Urban cowboy

The hotel's arcade shops sell foods, souvenirs, clothes and other items from the 49th state. Boyd, described by author and screenwriter Jack Sheehan as "an urban cowboy with the ever-present Stetson hat and string tie," was a nonstop worker who, even as a multimillionaire, would still clear tables, deal craps or work in the casino cage. He had begun working in an amusement park as a carny and pitchman for games of chance.

"Sam never got over being carny," said Perry Whitt, who first worked for him at the Flamingo and later became director of the Boyd Gaming Corporation. "(His tactics) always drew a lot of people in. He'd have flags and balloons and coupon books and huge birthday cakes and Sam didn't care if you had twenty dollars in your pocket or twenty thousand. He just wanted masses of people and he got them."

Sam Boyd emigrated from Oklahoma in the Depression years and learned his trade while working on gambling boats off the California coast. He got his start in Las Vegas in 1941, working at the Jackpot Club where Binion's Horseshoe now sits. He also worked at El Cortez, at El Rancho Vegas and at the Flamingo as shift boss after Bugsy Siegel was killed. For a time he was pit boss at the mob-infiltrated Thunderbird, which was topped by a neon sign in the shape of the mythical Navaho Indian bird.

"He was the best promoter you ever saw," says Rita Taylor, a chorus girl at the Mint in 1959 and now a Boyd Gaming executive. "It was always like a carnival or a party with people in hats and balloons everywhere." Sam Boyd died in 1995, and many of the multi-million dollar Boyd Gaming Corporation's employees are stockholders.

Diamond Jim Brady

An overhead bridge crosses the street beside the Aloha Cafe to the **Main Street Station** ⓬ (200 North Main Street, tel: 387-1896 or 800/713-8923), which boasts of its "turn-of-the-century opulence." Some of the stained-glass windows (surprisingly underlit) were originally given to Lillian Russell by Diamond Jim Brady and, along with beveled glass panels, came from the actress' Pittsburgh mansion. There are Bel-

BELOW: cool dude in a hot town.

gian street lamps from 1870, century-old chandeliers from the opera houses of Paris and San Francisco, and bronze doors from a Kuwaiti bank. Along the sidewalk, passers-by can peer into a beautifully preserved and antique-filled Pullman railroad car in which Buffalo Bill Cody lived as he toured the country a century ago with its guest quarters occupied, separately, by Teddy Roosevelt and Annie Oakley.

Here also is Downtown's only micro brewery, which produces a range of beers from light German ale to dark malty Porter. In the bar, TV screens show sports and music videos, and the pub serves food from lunch through to late-night suppers. Two other well-known Downtown landmarks are George L. Sturman's **Fine Arts Gallery** (Main Street and East Charleston, tel 384-2615) where the main collection focuses on the 1930s to 1980s and includes Dali, Warhol and Calder. Also on view are glass sculptor Dale Chiluly's paint-spattered sneakers, and a watercolor by Robert DeNiro Sr. **Luv-it Frozen Custard**, at the corner of Las Vegas Boulevard and Oakey since 1974, is a local favorite.

Beyond Downtown

At the corner of Las Vegas Boulevard and Washington Avenue is one of the state of Nevada's most venerable buildings, the **Old Mormon Fort**, in what is technically the **Old Las Vegas Mormon Fort State Historic Park** ⓭ (500 East Washington Avenue, tel: 486-3511, daily 8:30am–4:30pm). The fort was built by Brigham Young's pioneers in 1855 to protect missionaries and settlers en route to California. Inside the high adobe walls, a reconstructed tower looks over a plaza deserted except for a broken-down wagon and the iron pegs for throwing horseshoes.

BELOW: this purple coffee shop is one of the attempts to prettify Downtown.

The only surviving part of the original structure is the building nearest to the little creek which, rising from underground aquifers a few miles west, supplied a creek running through the fort, nourishing the poor soil in which the missionaries planted potatoes, tomatoes, melons, squash, grapes, peaches, barley and wheat. Some of these are grown today in a demonstration garden. After the Mormons left, a miner named Octavius D. Gass acquired the site along with other land to assemble a sizable ranch, subsequently bought by Archibald Stewart whose widow Helen ran the ranch after her husband was killed in 1884 and later sold the property to the railroad. The site on which the Stewart home stood is scheduled for excavation to unearth what may be underneath.

Map on page 216

A walk through time

The fort shares a wall with the **Las Vegas Natural History Museum** ⓮ (900 Las Vegas Boulevard North, tel: 384-3466, daily 9am–4pm, fee) whose hallway proclaims it to be "a walk through time in which each foot represents a million years." The animated dinosaur reproductions move convincingly and a 32-foot (10-meter) Tyrannosaurus Rex growls impressively when a button is pressed. Interactive exhibits include an African Rain forest feature ("To Africa" says the sign on the elevator) where spectators can create a thunderstorm against a backdrop of Mount Kilimanjaro and bring to life a savanna packed with zebra, gazelle, rhino, hippo, baboon and cheetah, all cohabiting peacefully at the neutral zone of the waterhole.

A large room is filled with animals and birds, lions, bison, leopard, antelope, musk ox, ibex, peacock, ostrich, geese, vultures and flamingo. The shimmering blue walls of the next is like a rippling ocean in which striped baby sharks

BELOW: a recreated living room in the Old Mormon Fort, Nevada's most ancient building.

GAMBLERS' BOOK SHOP

There's hardly any aspect of gambling or its history that the Gamblers' Book Shop (630 South 11th Street, tel: 382-7555) doesn't have something about on its shelves, and when Brooklyn-born manager Howard Schwartz can't find anything on a subject he usually commissions somebody to write it. "I have a lot of respect for people who buy books so they can understand the games," he says, admitting that he spends about 30 hours a week reading about different aspects of his chosen subject.

Many of the titles were written by John Luckman, who in 1964 with his wife Edna founded the store. It now stocks more than a thousand titles, plus all the manila folders on everything from card tricks to slot-machine crooks that have been amassed over the years.

About half of the store's sales derive from its extensive mailing list of 25,000 customers, whose demands are increasingly for computer games and videotapes. But whatever the subject, Schwartz can't emphasize enough the advantage of doing necessary homework. "This generation has a short attention span," he muses, "but knowing what you're doing allows you to slow down your losses." Fledgling gamblers who don't bother to educate themselves, he jokes, "might as well mail in their wallets."

swim in an open tank. Other fish swim in a separate aquarium, all compatible and "of the same size so no fish considers another a possible dinner." The sharks are fed at 2pm on Monday, Wednesday and Saturday.

Two huge sleepy pythons named Bonnie and Clyde sprawl behind glass. They are from Burma and said to have "highly developed heat sensors for detecting warm-blooded animals." Pythons naturally grow to a length of 24 feet (7 meters) and can devour animals as big as leopards. With a digestion like that, it's not surprising that one good meal might last them several months.

Leaflets are offered to parents with questions and suggestions to stimulate interest among younger visitors. In the **Young Scientists Center** there are exhibits challenging children to identify familiar aromas and teaching them about different tastes.

Something for the kids

There's plenty to engage the attention of adults in the nearby **Lied Discovery Children's Museum** ⑮ (833 Las Vegas Boulevard North, tel: 382-3445, Mon–Sat 10am–5pm, Sun 1–5pm), which shares the ground floor of the city's library. (Note the museum is pronounced "leed," not "lied.") If you ever wondered what a million pennies ($10,000) looks like, here's an exhibit. Also in the make-believe post office, customers can sort, weigh and mail packages.

Irresistible to all ages is the Discovery Grocery Store, which makes shopping a game and a musical pathway with which you can play a tune by jumping on different panels. There's a tube stretching up several floors, which you can put your head in and talk to hear the echo; an overhead ropeway with moving buckets that can be filled and emptied; sand in which to move rubber cacti

BELOW: kids check out the groceries at the Lied Discovery Children's Museum.

around; a place to pump bubbles up viscosity tubes or to draw yourself on grid sheets while looking in a mirror. Heavy boots can be donned for Planet Walking, which demonstrate the difference in gravity. What weighs 80 lb (36 kg) on earth would weigh 95 lb (43 kg) on Saturn, Uranus and Neptune, 188 lb (85 kg) on Jupiter, and 2,232 lb (1,012 kg) on the Sun. And maybe now they've got that Language Map in operation. It lights up, speaks, and shows the location where a particular language is spoken.

Map on page 216

Frontier town

"Work your claim until you have all the gold from it and do not gamble away the money," and "Do not make gold the most important thing in life," were among the nuggets of advice offered to miners in an 1853 letter exhibited in the **Nevada State Museum and Historical Society** ⓰ (Lorenzi Park, Valley View and Bonanza, tel: 486-5205, daily 9am–4:30pm, library weekdays only) which explores the history of Southern Nevada. Even though it's off the beaten track the museum is well worth a visit, if only for its mining exhibit and the relics from the days when this was still a frontier town. The boots of Rex Bell, the local rancher turned movie star who became governor and married silent screen star Clara Bow, accompany his picture on horseback.

A huge photo of Tonopah and a sheet of flame shooting skywards from a nuclear test are more dramatic, the latter beside an actual geiger counter which everybody has heard of but few have seen. Other exhibits are of long-gone casinos, the old Mormon settlement, wildlife varying from butterflies to Big Horn sheep, and an Anasazi community. Running nonstop is a video of training at the Army Gunnery School, the forerunner of Nellis Air Force Base. ❑

In the 1990s, Vegas attempted to lure families to Sin City by building "kid-friendly" resorts. Although these are successful, the trend since the millennium has been back to the adult market.

BELOW:
kidding around in the Nevada State Museum.

LEAVING LAS VEGAS

The Grand Canyon, Death Valley, Hoover Dam – the desert around Vegas is patterned with wonders

The arid expanses surrounding Las Vegas are patterned with wonders of the natural world, wonders that dwarf the man-made spectacle of Sin City. Perhaps the best known is the great Grand Canyon. A fissure 10 miles (16 km) wide and up to a mile deep, this work of sculpture by the Colorado River reveals aeons of the earth's evolution in layers of color.

The monumental Hoover Dam (still called the Boulder Dam by some, because of enduring antipathy to President Hoover), is definitely worth visiting. The dam's interruption of the Colorado River's flow results in the huge artificial Lake Mead, which offers cruises, nature walks and exceptional sunsets. In all the expanses of the desert, perhaps the strangest feature is State Route 375, which was dedicated in 1996 by Governor Bob Miller as the "Extraterrestrial Highway." It has earned this name by the frequency of UFO sightings in the vicinity.

The other-worldly life and landscapes of Death Valley and the Mojave Desert offer sights and experiences that are practically unrepeatable anywhere else in the world. Here is a landscape formed among some of the Earth's most extreme conditions, and extreme caution is advised when traveling *(see "Travel in the Desert," page 289).*

Hikes and trails lead to magnificent views of unique flora and fauna. The development of human habitation in these hostile environs is a testament to enterprise and determination. Throughout are small ghost towns, some preserved and some remodeled as theme-park style attractions. Thriving in the desert along with Vegas are more gambling resorts. Rounding off the attractions is Route 66, the legendary "Mother Road," built at a time when highway travel was glamorous and exciting.

Leaving Las Vegas? Welcome to a bold, brave and completely different world. ❑

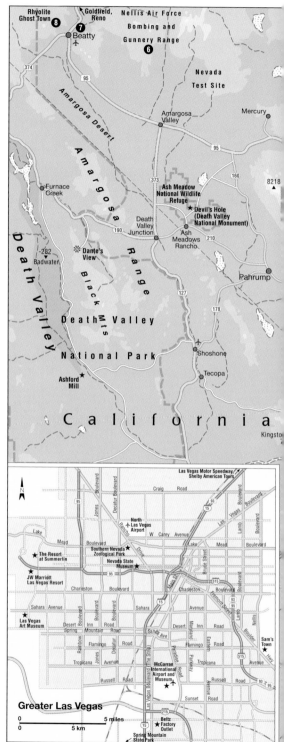

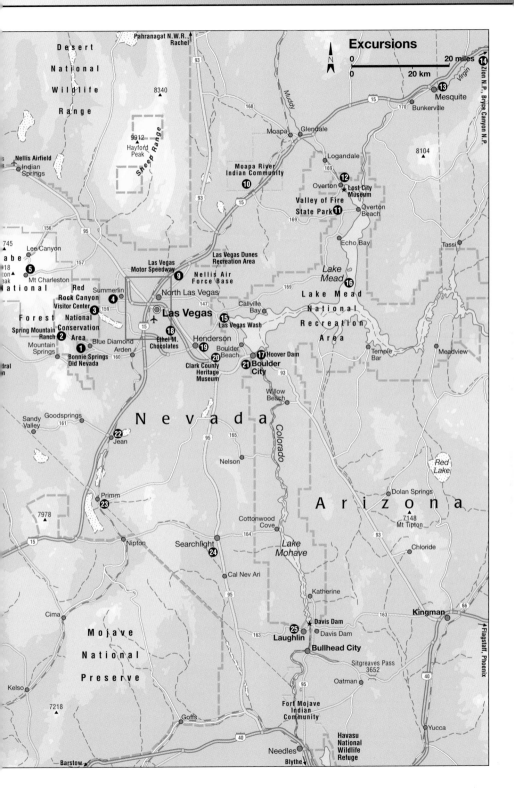

Excursions

N

0   20 miles
0   20 km

Desert National Wildlife Range

Pahranagat N.W.R.
Rachel
93
8340
168
Muddy
Moapa
Glendale
9912
Hayford Peak
Sheep Range
Moapa River Indian Community
⑩
93
15
Logandale
169
⑫
Overton
Lost City Museum
Valley of Fire State Park ⑪
Overton Beach
169

Nellis Airfield
Indian Springs
745
Lee Canyon
abe
918
ton
eak
⑤
Mt Charleston
156
95
157
Summerlin
Red Rock Canyon Visitor Center
④
159
Spring Mountain Ranch ②
Mountain Springs
Blue Diamond
Arden
Bonnie Springs Old Nevada ①
160
③ National Conservation Area

Las Vegas Motor Speedway
⑨
Las Vegas Dunes Recreation Area
Nellis Air Force Base
North Las Vegas
147
Callville Bay
Echo Bay
Tassi
Lake Mead ⑯
Lake Mead National Recreation Area
Las Vegas
⑮ Las Vegas Wash
Ethel M. Chocolates ⑱
Henderson ⑲
Boulder Beach ⑳
Clark County Heritage Museum
⑰ Hoover Dam
㉑ Boulder City
73
Temple Bar
Meadview

Nevada

Sandy Valley
Goodsprings
161
㉒ Jean
95
165
Nelson
Colorado
Willow Beach

7978
Primm
㉓
Nipton
Searchlight
164
Cottonwood Cove
㉔
Cal Nev Ari
95
Lake Mohave

Arizona
Dolan Springs
7148 Mt Tipton
93
Chloride
Red Lake

Cima
Mojave National Preserve
Kelso
7218
Goffs
40
Katherine
㉕ Davis Dam
Laughlin
Bullhead City
163
Kingman
66
Sitgreaves Pass 3652
Oatman
95
40
Fort Mojave Indian Community
Yucca
Havasu National Wildlife Refuge
Barstow
Needles
Blythe

15

Mesquite ⑬
Bunkerville
170
15
8104

Virgin
⑭
Zion N.P., Bryce Canyon N.P.

Flagstaff, Phoenix

RED ROCK CANYON LOOP

How to leave Sin City, visit an old Western town,
hike in a geological phenomenon and be back in town
in time to hit the Strip that night

Map
on pages
236-7

A 40-mile (63-km) loop from the Las Vegas Strip will take in most of the sites immediately to the south and west of the city. Begin with a drive south down Las Vegas Boulevard, past the Mandalay Bay casino. This will bring you to the first destination, the huge **Beltz Factory Outlet** (7400 Las Vegas Boulevard, tel: 896-5599) where brightly lit aisles are lined by familiar names like Samsonite, Royal Doulton, Reebok and Black & Decker among the 155 stores. Savings are promised with the "no middlemen, no mark-up" outlet ethos. There is ample parking space and a central food court. The glossy brochure is written in five languages, and a fleet of taxis line up outside.

Wild West

Only a few hundred yards beyond the outlet, opposite the site of a new casino, SR 160 heads west to the minuscule community of **Blue Diamond**, a company town for a gypsum producer, where SR 159 curves right through Red Rock Canyon, the ultimate destination. First comes **Bonnie Springs Old Nevada ❶** (tel: 875-4191), a *faux* Olde Western town whose motel (tel: 875-4400) has themed rooms ranging from Covered Wagon to Chinese. Everything, except for an apparently never-used chapel, is covered with dust and sports an old and probably intentionally decrepit appearance. There actually was a ranch here in 1843, used as a stopover to refresh passengers on wagon routes bound for California via the old Spanish Trail. Today's visitors throng to the subterranean wax museum, too dimly lit to read the captions below crude figures representing a mountain man, a missionary, a prospector, and Paiute Indians. Abraham Lincoln's lips move almost in synch with a recorded speech, presumably not recorded by Abe. Brigham Young, the explorer Jedediah Smith and President James Buchanan complete the motley group.

Lining the main street are a disused opera house and dingy shacks depicting a sheriff's office, a shaving parlor – "teeth pulled here" – and a general store doubling as a museum. Exhibits include tattered newspapers, an 1897 washing mangle and ancient medicine bottles. Where the street ends in a central square, a crowd gathers three times a day to watch a "melodrama" which closes with the mock hanging of two wisecracking bank robbers. Although there are a couple of cafe-saloons, the best place to eat is a restaurant beside the entrance overlooking a murky pond where swans and ducks swim and dive.

Spring Mountain Ranch ❷ (Blue Diamond Drive, tel: 875-4141) was the home of wealthy Vera Krupp, who raised cattle on thousands of adjoining acres. The ranch dates back a century to when moun-

PRECEDING PAGES: leaving Las Vegas; slots in the supermarket. **LEFT:** Summerlin and the Strat Tower. **BELOW:** take a bike to Bonnie Springs.

tain man Bill Williams, one of explorer John Fremont's guides, camped here. The original sandstone cabin and blacksmith's shop were built in 1864 and can still be visited. Along with the Old Mormon Fort in downtown Las Vegas, they are the oldest buildings in the valley.

Today's visitors begin their tour at the attractive modern ranch house (open daily 10am–4pm) built by Chester Lauck who played Lum in the famous early radio show, "Lum and Abner." Lauck built the 3-acre (1-hectare) reservoir still used for irrigation, naming it Lake Harriet after his wife, and bred racehorses on the ranch with his partner, screen actor Don Ameche.

The Krupp diamond

Charter companies make day excursions to Red Rock Canyon from Las Vegas.

Additions to the property, including the swimming pool, were added by Mrs Krupp, wife of the notorious German "cannon king" Alfred Krupp. In 1959, Vera was robbed at gun point in her living room, and a ring set with a 33.6 carat diamond was taken from her. The ring was recovered a few weeks later, and, after her death, bought by Richard Burton for $305,000 for his then-wife Elizabeth Taylor. The living room in question now serves as the **visitor center**.

In 1967, Howard Hughes bought the ranch as part of his Las Vegas spree, but probably never visited, although his deputy, Robert Maheu, occasionally entertained guests here. After one more owner, Spring Mountain Ranch was bought for $3.25 million by the Nevada state parks department, and is now used for summer concerts. There are guided tours, beginning at noon, and the picnic grounds are open until dusk.

BELOW:

greedily grazing at Blue Diamond.

More than 1 million visitors a year travel SR 159 to explore **Red Rock Canyon National Conservation Area ❸**. The 197,000-acre (80,000-hectare)

site is managed by the Bureau of Land Management. The informative and useful **Red Rock Visitor Center** (daily until 4:30pm, tel: 363-1921) is located at the end of the 13-mile (21-km) loop if you have come from Bonnie Springs, or at the beginning if you enter from West Charleston Boulevard. There are many day excursions from Las Vegas; if you opt to travel with ATV Action Tours, tel 566-7400 or 888/288-5200, you can explore some of the hidden dirt tracks in an off-road vehicle. Despite its desert appearance, the canyon is often a few degrees cooler that the hot streets of Las Vegas, and offers a tiny breeze, which is more than welcome in the middle of summer.

Map
on pages
236–7

Sculpted vistas

Red Rock Canyon really ought to be called "red-rock and green-tree canyon," because the far side of the loop is green and fertile compared to the arid beauty of the near side. Along the way are sculpted vistas, hidden waterfalls and desert vegetation, as well as bighorn sheep, coyotes, antelope, wild horses and burros. (Please remember not to feed the wild animals, or allow children to do so.) There are trails, both long and short, for hikers and cyclists; picnic areas; a campground (for permits, call 647-5050); and a rock climbing center (tel: 363-4533) which offers instructional classes.

Traces of the Paiute Indian tribe have been found at Willow Spring, where a well-preserved panel of five red-painted pictographs and petroglyphs survive. Some archeologists say that the paintings, "reflect the belief that the rock face was a permeable boundary between the natural and supernatural worlds… the door the shaman entered to visit the spirits." The magnificent colors of the ochre and gray morning landscape come from ferrous minerals

BELOW:
Summerlin and
other green
suburbs are
within easy reach
of the Strip.

Map on pages 236–7

in the rocks, and change color as the day progresses. When the evening shadows grow long, the canyon turns a deep terracotta red. After heavy winter rains, wildflowers are abundant and in late spring the air is filled with the aroma of blossoming cliffrose, a tall, attractive shrub covered with tiny, cream-colored flowers.

Adopt an endangered species

Mojave Desert flora and fauna are displayed both inside and outside the visitor center – the only place in the park where water is sold, so be sure to buy bottled water here before venturing further. Near the center is a poignant, homemade memorial to the victims of the September 11, 2001 terrorist attacks. A short Discovery Trail exhibits plants and some of their strategies for desert survival natural strategies like deep and widespread roots, tiny leaves or fleshy, succulent stems with waxy skin for water storage. Cactus sap acts as a kind of antifreeze to keep it from boiling on even the hottest days, and prickly spines deter attacks from creatures hoping to tap the moisture.

Behind the visitor's center are desert tortoises. Despite being on the endangered species list, tortoises are available for adoption, as long as you live in Nevada. This soil-colored desert reptile co-habits in a territorial area of less than a square mile for its life span of 50 to 100 years. They subsist on herbs grasses, cacti and flowers but are an easy source of food for predators such as foxes, coyotes and snakes. Eggs hatch in the fall and as the shells of young turtles does not harden, they are most vulnerable in their youth. It is illegal to take a desert tortoise from the wild but adoption can be arranged via the Tortoise Group (tel: 739-8043), which redistributes legally acquired former pets, some of which have outlived their owners.

Dominant shrubs like the creosote bush sprout yellow flowers whose nectar and pollen sustain millions of bees, as does the rabbit brush which blooms from August to October. The roundish, woody saltbush shrub is a common desert plant that sustains wildlife and the weedy, yellow sunflower known as groundsel has value in traditional medicine for Native Americans, as does the multi-use mesquite from which both food and rope have been processed.

Heading back towards Vegas on SR 159 offers - just north of the road – a chance to drive through **Summerlin ❹**. An expensive, self-contained suburb for 60,000 residents, it has lush, tropical landscaping and offers numerous plush, well-appointed golf courses among the resorts.

The **JW Marriott Hotel Resort** (Rampart Boulevard and Summerlin Parkway, tel: 869-7777 or 800/695-8284) has two lavish pools with lagoons, a spa, a casino and restaurants. Nearby are half a dozen golf courses Marriott has taken over the Resort at Summerlin (221 North Rampart Boulevard, tel: 869-7777, fax: 869-7771), comprised of two hotels: the Regent Grand Spa decorated in Spanish-Revival style with a giant spa; and the more formal Regent Grand Palms with its gourmet restaurant. Stopping at one of these resorts is perfect for a tranquil late lunch or early dinner before hitting the frenetic gaming rooms of the Strip.

BELOW: a bighorn sheep. **RIGHT:** blowing his own horn at Red Rock Canyon.

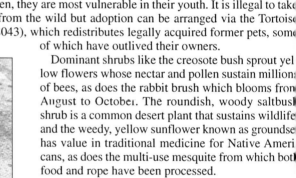

NORTH OF LAS VEGAS

Northwest of Las Vegas there are ski slopes and a ghost town, northeast, a lost civilization and blazing sandstone cliffs. But hey – is that a UFO hovering overhead?

To reach the refreshing slopes of a desert mountain, head north on US 95 and then west on SR 157. Rising to a peak of around 12,000 feet (4,000 meters), Charleston Peak at **Mount Charleston** ❺ is high enough to support both summer and winter activities – skiing and sleigh rides in winter, horse riding, wagon rides and hiking in the summer, when the temperature is typically in the 70s° F (21° C). This is one of the reasons Mount Charleston is such a popular summer day trip from the sweltering streets of Sin City, where temperatures are likely to be considerably higher. At other times of the year, people flock to the **Las Vegas Ski & Snowboard Resort,** (tel: 593-9500) with 10 ski trails spread over 40 acres (16 hectares) in **Lee Canyon**. The ski season lasts from late November until early spring.

Mount Charleston captures enough westerly precipitation to support varied vegetation. Sagebrush, crimson blooming cactus, yellow wildflowers, and bristle cone pines are among 30 species of plants endemic to the region. Named after two brothers who operated a sawmill a century ago, **Kyle Canyon** has a campground and RV site; there are other camping sites (reservations: tel: 877/444-6777) and a few picnic areas. Nearby is the **Mount Charleston Lodge** (tel: 872-5408), with log cabins available at reasonable rates.

LEFT: a member of Moapa Tribal Enterprises.
BELOW: Valley of Fire State Park.

Pioneer territory

A golf resort is emerging near the pleasantly rural **Mount Charleston Hotel** (tel: 872-5500) where a roaring fireplace dominates the huge lobby. The hotel has no casino but a good dance floor, and makes an ideal spot for a quick honeymoon if you happened to have gotten hitched in one of Las Vegas' chapels earlier in the day.

The glass-enclosed Cliffhanger Lounge and vast dining room offer grand mountain views from panoramic windows, as does the relaxing sauna. There is an adjoining nine-hole golf course. The hotel has a free pamphlet listing hiking trails ranging from less than a mile to a grueling 11-mile (18-km) loop to the mountain peak. There are scenic drives, hiking trails and horses for rent for those who seek to explore the **Toiyabe National Forest**, a unique example of forested mountains hemmed in by desert. Thousands of years ago as the water that once covered the valley dried up, plant and animal life retreated to the higher ground which today still supports deer, elk, wild turkey, wild horses and burros, bighorn sheep and even the occasional mountain lion.

Continuing north on US 95, the road skirts the western border of the 3.5 million-acre/1.5 million-hectare **Nellis Air Force Bombing and Gunnery Range** ❻, in an area known as Pioneer Territory. Originally built

Take to the slopes at the Las Vegas Ski & Snowboard Resort.

BELOW: cabins in the town of Mount Charleston.

to train B-29 gunners during World War II, it eventually became the training ground for the nation's ace fighter pilots. Many key military personnel assigned to Nellis during World War II later returned as civilians to take up permanent residency in Las Vegas. Today, thousands of active duty personnel, civilian employees, military dependents and military retirees are connected to Nellis. The base is only open to the public on one "open house" day each fall.

Almost 60 years ago, the first atomic bombs were tested at Yucca Flat, and the government's occupation of this area finally led to **Yucca Mountain** being selected as a repository for 77,000 tons of radioactive waste. The waste will be stored in supposedly "safe" canisters in concrete-lined chambers. Nobody knows just how safe this will actually be, particularly since the discovery that the mountain's interior is not as waterproof as had been thought.

The plan was vetoed by Nevada's governor but his veto was overridden by a vote in the Senate. Nuclear waste storage has been at more than 130 separate above-ground power plants and research labs; some of the opposition to the Yucca Mountain site has come from people worried about the hazards of transporting the waste across the country to Nevada.

Ghost town

Continuing north on US 95 through the Amargosa Desert – about 100 miles (160 km) of unpopulated, mostly barren terrain – you reach the small town of **Beatty ❼**. A museum (tel: 775/553-2303, daily 10am–2pm) is on Main Street, as well as an information center (tel: 775/553-2424). Here SR 374, within ten minutes' drive, leads past the battered hillside ruins of **Rhyolite ❽**. At the turn of the 19th century this was a prosperous mining community, home to an opera

house, four banks, newspapers and three railroads. But now Rhyolite is a ghost town. The ruined Cook Bank Building is the subject of many photographs, as is Tom Kelly's house, built entirely from bottles. Every spring there's a Resurrection festival at which participants dress in period costumes. The area is rife with abandoned mine shafts and it's as well to regard the warning: "the combination of water in the mine, rotting ladders, cave-ins, bad air, old explosives and rattlesnakes should always be foremost in your mind."

Map on pages 236-7

On the road to Reno

Many of the town's early investors were from Tonopah, and on Labor Day in 1906 most of them were in **Goldfield**, then the biggest city in the state, to see Battling Nelson and Joe Gans in the World Lightweight Championship fight. After 42 bloody rounds, Gans was fouled in a clinch, "as dirty a foul as was ever witnessed by spectators at ringside," reported the *Goldfield Sun*. Promoter Tex Rickard took $72,000 at the gate for his first big event, and a few years later he was organizing fights at New York's Madison Square Garden.

A famous gambler named George Wingfeld also got his start here. Winning enough at the faro tables to invest in mining shares, he eventually moved to Reno, from which he manipulated the state's financial and political affairs for many years. In 1908 he spent half a million dollars building the **Goldfield Hotel** which still dominates the town.

From Rhyolite, SR 374 continues west right through the middle of Death Valley *(see page 307)*. US 95 continues north, and eventually leads to a turn-off for that other major Nevada gambling town, **Reno**. Heading south along the same road will lead back to Las Vegas.

BELOW: never forget this is Nevada.

RENO

Reno (446 miles/718 km northwest of Las Vegas) trumpets itself as "The Biggest Little Town in the World," with an arch of neon Downtown. It does, in fact, offer a pretty broad range of entertainment, recreation, diversion and occupation. McNally, the US road map makers, recently declared the Reno and Lake Tahoe area the top US destination for outdoor recreation. Excellent opportunities for hiking, biking, climbing, golf, water sports, skiing and snowboarding are all located nearby.

The green baize tables and shiny slots still have huge pulling power, and just as Las Vegas is the gambling mecca for Angelenos, Reno is the gaming resort of choice for San Franciscans. But as well as the fun of gambling, shows and super-swift divorce, Reno offers a pretty full cultural life. There is an opera society, and at least two groups of players mount outdoor summer Shakespeare festivals. Many of the old-school Las Vegas casino hotels are represented by sibling establishments here. There is a Circus Circus, a Harrah's, and a Flamingo Hilton. The Eldorado is a favorite with many visitors for its atmosphere, service and value.

The downtown arch is in fact the Little Town's second; the original arch from 1926 is on show at the National Automobile Museum (tel: 775/333-9300).

Overton's Lost City Museum traces the history of the Anasazi Indians.

Northeast of Las Vegas

The fastest route from Las Vegas northeast is via Interstate 15, which soon passes the **Las Vegas Motor Speedway** (tel: 644-4444). The Speedway features celebrity races, NASCAR events, MotoX and even hosts events like the George Strait Chevy Truck Country Music Festival. Track tours are available from Mondays to Fridays 9am–4pm. If the idea of all that speed starts a thrill in your veins, the track occasionally offers "test and time" events. Show up with a street-legal car that passes a technical inspection and you can try it on the track and get an official report. It's advisable to arrive with an alternate ride home – your car may not be quite so technically excellent after you've thrashed it up the track. If you're even more serious, the Speedway offers a range of training courses, from three-hour sessions to some lasting three days.

Flanking both sides of I-15 are the grounds of **Nellis Air Force Base**, where fighter pilots have been trained since World War II. A left turn north off I-15 leads to US 93, which runs along the eastern border of the Nellis Air Force Bombing and Gunnery Range. Beyond the **Pahranagat National Wildlife Refuge**, US 93 bumps into what some consider the strangest feature of this alien desert landscape, SR 375. Also known as the **Extraterrestrial Highway**, SR 375 has been the site of many more than the usual number of UFO sightings on deserted highways.

The little community of **Rachel**, little more than some trailers and a bar called the Little A'e'Inn, is a rallying point for UFOlogists from around the world. Their credibility is strengthened by rumors that the Air Force studies alien visitations at nearby **Groom Lake**. The very existence of any such facility is officially denied. Needless to say the base – where top-secret aircraft are tested –

BELOW: the Extraterrestrial Highway has been the site of several UFO sightings.

is heavily guarded and intruders are arrested. Back down on I-15 and still heading northeast, the road slices through the **Moapa River Indian Community** ⑩, or technically, a corner of it. The reservation is not open to the public, but Native Americans man a stand where souvenirs can be purchased.

A right-hand turn off the highway along SR 169 loops through the spectacular **Valley of Fire State Park** ⑪, the name derived from the jagged sandstone cliffs which appear to be ablaze in sunlight. A leaflet is available from the toll booth at the entrance and also from the wonderfully sited **Visitor Center** (daily 8:30am–4:30pm, tel: 397-2088) about midway through the route. Take plenty to drink as even the center is sometimes without water and has no soft drink machines. **Mouse Tank**, a trek of almost half a mile from the road, is where Paiute Indians used to drink from rainwater collected in the stone basin. Carvings and petroglyphs can be seen, mostly around **Atlatl Rock**, depicting a prehistoric hunting tool, forerunner of the bow and arrow. Several movie companies have taken advantage of the spectacular scenery. Movies set in the park include *The Professionals* starring Lee Marvin, Burt Lancaster and Jack Palance, many *Star Wars* scenes and *Star Trek: Generations*.

Lost City

Where SR 169 leaves the Valley of Fire State Park is **Overton** ⑫, a small town in which the **Lost City Museum** (daily 8:30am–4:30pm, tel: 397-2193) documents the history of the long-lost Anasazi Indians. Living in the area for centuries, they left as long as 800 years ago, probably because of a prolonged drought. Ironically, the area that was home to the Anasazi is now beneath the waters of Lake Mead.

Map on pages 236–7

ATVs (all terrain vehicles) are a great way to explore.

BELOW: plane display at Nellis Air Force Base.

Map on pages 236-7

The museum exhibits some of the beads, polished shells and, intriguingly, bone gambling counters, salvaged by archeologists before the lake and Hoover Dam were built. In Overton on North Moapa Valley Boulevard are the funky Overton Motel (tel: 397-2463) and a Best Western (tel: 397-6000).

In the northern arm of Lake Mead are two waterfront resorts about ten miles apart. For those with time, the meandering **Northshore Scenic Drive** offers attractive scenery and occasional sight of bighorn sheep. Following it south curves around the lake and eventually ends up near Lake Mead marina and the chance to catch a boat to Hoover Dam *(see page 256.)* On the way, you can take smaller roads to **Overton Beach** (tel: 394-4040), **Echo Bay Resort & Marina** (tel: 394-4000), or to **Callville Bay**, originally established by Anson Call in 1864 as a freight outlet for Colorado River steamboats.

Mesquite

At **Logandale**, a mile or two north of the town of Overton, jeeps and four-wheel drive ATVs are available to rent from Valley of Fire Adventures (tel: 800/519-2243). An off-road vehicle is an exhilarating way to explore the fascinating trails and canyons of the Logandale Trail System. Cold drinks are provided, but take your own lunch and stop to enjoy the ancient petroglyphs.

BELOW:
Eureka casino in the town of Mesquite.
RIGHT:
flying the flag.

North of Logandale, SR 169 runs into I-15 which enters Arizona at the resort town of **Mesquite ⑬**, on the Virgin River, which has achieved some notoriety for its July Running of the Bulls Festival, based on the famous 400-year-old event in Pamplona, Spain. After recent poor attendance, however, the festival's future is in some doubt. Moving the Running of the Bulls to spring is being considered, and also making it a one-day event.

I-15 continues northeast and just skims the tip of Arizona before plunging into the state of Utah. Turn-offs lead to the majestic **Zion National Park ⑭**. From afar, the park's enormous buttes and domes rise like temples beckoning the faithful. From up close, its sheltering walls seem to offer a protected sanctuary. For the Mormon settlers who came here in the mid-1800s, the land seemed to be Zion, "the Heavenly City of God." As a national park since 1919, Zion continues to draw millions of "worshippers" to marvel at the extraordinary geology and natural beauty. The park's dominant rocks are the sheer, creamy-pink **Navajo Sandstone cliffs**, which reach 2,200 feet (671 meters) in height. The **Zion Canyon Visitor Center** is just inside the south entrance.

A little further on is **Bryce Canyon National Park**. Plan to spend at least a day here to take full advantage of the summer ranger programs and exhibits in the **visitor center**, as well as the experiences to be had in a park whose elevation ranges from 6,600 to 9,100 feet (2,000 to 2,775 meters.) Bryce has two pleasant campgrounds as well as the rustic **Bryce Canyon Lodge** (closed in winter), built in the 1920s by the Utah Parks Company. (To stay here, book aat least six months ahead.) With a shorter time frame, it's possible to view the park's highly eroded cliffs along an 18-mile (29-km) scenic drive following a plateau through ponderosa pines and summer wildflowers. ❑

LAKE MEAD AND HOOVER DAM

This giant lake in the desert offers unlimited recreational opportunities all year round. It was only made possible by a masterpiece of 1930s engineering

The most popular day trip from Las Vegas is to Lake Mead and Hoover Dam, about 35 miles (56 km) to the southeast. Sightseeing excursions can be arranged from Las Vegas by light airplane, by helicopter or by bus if you don't have access to a car. If you're traveling by road, stops can be made at Henderson and Boulder City *(see pages 260 and 262)*, probably best appreciated for their museums after a trip to the dam. Also on the way is the opulent **Lake Las Vegas Resort** (tel: 565-0211), a $7 billion development. The entrance is off SR 147, locally known as Lake Mead Drive. At the Discovery Center (tel: 564-1600) near the entrance a free video, *Out of the Blue*, is shown continuously, depicting the development of this European-style waterfront village. When the project is completed in 2010, the 3,600-acre (1,500-hectare) project will have 5,500 homes arranged in five neighborhoods.

Already in operation is the 496-room **Hyatt Regency** (tel: 800/554-9288). Decorated in hues of aqua, cayenne and gold with two-story arched windows, and with upper galleries overlooking the courtyard in a Mediterranean style, it offers a spa, a fitness center, two swimming pools with cabanas and a water slide, a sandy beach, a casino and five restaurants including the Marrakech Express 24-hour coffee shop. Julia Roberts and Billy Crystal's movie *America's Sweethearts* was filmed here shortly after the hotel opened in 2001.

LEFT: a Nevada Wildlife boat cruises along Lake Mead.
BELOW: angling is encouraged.

Private casbahs

Montelago Village, at the west end of the lake, opened in late 2002, centered around the **Ritz Carlton** hotel. Around 75 of the rooms are in a bridge, styled after the Ponte Vecchio in Florence, with an arcade of classy shops. There are 47 suites with lake or mountain views and four larger "casbahs," with private entrances. The beach area, with a lawn and picnic areas, was constructed with 350 tons of imported white sand. Overlooking it all is the hilltop Monte Catini, an exclusive development with only 19 residences in the $3 million range, all named after Renaissance families.

The complex, with a lakefront walkway, cobbled streets, shops and the **Reflection Bay Golf Club** designed by Jack Nicklaus, is likely to become a tourist attraction in its own right. It has already proved an attractive lure for successful corporate types, including the head of a certain supermarket chain, a former pro auto racer, a football Hall-of-Famer and Celine Dion, who established a home base for her three-year residency at Caesars Palace.

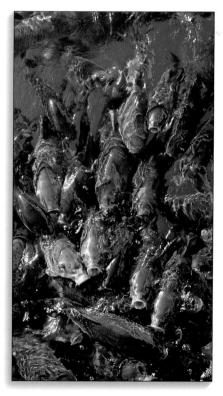

There are ample opportunities for boating on the lake.

The **Las Vegas Wash** N, wetlands between Lake Las Vegas and Lake Mead, are a prime spot for nature-viewing, providing for birds and other creatures an oasis refuge from the desert. At the eastern end of Tropicana Avenue, a parking area affords access to the Duck Creek Trail, part of a 165-acre (66-hectare) preserve dotted with "sitting shelters" in which to wait for waterfowl to appear.

Four miles (6 km) before reaching Lake Mead, a casino-hotel called the **Hacienda** (Highway 93, Boulder City, tel: 293-5000 800/245-6380) has replaced the famous Gold Strike, which burned down. Like its predecessor, it has proved very popular with locals, especially those from nearby Boulder City, where gambling is not allowed.

Lake Mead

Lake Mead N, with a jagged shoreline of 550 miles (885 km), contains enough water to cover the entire state of New York to a depth of about 1 foot (0.5 meters). The lake is 500 feet (152 meters) at its deepest point in late fall and early spring, but averages about 200 feet (61 meters) deep for its 100-mile (160 km) length. The water has an average daytime temperature of 86° F (30° C) in summer, so visitors hanging their beer and soda over the side of a boat to cool find the drinks come up warmer than when they went in. The recreational areas on and around the lake attract 9 million visitors a year.

BELOW: burning brown and ochre hills hide Lake Mead from view.

The first glimpse of the lake, when arriving from Las Vegas, is a refreshment. Turning off just before Boulder City, the hot, desert landscape becomes more gentle. A sudden curve, a hill and from the top, the lake – ice-blue against brown rolling hills. The drive to the marina is through the fragrant national park, with more coyotes and mountain goats than people.

At the marina, **Lake Mead Cruises** (tel: 293-6180) offer a variety of excursions (most available with hotel pick-up in Las Vegas). The *Desert Princess* is a pretty, triple-decked paddle wheeler and the largest boat on the lake. Throughout the year she hosts 90-minute cruises, plus weekend dance cruises, and lunch and dinner cruises. The two-hour dinner cruise is particularly pleasant, with appetizing entrées and a well-stocked bar. After a turn-around at Hoover Dam, the return to the marina is timed for the the setting of the sun behind the ochre- and chocolate-colored hills.

Map
on pages
236–7

Fast-moving cat

More adventurous is the *Velocity*, a fast-moving 57-foot (17-meter) catamaran that gives spectacular close-up views of canyon walls and occasional glimpses of wildlife. On this six-hour cruise, passengers can follow the pilot's narration through headphones as the boat zips through areas with names like Iceberg Canyon or to God's Pocket near the Grand Canyon, pausing for lunch and swimming at far-flung Sandy Point. The catamaran has open windows but no air-conditioning. Normally, the breeze off the lake is cool enough for comfort, but in the fiery months of June, July and August, anyone sensitive to heat might prefer to opt for the climate-controlled *Desert Princess*.

Nevada Highway 169, which is also called the **Northshore Scenic Drive**, runs for miles along the shore, then heads north towards Overton Beach and the Valley of Fire State Park *(see page 249)*. There are no roads on the south side.

Angling on the lake goes on year round but a license is required. The lake has many camping spots and there are several places that offer boat rentals and provisions for overnight camping. Houseboats can also be rented.

BELOW:
there are a variety
of different cruises
to be taken aboard
the *Desert Princess.*

Map on pages 236–7

Hoover Dam took less than five years to complete.

Hoover Dam

Straddling the Arizona–Nevada border, **Hoover Dam ⑰** is anchored to the rugged volcanic walls of the Black Canyon and towers 726 feet (221 meters) above the Colorado River. It was for years, and occasionally still is, known as Boulder Dam. This was because of the unpopularity of the 31st president, Herbert Hoover, who had largely been responsible for the successful outcome of a series of highly delicate negotiations to push the project forward.

Dedicated by President Franklin D. Roosevelt in 1935, the Hoover Dam was built primarily as a flood-control measure, but with 17 generators, it was able to produce enough energy to supply a million residences for 20 years. The lake that resulted from filling the deep canyons behind it supplies nearly 25 million people with water, including Las Vegans. After the snow melts in the Rocky Mountains, the runoff pours into the 1,400-mile (2,250-km) long Colorado River, roaring through the Grand Canyon before beginning its 100-mile (160-km) journey into Lake Mead. This is where Hoover Dam halts its flow. The river heads south, providing the state border with Arizona all the way into Lake Mohave, which is blocked at the southern end by the **Davis Dam**.

Masterpiece of engineering

A visit to the dam is more rewarding than it might first seem. A masterpiece of engineering, it has striking sculptures by Oskar J.W. Hansen which might well be the largest monumental bronzes ever cast in the United States. After the tightening of security following the September 11, 2001 disaster, tours inside the dam itself were suspended, but a two-hour Discovery Tour has been introduced where visitors – there are a million each year – are treated to a talk inside the circular, state-of-the-art **Visitor Center** (last tour 3:30 pm, tel: 294-3523). After a 25-minute movie including vintage film of the dam's construction, an elevator takes visitors to a scenic overlook.

Before the river could be managed, its waters had to be divided equally among the six states it serves, an apportionment that was made by the creation of the Colorado River Compact in 1922. Mexico was later allocated a share in a treaty made in 1944. More than one and a half million acres (607,000 hectares) of land are irrigated in the United States and Mexico by management of the water.

Construction of the Hoover Dam cost $60 million, a huge figure at the time (though less than four percent of the cost of Bellagio), and workers were kept busy for four years, enduring exacting conditions under the supervision of a veteran dam builder, Frank T. Crowe. When Will Rogers came to visit he asked how many men were working on the dam. Crowe said, "About half of them." Rogers replied: "Mr Crowe, I'm supposed to be the comedian."

The dam, 660-feet (200-meters) thick at its base, and 45-feet (14-meters) thick at the top, required 4.5 million cubic yards (3.5 million cubic meters) of concrete. Because of the heat generated by concrete as it settles, the concrete was first poured into a series of interlocked columns inset with miles and miles of tubes through which cooling water flowed. ❑

HENDERSON AND BOULDER CITY

Map
on pages
236–7

*Two different towns lie only a short distance from Vegas.
Henderson is fast-growing and fast-moving, while Boulder City
feels like a sleepy community in the Midwest*

Henderson and Boulder City could hardly be more different – from each
other or from Las Vegas. Henderson, one of the US's fastest growing
cities, is now primarily a service suburb for Vegas. The landscape turns
from desert scrubland to subdivision so fast that maps are updated every year,
and taxi drivers are perpetually lost. Many hotel, casino and other service staff
make the 13-mile (21-km) commute to the Strip or Downtown at least once a
day. Boulder City is older and distinctly more genteel. Growth is restricted to
120 inhabitants per year by city ordinance.

On the way to Henderson (about 9 miles/14 km southwest on Interstate 515),
the 50-room **Sam's Town** (5211 Boulder Highway, tel: 456-7777) has something
for everybody. The rooms are decorated in a "19th-century southwestern theme,"
and two huge RV parks have swimming pools, spa, laundry, pet runs and clubhouse. A complimentary shuttle runs (8:30am–11pm) to downtown Las Vegas
casinos. The hotel's A Place for Kids (tel: 450-8350, daily noon–midnight, till
10pm Sundays) offers computer and art centers, group games and a quiet area.
For a fee, children (3–12) will be supervised at play.

LEFT:
casino cowboy.
BELOW:
Bob will be happy
to serve you.

Yummy factory

Northwest of Henderson is the factory that produces
Ethel M. Chocolates ⓲ (1 Cactus Garden Drive, tel:
888/627-0990. Around 60 different varieties of the
yummy candy are made here, including a "chocolate
postcard" bearing your own personal photograph. Visitors can watch some of the chocolate production on
a self-guided tour between 8:30am and 7pm every
day. A ton and half of chocolates are typically enrobed
in the course of a shift and the company's 70 stores
throughout the West have at least $150 million annual
sales. Employees, of whom there are now 200, are
given sensory training that includes learning which
flavors are tasted on which parts of the tongue.

The company is owned by the mother of "Mr Mars
Bar," the reclusive Forrest Mars, whose worldwide
business grew from his parents' candy store in
Tacoma, Washington.

Mars was described by author Joel Glenn Brenner
as "the Howard Hughes of candy." In his book, *The
Emperors of Chocolate: Inside the Secret World of
Hershey and Mars*, Brenner says that Forrest, now in
his 90s, lives mostly in Miami but for about two
months of the year stays in a penthouse above the Las
Vegas factory – watching the employees through one-
way mirrors. Forrest established the factory in Nevada
"because it is one of the few states that allowed the

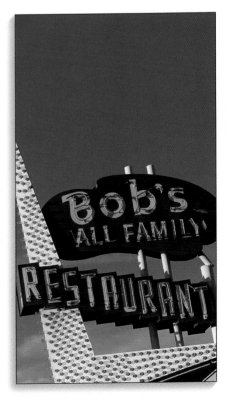

sale of liqueur-filled cordials." The adjoining cactus garden of the chocolate factory has many varieties of prickly plants – it's a good place to learn to identify them – and receives about 700,000 visitors a year.

Henderson

North of Henderson, the hilltop **Green Valley Ranch** (2300 Paseo Verde Parkway, tel: 614-5283), has a 10-screen cinema, an Irish-style pub and a pancake house. Claiming inspiration from a typical Argentinean *estancia,* it is aimed squarely at a local, middlebrow audience. The city of **Henderson** ⓘ began as a satellite of Las Vegas when the latter's population was a mere 8,500. Henderson's infra-structure cannot keep up with its current rapid-fire expansion, and doctors and teachers are welcomed with open arms.

Henderson's earlier development was spawned by the US Defense Department's partnership with Cleveland entrepreneur Howard Eells for the production of magnesium. At first, many of the 13,000 workers lived in shacks, trailers and tents along the Boulder Highway in a community known as Pittman, but the company town of Henderson soon came into being with a bill pushed through the Senate allowing residents to buy their homes. A **Farmer's Market** is held on Water Street from 4pm on Thursdays, and several Henderson hotels have collaborated to offer golf packages at half-a-dozen local links. Call (800) 481-7890 for information.

Thousands of panes of stained glass are subtly lit to denote the passing day in the ceiling of **Sunset Station Hotel Casino** (1301 West Sunset Road, Henderson, tel: 547-7777). Iron balconies, windows and weathered brick give the sense of a stroll in a Spanish village. The Mediterranean architecture is enhanced

BELOW:
employees of the
Ethel M. Chocolates
factory are given
sensory training.

by a bar in the style of Spanish architect Antonio Gaudí. The 457-room hotel has a microbrewery, a 13-screen movie theater and an outdoor amphitheater.

Between Henderson and Boulder City is Southern Nevada's first museum, set up in 1949 by Anna Parks who, with her husband Gene, had opened a mortuary in Boulder City in 1932 for the remains of those killed during the construction of Boulder Dam.

Map on pages 236-7

Native American goods make great souvenirs to take back home.

Pioneer life

The museum was the forerunner of the **Clark County Heritage Museum ㉑** (1830 South Boulder Highway, just before Lake Mead Drive, tel: 455-7955, daily 9am–4:30pm), which can be reached easily by taking the Boulder Highway route into Henderson. In the lobby are shelves of interesting books about Native Americans and the geology of the region.The history of Southern Nevada is shown in exhibits which begin with a diorama of the desert as it was 12,000 years ago, with petrified logs on sandy wastes, turtles, cacti and a tall extinct beast described as a camelope. A Pauite camp is displayed with rabbit pelts woven into a blanket, baskets, and other craftwork.

The pioneer life of trappers, farmers and ranchers is represented by a woman sitting in her kitchen beside a big spinning wheel and a baby in a rocker. Other exhibits are diverse: there's Fanny Soss' 1930 dress store, the first local shop with window mannequins, as well as a depiction of the notorious Block 16, the downtown Las Vegas area where low-class saloons and gambling dives abutted on the Arizona Club with a second-floor brothel. Singer Ella Fitzgerald donated two of her dresses to the collection on casinos, which includes items from the Tropicana, the Hacienda and the Thunderbird.

BELOW: a subdivision in Henderson, one of the fastest-growing areas in the US.

Boulder City

Established mainly because the government wanted to keep men building the nearby Hoover Dam away from hard liquor, gambling and prostitution, pretty **Boulder City** ㉑ (pop: 15,500) still has no gaming, no neon and a strictly controlled growth policy. When the town was created, the Secretary of the Interior appointed Tennessee-born Sims Ely, a former newspaper editor, to be city manager of Boulder City and he proved to be a strict guardian of the city's morals. Cars were searched at the entrance to town and impounded if liquor was found. Alcoholic beverages were not legalized until 1969 and gambling and prostitution are banned to this day. Off-duty workers went to Las Vegas for entertainment – although a (still-existing) casino called the **Railroad Pass** was quickly erected in 1931 west of town, making it one of the state's oldest gaming houses. Sims, who died in 1954, had totally dictatorial powers – a "little Hitler" – one worker called him, giving orders to the police and granting or refusing all commercial or residential leases.

Today, the little town is proud of its history and strives to preserve its small town atmosphere. The speed limit announces the countdown – from 65 miles an hour on the main road down to 15 miles in town – all advertised in ever-decreasing increments. One local tale is that, for a while at night time, a police car was stationed just outside the city limits to enforce the speed countdown. The shadowy figure inside the car wasn't a real cop but a dummy, and kids loved to "decapitate" him for kicks.

BELOW: don't take wooden nickels from this man.

The town's charm is best discovered in the historic district. Centered around the Boulder City Theater on Arizona Street, the attractive little houses with red-tile roofs and stuccoed walls on nearby Cherry and Birch streets were built to

HIKING, BIKING AND BIRDWATCHING

A recent survey established that about eight million of Las Vegas' annual visitors – about 22 percent – visit public lands and recreational areas around the Las Vegas valley. What might sound like an unlikely stop is Henderson's 147-acre (60-hectare) Water Reclamation Facility (Moser Drive, near where Sunset intersects the Boulder Highway, tel: 566-2940, daily 6am–3pm), which has been designated as a Bird Viewing Preserve where a local branch of the Audubon Society has documented 200 different species. Early morning is the most rewarding time to visit. The hills north of Boulder City are a mecca for mountain bikers. Well-established trails now have approval from the city, which maintains a road to the top of what locals call Radar Mountain. At its base are a shower and washroom. The International Mountain Biking Association has certified Bootleg Canyon as a rare "epic" ride. Hikers can explore the Historic Railroad Trail from the Visitor Center at US 93 and Lakeshore Drive, just east of Boulder City. Part of the trail runs through tunnels built to ferry construction materials to Hoover Dam. Wilderness lovers can canoe and kayak along the Colorado River south of Hoover Dam with the help of Down River Outfitters (1631 Industrial Road, Boulder City, tel: 800/748-3702).

Map on pages 236-7

house employees of the dam's power companies. The houses were eventually auctioned off for about $75,000 each, but the area looks much the same, with its trees, sidewalks, a diner and a pizza parlor, a complete contrast to Sin City only 23 miles (36 km) away. By 9pm all is quiet – even the McDonalds on the strip mall outside town shuts early.

A life-sized climber doggedly conquers a canyon wall in the **Boulder City Hoover Dam Museum** (1305 Arizona Street, tel: 294-1988, daily 10am–5pm, Sun noon–5pm), offering an imaginative demonstration of the day-to-day tasks of building the dam. It's a pleasant little museum where you can play your part in an old debate by casting your vote for the name "Hoover Dam" or "Boulder Dam." An ancient switchboard allows visitors to plug in and listen to residents reminisce about the old days. A film shows how hard the men worked – "muckers" shoveled out after each blast with short-handled spades called banjos for just $4 a day. The café serves buffalo burgers and a cowboy breakfast named after Will Rogers, who played in the town's theater in 1935.

Famous hotel

The museum, and a gallery showing the work of local artists, are situated inside the refurbished, 22-room **Boulder Dam Hotel** (tel: 293-3510). Here the friendly atmosphere of a bed-and-breakfast inn has welcomed guests including John Wayne, Doris Day, Shirley Temple, Bette Davis and Dean Martin. It's a good base for tours of the dam, or excursions on the lake. Lake Mead Air (tel: 293-1848) operates flights to the Grand Canyon from the city's airport.

From Boulder City, it's easy to pick up US 95 and head for the gambling mecca, Laughlin *(see page 268)*. ❑

TIP

Unless otherwise stated, all telephone numbers in this book are preceded by the code 702.

BELOW: the hills around Boulder City provide "epic rides" for mountain bikers.

GAMBLING TOWNS

*Deep in the desert, in towns called Primm and Laughlin
and Jean, the soft shuffle of cards mingles with the
unmistakable sound of money being lost and won*

Map on pages 236–7

The gambling town of Primm is 43 miles (69 km) southwest from Las Vegas along Interstate 15 and just inside the Nevada border with California. On the way are several pleasant distractions and diversions. The town of **Jean ㉒**, 34 miles (55 km) southwest, has two major casinos, the 300-room **Nevada Landing** (tel: 387-5000 or 800/628-6682), built to look like a ship, and the **Gold Strike** (tel: 477-5000 or 800/634-1359), which has a sauna in turn-of-the-19th-century style. Plans are underway for an international airport between Jean and Primm, confirming the area's new-found status. The airport is scheduled for completion in 2006.

Eight miles (13 km) northwest of Jean, along SR 161, is **Goodsprings** (pop: 232). Once a gold-mining town, it is still the home of the old **Pioneer Saloon**, where Clark Gable awaited news of his wife Carole Lombard after her plane crashed into nearby Mount Potosi. "This is where the stars come to take a break from Las Vegas," says one regular, Elvis impersonator Lary Glen Anderson. The Pioneer Saloon is one of the oldest buildings in the state, and posters on the bullet-riddled tin walls hint at the bar's rowdier days.

South of SR 161, across the Spring Mountains, is Sandy Valley. Appealing to lovers of the outdoors is the **Sandy Valley Ranch** (tel: 631-1463), which offers trail rides and the opportunity to work alongside cowboys in a cattle round-up.

Primm

Time was when the only thing in **Primm ㉓** (former name: Stateline) was a two-pump gas station run by a crusty character known as Whisky Pete. His memory lives on in the name of **Whisky Pete's** hotel-casino (100 West Primm Boulevard). The hotel's soaring towers unexpectedly stand above the flat terrain surrounding it, earning it the nickname, the Castle in the Desert. Pete's has 800 rooms, a 700-seat showroom and a pool with a waterslide. It is linked by monorail to two other casinos, **Buffalo Bill's** (31700 South Las Vegas Boulevard) with its red-barn architecture, and **Primm Valley** (31900 South Las Vegas Boulevard), which resembles San Diego's famous turreted Hotel del Coronado. All three share the same telephone numbers: 386-7867 or 800/386-7867.

Straddling Interstate 15, this trio of casinos is collectively known as the **Primadonna Casino Resorts**, now owned by MGM-Mirage. The company bought the Dry Lakes Lotto Store, just over the state line and the leading outlet in the entire state for selling California lottery tickets ($6.2 million of them). Twin golf links, the **Desert Course** and the **Lakes Course**, both designed by golf-course architect Tom Fazio, are only a couple of miles away, adjacent to I-15 in California.

LEFT: Nevada Landing casino in the town of Jean.
BELOW: blue in Jean.

Buffalo Bill's – whose pool is in the shape of a buffalo silhouette – is a maze of corridors, and is very popular, with a busy check-in line even at midnight. The interior is heavy on Old Western style, with a Hangman's Bar and the start of a themed log-flume ride which takes riders on a five-minute journey soaring high into the sky before descending downward from Primm's Peak and crossing paths several times with America's highest roller coaster, the Desperado. The flume logs float past animatronic old prospectors and stuffed animals, while a vulture keeps a beady eye on the proceedings.

Desperate ride

On a breathtaking three-minute ride, **Desperado** drops 225 feet (69 meters) at 55 mph (88 kph), then another leap more than half that distance, reaching speeds of 85 mph (136 kph) with the feeling of free-falling. A Utah firm, Arrow Dynamics, which collaborated with Walt Disney to produce many of the Disneyland rides in the 1950s, created the five-coach magenta, yellow and blue trains to resemble bullet trains. They carry 30 passengers each and can accommodate almost 900 riders per hour. Another trip, scarily realistic, is across bumpy desert trails in the **Ghost Town Motion Simulator Theater**. There's also a first-run movie theater, a weekend comedy club, an arena for concerts, a bowling alley, a swimming pool, golf course and three restaurants.

BELOW:
get a new outfit at
this upscale outlet
in Primm.

Adjoining Primm Valley, the upscale **Fashion Outlet of Las Vegas** has shops with discount fashions by Calvin Klein, Versace, Ralph Lauren and others. A shuttle bus runs from the MGM Grand on Las Vegas' Strip in order to transport card-carrying retail therapists. The trip takes 45 minutes each way, and around three return journeys daily are made. Call 874-1400 for a schedule.

Between the casino and the clothing mall is a museum strong on gangster exhibits. On view is the restored armored Lincoln car that was custom built for Dutch Schultz, known as "the Bronx Beer Baron," who was killed in a bloody gang feud the following year. Schultz ran bootlegging routes, owned breweries, speakeasies and policy rackets in New York during the 1920s and 1930s. Schultz was said to be making $20 million a year during the Depression.

Map on pages 236–7

Bonnie and Clyde

More famously are mementoes from the life of Bonnie and Clyde, the young couple who during the 1930s robbed gas stations, restaurants and small-town banks in Texas, Oklahoma, New Mexico and Missouri. Exhibits including original newspapers with the notorious couple featured in headlines and stories, a necklace, a belt and mirror that Clyde made during a prison term, which had lain forgotten in a storage depot until recently.

Bonnie and Clyde, portrayed by Warren Beatty and Faye Dunaway in the 1967 movie, came to an inglorious end on May 23, 1934 when – betrayed by a friend – they ran into a police ambush. No fewer than 168 rounds of ammunition, 15 guns and two bodies were recovered from the car when the shooting finally stopped. The bullet-riddled Ford is on view here along with Clyde's blood-stained shirt.

A letter adorns the dark gray Ford that Clyde Barrow stole in Topeka a few weeks before his death. "While I still have breath in my lungs," he wrote to Henry Ford, "I will tell you what a dandy car you make. I have driven Fords exclusively when I could get away with one. For sustained speed and freedom from trouble, the Ford has got every other car skinned."

Keno is one of the easiest games to play, but also pays some of the lowest odds in the house.

BELOW: Buffalo Bill's casino, Primm

Towards Laughlin

From Las Vegas, take US 95 south past Henderson and Boulder City *(see pages 260–63)*. Roughly halfway between Las Vegas and Laughlin is the former mining town of **Searchlight** ㉔. Its heyday was the early 20th century when the town had a railway line, a power plant, several hotels and a dairy, all from the success of gold and silver mines, most of which soon petered out.

Continuing south on US 95, almost to the southern tip of Nevada, SR 163 east continues to Laughlin, which itself is within a metaphorical dice throw of both California and Arizona. **Laughlin** ㉕ 95 miles (152 km) southeast of Vegas, is younger than Sin City but just as much of a gambling mecca, and because of its location on the Colorado River, somewhat more intrinsically scenic. An estimated 3,000 cars a day travel to Laughlin from Las Vegas, and another 2,500 from California, the latter coming mostly from the San Diego or Palm Springs areas. Laughlin sees six million visitors a year, and land along the river bank now fetches as much as $1.5 million an acre ($3.7 million a hectare). Hotel rooms, though, are considerably cheaper in Laughlin than in Las Vegas, usually dropping very low in the blisteringly hot summer months.

Until the casino era, the debilitating heat kept the region's population sparse. From the earliest days, most of the locals were Mojave Indians who had adjusted to the unpredictable river's flow, as it shriveled to a trickle in summer, or swelled to a raging, crop-ravaging torrent at other times of the year.

There are nine hotel-casinos beside the Colorado River, all connected by a pleasant **River Walk**, with a riverboat service operating as a water taxi. Paddle-wheel riverboats operated by Laughlin River Tours (tel: 298-1047) run up and down the river from docks at the Flamingo Hilton and Edgewater casinos, which

BELOW: kids cooling it in the desert.

is also the starting point for helicopter tours (tel: 271-4533). The *USS Riverside* (tel: 227-3849) makes five 75-minute cruises down the river daily between 10:30am and 6:30pm. Jet skis can also be rented for adventures on the water.

Map
on pages
236–7

Dealer grad makes good

It all began with Don Laughlin in the early 1960s. Looking for a new challenge, he piloted his plane south from Las Vegas along the Colorado River. While he was still at school in Minnesota, Laughlin had built a business putting slot machines in local bars, from money he had made trapping mink. He attended dealers' school in Las Vegas, worked at several casinos and eventually bought and sold one. Fully aware that owning a casino close to a state line would give him a head start, he checked out possible sites. "I saw a lot of little communities like Kingman and Needles," he recalls, "and gambling was not legal in either California or Arizona," where those towns are located.

He settled for a place where he found a boarded-up eight-room motel, bought the surrounding 6 acres (3 hectares) of riverside land for $235,000 and moved his family into four rooms. Today, the man who started by offering all-you-can-eat chicken dinners for 98¢ is a multi-millionaire, the owner of numerous Rolls Royces, two helicopters and the Bullhead airport across the river. He built the bridge connecting Laughlin, Nevada to Bullhead City, Arizona *(see page 276)*, a bridge that is crossed by up to 25,000 vehicles a day. He started small, saying, "You don't need to be big to attract gamblers."

When a US Postal Service inspector insisted the fledgling town be given a name, Laughlin followed his advice and gave it the family name. This decision is indicative of his business philosophy. "The Riverside is a friendly, fam-

BELOW:
casinos by the
Colorado River,
Laughlin.

ily operation." he says. "We are the natural heir to a market that corporations alienate." Nevertheless, he maintains tight security. "A casino always operates with a cageful of cash for ransom," he observes, "and the bad guys know that." A local reporter visiting the 1,405-room **Riverside Resort** (1650 South Casino Drive, tel: 298-2535 or 800/227-3849) found the entrepreneur watching the progress of the empire he was building through his binoculars.

2 hopeful 2 B 4 gotten – 4 now, at least.

On the Riverside's ground floor, the Watch Man claims to be the world's largest watch store with 20,000 watches all under $20, mostly famous brands and in categories such as dog watches, Route 66, Betty Boop, sports teams and Elvis. Always hidden in plain sight is a genuine Rolex, which is sold for $19.97 if found. The hotel has a 34-lane bowling alley, six-screen theater and a supervised Kid Kastle, open 10am to 11pm, till midnight on weekends. There are movies, food and free arcade games; parents pay a small hourly rate.

All aboard

The **Ramada Express** (tel: 298-4200 or 800/243-6846), the only hotel across the street from the water, offers free rides around its 17-acre (7-hectare) property on a steam locomotive, which also shuttles customers to and from the parking lot. One third of the hotel's 1,500 rooms are for adults only, i.e. no kids.

BELOW:
having more fun
than most.

The third-floor **Auto Collection** includes John Wayne's 1966 War Wagon used on his ranch, and which he took with him on an African safari, and the blue marriage-trap seen in *The Quiet Man*, a film he made in 1952 with Maureen O'Hara. There's a 1923 hot-rod race car with all working parts visible; Don Laughlin's 1931 Ford Roadster with its "OLD TIME" license plate; a 1904 two-cylinder Holsman car, and some late 1800s gaming tables.

The hotel, intensely patriotic with its daily flag-raising ceremony at 7am, is particularly sympathetic to war veterans to whom it gives special slot-club cards and decorative pins. Upstairs, the **Veterans Museum** (daily 10am–3pm) houses a collection of war relics.

Map on pages 236–7

Native American art

The **Edgewater** (2020 South Casino Drive, tel: 298-2453 or 800/677-4837), where some jackpots pay off in silver coins, displays huge posters on its exterior wall advertising its Krispy Kreme donut outlet; the donuts themselves are prizes in its daily Elvis Slots Tournament. The casino has some unusual slot machines topped with "hurricane indicators" which display a storm that increases with each win, ending hopefully with a flood of coins. In the casino are statues of Kokopeli, a Native American spirit of the Southwest, reputed to bring luck. There's also a Kokopeli Lounge, the scene of free bingo from Tuesday to Thursday, and an attractive second-floor bar overlooking the water. Located at river level is a store named Petroglyphs, which specializes in Native American art, pottery and jewelry.

The **Colorado Belle** (2100 South Casino Drive, tel: 298-4000 or 800/477-4837), designed to resemble a 19th-century riverboat with fancy ironwork railings and balconies overlooking the water, has a Mississippi Lounge and Mark Twain's Chicken and Ribs. Near the swimming pools is a man-made waterfall.

Harrah's (2900 South Casino Drive, tel: 298-4600 or 800/427-7247) styles itself as a Mexican village, its casinos – one non-smoking – decked with *papier mâché* tropical birds and hand-painted flowers. Colorful wall murals depict rural south-of-the-border scenes and games of chance, and there's the Cabo

BELOW: steam around the hotel grounds in the *Lucky Lady*.

Map on pages 236–7

Café, Rosa's Cantina and a bar named Margaritaville. In addition to two pools, the hotel maintains its own private sandy beach in a natural cove and offers daily river cruises in the Del Rio Yacht. The 1,900-room **Flamingo Laughlin** (1900 Casino Drive, tel: 298-5111 or 800/352-6464), a clone of its Las Vegas namesake, has an outdoor amphitheater as well as an indoor showroom, three tennis courts and six restaurants.

24-hour buffet

The **River Palms**, formerly the Gold River (2700 Casino Drive, tel: 298-2242 or 800/835-7903), has the only 24-hour buffet in town, and a gourmet restaurant set around pine trees, a stream and a 300-foot (91-meter) beach. The producers of the film *Leaving Las Vegas* chose Laughlin as a set because they found it more relaxed than Vegas itself. Much of the movie was shot in the River Palms.

The Golden Nugget (2300 Casino Drive, tel: 298-2242 or 800/950-7700) – a sister to its Vegas namesake – stages poker tournaments. It was converted in 1988 from the Nevada Club by Steve Wynn, who bought it for $40 million. The 300-room hotel has a refreshing rainforest atrium with towering palms, cascading waterfalls, a big brass cage with mechanical talking birds, and a self-playing piano in the lobby.

Carved wooden figures sit at tables outside the 416-room **Pioneer Hotel & Gambling Hall** (298-2442 or 800/634-3469), which offers an "old fashioned" Sunday champagne brunch in Granny's Gourmet Room. As befits the name, it sports a Western motif with a Boarding House restaurant, Fast Drawer snack bar and Sassy Sue's Saloon. The croupiers wear sheriff's badges. The only gambling venue without a hotel attached is the **Regency Casino** (298-2439), which has a piano bar and offers breakfast 24 hours a day.

BELOW: the Pioneer emphasizes its Western motif with bars like Sassy Sue's Saloon. **RIGHT:** cowboy strikes a cool pose.

All the hotels offer nightly entertainment and plenty of eating places. Diners at the Riverside and the Flamingo can watch ferries on the river, and the Ramada has a steak house set in a Victorian parlor railroad car. Special events tend toward the macho, with 600 cowboys competing in five days of rodeo events such as riding, roping and bull wrestling in late March; top bull riders compete for a $100,000 purse at the Laughlin Shoot-Out in September. There is speedboat racing on the Colorado River in early June, while thousands of motorcycle enthusiasts turn up in April for an annual "rumble in the desert."

A free shuttle runs from most of the casinos to the two-story **Horizon Outlet Center** (1955 South Casino Drive, tel: 298-0081), open 9am–8pm, 10am–6pm Sundays. The center has 55 factory outlets and a food court.

As in other parts of the United States, Native American Indian tribes are looking to carve out some of the staggering profits available from gambling. The **Avi** (10000 Aha Macay Parkway, tel: 535-5555 or 800/284-2946), 9 miles (15 km) from Laughlin, is run by the Fort Mojave tribe. The hotel was the first Indian-owned casino in Nevada, and it has a Southwestern and Indian theme. In the tribal language of the Fort Mojave Indian, the name of the casino, Avi, means "something of value." ❑

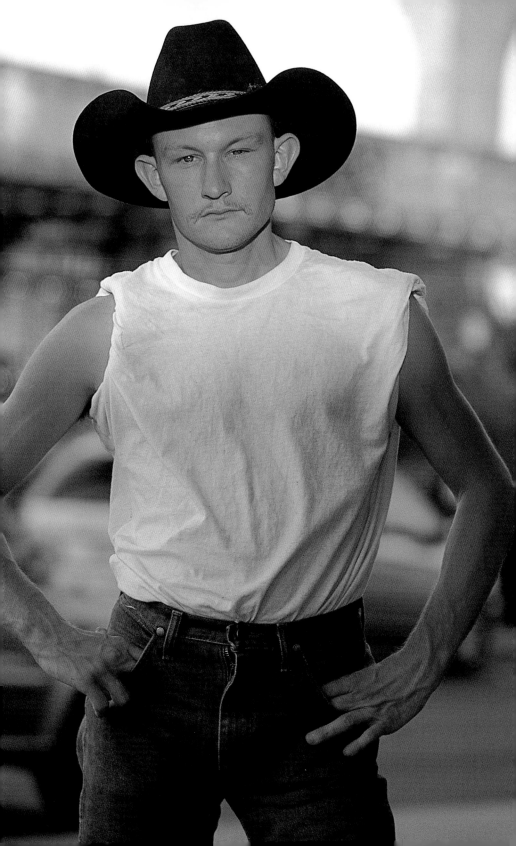

LONDON BRIDGE AND ROUTE 66

Map on page 278

Nostalgia is the name of the game on this route,
which takes in a 19th-century bridge transported from Europe,
and America's most potent reminder of the innocent 1950s

This route takes in some of the sights in the state of Arizona, starting out by the banks of the mighty Colorado River. The river, an aquatic playground in a land that averages a mere 3 inches (8 cm) of rain annually, forms the border between Nevada, California and Arizona. Retirees and snowbirds (people from wintry climates in search of winter warmth) are attracted by the year-round sunshine, carefree lifestyle, easy access to casinos and endless outdoor recreation. Thankfully, at least some of the river's extraordinary biodiversity has been protected at nearby wildlife preserves, hard-working places that maintain and preserve vital wetland habitats inhabited by migrating birds, as well as the resident flora and fauna.

Some of the chapters in this book easily combine to make tailored excursions, for instance, hooking up at Williams, Arizona for a trip to the Grand Canyon *(see page 293)*. Anyone who wants to head straight for Route 66 at Kingman from Hoover Dam *(see page 256)* and skip London Bridge entirely can stop off at one or both of the following very different sites.

LEFT: 1955 Chevy Bel-Air.
BELOW: North American lynx.

Keepers of the Wild

US 93 runs southeast from Hoover Dam to join Route 66 at Kingman. About halfway to Kingman, at milepost 27, is the **Keepers of the Wild** (tel: 928/767-4004), a tranquil 35-acre (14-hectare) animal haven for endangered species. Founder Jonathan Kraft has developed a refuge for animals which have been rescued from neglect and abuse. A deli, an ice-cream counter and a souvenir shop all help to finance the hard-working, non-profit sanctuary, which already cares for tigers, cougars, leopards, foxes and emus, among other exotic beasts.

Further south down US 93 heading towards Kingman is the turn-off to **Chloride ❶**, where the colorful mining legacy of the region is well preserved. Home to as many as 2,000 people during its 1860s boom, Chloride's name derives from the silver-chloride ore extracted from mines in the nearby Cerbat Mountains. Only a few hundred residents remain in the rustic, frontier-style buildings, but at the end of June each year the town comes alive during Old Miners Day. Festivities are marked by burro rides, a swap meet, a crafts fair and a parade. An old-time melodrama is performed at the Silverbelle Playhouse (tel: 928/565-2204) on the first and third Saturday of each month between March and May. The theater is dark during the hot summer season, then resumes productions again between September and November.

Bullhead City

Since gambling is such an integral part of this book, it would be a shame to miss out **Bullhead City ❷**, the small town connected by a bridge over the Colorado River to the flashier gambling town of Laughlin, Nevada *(see page 268)*. Many people who want to hit the tables in Laughlin actually stay in Bullhead City, as room rates are often less expensive. But the two towns are virtually intertwined. Don Laughlin, the namesake and prime mover of the gambling mecca, owns the **River Queen Motel** (tel: 800/754-3214) in Arizona, which is connected to his Riverside Hotel in Nevada by a free shuttle boat. Restaurants in both towns are supplied with steaks from the Laughlin family's ranch deep in Arizona's Hualapai Mountains.

Most years, Laughlin and Bullhead City register at least 30 days when one or the other is the hottest city in the US. A popular excursion from either town, especially during these periods, is via SR 163 to **Davis Dam** at the southern tip of Lake Mohave. From there, it's a short drive north along the Katherine Spur Road to the Lake Mojave Resort at **Katherine Landing** (tel: 928/754-3245, where there are boat rentals, eating places, places to stay and RV campgrounds. At the town of Katherine itself, a gold mine operated from about 1900, producing $12 million of ore before it closed in 1942. Steamboats navigated the river, delivering supplies to the miners and returning filled with precious ore. In the previous century, sternwheelers had operated from what is now Bullhead City, charging travelers $44 for a trip that first headed south then onwards by coach to San Francisco.

Bullhead City has two 9-hole and three 18-hole golf courses, as well as the **Colorado River History Society Museum** (tel: 928/754-3399, open Tues–Sun

BELOW:
London Bridge
was built in 1824.

9am–4pm, donations welcome.) Outside the museum is a replica of the old Katherine gold mine; inside are artifacts of the Mojave tribes, gold mine exhibits, and minerals and gemstones.

From Bullhead City, SR 95 south skirts the Fort Mojave Indian Community and gives a nod to Oatman, where Route 66 can be picked up later. For now, the destination is the improbable "instant city" of **Lake Havasu City ❸**, about 150 miles (241 km) southeast of Las Vegas. The town was developed on the Colorado River during the early 1960s by the late tycoon Robert McCulloch. McCulloch's chain-saw factory moved from here to Tucson years ago but not before his town acquired its greatest single attraction: **London Bridge**. Yes, the same arched structure built in 1824 across the River Thames in England.

Map on page 278

London Bridge is standing up

The tycoon bought London Bridge for $2.5 million in 1968. It took three years to dismantle and ship to the Arizona desert, then an additional $7 million to rebuild it on a peninsula jutting into the lake block by sequentially numbered block. Rumor has it McCulloch thought he was buying the infinitely more decorative Tower Bridge. His feelings on October 10, 1971 – the day the less-graceful London Bridge was dedicated – are not recorded.

Despite its unlikely relocation, this is an authentic piece of history: note the scars made on the stones by German fighter aircraft in World War II. Next to the 900-foot (275-meter) span is the **English Village**, a tourist-oriented promenade of shops and restaurants decked out in an "old London" theme. The city itself has thrived and become home to more than 45,000 year-round residents, including many retirees. It is also home to the **Creative Cultural Center** (tel: 928/855-

Lake Havasu is said to be the personal watercraft capital of the world. Havasu is a Native American term meaning "blue water."

BELOW: each brick on the bridge was given a number so it could be reassembled in the desert.

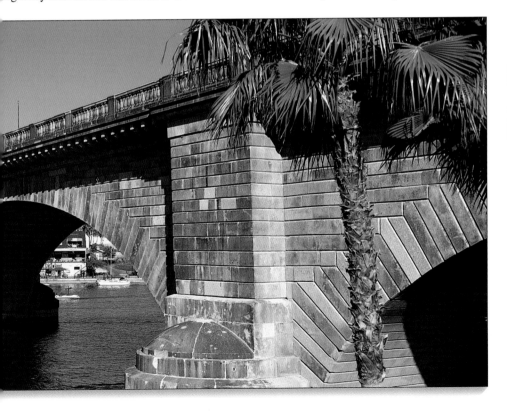

7300), which tells stories of the local Indians. A full spectrum of water recreation, golf courses, tennis courts and related services is a feature of the community. Although you can hike up nearby Crossman Peak, most of the action is on **Lake Havasu**, a 45-mile (72-km) long artificial lake ("havasu" is a Native American term meaning "blue water.")

Dubbed the "personal watercraft capital of the world," each year Lake Havasu hosts the top personal watercraft racers for the Skat-Trak Watercross World Championships. Like others in the area, this reservoir is extremely popular with the Spring Break crowd during March and April, when thousands of party-hungry college students arrive.

Angling for a catch

Anyone seeking more sedate pursuits may enjoy the angling opportunities; the lake has an abundance of striped bass, black crappie, bluegill and rainbow trout. It's also been the recipient of the largest freshwater fisheries program of its kind in the US. Since the program's inception in 1992, local anglers have reported a widespread increase in the size and quantity of the lake's Striper and largemouth bass.

Other tranquil possibilities are nearby in **Buckskin Mountain State Park**, **Bill Williams National Wildlife Refuge** and **Lake Havasu State Park**, each protecting scenic areas and key ecosystems along this stretch of the river. The parks provide a mix of boat-launch ramps, campgrounds, swimming beaches, picnic areas and hiking trails. **Parker Dam**, which impounds the Colorado River about 20 miles (32 km) south of Lake Havasu City, is not as architecturally stunning as the Hoover Dam, although workers were required to dig an amaz-

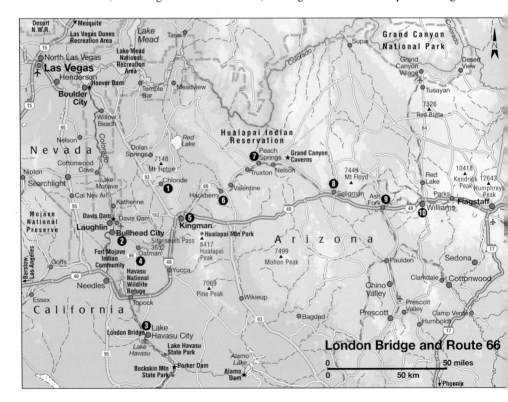

London Bridge and Route 66

ing 230 feet (70 meters) into bedrock below the river in order to make the structure secure. Free, self-guided tours are available on the west side of the dam (tel:
760/663-3712, open daily 8am–5pm.)

Map
on page
278

Route 66

Route 66, the most famous road in America, is at times overrun by Interstate 40.
But there is still enough of the old road remaining to get the feel of a by-gone
age. From Parker Dam, head north back up SR 95 to join the "Mother Road" at
the little town of **Topock**, where, were you to head west, Route 66 (and the
interstates which have been laid on top) would take you almost all the way to
Los Angeles. Instead, head north through 20 miles (32 km) of desert scrubland
to the first stop east, the town of **Oatman ❹**.

Originally a tent camp in 1906 to service the gold mine, Oatman collapsed
almost overnight when gold prices slumped. The town remains locked in the past
so far as its appearance is concerned: an ancient western town with sagging
wooden shacks lining the solitary unpaved street, on which amusing mock gun-
fights are conducted daily. Across from Fast Fanny's (clothes, sunglasses, post-
cards), a bed on wheels promotes the annual Great Oatman Bed Races which are
held during the "cool" of January (summer temperatures can reach 118° F/48°C,
which prompts an annual Sidewalk Egg Fry celebration).

*The "Main Street of
America" stretches
over eight states and
three time zones.*

More than half a million visitors come to look around Oatman every year,
many of them to attend the Gold Camp Days in September or the International
Burro Biscuit Toss on Labor Day. The miners turned their burros loose in the
mountains and there are always still a few wandering around town. Photogra-
phers love it; Oatman has been the scene of several films, including *How the*

BELOW: gunfight at
the Oatman corral.

West was Won and *Universal Soldier*. The 1926 Mission Inn, next to a sidewalk display of life-sized wooden bears, is the popular place to eat, serving wonderfully substantial, cholesterol-laden breakfasts, the sort that trendy westerners only dream about in these modern health- and diet-obsessed times.

Clark Gable slept here

The doddering 1902 **Oatman Hotel** (tel: 928/768-4408), its walls plastered with photographs, newspapers and movie posters, makes no concession to modern comforts such as television – or even water – in the rooms but is an irresistible place to stay. History rules here, not luxury. Clark Gable and Carole Lombard spent their honeymoon night in Room 15 after being married in Kingman, and the simple room is preserved as a sort of shrine (it costs around $20 extra) with pictures of the pair on the walls and a pink nightdress draped over a chair. There's a cosy bar downstairs but no food after 6pm when (for most of the year) restaurants and shops close up tight.

From Oatman (Route 66 is called "Oatman" as it leaves that town), the highway twists and winds through hills in a way which many an old Model T Ford was obliged to struggle backwards. It finally reaches the 3,652-foot (1100-meter) summit of **Sitgreaves Pass,** named, like the Beale Wagon Trail, for a mid-19th century Army surveyor. On the other side of the pass, Route 66 crosses a desolate, rocky wilderness in a series of seemingly endless switchbacks and blind curves that is laughingly known as "the fun run."

About 25 miles (40 km) northeast of Oatman is the city of **Kingman ❺**, sprawling in the brown plain of the Hualapai Valley. Established as a turquoise-mining center and railroad stop, the town now mainly serves highway travelers

BELOW: the long and occasionally winding road is part of modern American folklore.

and retirees. Kingman is where the tubby, gruff-voiced movie star Andy Devine was born, and he is much celebrated. The main street is named after him, and Devine fans should seek out the history museum *(see below)*, where an entire room is devoted to the actor. On this and the adjoining Beale Street are the oldest buildings, including the **Beale Hotel** where Clark Gable and Carole Lombard were married. Kingman's **Route 66 Museum** is in a converted powerhouse, and one of its exhibits is a recreation of a small-town Main Street, complete with 1950s yellow Studebaker car. The region's history from prehistoric times to the present is represented in the worthwhile **Mohave Museum of History and Arts** (400 W. Beale Street, tel: 928/753-3195, open Mon–Fri 9am–5pm, Sat–Sun 1–5pm). See a detailed replica of a Mohave Indian village, an impressive collection of carved turquoise and, of course, loads of stuff about Andy Devine.

Map on page 278

Get your kicks here

Adjacent to the museum is the **Kingman Visitors Center** (open Mon–Fri 8am–5pm, Sat 9am–4pm, Sun 10am–3pm), offering information about several historic sites in the area. Fourteen miles (23 km) southeast is pine-forested **Hualapai Mountain Park** (tel: 928/757-3859, fee), a pleasant enclave that rises to 8,500 feet (2,600 meters) above sea level, with scenic hiking trails, a campground and picnic areas. At **Hackberry ❻**, the owners of the general store (which doubles as a useful visitor center) have established a Bobby Troup Memorial Oasis, in memory of the author of the song *Route 66*. Good cooking can be found at the Frontier Café in **Truxton**, while the oldest operating garage on Route 66, together with some abandoned motels and the Hualapai Tribal headquarters, are in **Peach Springs ❼**.

BELOW: Kingman's museum of the Mother Road is in a coverted powerhouse.

THE MOTHER ROAD

John Steinbeck called Route 66, "The Mother Road, the road of light," and it did almost as much to bring the romance of road travel to Americans as Henry Ford himself.

Cyrus Stephens Avery, born in 1871 in Stephensville, Pa, was leader of the American Association of State Highway Officials. The group's San Francisco meeting in 1924 began the quest to link "a comprehensive system of through interstate routes." The road opened in 1927.

Winding 2,400 miles (3,862 km) from Grant Park in Chicago, Illinois to Ocean Avenue in Santa Monica, California, the tarmac ribbon stretches over eight states and three time zones. It incorporated the old Pontiac Trail, the Osage Indian Trail, the Ozark Trail, the Grand Canyon Route and the Will Rogers Highway.

The "Main Street of America" was promoted to the public by a foot race from Los Angeles not only to Chicago but on to New York with a prize of $25,000. Almost 300 runners set out on March 4, 1928 and 55 of them crossed the line 3,422 miles (5,500 km) and 87 days later. Andy Payne from Oklahoma was the winner.

The neon signs of the motor courts and motels, the diners and the old Burma-Shave signs of Route 66 are soulful symbols of modern American folk memory.

Twenty-five miles (40 km) west of Seligman is **Grand Canyon Caverns** (tel: 928/422-3224, open daily 8am–6pm, 9am–5pm in winter), into which early visitors paid 25¢ to be lowered 150 feet (45 meters) by rope. Today, there's an elevator and well-lighted paths instead of rope.

Highway history

At **Seligman ❽**, Route 66 – the solitary main street – is lined with irresistibly fascinating gift shops devoted to the highway's history. One of them is run by Myrna Delgadillo whose father, Angel, is a hero to fans of the road. The walls of his barber shop (which doubles as a **visitor center**) are covered with business cards from all over the world and a day rarely passes by without some stranger seeking him out. It was Angel who got the state's Historic Route 66 Association off the ground and revived attention in a dying Seligman after the town was bypassed by the interstate. As a poem in Arizona's *Route 66 News* phrased it.

Angel Delgadillo and his older brother Juan were stranded by the interstate/Life in Seligman was dying from malnutrition but they knew their dream couldn't wait.

Born and raised in the town, Angel is apt to reminisce about the early days, recalling that when the Okies came (Oklahoma refugees from the 1930s Dust Bowl famine), he could guess their relative wealth by how many mattresses sagged over the sides of their overloaded trucks. Angel's brother Juan operates the **Snow Cap Drive-In** next door, at the rear of which a "garden" of oddities includes two old-fashioned wooden outhouses equipped with modern plumbing. Seligman's gift shops carry every conceivable type of souvenir from US 66 highway signs, "Mother Road" license tags, oil company signs, ancient Coca

BELOW: Juan Delgadillo in his Snow Cap Drive-In; brother Angel fought for state recognition of Route 66.

Cola ads and bottles as well as the familiar inscribed mugs, glasses and T-shirts. There's a vast range of books about the road, some esoteric like the *Gas Pump Collectors' Guide* and, of course, Frank Rowsome's well-known collection called *the verse by the side of the road.*

Map
on page
278

Burma Shave signs

Everybody was sad to see the jokey, slogan-filled red-and-white Burma Shave ads disappear, as they proved to be just one more nail in the coffin of the vibrant Mother Road. As early as 1930, the company had been spending $65,000 a year on the signs, which were ranged along the road with the phrase of a jingle on each sign that could be read at driving pace.

It was not only passing drivers who enjoyed them: friendly relations had been established with hundreds of farmers on whose land the signs appeared. Although rentals rarely topped $25 per year, many farmers were so proud of the signs that they made their own repairs when necessary. Cows were generally good companions, but horses, apparently, found them to be perfect back-scratchers – until the company raised the height of the signs.

There was never a chance that Burma Shave would run out of jingles. An annual contest offering $100 for each printable slogan drew more than 50,000 entries. The company's directors would meet in not-so-solemn conclave to whittle down to the best 1,000 stanzas. Winners included handy driving hints like, *Don't take a curve/at 60 per/We hate to lose/A customer* and *Remember this/if you'd be spared/Trains don't whistle/Coz they're scared.* Of course, there were thousands of entries that were too risqué to be used, like: *Listen, Birds/These Signs Cost Money/So Roost a While/But Don't Get Funny.*

A Burma Shave sign (in the background) always lightened the journey of a traveler on the Mother Road.

BELOW: angels and snow near Williams, Arizona.

TIP

If time is tight, take the Grand Canyon Railway from Williams. Not only does this bypass all the tour buses hogging the roads to the canyon, but chugging up the mountain in a steam-driven locomotive is an evocative way to appreciate the past.

Small as it is, Seligman includes enough sites for a **20-minute walking tour**, for which a free leaflet is available at Angel Delgadillo's barber shop. Sadly, many places have burned down over the years, but visitors might care to note the 1932 **Deluxe Motel** on the main street, the Black Cat Bar (1936) at the western end of town and the boarded up, pseudo-Tudor Harvey House restaurant still standing beside the rail tracks.

Stage coaches and railroads

Somnolent **Ash Fork ❾**, a stage coach depot until the arrival of the railroad in 1882, was a regular stop along Route 66 until being bypassed by the interstate. A Confederate flag flies over the Route 66 Grill. One of the adorable Harvey Girls (waitresses in the Harvey House restaurants along the Santa Fe Railroad line) lived nearby until her death. She donated several artifacts from the defunct Harvey House chain to a fledgling museum in a huge, empty warehouse beside the tourist office.

A former railroad despatcher, Dan Ayres, who has a print shop in town, is the author of a series of "railway novels." Half a dozen sandstone companies, whose flagstone wares are piled high around the station, mine the surrounding mountains for an earth-colored stone which is shipped nationwide.

The next town has its main street on Route 66. It is named **Williams ❿**, after Bill Williams (1787–1849), an early fur trapper whose 8-foot (3-meter) statue stands at the west end of town. The excellent *Route 66 Magazine* is published here in Williams, which is also the main departure point for the Grand Canyon (*see photo on page 303*). The **Grand Canyon Railway** (tel: 800/THE TRAIN) makes a daily trip at 10:30am. The 2½-hour trip each way – by vintage steam

BELOW:
Seligman Suzy Q.
RIGHT:
buy malts and
soda pop here.

locomotives in summer, diesel locomotives the rest of the year – allows three hours at the canyon itself. Near the railroad depot is the **Fray Marcos Hotel** (tel: 928/635-4010), a now-restored rare operating unit of the once-ubiquitous Harvey House chain which an English immigrant, Fred Harvey, established in the 1880s along the route of the Santa Fe line, revolutionizing the then-abysmal standards of railway food. One of Harvey's basic rules was that the coffee – served by smiling waitresses in black dresses and spotless white aprons and bows – was remade every two hours, even if the urn was still full. For 75¢, customers could choose from seven entrées – and ask for more.

Map on page 278

Twisting the night away

A tan-colored 1953 Cadillac and lifesize cutouts of James Dean and Marilyn Monroe sit outside **Twisters**, a self-proclaimed "Back-to-the-'50s" diner which displays hundreds of snapshots of families taken on the route, along with an old glass-topped Sky Chief gasoline pump converted into a holder for Route 66 souvenirs. There's an overpowering smell of chilli and a menu offering a dozen different shakes, malts, floats and cherry phosphates. For those seeking more conventional fare, the best-known restaurant in town, **Rod's Steak House**, has been serving customers along Route 66 for more than half a century.

Farther east toward Flagstaff, Route 66 is mostly unsurfaced and not very well maintained, but it does have the distinction of containing the highest point of the route at 7,300 feet (2,225 meters) above sea level. This is about a mile or two before the town of **Parks**, where the Parks in the Pines general store has been in business for more than 80 years. From here, Route 66 becomes Interstate 40 as far as **Flagstaff**, the biggest town in northern Arizona. ❑

BELOW: making a splash.

TRAVEL IN THE DESERT

The scale of the desert is like no other, with unqiue flora and fauna. These evocative expanses can be best appreciated by following a few basic precautions

Exploring in the desert is a fabulously memorable experience, and well worth taking the time to do. The sheer scale is awesome, and the landscape, flora and fauna can rarely be seen elsewhere. It can also be very dangerous and inhospitable for the unwary or unprepared. The smallest mishap in the desert, such as a flat tire or a twisted ankle, can become life-threatening; the AAA (American Automobile Association) produces a checklist for desert driving that is always useful to have. Desert distances are vast, conditions can be harsh, and the chances of finding anyone to help are negligible. If you plan to leave the beaten track, it is a good idea to leave word with somebody, along with an estimate of your route, and when to expect you to return.

The chances of getting cellphone coverage are fairly slim, but it could save your life, so if you have a phone, make sure it's charged up and take it. Also, keep careful track of your progress on the map, using the odometer. If you have to call for help you need to be able to give your location as precisely as possible.

Writing on a website, a New Jersey resident making his first visit was surprised by some of the things that he didn't find in the desert. These included: car rentals, restaurants, hospitals, service stations, gas stations, muffler, brake or tire shops, places to get water or food, highway call boxes, cops – in fact, any other people at all. On his return, he said "we were incredibly lucky" to get back safely. Even so, he also said that he was planning a return visit.

PRECEDING PAGES: palm trees near Furnace Creek Inn, Death Valley. **LEFT:** purple prickly pear cactus. **BELOW:** a four-wheel drive vehicle is perfect for the desert.

Death Valley wheels

Any vehicle will be tested to the extreme by the temperatures and terrain, so if possible take a serious offroader with high ground clearance, four-wheel drive and large wheels. A saloon in good condition should get you there and back with no trouble, but be careful if you leave the paved highway. If wheels get stuck in sand or mud, it is often easier to get out in reverse, rather than going forward. Wood, rocks, blankets or carpets under the wheels can help to give traction. Wheels are more likely to grip when turning slowly, and spinning will make them dig deeper in, so take your time. Sometimes, deflating tires can help.

Whendriving off-road, low-tire pressure will give the best flotation and traction in soft ground, high-pressure is best for rocks and paths. Salt flats can be deceptive. A strong crust sometimes disguises soft, salty mud beneath. If in doubt, it's best to scout the area on foot first, checking the ground with a stick before driving over it.

If your vehicle does break down, your best chance is usually to stay with it. The car can help provide shelter and warmth at night, and it is easier for potential help to spot a car. Switch off the car's interior

Most desert plants have thin or tiny leaves; these retain moisture better.

BELOW: the desert responds to winter rains with generous bursts of color.

lights and anything else that might consume battery power. *In extremis*, the doors and hood can be removed and made into a shelter. In any event, keep calm. Panic can raise body temperature and cause dehydration, and water is the most precious resource. Humans can survive for up to four weeks without food, but only 7 to 10 days at most without water. If you get truly stuck, survival priorities are to conserve water and energy. Eat as little as possible, since eating makes you thirsty and takes up energy. Keep your mouth closed and breathe through your nose, and rest while the sun is up.

If you must set off from the vehicle, travel when it is coolest; before 10am and after 4pm and stick to trails that seem well traveled. Arid areas are often crisscrossed with trails that lead nowhere. Make a map before you start, marking carefully where you have been, as distances in the desert can be hard to judge.

Watering holes

If you run out of water, there is some to be found in the desert. Dry stream beds sometimes have water just below the surface. Also, near trees or green vegetation, at the base of a hill or the bottom of a canyon, there can be sources of water below the ground. Don't waste time and energy digging more than a few feet down, since some vegetation has roots that can reach 20 feet (6 meters) or more below ground level. Also be wary of the appearance of water near the horizon, as this can turn out to be a heat-haze mirage. A plastic sheet spread on the ground or under metal auto hoods may yield condensation early in the morning; if so, sponge it up with a cloth. Early in the day, you can build a solar still by digging a hole 3 feet deep by 3 feet wide (1 meter by 1 meter). Half-fill the hole with green vegetation and make it airtight by covering with a piece of

DESERT ESSENTIALS

Here are a few essential items no desert traveler should be without:

A good quality, large-scale map
A compass (best not to rely on GPS receivers alone)
A hunting knife, and a multi-tool penknife
Plenty of water (the car radiator might need some)
Dry or canned food
Matches
First-aid and snakebite kit
Iodine for first-aid and water purification
Blankets
Clothing that is light, both in weight and color
Clothing made of natural fibers that breathe, preferably loose-fitting to allow air to circulate
A shovel
Plastic sheets to help collect water
Spare gas in a safe jerry-can
Spare tire (check that it's in good condition)
Tire pump and puncture repair kit
Spare oil (some cars need a lighter oil in extreme heat)
Spare radiator hoses and belts for the motor
Basic car tools, including a jack and wheel-brace

Map on pages 236–7

plastic, anchored at the edges with stones or sand. Weight the center with a stone wrapped in cloth so that it doesn't get hot and melt the plastic. Place a tin can under where it sags to collect the condensed moisture. Two or three drops of iodine or bleach will purify a quart of water in about 30 minutes.

To attract attention, bright clothing, colorful tarps, smoke by day and fire at night can all be seen for long distances. Mirrors and shiny objects, even tin cans, can reflect the sun for a long way. Sweep the horizon occasionally in this way to attract attention.

Hiking for fun and safety

As long as safety rules are followed, careful hikers will find the Mojave Desert a generally benign and fascinating place to visit. Desert flowers, cacti and wildlife are unlike those seen elsewhere, especially if you venture off the highway.

An important rule is: never put your hands or feet into holes in the ground, cracks in the rocks or any other places where you can't see what's inside. There are many species of insects that can inflict painful or even dangerous bites, including scorpions, desert tarantulas, recluses and black widows and they hide from the heat in dark places. Additionally, the Mojave Desert sidewinder is a venomous rattlesnake, common around Las Vegas, although rarely seen. Generally, insects and reptiles leave you alone as long as you leave them alone. If they are interfered with, though, they will defend themselves, and this can include when they have been stepped on accidentally. Be sure to wear sturdy boots, and it doesn't hurt to carry a stick. If you intend to go on any type of hike, plan to take as much water as you can comfortably carry, plus lots of sunscreen, a sun hat, and the essentials listed opposite. ❑

BELOW: water on salt flats, Death Valley.

THE GRAND CANYON

*The Grand Canyon is one of the seven wonders of the world,
and nearly 5 million people a year travel to
gaze into this mighty gash in the earth*

Map
on page
294

The Grand Canyon is one of the most popular excursions for visitors from Las Vegas, and it is certainly one of the world's more spectacular natural phenomena. More than 270 miles (434 km) long and averaging 10 miles (16 km) in width, the canyon reaches depths of 5,700 feet (1,700 meters) which passes through five of the seven temperate zones, each with their own distinct ecologies. A groove cut straight into the earth, strata of red and yellow sandstone, sandwiching layers of dark granite and pale limestone plunge thousands of feet to what appears to be a trickling stream at the bottom of the fissure. Just as it takes time for a person's eyes to adjust to extremes of light and dark, those eyes begin wakening to the immense scale as you realize that that "trickling stream" is the mighty Colorado River. Everywhere is nature at its boldest and proudest – from the butterflies and squirrels, to magnificent, soaring eagles. The Grand Canyon can make a frantic, darting rubbernecker out of any newcomer, but a sagacious forest ranger advises, "If you keep your head still, you'll see everything that moves."

The region became a national park in 1919, but it had been widely known well before that, discovered by a member of explorer Coronado's 1540 expedition. Army Lieutenant Joseph Ives claimed in 1857 to have been in the first and, he said at the time, he "will doubtless be the last party of whites to visit this profitless locality." He declared the region "valueless" and said that after entering there was nothing left to do but leave. Nevertheless, in 1869 geologist John Wesley Powell, a one-armed Civil War veteran, led a four-boat flotilla on an exploration of the Green and Colorado rivers. On a subsequent expedition, Powell, who later went on to head the Bureau of Ethnology, was accompanied by photographer John K. Hillers, and his pictures of the mighty canyon captured the world's imagination.

LEFT: hikers can choose a rigorous or an easy trail.
BELOW: parts of the Inner Canyon are similar to the desert.

Getting there

Tour companies from Vegas conduct excursions to, flights over, boats along and helicopters through the Grand Canyon. By road, it is a day's drive from Las Vegas, whether you go northeast and then south via Interstate 15 and then SR389 to Fredonia, or head south on US93 to Kingman, then east on Interstate 40 to Williams. Williams is the departure point for the Grand Canyon Railway *(see pages 284–5)*, which is a very pleasant way to arrive at the canyon, avoiding the crowds on the road. If you're driving from Williams, continue north on SR 64 and follow I-180.

Some tour companies offer the round trip in one hurried day from Vegas and back. Scenic air tours are expensive, but they usually fly out over the Hoover Dam and along, if not in, the canyon itself. The depar-

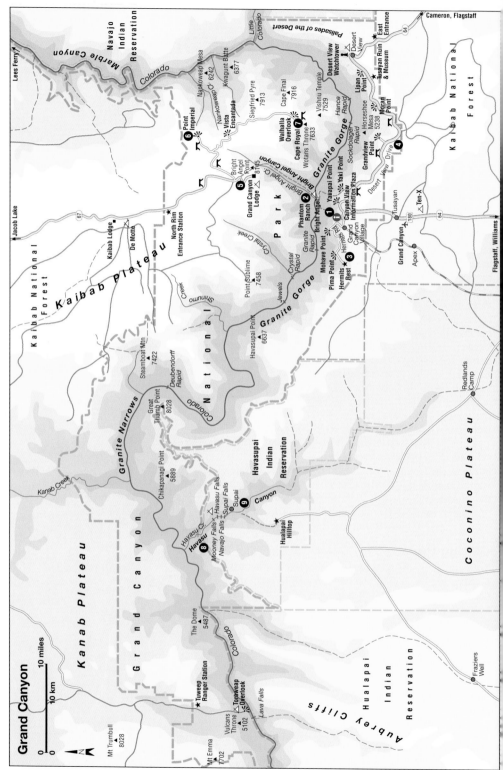

Grand Canyon

ture for all boat trips "down the Grand," as the boatmen say, is 15 miles (24 km) below Glen Canyon Dam at **Lees Ferry**, upstream from the mouth of the Paria River. A rigorous four-day hike goes upstream through spectacular **Paria Canyon Narrows** where sheer sandstone walls only 150 feet (46 meters) apart rise 1,000 feet (300 meters) high.

Map on page 294

Ancient elements

The ancients spoke of four basic elements – earth, water, wind and fire. But at the Grand Canyon, another element must be added – light. It is light that brings the canyon to life, bathing the buttes and highlighting the spires, infusing color and adding dimension, creating beauty that takes your breath away. Where else are sunrise and sunset the two biggest events of any day? In early morning and late afternoon, the oblique rays of sunlight, sometimes filtered through clouds, set red rock cliffs on fire and cast abysses into purple shadow.

The canyon is rightfully one of the seven wonders of the world. Nearly 5 million people a year arrive at its edge and gaze down into this yawning gash in the earth. But the approach to the canyon gives no hint of what awaits. The highway passes a sweeping land of sagebrush and grass, through dwarf pinyon and juniper woodland, and into a forest of tall ponderosa pines. Then, suddenly, the earth falls away at your feet. Before you stretches an immensity that is almost incomprehensible.

The canyon is negative space – it's composed as much by what's not there as what is. After taking time to soak in the scene, eyes rove down to the bottom, where the Colorado River appears to trickle like a stream. Though it looks small from this elevation, 7,000 feet (2,100 meters) above sea level, it is in fact, one

Frolicking in a canyon stream after a tough trail hike.

BELOW:
air tours from
Vegas fly over
Hoover Dam and
into the canyon.

*People's reactions to
their first sight of the
Grand Canyon vary.
Some burst into
tears. Some laugh
with delight. One
visitor said, "I never
wanted a drink so
bad in my life."*

of the great rivers of the West. And, unbelievable though it may seem, the river is the chisel that has carved the Grand Canyon. The Colorado rushes through the canyon for 277 miles (446 km), wild and undammed. Over several million years, it's been doing what rivers do – slowly but surely eroding the canyon to the present depth of 1 mile (2 km).

To the east, the scalloped skyline of the Palisades of the Desert defines the canyon rim. To the north, about 10 miles (16 km) as the hawk flies, is the flat-lying forested North Rim. To the west, the canyon's cliffs and ledges, cusps and curves extend as far as the eye can see, with only distant indigo mountains, nearly in Utah, breaking the horizon. **Grand Canyon National Park** is more than a million acres (400,000 hectares) of land, and this view encompasses only about a quarter of the entire canyon.

People's reactions to their first sight of the Grand Canyon vary. Some are speechless. Some are brought to tears. Still others, such as early visitor Gertrude B. Stevens, have been overcome in other ways: "I fainted when I saw this awful looking cañon," she declared. "I never wanted a drink so bad in my life."

But with more than the average four-hour stay, a person can begin to explore the minutia of this miraculous place, savoring different moods throughout the hours of the day, as the light constantly changes the face of the canyon.

South Rim

BELOW: mule deer
grazing at the
South Rim.

Most visitors first see the Grand Canyon from the **South Rim**, the area that is open all year round and offers the most accommodation. The best place to start is at the **Canyon View Information Plaza ❶**, accessible by free shuttle bus. This open, spacious center features wall-size maps, exhibits and books that set

the canyon in a larger context and help orient visitors. Rangers there can answer specific questions. From the plaza, it's a short stroll out to **Mather Point**, for that virgin glimpse of the canyon. Back at the plaza, buses run at frequent intervals all day to the many overlooks along the rim. Other buses go to trailheads to drop off day hikers and backpackers.

Map on page 294

By extending the public transportation system, the National Park Service is aiming to get people out of their cars, and get cars and development away from the rim, seeking to restore that invigorating sense of discovery. Now, the ravens are taking back their rightful place, soaring over the dizzying abyss and croaking their calls of greeting.

The historic buildings on the rim, most of them of native stone and timber, will stay in place, however. One is the **Yavapai Observation Station**, on the next point west of Mather. One entire wall of this small museum and bookstore is glass, affording a stupendous view into the heart of the canyon – slices of the Colorado River, a 1928 suspension bridge, Bright Angel Campground and **Phantom Ranch ❷**, tucked at the very bottom.

Hermits Road

From here, a paved path along the rim leads to the village area, where shuttle buses head out along the 8-mile (13-km) **Hermits Road ❸** (which is also called **West Rim Drive**). Constructed in 1912 as a scenic drive, it offers several overlooks along the way. At Trailview Point, you can look back at the village and the Bright Angel Trail switchbacking down to the river. Indian Garden, a hikers' campground shaded by cottonwoods, is visible 4½ miles (7 km) down the trail. The Bright Angel Fault has severed the otherwise continuous cliff layers that

BELOW:
dawn at Yaki Point, South Rim.

TIP

First-time hikers need to pace themselves accordingly. Descending into the Grand Canyon is the reverse of climbing a mountain; the longest haul comes at the end, when muscles are tired and feet are sore.

block travel in the rest of the canyon, providing a natural route for hikers. In the morning, mule trains plod into the canyon, bearing excited greenhorns who may wish they'd gone on foot before the day is done. The trail is also the route of a pipeline that pumps water from springs on the north side up to the South Rim. The benefit of that reliable water supply makes the **Bright Angel Trail** favored among canyon hikers, especially in the heat of summer. But be aware that flash floods have been known to wash out parts of the trail and the pipeline, hampering delivery of that most precious commodity in this semi-arid land.

Infinite complexity

Other recommended points along Hermits Road are **Hopi**, **Mohave** and **Pima**. From each vista different isolated buttes and "temples" present themselves. There is the massive formation called the Battleship, best seen from **Maricopa Point**. There's Isis and Osiris, Shiva and Brahma. These overblown names were bestowed by Clarence Dutton, an erudite geologist with the early US Geological Survey and protégé of Major John Wesley Powell. Dutton's classical education inspired names with this Far East flavor. He wrote that all the canyon's attributes, "the nobility of its architecture, its colossal buttes, its wealth of ornamentation, the splendor of its colors, and its wonderful atmosphere… combine with infinite complexity to produce a whole which at first bewilders and at length overpowers."

At **Mohave Point** on a still day, you can hear the muffled roar of crashing waves in Granite and Hermit rapids on the Colorado. With binoculars, it may be possible to spy boaters bobbing downriver in rubber rafts. The road ends at **Hermits Rest** with a gift shop, a concession stand and restrooms. This is also

BELOW: Native American crafts at the Hopi House, South Rim.

Map on page 294

where hikers head down the **Hermit Trail**, one of the more accessible back-country trails beyond the main corridors of Bright Angel and South Kaibab. It's about 8 miles (13 km) down Hermit Canyon to a lovely streamside camp for overnight hikers.

The Santa Fe Railway built the camp as a destination for tourists who arrived on mules, while supplies were shuttled 3,000 feet (900 meters) down a cable from the rim. In those days, according to author George Wharton James, the camp furnished accommodation "to meet the most fastidious demands." The "hermit" was a Canadian prospector named Louis D. Boucher, who settled at an idyllic spot called Dripping Springs, off the Hermit Trail. Known for his flowing white beard and a white mule named Calamity Jane, Louis kept mostly to himself. He prospected a few mining claims, escorted tourists now and then, and by all accounts grew amazing fruits and vegetables down in the canyon.

Desert View Drive

Returning to the village, another road, **Desert View Drive ❹**, follows the canyon rim for 25 miles (40 km) to the east. Overlooks along the way display still more spectacular canyon scenery. From **Yaki Point**, the panorama includes the massive beveled surface of **Wotans Throne**, and beside it graceful, pointed **Vishnu Temple**. The other main hiking route, the popular **South Kaibab Trail**, departs from near Yaki Point, snaking down the side of **O'Neill Butte** through a break in the Redwall Limestone, down to Bright Angel Campground and Phantom Ranch.

Farther east, **Grandview Point** looks down on **Horseshoe Mesa**, site of early copper mines. The **Grandview Trail** starts here, built by miners to reach the ore.

BELOW: trips by mule or horse can be taken into the canyon.

But even a short walk will reveal that no matter how pure the ore, hauling it out was not a profitable enterprise. Grandview was among the first destinations for early tourists to the canyon, who stayed at Pete Berry's Grandview Hotel. One of the regulars there was old John Hance. He arrived at the canyon in the 1880s and built a cabin near **Grandview**.

For a time, John worked an asbestos mine on the north side of the river but quickly realized that working the pockets of "dude" visitors was more lucrative. "Captain" Hance regaled rapt listeners with tales of how he dug the Grand Canyon, how he snowshoed across to the North Rim on the clouds, and other fanciful yarns. His stamp remains on the canyon – there is a Hance Creek and Hance Rapid, and the **Old** and **New Hance Trails**, rugged routes that drop down into the canyon from Desert View Drive.

Don't feed the wildlife

In addition to great views and good stories, the drive in this area also gives a look at stands of wonderful old ponderosa pines. These cinnamon-barked giants grow back from the rim, here benefiting from slightly higher elevation and increased moisture. Their long silky needles glisten in the sunlight, and a picnic beneath their boughs is a delight. Grazing mule deer and boisterous Steller's jays may be your companions, along with busy rock squirrels looking for handouts. Resist the temptation; feeding wildlife is dangerous to them and strictly prohibited. The trees growing on the very brink of the rim are Utah junipers and pinyon pines. Sculpted by the wind, they cling to the shallow, rocky soil, never attaining great heights, though they can be very old. The warm, dry air rising up from the canyon explains their presence.

BELOW: be alert to sidewinder rattlesnakes.

In certain good years, pinyon pines produce delicious, edible brown seeds. People gather them, and so do many small mammals and birds. One bird – the dusky-blue pinyon jay – shares an intimate relationship with the tree. The jays glean nuts from the sticky cones, eating some and caching others. Inevitably, some of the nuts are forgotten and grow into young pinyon pines.

Map on page 294

North side

From the lodge, a short trail goes to **Bright Angel Point ❺**. Though you're still looking at the same canyon, the north side's greater depth and intricacy are immediately apparent. This is due partly to the Grand Canyon's asymmetry: the Colorado River did not cut directly through the middle of the Kaibab Plateau but slightly off-center to the south. Also because of its greater height and southward tilt, more water flows into the canyon here than away from it as on the South Rim. Thus the northern side canyons are longer and more highly eroded. The **North Kaibab Trail** along **Bright Angel Creek**, for example, is 14 miles (23 km) long, twice the distance of the corresponding trail on the south side. While many people take the North Kaibab all the way down to the river for overnight stays, this trail also lends itself to wonderful day hikes. Other shorter walks on the rim include the **Transept, Widforss** and **Ken Patrick Trails**.

A drive out to **Point Imperial ❻** and to **Cape Royal ❼**, on the only other paved road, are well worth the time. At 8,800 feet (2,700 meters), Point Imperial is the highest prominence on either rim of the canyon. Its eastward-facing view showcases Mount Hayden, Kwagunt Butte and Nankoweap Mesa in the **Marble Canyon** portion of Grand Canyon. From there, the road goes out to **Cape Royal**, where it ends. Clarence Dutton also named this promontory; his

Coyotes in the canyon are sometimes heard at sunset.

BELOW: Desert View Watch Tower.

description of sunset there strains even his exuberant prose: "What was grand before has become majestic, the majestic becomes sublime, and ever expanding and developing, the sublime passes beyond the reach of our faculties and becomes transcendent."

Into the canyon

With the first step down into the Grand Canyon, the horizontal world of the rims turns decidedly vertical. A walk down a trail, even for a short distance, is really the only way to begin to gain a fuller appreciation of the canyon's great magnitude and antiquity.

A word to the wise, though. Adequate preparation for this backcountry experience is essential. A Grand Canyon trek is the reverse of hiking in mountains: the descent comes first, followed by the ascent, when muscles are tired and blisters are starting to burn. And no matter what trail you follow, the climb out is always a long haul against gravity – putting one foot in front of the other and setting mind against matter. For first-time hikers, the maintained corridor trails are highly recommended: the Bright Angel, or the South or North Kaibab. Also be aware that all overnight hikes require a Park Service permit, whereas day hikes do not.

There are two other critical considerations – heat and water. As you descend into the canyon, you pass from a high-elevation, forested environment into desert. Temperatures in the inner canyon are routinely 20 degrees warmer than the rim – from June to September that means upwards of 110° to 120° F (43° to 49° C) when deep below. That kind of unrelenting, energy-sapping heat, coupled with a shortage of water, can spell disaster for the unprepared. In summer, each

BELOW: cowboy on a lonesome trail.

Map on page 294

person should carry – and drink – a minimum of a gallon (4 liters) of water apiece. Along with water, a hiker should eat plenty of high-energy foods and take frequent rest stops. A hat, sunscreen and sunglasses are necessary items. To avoid the extreme heat, hike in early morning and early evening. Or avoid summer altogether and go in spring or fall, which are the best times for an extended canyon hike.

The Inner Canyon

Dropping below the rims into the canyon's profound silence, you enter the world of geologic time. Recorded in the colorful rock layers is a succession of oceans, deserts, rivers, and mountains, along with hordes of ancient life forms that have come and gone. The cap rock of the rims, the Kaibab Limestone, is 250 million years old, and is the youngest layer of rock in the Grand Canyon. Every layer beneath it is progressively older, down to the deepest, darkest inner sanctum of black schist; metamorphic rock that is transformed through massive heat and pressure, that rings in at close to 2 billion years.

As you put your nose up against the outcrop, you'll notice that this creamy-white limestone is chock-a-block with sponges, shells and other marine fossils that reveal the origin in a warm, shallow sea. The next obvious thick layer is the Coconino Sandstone. Its sweeping crossbeds document the direction of the wind across what were once sand dunes as extensive as those in today's Sahara Desert. It isn't hard to imagine this, because already, even in this first mile of the trail, the canyon begins to look and smell like the desert – dry, dusty and drenched with sun. Beneath the Coconino is the Hermit Shale – soft, red mudstone that formed in a lagoon environment. Underlying the Hermit is the mas-

The Grand Canyon Railway resumed running in 1989, after a 21-year absence. The day excursion allows about three hours at the canyon.

BELOW: Grand Canyon Railway leaves from Williams, Arizona.

sive Supai Formation, 600 feet (180 meters) thick in places, the compressed remains of mucky swamp bottom 300 million years past. The Redwall Limestone is always a milestone on a Grand Canyon hike, passable only where a break has eroded in the 500-foot (150-meter) high cliffs. Beneath the Redwall are the Muav Limestone, Bright Angel Shale, and Tapeats Sandstone – a suite of strata that indicate the presence of, respectively, yet another ocean, its nearshore, and its beach.

Throughout most of the canyon, the tan Tapeats reclines atop the shining iron-black Vishnu Schist, the basement of the Grand Canyon and arguably its most provocative rock. At the bottom, embraced in the walls of schist, are the tumbling, swirling waters of the Colorado River, the maker of this, its greatest canyon. The river, aided by slurries of rock and water sluicing down tributary canyons, has taken only a few million years to gnaw down into the plateau to expose almost 2 billion years of earth history.

Soak hot feet in the cool water. Listen to boulders grinding into gravel on their way to the sea. Consider these old rocks in this young canyon. Ponder our ephemeral existence in the face of deep time.

Havasu Canyon

Havasu ❽, a side canyon in the western Grand Canyon, has been called a "gorge within a gorge." Within it flow the waters of **Havasu Creek**, lined with emerald cottonwood trees and grapevines and punctuated by travertine falls and deep turquoise pools, paradise in the midst of the searing desert of the Grand Canyon. A visit is an unforgettable experience, a gentle introduction to the Grand Canyon and to the Havasupai Indians, the "people of the blue-green

BELOW: raft trips can be organized from Las Vegas.

Map on page 294

water," who have made their home in this spot for at least seven centuries.

Getting there is no easy matter. The journey requires a 62-mile (100-km) drive north of Route 66 (about 190 miles/300 km from the South Rim) to a remote trailhead, then an 8-mile (13-km) hike or horseback ride to the small village of **Supai** ❾ on the canyon bottom.

Shangri-la

The pace at Supai is slow and easy. Development is limited to a small café, general store, post office, school, tourist lodge and tribal museum. Mail and supplies arrive by mule or horse (and these days by helicopter and Internet). In past times, the Havasupai partook of what the land offered. Evidence is seen along the trail in large rock piles, the pits used year after year for roasting the sweet stalks of agave. In their rocky homeland are distinctive natural features that hold great significance to the Havasupai. Rising high above the village is a pair of sandstone pillars known as Wigleeva. To the Havasupai, these are their guardian spirits; as long as they are standing, the people are safe.

About 1½ miles (2.5 km) beyond the village is the first of the famous waterfalls – **Navajo Falls**. A short distance beyond is 100-foot-high (30-meter) **Havasu Falls** and the campground. The trail continues on to **Mooney Falls**, known as the Mother of the Waters to the Havasupai. To go farther down canyon requires a steep descent next to the falls on a water-slickened cliff face, with the aid of a chain railing. It's another 3 miles (5 km) to **Beaver Falls**, a popular day hike for boaters coming up from the river to frolic in the beautiful pools. Those who make the journey know why Havasu is often called the Shangri-la of the Grand Canyon. ❑

BELOW:
Havasu Falls,
Havasu Canyon.

DEATH VALLEY AND THE MOJAVE DESERT

Despite being one of the harshest environments on the planet, over 900 species of plants, birds and animals manage to survive in these arid expanses

Map on page 308

O ne of the lowest spots on earth and a merciless environment, Death Valley is a unique experience: vast bowls of dry-red sand and rock, blue and cold desert nights, yucca and Joshua trees, and even tiny clumps of hardy human habitation. An almost alien landscape makes the force of life that survives here all the more admirable. Two varieties of a tenacious bird species, Costa's hummingbird and the blackchinned hummingbird – of the family *trochilidae* – are at home in these arid parts. They can be found in washes, chaparral and dry canyons around dry riverbeds in the Mojave Desert. Costa's hummingbird is about 3 inches (76 cm) long with a glistening amethyst head, a green luminescent back and dark green tail feathers.

The blackchinned hummingbird is about the same size, and the male has an iridescent violet band around its neck that often appears black. These amazing birds flap their wings more than 70 times a second with enough force to allow them to hover, fly backward, side-to-side and even upside down. They can use spider webs to make their nests, in which they lay pea-size eggs. Hummingbirds seek out bright flowers on which to feed, and most often prefer red blossoms. These include Chuparosa, Bigelow Mimulus and Giant Four-O'-Clocks.

Pahrump

Heading south down the Las Vegas Strip and onto SR 160, then beyond the turn-off for Red Rock Canyon for an hour's drive will bring you to **Pahrump ❶**, 62 miles (100 km) west of Las Vegas, and a good stopping point on the way to Death Valley.

The name Pahrump is a Paiute Indian word that means "big springs," or "water rock," and big they are – the town sits above America's largest aquifer, estimated at over 200 feet (60 meters) in average depth. This fertile area accounts for the only winery in Nevada, the **Pahrump Valley Winery** (tel: 775/727-5900), which conducts tasting sessions and free tours most afternoons. Open to visitors daily 10am–4:30pm, the winery has a restaurant offering live music on weekends and in October, celebrates a Grape Stomp and Jazz Festival.

Pahrump also has a speedway (tel: 775/727-7172) with go-cart racing and occasional stock-car rallies. Nearby are two golf courses: **Willow Creek Golf Course** (775/727-4653), set in the middle of 10 lakes, and **Lakeview Executive Golf Course** (775/727-5388), whose 82 acres (33 hectares) house seven lakes. The town is known to radio listeners across America as the home of talk-show host Art Bell,

LEFT:
the barren salt flats of Badwater, Death Valley.
BELOW:
be sure to gas up before you go.

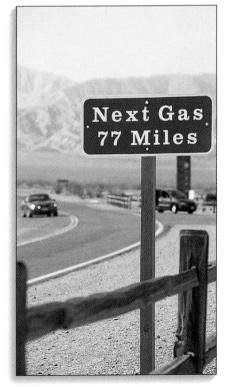

Next Gas 77 Miles

whose program is syndicated to over 530 stations and deals with UFOs and other offbeat subjects. Accommodation includes a **Best Western** (1101 South Highway 160, tel: 775/727-5100 or 800/528-1234); also **Terrible's Lakeside** (Homestead and Thousandaire, tel: 775/751-7770) with 167 spaces for RVs in campgrounds beside a lake offering canoeing, paddleboating, swimming and fishing, and the **Saddle West Hotel Casino** (tel: 800/433-3987) with 80 RV spaces and a 24-hour cafe.

Pahrump Nugget (tel: 775/751-6500) on the main street has a steakhouse, buffet and coffee shop, while the **Mountain View Casino** (tel: 775/727-7777) has a restaurant, a bowling alley and a lounge. **Terrible's Town Casino** (tel: 775/751-7777) has a 24-hour restaurant, a food court and a Sports Book, in case you're there and fancy a flutter on Super Bowl weekend.

Two surprisingly elegant brothels nestle discreetly out of town along Homestead Road. Nevada law allows prostitution. It is the only state in the US to do so, and only in counties with populations less than 200,000, though some coun-

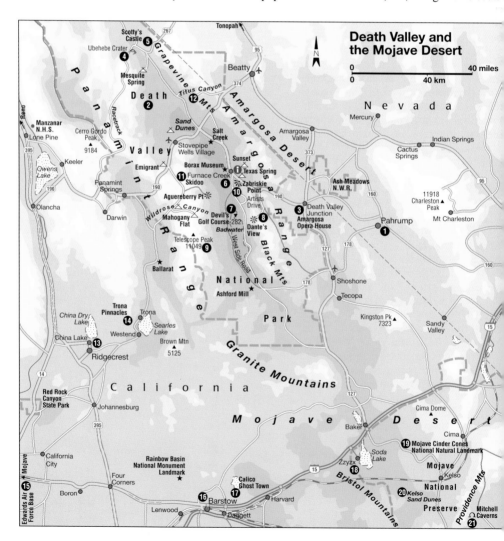

Death Valley and the Mojave Desert

0   40 miles
0   40 km

ies eschew the option. In all, there are around 25 legal establishments in the state. Soliciting is illegal in any public place in Nevada, as is any form of advertising of prostitution, though legal brothels are listed in the Yellow Pages.

Twenty-four miles (38 km) northwest of Pahrump, the **Ash Meadows National Wildlife Refuge**, with its crystal-clear springs and streams, is a popular place for bird watchers.

From Pahrump, you can drive north and then west to SR 190 which leads to Furnace Creek in Death Valley, or take SR 372 and then SR 178 down to the tiny community of **Shoshone** with another entrance into the park. Shoshone calls itself "the oasis where Death Valley began." During the 1920s, tourists arrived here on the Tonopah and Tidewater Railroad. The **Shoshone Inn** (tel: 760 852-4335) has a pool and there's a general store and museum. The route back to Las Vegas is via Tecopa and the Old Spanish Trail Highway. **Tecopa**, named after local Indians, is where several hundred camping sites adjoin a mineral hot springs. Nearby opal beds, cliff-side amethysts and petrified wood have been attracting an increasing number of gemologists and rock hounds. A short diversion could be made from Tecopa to the **China Ranch Date Farm**, a working family ranch in the middle of cottonwood trees.

Death Valley

The fearsome reputation of **Death Valley National Park ➋**, first established as a national monument in 1933, seems to attract as many as it intimidates. The valley, and in particular, **Badwater**, at 282 feet (86 meters) below sea level, is the lowest spot on dry land in the US. The daily high average temperature in July of 116° F (47° C) is exceeded only in the Libyan Sahara Desert. Temperature

Map on page 308

Help Smokey the Bear by putting out all matches and campfires.

BELOW: the road to nowhere through Death Valley.

highs commonly pass 120° F (49° C). May to October is one continuous heat wave, yet hikers and naturalists come to visit all year long. From autumn through spring, however, the climate is ideal for exploring, with daytime temperatures ranging between 60° to 70° F (about 15 to 25° C). Skies are usually bright.

Despite the harshness of Death Valley's environment, about 900 different species of plants grow here, some throwing down roots 10 times the height of a man. After the spring rains, the valley blooms with desert star, poppies, verbena and evening primrose, which can be admired at lower elevations between mid-February and mid-April. From then until early May, the most blooms of lupins and daisies can be found between 2,000 and 4,000 feet (610 to 1220 meters) in the Panamint Range. Above 4,000 feet (1220 meters), blooming time lasts into the month of June.

Once upon a time

This 120-mile long (193-km) valley is the result of a geological phenomenon. At least 5 million years ago the deep gap between the Funeral and the Panamint mountains was created by earthquakes, and the folding of the earth's crust created technically not a valley, but what geologists call a *graben*. When the vast, cool sea created by the Ice Age evaporated, the alternating layers of mud and salt were cut off from cooling breezes by the surrounding mountains, and this basin 4 to 16 miles (6 to 26 km) wide was left to parch with an annual rainfall of less than 2 inches (50 mm).

Virtually all the water supply for Furnace Creek and other desert areas comes from the underground aquifer that dates back to the last Ice Age, a non-renewable resource which will eventually run dry.

BELOW: the improbable Amargosa Opera House.

Map
on page
308

Coming from Pahrump, the key spot to head for is **Death Valley Junction** on California SR 190, where the remarkably decorated and equally improbable **Amargosa Opera House ❸** (tel: 760/852-4441) has Saturday night performances and 12 basic hotel rooms. Be sure to book tickets ahead, as the opera house can get surprisingly busy. From here, SR 190 leads to Furnace Creek. Alternatively, if you're coming from Beatty, Nevada on US 95, take SR 374 down to **Stovepipe Wells Village** (tel: 760/786-2387) where there's a service station and an 81-room hotel, complete with pool and RV facilities. To the north are two of the park's main attractions. The first is the **Ubehebe Crater ❹**, a kind of inverse volcano, a crater 500-feet (152-meters) deep formed by a giant explosion of trapped steam around 4,000 years ago.

Castle in the desert

The second is **Scotty's Castle ❺** (tel: 760/786-2325), a 25-room recreation of a Spanish-Mediterranean villa. The palace was started in 1926 and completed in 1931, and it is now Death Valley's biggest visitor attraction. The castle is operated by the National Park Service, who run hourly tours. During its construction the castle employed 2,000 workmen, all at the expense of a young Chicago millionaire, Albert Johnson. He had been charmed into investing thousands of dollars in a fruitless search for gold by Walter Scott, an affable roustabout popularly known as "Death Valley Scott."

Despite years of patience for no reward of a successful gold strike, Johnson built his summer retreat in the valley, generously making room for his dubious prospector friend, Scott, and filling the castle with beautiful continental furnishings and *objets d'art*. The Chicago financier and his wife lived at the cas-

BELOW: murals on walls inside the opera house, Death Valley Junction.

tle for many years off and on, until Johnson's death in 1948. Scott died in 1954 and is buried along a trail just behind the castle. To make the tour a more authentic experience, park rangers dress up in period clothes of the 1930s.

The **Visitor Center** at **Furnace Creek** ❻ (tel: 800/365-2267) is open daily all year round. The very elegant **Furnace Creek Inn** (tel: 760/786-2362), with two swimming pools and three restaurants, was built in 1927 by the Pacific Coast Borax Company. It has an 18-hole golf course which is – like most things in the valley – the lowest on earth. As you tee off on the 9th hole, you can call in your lunch order and, at the next hole, drive your cart up a ramp for collection to eat at one of the outdoor tables.

Devil makes a hole-in-one

Caddies are not available in the valley's other links, the **Devil's Golf Course** ❼, an otherworldly expanse of rugged salt crystals which lies between the former site of the Eagle Borax mill, southwest of Badwater, and the borax works just north of Furnace Creek. At the latter, the **Harmony Borax Works**, an old cleanser-processing plant has been restored to illustrate to visitors the 19th-century manufacturing method.

Beginning in 1873, borax – a white, crystalline substance made into soap and used as a flux, cleansing agent and antiseptic – was a major product of the valley. It was transported out by wagons, then hauled by 20-mule team for 165 miles (265 km) to Mojave. The company established resting stations, and provided water tanks and feed boxes every 16 miles (25 km). Eventually the price of borax was undercut by producers in Italy, and the Death Valley borax companies shut down operations.

BELOW: the elegant Furnace Creek Inn.

Overlooking Badwater to the east is **Dante's View** (5,475 feet/1,669 meters) and in the west, **Telescope Peak** ❾, the highest point in the Panamint Range (11,049 feet/3,368 meters). Among Death Valley's other natural beauty spots are **Zabriskie Point** ❿, southeast of Furnace Creek in the Black Mountains and made famous in the late 1960s by a movie of the same name directed by Michelangelo Antonioni; **Artists Drive**, and the **Golden Canyon**, with vivid displays of color among old outcroppings.

Death Valley's human population of 200 or so are indomitable to say the least, enduring terrific heat and isolation. The nearest big community is Las Vegas, 140 miles (225 km) away, but there are now grocery stores and gas stations only 60 miles (96 km) away in Pahrump. Local television reception is mediocre. One compensation for all this isolation is the glorious sunrises – look east toward the Amargosa Range. Sunsets are best from Dante's View, Zabriskie Point and Badwater.

23 Skidoo

A now-deserted mining town off Emigrant Canyon Road was **Skidoo** ⓫, its name derived from the phrase "23 Skidoo." (The town was 23 miles/37 km from Telescope Peak.) Skidoo is famous for its "million dollar slope" from which $1 million in gold ore was taken early in the 20th century – "it could be scraped out in wheelbarrows," boasted its former owner.

But Skidoo has found even more of a place in legend as "the town that hanged its killer twice," after an incident in which a drunken saloon keeper killed a popular town banker. Skidoo's citizens were wary of what kind of justice might be administered from the nearest lawmen at Lone Pine, so they took it upon

Map on page 308

Zabriskie Point lookout is a short distance uphill from the parking area.

BELOW:
Zabriskie Point became famous because of a 1969 art-house movie of the same name.

Native Americans utilized every bit of the Mojave yucca, making rope from the leaves, eating the petals and grinding the seeds into meal.

BELOW: guest bedroom, Scotty's Castle **RIGHT:** Main Hall, Scotty's Castle.

themselves to hang the killer. The next day – when a reporter from the *Los Angeles Herald* arrived, they dug up the body and hanged the man again so the newsman could get a headline-grabbing picture.

Unlikely as it may seem, parts of Death Valley are extremely popular with hikers, in particular the steep and narrow **Titus Canyon ⑫**, off SR 374 a few miles before Beatty in Nevada. The deserted ghost town of **Leadfield** can be inspected along the way. A narrow, dirt road winds through the canyon which the park service suggests should be negotiated with a four-wheel drive, or in a vehicle with a high ground clearance. Other hiking and backpacking trails include the 5-mile (8-km) round trip from Golden Canyon to Zabriskie Point; the 2 mile (3 km) round trip to the **Keane Wonder Mine** (which can be visited and is located off the Beatty Cut-Off Road, 16 miles/26 km northeast of the Visitor Center); and the 14½-mile (23-km) round trip through **Mosaic Canyon** off SR 190, just west of Stovepipe Wells.

Ghost town

State Route 190 runs into the Panamint Range, some of whose rugged canyons bustled with life in 1873. The now-abandoned town of **Panamint** came into being when the robbers of a Wells Fargo express discovered silver while hiding out in Surprise Canyon. Persuading two state senators to make a deal with the stage-coach company in return for part-ownership of the silver lode, they presided over an instant boom town with stores, saloons, boarding houses and banks – all along a main street that occupied the entire width of the narrow canyon. Within a year the boom was over but, perhaps with their own past careers in mind, the canny miners cast their silver in the form of 700-lb (318 kg)

cannon balls in order to ship out booty, a burden too heavy for robbers to carry away. Indian Ranch Road, an unpaved track off the Trona-Wildrose road and which forks off up Surprise Canyon, continues down to **Ballarat**. Only crumbling adobe walls and ruined shacks remain here of what was a supply town for the miners, to which the stagecoach used to run all the way from Johannesburg. Sixty-five miles (105 km) northwest on SR136, then a little farther north on US 395 is **Lone Pine**, a picturesque village that has been a popular location for Hollywood westerns.

Map on page 308

China Lake ⑬ is a dry basin to the south, near Ridgecrest and off US 395. It is best known as the focus of the important China Lake Naval Weapons Center. Near the main gate of the naval station is the small **Maturango Museum**, open on Saturday and Sunday afternoons.

The museum occasionally conducts public field trips for the study of aboriginal rock inscriptions found nearby, as they are perhaps the best such collection in the state. As a result of discoveries at China Lake, some scientists are beginning to say that humans migrated from Asia at least 40,000 years ago, and perhaps as long as 100,000 years ago.

Spooky stone spires

Not far from China Lake are the **Trona Pinnacles ⑭**. This great pincushion of ancient limestone columns in the middle of the Mojave Desert is both rare and bizarre. The spooky stone spires are "national natural landmarks," probably the most outstanding example of tufa formations in North America and a challenging moonscape for hikers and rock climbers.

The tufa Trona Pinnacles are situated on the west side of the bleakly awe-

BELOW:
Scotty's Castle took 2,000 workmen five years to build.

some **Searles Lake**, access to which is via State Highway 178 north from Johannesburg. Camping is permitted at the Pinnacles. South of China Lake along SR 14 is **Red Rock Canyon State Park**, an unusual camping and picnic spot which, despite its geological importance, has remained relatively unexplored. (Do not confuse this with the popular Red Rock Canyon National Conservation Area located on the outskirts of Las Vegas.)

Here in this isolated but handsome state park, great, brightly colored columns of sandstone rise off the desert floor on either side of the highway, sculpted towers in the foothills of the eastern Sierras. These towers were once the home of a desert Indian tribe now known only as "the Old Ones."

Much later, about the middle of the 19th century, desert prospectors began to discover gold nuggets on the surface of the dry stream beds, and traffic to the region picked up considerably. The finds led to a mini-boom in the area, and about $16 million worth of ore was subsequently removed, including one massive 5-lb (2-kg) nugget.

On weekends, state rangers give guided nature walks around Red Rock. Picnic tables and about 50 primitive campsites are provided for tents and recreational vehicles. Visitors must bring their own food and water, however, as there are no concessions or vendors operating inside the park.

The Mojave Desert

The Mojave Desert, named after the southwestern Indians, and pronounced "*mo-hahv-ee*," lies between US 395 and Interstate 40, adjoining the Nevada state border. The desert means different things to different people, and has become a battleground of conflicting interests between backpackers, miners, ranchers, scientists, environmentalists and off-road vehicle enthusiasts.

Visitors come to escape the confines of urban life. They also come to experience for themselves the truth about one of the most famously desolate, challenging landscapes in the Americas. Explorer Juan Bautista de Anza experienced the Mojave's fiery natural furnace, and in his diary in 1775 referred to the region as Tierra del Muertos, literally, "Land of the Dead." The first would-be settlers who had the misfortune to wander in here, on their way to join the 1849 Gold Rush, found this to be only too true.

The Mojave covers an enormous amount of land – roughly as much as the states of Massachusetts, Connecticut and Rhode Island combined. It's easy to get lost and, with conventional vehicles, to get stranded off the main roads. Water can usually be found if one is equipped to dig deep enough, as the native Shoshone Indians knew very well, but very few visitors know anything about survival techniques and what's safe to eat.

The *WPA Guide* in 1939 reported that August travelers found "intense heat" even at altitudes above a thousand feet (300 meters) over the valley. It advised experienced travelers to regularly estimate the temperature by putting their hand outside the car and checking how long it took the sunlight "to cause a sharp pain at the base of the nails."

BELOW:
Calico Ghost Town is not a mirage.

Astronauts

At the often deserted junction of SR 14 and 58 is the small desert town of Mojave. From borax to the B-1 bomber, this place has seen more history than towns many times its size. Located near to Edwards Air Force Base, Mojave was part of the Antelope Valley aerospace boom, serving as a bedroom community for the aerospace workers, as well as those employed in agriculture and railroads. The winter season is its busiest time when weekend skiers, heading to and from Sierra slopes, pack the motels and roadside cafes.

Tours of **Edwards Air Force Base** ⓯ are available by appointment (tel: 661/ 277-1110), and are a rewarding diversion for anyone remotely stirred by the adventure of flight or space travel, since a great deal of US aerospace history was made here. Many of the astronauts in the *Mercury, Gemini* and *Apollo* space programs were recruited from among the USAF and US Navy test pilots who flew here, notably Alan Shepard, the first American into space, Gordon (Gordo) Cooper, and Virgil (Gus) Grissom, who was tragically killed in the *Apollo 1* disaster. The whole story is brilliantly told in Tom Wolfe's book, and the movie of the same name, *The Right Stuff*. The astronauts flew in the company with the hero of them all, WWII P-51 ace Chuck Yeager, played in the movie by Sam Shepherd.

Edwards was also the landing site for the first space shuttle mission, and many since. Although there is usually very little notice of the shuttle landing at Edwards, they do often open the base for visitors to watch the landing. If your visit could coincide with a possible landing, call NASA's public information line (tel: 661/276-3520) in advance for information.

"Area 51," legendary among UFOlogists, is said to be located at Edwards,

TIP

If your visit to the desert coincides with a space-shuttle landing, call NASA's information line, tel: 661/276-3520 for details on watching the landing from Edwards Air Force Base, the site of the first mission.

BELOW: Calico Ghost Town.

Map on page 308

although not by staff at the base itself, who categorically deny its existence.

East along I-15, **Barstow ⑯** is a bustling desert town made slightly famous in the line "Kingman, Barstow, San Bernadino," from the song *Route 66* by Bobby Troup; now it mostly serves the military community. There is a stretch of motels, gas stations, grocery and general stores, and this is a good base for stocking up on supplies. Nearby, dedicated paleontologists are still carrying on the work of the late Dr Louis Leakey, leader of a team of eminent scientists who believed they had found a prehistoric "tool factory" some 200,000 years old. The **Calico Early Man Site** is open to the public, with occasional tours. Arrangements can be made at the Federal Bureau of Land Management in Barstow. Calico itself was established by the silver miners of the 1880s. Their boom-town has been given a new lease of life by the imaginative restoration of Los Angeles' Walter Knott of Knott's Berry Farm fame. It is now known as the **Calico Ghost Town ⑰** (tel: 760/254-2122). Half history and half Hollywood, Calico is a themed amusement park where visitors can explore mining tunnels, ride the ore train and browse in old-fashioned dry-goods shops.

Mojave National Preserve

A place with a name like **Zzyzx ⑱** (pronounced *zizz-ex*) deserves consideration for a detour. Travel for 60 miles (97 km) east of Barstow along Interstate 15, then 4 miles (6 km) south along the shore of **Soda Lake**, usually a dry lake bed, to the **Desert Studies Center**. During the 1940s and 1950s, this old cavalry outpost site was a health club run by a man named Doctor Curtis Springer. Rather eccentric, the good doctor wanted the last word on everything, and his last word on the town's name was Zzyzx. In 1976 the resort was turned into a university research station A spring-fed pond and nearby marshes shelter the rare Saratoga Springs pupfish and Mojave tui club.

A few miles farther east, **Kelbaker Road** threads through a desolate area of cinder cones and lava beds now designated as **Mojave Cinder Cones National Natural Landmark ⑲**. Plan to stop at **Kelso**, site of the grand, Spanish-style, Union Pacific Railroad depot built in 1942. Farther along you'll pass the 600-foot (183-meter) high **Kelso Sand Dunes ⑳**, the third highest dune system in the country. This is the location of the "singing sand dunes," which hum or boom when they are in motion.

The road then climbs through a boulder-choked pass separating the Granite and Providence mountains, and descends toward Interstate 40. Double back towards Kelso and turn right on **Kelso-Cima Road**, which curves upward past **Cima Dome**, a gently sloping geological "blister" of monzonite, a granite-like rock, that covers 75 square miles (194 square km). You'll also pass one of the finest Joshua tree forests in California, which some people feel is even more impressive than Joshua Tree National Park itself.

Mitchell Caverns ㉑ is an intricate network of some 40,000 limestone caves. From mid-September to mid-June, tours are conducted by park rangers, while the short, self-guiding **Mary Beal Nature Trail** can be taken from near the **visitor center**. ❑

INSIGHT GUIDES
Travel Tips

CONTENTS

Getting Acquainted

The Place

Area: About 84 square miles (32 square km).
Time Zone: Pacific Standard Time (Pacific Daylight Time in summer). Vegas is in the same time zone as California; 8 hours behind London and 3 hours behind New York.
Currency: US dollars (US$). Automated teller machines (ATMs) are located throughout the city and in most major casinos, many of which also accept travelers' checks and cash foreign currency. There are many check-cashing services, which accept foreign checks.
Weights and Measures: The US uses the Imperial system of weights and measures. Metric weights and measures are rarely used.
Electricity: 110 volts.
Dialing Codes: International 001. Local codes: the area code in Las Vegas and Clark County is 702. The area code through the rest of Nevada is 775.

Gaming Economy

The Las Vegas economy is based on tourism and gaming. Casinos earn more than $7.3 billion annually in Clark County and more than $9 billion across the state. Clark County has issued more than 1,700 gaming licenses, and contains nearly 5,000 live table games. including poker and craps. Slot machines are allowed in many convenience stores, and gaming chips have been known to turn up in the collection plates of local churches near the Strip.

Climate

Located in the Mojave Desert, Las Vegas has relatively hot and dry weather most of the year. Most of the city's annual rainfall of about 4.13 inches (10.64 centimeters), comes in winter. The monsoon period in the Mojave Desert falls from July through September with frequent thunderstorms bringing lightning and heavy downpours. The drenching rains, though fleeting, can create dangerous flash floods, and motorists and pedestrians are cautioned never to cross running water, flooded washes or roads after a storm.

The average monthly temperature is 56°F (13°C)–80°F (27°C). Summer temperatures are often over 100°F (38°C) in the day and 75–85°F (26–30°C) at night, but heatwaves of 117°F (47°C) can occur in Las Vegas. The heat is dry as the city has low humidity.

Although it rarely drops much below freezing, the Las Vegas Valley occasionally has winter snow. An average year sees 212 clear days, 82 partly cloudy days and 71 cloudy days, with rain in winter and spring. The mildest Las Vegas weather is generally from October through April or May.

Geography

Las Vegas is located in Clark County in the extreme south of the state of Nevada.

The small city of Las Vegas centers on the populations of Las Vegas, North Las Vegas and Henderson. The boundaries of these are divided by substantial islands of county land, which also surrounds the metropolis. Drivers traveling on the extensive road network around Las Vegas will find it difficult to know when one city stops and another starts. All are located in the Las Vegas Valley, and from the air appears as one vast city amid the barren emptiness of the 25,000-square mile (10,000-square km) Mojave Desert.

Clark County covers 7,881 square miles (3,000 square km) at

Facts and Figures

- More than 35 million travelers visit Las Vegas annually, including nearly 4 million convention delegates.
- There are more than 126,000 hotel and motel rooms in Las Vegas, with an average daily room rate of $85.
- The average age of Las Vegas visitors is about 48. Only 12 percent of visitors are under 21.
- Around 26 percent of Las Vegas visitors are from Southern California. About 12 percent are from other countries.

the southern end of the state and is about the size of Massachusetts. Boulder City, about 30 miles east of Las Vegas, is also considered part of the metropolitan area of the city.

Population

Las Vegas has more than 506,000 permanent residents. Clark County has about 1.5 million residents and is part of the designated Las Vegas population, as is a portion of Nye County in Nevada and Mojave County in Arizona.

Between 5,000 and 8,000 people move into Las Vegas each month, making it one of the fastest-growing areas in the US.

Government

Nevada has two US senators; two US representatives; a 21-member state senate; a 42-member assembly; a governor and a lieutenant governor. Clark County has a seven-person board of commissioners that employs a county manager, and the city of Las Vegas has a mayor and a six-person city council that hires a city manager. Other cities in Clark County also have separate city councils.

Planning the Trip

What to Bring

Dress is almost universally casual, although some upscale restaurants require smart attire. While light clothes are essential for summer, warm coats and sweaters are needed in winter and a jacket may be advisable for cooler summer nights. Rain can be expected in winter and spring. During the hot season it is advisable to wear a hat and sunglasses.

Entry Regulations

VISAS AND PASSPORTS

A passport, a passport-sized photograph, a visitor's visa, proof of intent to leave the US and, depending on your country of origin, an international vaccination certificate are required of most foreign nationals. Visitors from a few European countries staying less than 90 days no longer need a visa. Vaccination certificate requirements vary, but proof of immunization against smallpox or cholera may be necessary. Canadian and Mexican citizens, and British residents of Canada and Bermuda, are normally exempt but it is wise to check.

Since September 11, 2001, security measures are in place, and are subject to change without notice. Foreign nationals should carry photo ID most of the time.

CUSTOMS

Meat or meat products, illegal drugs, firearms, seeds, plants and fruits are among prohibited goods. Also, do not bring in any duty-free goods worth more than $400 (Americans) or $100 (foreign travelers). Visitors over 21 may import 200 cigarettes, 3 lb (1.3 kg) of tobacco or 50 cigars and 34 fl oz (1 liter) of alcohol.

Non-residents may import, free of duty and internal revenue tax, articles worth up to $100 for use as gifts for other persons, as long as they remain in the US for at least 72 hours and keep the gifts with them. This $100 gift exemption or any part of it can be claimed only once every six months. It can include 100 cigars, but no alcohol. Do not have the articles gift wrapped, as they must be available for customs inspection.

If you are not entitled to the $100 gift exemption, you may bring in articles worth up to $25 free of duty for your personal or household use. You may include any of the following: 50 cigarettes, 10 cigars, 150 ml of alcohol, or 5 fl oz (150ml) of alcoholic perfume or proportionate amounts. Articles bought in duty-free shops in foreign countries are subject to US customs duty and restrictions but may be included in your exemption.

For a breakdown of customs allowances contact the United States Customs Service, PO Box 7407, Washington, DC 20044. Tel: 202/514-4316.

Health

Health care is extremely expensive, so visitors should always have comprehensive travel insurance to cover any emergencies.

Money

Credit cards are accepted almost everywhere, although not all cards at all places. Along with out-of-state or overseas bank cards, they can also be used to withdraw money at ATMs (automatic teller machines) which are marked with the corresponding stickers (i.e. Cirrus, Plus, Visa, MasterCard, American Express, etc.)

If cashing travelers' checks, be sure to bring along your passport.

Tax

Shoppers in Clark County pay about 8.25 percent in taxes for all non-food items, or for food items purchased already prepared such as in a restaurant. There is often a slight difference between the tax in Clark County, the city of Las Vegas, Henderson, North Las Vegas, Boulder City, Mesquite, Laughlin and other areas of the state.

Getting There

BY AIR

McCarran International Airport, 5757 Wayne Newton Boulevard, tel: 702/261-5211, is the hub for air travel into and out of Southern Nevada. It is particularly busy on weekends.

BY TRAIN

There is no train servicer at this time although there are rumors that eventually services will be resumed to and from Los Angeles.

BY BUS

The national bus line, Greyhound (tel: 800-231-2222), operates daily services to Las Vegas from most parts of the country. The Downtown depot of Greyhound is at 2200 South Main Street (tel: 384-9561). There are several hotels and motels within walking distance.

BY CAR

Around 26 percent of Las Vegas visitors are from Southern California. Those who come by car usually follow Interstate 10 from LA (or I-215 from San Diego) to join I-15 north of Riverside. At Barstow, I-15 is intersected by US 58 which takes travelers from the northwest. Traffic on I-15 is fast moving, mainly through desert, and there are many accidents. From the north and northwest, the most direct route into Las Vegas is US 95.

Practical Tips

Business Hours

Las Vegas is a 24-hour city. Casinos, hotels, many liquor stores, bars, numerous restaurants, grocery stores and other shopping outlets never close. Banks keep regular hours, generally 9am to 5pm, but some branches are open on Saturday and a few even on Sunday. Most major shopping malls are open from 10am to 10pm every day including Christmas Day and New Year's Day.

Photography

Taking photographs is an imperative for most visitors who otherwise find it hard to explain Las Vegas to friends and family back home. There are numerous camera shops that handle all types of film and equipment, and there are places to have film developed in an hour on almost every street corner and in most supermarkets.

Photography inside casinos or showrooms is strictly prohibited. In the early days there was such a stigma attached to gaming that customers would get upset if anyone took photographs, in case a picture of them sitting at a blackjack table appeared in their newspaper. Particularly obliging pit bosses or security guards might give you a wink and turn their backs *if you ask first*.

In showrooms, the performers and casino big shots believe that while customers have paid for the right to watch a live performance, it doesn't give them the right to take pictures and perhaps sell the photo to others. Many showbusiness people have spent large sums of money registering the right to make money off their faces, and they don't want just anyone taking their picture.

In some shows, a photographic flash going off at a critical moment could be hazardous for performers, so cameras are banned. However, some performers, such as Wayne Newton at the Stardust, will walk through and greet the audience, when photography is encouraged.

Religious Services

There are more than 500 churches and synagogues in Las Vegas representing more than 40 faiths. Casino gaming chips are found in donation baskets nearly every day at two Roman Catholic churches a few hundred yards from the Strip.

Apostolic
Bible Way Fellowship Church, 490 Bewie Drive. Tel: 631-4990.
Mountaintop Faith Ministries, 2845 Lindell Road. Tel: 367-1636.
New Life Christian Center, 1229 Carson Avenue. Tel: 387-5433.

Public Holidays

Although Las Vegas recognizes all major public holidays in the US, it makes little difference to the casual visitor. Most government offices, including federal, county and city, close on holidays, but the majority of businesses that cater to tourists never close. Most major holidays occur on the Monday closest to the celebration date. On most 3-day weekends, Vegas becomes very crowded.
● **New Year's Day** January 1
● **Martin Luther King Day** Third Monday in January
● **President's Day** Third Monday in February
● **Labor Day** First Monday in September
● **Independence Day** July 4
● **Veterans' Day** November 1
● **Christmas Day** December 25

Telephone Numbers

Unless otherwise stated, all telephone numbers in this book start with the code 702. When dialing within Las Vegas, the code is not used. When calling outside the area, even if the code is still 702, you must dial it.

Truth Christian Ministries, 3840 El Camino . Tel: 382-8781.

Assemblies of God
Church on the Street, 913 Ogden Avenue. Tel: 474-4439.
Desert Breeze Community Church, 3655 South Durango Drive, Tel: 838-6213.
Green Valley Christian Center, 711 Valle Verde Court, Henderson. Tel: 454-2722.

Baptist
Community, 245 East Foster Avenue, Henderson. Tel: 565-0071.
Macedonia, 2600 Clayton Street, North Las Vegas. Tel: 646-9075.
Second Baptist Church, 500 Madison Avenue. Tel: 648-6155.
Warm Springs, 2075 East Warm Springs Road. Tel: 361-7070.
Calvary Southern, 1600 East Cartier Avenue, North Las Vegas. Tel: 649-2644.
First Baptist Church of the Lakes, 9125 Spring Mountain Road. Tel: 254-3234.

Buddhist
Buddhaya Nandharam Temple, 5320 Kell Lane. Tel: 437-3320.
Nevada Buddhist Association, 4189 South Jones Boulevard. Tel: 252-7339.

Roman Catholic
Guardian Angel Cathedral, 302 Cathedral Way. Tel: 735-5241.
Shrine of the Most Holy Redeemer, 55 East Reno Ave. Tel: 891-8600.
St Thomas More Catholic Community, 130 North Pecos Road. Tel: 361-3022.
St Viator, 2461 East Flamingo Road. Tel: 733-8323.

Church of Jesus Christ of Latter-Day Saints

Nevada Las Vegas Mission, 3675 McLeod. Tel: 794-0365.

Episcopal

Episcopal Diocese of Nevada, 2100 South Maryland Parkway. Tel: 737-9190.
St George Episcopal Church, 7676 West Gilmore. Tel: 647-8740.

Interdominational

Grapevine Fellowship, 2323 South Nellis Boulevard. Tel: 431-8463.
Jubilee Christian Center, 4130 South Sandhill. Tel: 433-4941.

Jehovah's Witness

Sunrise Congregation, 6080 East Owens Avenue. Tel: 438-8400.

Lutheran

Christ Lutheran Church Elca, 111 North Torrey Pines Drive. Tel: 870 1421.
Good Samaritan Lutheran, 6500 West Flamingo Road. Tel: 873-3589.

Eastern Orthodox

Antiochian Orthodox Church, 5719 East Judson Avenue. Tel: 452-1299.
St Paul Orthodox Church, 5400 Anne Oakley Drive. Tel: 898-4800.

Presbyterian

First Presbyterian, 1515 West Charleston Blvd. Tel: 384-6302.

Synagogues

Temple Beth Sholom, 10700 Havenwood Lane . Tel: 804-1333.
Temple Beth AM, 9001 Hillpointe Road. Tel: 254-5110.

Hospitals

Desert Springs Hospital Medical Center, 2075 East Flamingo Road. Tel: 733-8800.
Lake Mead Hospital and Medical Center, 1409 East Lake Mead Boulevard, North Las Vegas. Tel: 649-7711.
St Rose Dominican Hospital, 102 East Lake Mead Drive, Henderson. Tel: 616-5000.

Emergency Numbers

● **All emergencies**: 911
● **Police:**
Metropolitan Police Department, 400 Stewart Avenue. Tel: non-emergency 795-3111 or 229-3111.
North Las Vegas Police Department, 1301 East Lake Mead Boulevard, North Las Vegas. Tel: 633-9111.
Henderson Police Department, 240 South Water Street, Henderson. Tel: 565-8933.
Boulder City Police Department, 1005 Arizona Street, Boulder City. Tel: 293-9224.
Nevada Highway Patrol Tel: 486-4100.
Nevada Gaming Control, 555 East Washington. Tel: 486-2000.
● **Ambulance Dispatch Center** Tel: 384-3400.
● **Alcoholics Abuse Hotline** Tel: 800/222-0199.
● **Alcoholics Anonymous**, 1431 East Charleston Avenue. Tel: 598-888.
● **Domestic Violence Hotline** Tel: 646-4981.
● **Drug Abuse Prevention** Tel: 799-8402.
● **Gamblers Anonymous** Tel: 385-7732.
● **Poison Control** Tel: 732-4989.
● **Rape Crisis Hotline** Tel: 366-1640.
● **Suicide Prevention Hotline** Tel: 877/885-4673.

Summerlin Hospital Medical Center, 657 Town Center Drive. Tel: 233-7000.
Sunrise Hospital and Medical Center, 3186 South Maryland Parkway. Tel: 731-8080.
University Medical Center, 1800 West Charleston Boulevard. Tel: 383-2000.
Valley Hospital, 620 Shadow Lane. Tel: 388-4000.

Security

Las Vegas is a relatively safe city despite the fact that it is awash in cash. In addition to the Metropolitan Police Department, which patrols nearly all areas, there are separate police departments in North Las Vegas, Henderson and Boulder City. Other police agencies include Nevada Gaming Control officers, who are responsible for keeping gaming on the up and up, and the Federal Bureau of Investigation (FBI), which investigates federal crimes.

Every casino has its own armed security force who protect customers and the interests of the casino. If you have any problem inside the hotel, your first stop should be with security, although the chances of retrieving lost property are not especially good.

At no time should you leave any cash or belongings unattended. There are those who prey on the unsuspecting. For the most part, visitors to Las Vegas are safe in all casino areas including the street in front of the resorts, but, as in most cities, it is unwise to travel at night in areas that are not well lit.

Media

PRINT

There are two major daily newspapers in Las Vegas, the *Las Vegas Review-Journal* and the smaller *Las Vegas Sun*. Although the papers are editorially separate, they share advertising and printing facilities. Several other alternative publications are available, including weekly newspapers and magazines, most of which are free.

TELEVISION

There are numerous TV stations in Vegas as well as the national CBS, NBC and ABC. There is also the FOX network, and the UPN network, an entertainment channel; a local government channel; and a few Spanish channels.

Postal Services

Postal authorities are available to respond to questions or concerns

24 hours a day, seven days a week by calling 800/275-8777. There are branches of the post office throughout the Las Vegas Valley, but the main post office is located at 101 East Sunset Road, a stone's throw from McCarran Airport.

Tourist Offices

There are six public tourist offices throughout Clark County. These provide excellent information for Las Vegas travelers and often have discount coupons for any number of activities in the area. They can all be accessed through the Internet at **www.lasvegas24hours.com**, the website of the Las Vegas Convention and Visitors Authority (LVCVA). Everything you need to know about Las Vegas can be found here including an events calendar, detailed maps of the area and visitor and convention information. The six tourist offices are:
Las Vegas Visitor Information Center, 3150 Paradise Road. Tel: 892-7573.
Las Vegas Chamber of Commerce, 3720 Howard Hughes Parkway. Tel: 735-1616. Fax: 735-2011.
Boulder City Visitor Information Center, 100 Nevada Highway, Boulder City. Tel: 294-1252.
Jean Visitor Information Center, Interstate 15, Exit 12, PO Box 19470, Jean. Tel: 874-1360.
Laughlin Visitor Information Center, 1555 Casino Drive. Tel: 298-3321.
Mesquite Visitor Information Center, Interstate 15, Exit 122, 460 Sandhill Boulevard, Mesquite. Tel: 346-2702.

Special Facilities

DISABLED TRAVELERS

If you have a physical disability and need special accommodation requirements, your reservation agent or hotel ADA coordinator can help you find a room. Most showrooms have assistive listening devices and wheelchair accommodations, as do most restaurants and lounges.

For more information you should contact the properties concerned directly. Many casinos have slot machines and table games with wheelchair access.

If you rent a car, you should bring your hometown parking permit, or request a free 90-day permit through the city of Las Vegas at the Parking Permit Office, tel: 229-6431.

Lift-equipped shuttles are available to and from McCarran International Airport, which also has TTYs for the hearing impaired.

GAY TRAVELERS

The **Gay and Lesbian Center**, 953 East Sahara Avenue, Suite B 25, tel: 733-9800, is generally staffed seven days a week. The office provides a guide to local bars which includes:
Badlands Saloon, 953 East Sahara Avenue. Tel: 792-9262. An easy-going neighborhood bar with very friendly staff.
Cobalt, 900 Karen Avenue. Tel: 693-6567. Attracts all types with a variety of special shows and programs.
FreeZone, 610 East Naples Drive. Tel: 733-6701. The most popular bar for women, but also a hit with men on boys' nights and weekends. Check out the What a Drag show.
Hamburger Mary's, 4503 Paradise Road. Tel: 735-4400. A great place to eat and hang out for both the gay and straight crowd. Holds tons of special events.
Las Vegas Eagle, 3430 East Tropicana Avenue. Tel: 458-8662. Home of the "infamous" Underwear Nights on Wednesday and Friday.
Las Vegas Lounge, 900 Karen Avenue. Tel: 737-9350. Las Vegas' only transgender bar. Has fantastic shows and a great crowd.
Sasha's, 4640 Paradise Road. Tel: 735-3888. The most diverse live entertainment in town. Featuring the longest-running drag show cast.
Spotlight Lounge, 957 East Sahara Avenue. Tel: 696-0202. A favorite with locals. Lots of community events, and friendly laid-back staff.

Getting Around

Orientation

Although casinos, hotels, attractions and activities are spread virtually everywhere throughout the Las Vegas Valley, there are essentially two main areas where travelers will find the highest concentration of places to stay, sights to see and things to do, all of which are designed to entertain visitors and make their stay in Las Vegas enjoyable. These two are the Las Vegas Strip and downtown Las Vegas. To reach the Strip, tourists need only travel south on the Boulevard. It starts at Sahara Avenue. Travelers coming from the West will, of course, arrive at the Strip first, it being one block east of Interstate 15.

Downtown starts at Jackie Gaughan's Plaza Hotel Casino and runs east on Fremont Street for several blocks. Five blocks from the Plaza, Fremont Street intersects with Las Vegas Boulevard.

From the Airport

McCarran International Airport, 5757 Wayne Newton Boulevard, tel: 261-5211, is about 1 mile (1.5 km) from the Strip and about 5 miles (8 km) from downtown Las Vegas. A taxi ride from McCarran to the Strip costs about $10; the fare to Downtown can run up to $20. A shuttle service runs continually and costs much less.

Some airborne sightseeing excursions to the Grand Canyon and elsewhere take off from the North Las Vegas Airport, 2730 Airport Drive, tel: 261-3800. The NLV Airport is easily accessible by cab.

Taxis

All taxi service in Las Vegas is heavily regulated by the Nevada Taxicab Authority (tel: 486-6532). There is a limited number of companies and the service is metered. Unlike in most cities, Las Vegas cabs are prohibited by law from picking up hailing customers on the street. Not that it doesn't occasionally happen, but don't feel snubbed if you hail an empty cab but it doesn't stop to pick you up. However, there are nearly always taxi lines at the airport, major hotels on the Strip and Downtown; also at some restaurants. They can also be ordered by telephone 24 hours a day. Services include:

A Cab. Tel: 369-5686.
A-North Las Vegas Cab. Tel: 643-1041.
ABC Union Cab. Tel: 736-8444.
Ace Cab. Tel: 736-8383.
Checker Cab. Tel: 873-2000.
Deluxe Taxicab Service. Tel: 568-7700.
Desert Cab. Tel: 386-9102.
Designated Drivers. Tel: 531-6959.
Henderson Taxi. Tel: 384-2322.
Lucky Cab Company of Nevada. Tel: 477-7555.
Nevada Yellow Cab Corporation. Tel: 933-2141.
Star Cab Co. Tel: 873-8012.
Western Cab Company. Tel: 736-8000.
Whittlesea Blue Cab. Tel: 384-6111.

Trolleys and Buses

A trolley on wheels mainly for the convenience of tourists connects many of the Strip resorts with each other but this is not well publicized; look for a sign or a bench at the side or even the back of a particular casino. The trolley operates from 9:30–1:30am on a 2-hour loop system and a trolley (supposedly) arrives every 15 minutes, but it is a slow way to get around. Be sure to have the exact fare.

Public transportation is provided by Citizen's Area Transit (CAT) buses, which can be found in the Las Vegas Valley including Boulder City, Mesquite and Laughlin. A guide detailing routes, scheduling and service is available by calling CAT-RIDE (tel: 228-7433). There are customer service representatives at that telephone number who can help plan a trip. CAT operates 5.30am–1.30am daily on residential routes. Some routes run 24 hours a day, and some only during peak service hours Monday to Friday, except major US holidays.

Helpful CAT phone numbers are 228-7433 (CAT-RIDE) for transit information; 676-1500 for RTC administrative offices; and 228-7433 for lost and found. Websites include www.rtc.co.clark.nv.us for general RTC information, and www.catride.com for CAT information.

All buses have electronic fareboxes that accept dollar bills and coins, but do not give change. If you plan to transfer to another bus to complete your one-way trip, ask the driver for a transfer.

Monorail

The RTC's much-anticipated monorail system is now under construction. The first phase, with a possible completion in 2004, will extend from Tropicana Avenue to Sahara Avenue. The second, which will go from Sahara Avenue to Downtown will (perhaps) be completed in 2007. The project will connect with many CAT bus routes.

Currently, there is a free private monorail system between the MGM Grand and Bally's Las Vegas; also one connecting Excalibur, the Luxor and Mandalay Bay.

Sightseeing

LIMOUSINES

Cruising the Las Vegas Strip in a limousine is a exciting way to see the sights and provides the ultimate in traveling luxury. As with taxis, the limousine service in Las Vegas is strictly regulated. However, unlike taxis, limousines are not metered. The cost is agreed upon at rental.

A Luxury Limo Referral Service. Tel: 737-8899.
Ambassador Limousine. Tel: 888/519-5466.
Bell Transportation. Tel: 383-7060.
Fox Limousine Inc. Tel: 597-0400.
Larson's Van Service. Tel: 456-4791.
Las Vegas Limousines. Tel: 888/696-4400.
Lucky 7 Limousines. Tel: 739-6177.
On Demand Sedan and Limousine Service. Tel: 386-2715.
Presidential Limousine. Tel: 800/423-1420.
Rancho Limousine Service. Tel: 645-7634.
Rent-A-Limo. Tel: 597-9696.
Vegas Now (Door-to-Door Travel). Tel: 765-6552.

CHARTERS AND TOURS

Adventure Charters and Tours, 1305 North Main Street. Tel: 385-0500 or 800/255-5482.
ATV Action Tours, 175 Cassia Way, Henderson Tel: 566-7400 or 888/288-5200. Off-road vehicle tours to Red Rock Canyon, Death Valley and others.
Bell Trans/Limousines and Buses, PO Box 15333. Tel: 382-7060 or 800/274-7433. www.bell-trans.com.
Coach USA, 4020 East Lone Mountain Road. Tel: 644-2233 or 800/559-522. www.Paulina.salen@coachusa.com
Gold Carriage Charter and Tour, 1305 North Main Street. Tel: 383-8160.
Greyhound Charter Service, 200 South Main Street. Tel: 800/454-2487.
Lake Mead Cruises, 480 Lakeshore Road, Boulder City Tel: 493-9765.
Travelways, 1455 East Tropicana Avenue. Tel: 739-7714.
Vegas Now, 1350 East Flamingo Road. Tel: 765-6552 or 877/669-6900. www.vegasnow.com
World Bus Tours, 3500 West Naples Drive. Tel: 597-5545, 888/931-2432.

AIR TOURS

A Tour 4U, 8981 Fort Crestwood Drive. Tel: 233-1627, 888/609-5665. www.atour4u.com

Air Vegas Airlines, 1400 Executive Airport Drive Suite A, Henderson. Tel: 736-3599 or 800/255-7474. www.airvegas.com

Grand Canyon Discount, 2990 East Oquendo Road. Tel: 433-7770 or 888/600-8281. www.gcflight.com

Heli USA Flights, 275 East Tropicana Avenue, Suite 200. Tel: 736-8787 or 800/359-8727. www.heliusa.com
Tours over the Strip, to the Grand Canyon and others.

Maverick Helicopters, 6075 Las Vegas Boulevard South. Tel: 261-0007. www.maverickhelicopter.com

Papillon Grand Canyon Helicopters, 245 East Tropicana Avenue. Tel: 736-4359 or 888/635-7272. www.papillon.com

Scenic Airlines, 2705 Airport Drive, North Las Vegas. Tel: 638-3291 or 800/634-6801. www.scenic.com

Sundance Helicopters, 5596 Haven. Tel: 736-0606 or 800/653-881. www.helicoptour.com

Car Rental

Many rental car companies have outlets at McCarran Airport on Rent A Car Road. Some companies have offices inside hotels.

There is little difference between Nevada driving regulations and other US states. All speed limits are posted, seat belts are required and their use is strictly enforced, and drivers can turn right on a red light. One major difference about Nevada roads is the center lane, which is not used for travel but for left-hand turns only.

Nearly every major hotel in the state has free valet parking which, although optional, is usually rewarded with a tip of $1 or $2 per car every time you park.

A Lloyd's Rent-a-Car, 3735 Las Vegas Blvd South. Tel: 795-4008 or 800/795-2277. www.xpressrac.com

AA Prestige Auto Center, 1719 Industrial Road. Tel: 388-7580.

Alamo Rent-A-Car, 6855 Bermuda Road. Tel: 263-8411, 800/462-5266. www.goalamo.com

Avis Rent A Car, 5164 Rent A Car Rd. Tel: 261-4038, 800/822-3131.

Budget Car and Truck Rental, 5188 Paradise Rd. Tel: 736-1212 or 800/922-2899. www.budgetvegas.com

Dollar Rent-A-Car, 5301 Rent A Car Road. Tel: 739-8408 or 800/826-9911. www.dollarcar.com

Enterprise Rent-A-Car, 5032 Palo Verde Road. Tel: 795-8842 or 800/736-7222.

Express Rent A Car, 3735 Las Vegas Boulevard South. Tel: 795-4008.

Hertz Rent A Car, 5300 Rent A Car Road. Tel: 736-4900 or 800/654-3131. www.hertz.com

National Car Rental, 5233 Rent A Car Road. Tel: 261-5391 or 800/227-7368. www.nationalcar.com

Rent A Limo, 4990 South Paradise Road. Tel: 791-5466.

Rent A Wreck, 2310 Las Vegas Boulevard South. Tel: 474-0037 or 800/227-0292.

Thrifty Car Rental, 376 East Warm Springs Rd. Tel: 896-7600 or 800/8847-4389. angela@qualcar.com

Motorhomes

Bates Motor Home Rental Network, 3690 South Eastern Avenue. Tel: 737-9050 or 800/732-2283. www.batesintl.com

El Monte RV, 13001 Las Vegas Blvd South. Tel: 269-8000 or 800/269-8600. www.elmonterv.com

Sahara RV Center, 1518 Scotland Lane. Tel: 384-8818 or 800/48?-6494. www.sahararv.com

Motorcycles

Eagle Rider-Las Vegas Motorcycle Rentals, 5182 South Arville St. Tel: 888/916-7433. www.eaglerider.com

Las Vegas Harley-Davidson, 2605 South Eastern Avenue, tel: 431-8500. www.lvhd.com

Street Eagle Las Vegas, 6330 South Pecos Road. Tel: 346 8490. www.streeteagle.com

Where to Stay

Las Vegas hotel rates vary enormously but one constant is that hotel rooms cost more on weekends. Understandably, they also tend to go up and down depending on demand with few bargains available, for example, when a big convention is in town.

At other times there are sometimes astonishing deals but it may be necessary to consult the travel pages of an American newspaper – especially good is the Sunday edition of the *Los Angeles Times* – to find them. That is where you will also find ads listing free 800 telephone numbers and such websites as **Vegas.com** and **hotels.com** which will sometimes offer a choice of as many as 100 hotels from as low as $30 per night. As a rule, downtown Las Vegas is cheaper than the Strip but there are often comparable bargains to be found on the latter.

The Strip

RESORT HOTELS

Room rates in Strip resorts vary enormously depending on the time of the year, the day of the week and whether special offers are in force. The dollar signs here are a very approximate guide only.

Aladdin Resort & Casino
3667 Las Vegas Boulevard South. Tel: 785-5555 or 877-333-WISH. Fax: 736-7107. **$$$**

Algiers
2845 Las Vegas Boulevard South. Tel: 735-3311 or 800/732-3361. Fax: 792-2112.
A quiet haven with pool and patio café but minimal slot machines, across from Circus Circus. **$$**

Bally's Las Vegas
3645 Las Vegas Boulevard South.
Tel: 739-4111 or 800/634-3434.
Fax: 967-4405. **$$$**
Barbary Coast
3595 Las Vegas Boulevard South.
Tel: 737-7111 or 888/227-2279.
Fax: 894-9954. **$$$**
Bellagio
3600 Las Vegas Boulevard South.
Tel: 693-7111 or 888/987-6667.
Fax: 792-7646. **$$$$**
Boardwalk Casino-Holiday Inn
3750 Las Vegas Boulevard South.
Tel: 735-2400 or 800/635-4581.
Fax: 739-8152. **$$**
Caesars Palace
3570 Las Vegas Boulevard South.
Tel: 731-7110 or 800/634-6661.
Fax: 731-7172. **$$$**
Circus Circus
2880 Las Vegas Boulevard South.
Tel: 734-0410 or 800/444-2472.
Fax: 734-5897. **$$**
Excalibur
3850 Las Vegas Boulevard South.
Tel: 597-7777 or 800/937-7777.
Fax: 597-7009. **$$**
Flamingo Las Vegas
3555 Las Vegas Boulevard South.
Tel: 733-3111 or 800/732-2111.
Fax: 733-3353. **$$$**
Four Seasons
3960 Las Vegas Boulevard South.
Tel: 632-5000 or 877/632-5000.
Fax: 632-5195. **$$$$**
Hard Rock
4455 Paradise Road.
Tel: 693-5000 or 800/693-7625.
Fax: 693-5010. **$$**
Harrah's
3475 Las Vegas Boulevard South.
Tel: 369-5000 or 800-HARRAHS. **$$**
Imperial Palace
3535 Las Vegas Boulevard South.
Tel: 731-3311 or 800/634-6441.
Fax: 735-8578. **$$**
Las Vegas Hilton
3000 Paradise Road.
Tel: 732-5111 or 800/732-7117
Fax: 794-3611. **$$$**
Luxor
3900 Las Vegas Boulevard South.
Tel: 262-4000 or 800/288-1000
Fax: 262-4404. **$$**
Mandalay Bay
3950 Las Vegas Boulevard South.
Tel: 632-7777 or 877/632-7000.
Fax: 632-7108. **$$$**

MGM Grand
3799 Las Vegas Boulevard South.
Tel: 891-7777 or 800/929-1111.
Fax: 891-1030. **$$$**
The Mirage
3400 Las Vegas Boulevard South.
Tel: 791-7111 or 800/627-6667.
Fax: 791-7414. **$$$**
Monte Carlo
3770 Las Vegas Boulevard South.
Tel: 730-7777 or 800/311-8999.
Fax: 730-7250. **$$$**
The New Frontier
3120 Las Vegas Boulevard South.
Tel: 794-8200 or 800/421-7806.
Fax: 794-8445. **$$**
New York-New York
3790 Las Vegas Boulevard South.
Tel: 740-6969 or 800/693-6763.
Fax: 740-6920. **$$$**
Paris Las Vegas
3655 Las Vegas Boulevard South.
Tel: 946-7000 or 888/266-5687.
Fax: 946-4405. **$$$**
The Venetian
3355 Las Vegas Boulevard South.
Tel: 414-1000 or 888/283-6423.
$$$$

NEARBY CHOICES

King Albert Motel
185 Albert Avenue.
Tel: 732-1555 or 800/553-7753.
Pool, kitchenettes, laundromat. **$**
Motel 8
3961 Las Vegas Boulevard South.
Tel: 798-7223.
Opposite Mandalay Bay. **$**
Motel 6
195 East Tropicana Avenue.
Tel: 798-0728. Three blocks from
the Strip, near the airport. Pool,
plenty of parking, food shop. **$**
Viva Las Vegas
1205 Las Vegas Boulevard South
Tel: 384-0771 or 800/574-4450.
www.vivalasvegasvillas.com
Funky, light-hearted motel near the
Strat Tower with themed rooms,
wedding chapel, parking. **$**

Booking a Room

Most large hotels have smoking
and non-smoking floors. Be sure
to ask when reserving a room.

Downtown

Downtown Las Vegas is about
10 miles (16 km) from McCarran
International Airport.

HOTELS

Golden Nugget
129 East Fremont Street.
Tel: 385-8362 or 800/634-1454.
Fax: 386-8362.
www.goldennugget.com
The most upscale of the Downtown
properties. Shopping, salon,
exercise facilities, swimming pool,
airport shuttle, concierge desk, five
restaurants, buffet, room service,
cable TV. **$$**
**Binion's Horseshoe Hotel and
Casino**
129 Fremont Street.
Tel: 392-1600 or 800/237-6537.
Fax: 382 5750.
Home of the famous World Series
of Poker. Shopping, pool, concierge
desk, seven restaurants, buffet,
room service and cable TV. **$**
California Hotel and Casino
12 Ogden Avenue.
Tel: 385-1222 or 800/634-6505.
Fax: 388-2610. www.thecal.com
Hawaian decor. Shopping,
swimming pool, concierge desk,
three restaurants, room service and
cable TV. **$**
**Castaways Hotel, Casino and
Bowling Center**
2800 Fremont Street.
Tel: 385-9123. Fax: 385-9154.
www.castaways.com
Bingo parlor, 105 bowling lanes,
business services, swimming pool,
airport shuttle, concierge desk,
three restaurants, buffet, room
service, cable TV and data port. **$**
El Cortez Hotel and Casino
600 East Fremont Street.
Tel: 385-5200 or 800/634-6703.
Fax: 385-1554.
www.jackiegaughan.com
Salon, huge casino, concierge desk,
restaurant and room service. **$**
Fitzgeralds Casino and Holiday Inn
301 Fremont Street.
Tel: 388-2400 or 800/724-5824.
Fax: 388-2478.
www.fitzgeralds.com

Rooms with computer ports, safe and 25in TVs with cable, airport shuttle, concierge desk, five restaurants, buffet, room service. **$**
Four Queens Casino and Hotel
Tel: 385-4011 or 800/634-6045.
Fax: 387-5185.
www.fourqueens.com
Two restaurants, room service and cable TV. **$**
Fremont Hotel and Casino
200 East Fremont Street
Tel: 385-3232 or 800/634-6460.
Fax: 385-6229.
www.fremontcasino.com
Shopping, five restaurants, room service and cable TV. **$**
Golden Gate Hotel and Casino
1 Fremont Street.
Tel: 385-906 or 800/426-1906.
Fax: 393-9681
Built in 1905, it is the oldest hotel and casino in Las Vegas. Noted for its 99¢ shrimp cocktails. Two restaurants, cable TV and a coffeemaker. Sunday–Thursday **$**, Friday–Saturday **$$**
Lady Luck Casino and Hotel
206 North Third Street.
Tel: 477-3000 or 800/523-9582.
Fax: 366-9602. www.ladyluck.com
Suites with Jacuzzis, attractive garden with poolside rooms, four restaurants, room service and cable TV. **$**
Las Vegas Club Casino Hotel
18 East Fremont Street.
Tel: 385-1664 or 800-634-6532

Price Categories

Rates are for a hotel room, using the lowest standard rate. Suites start at a higher rate.

$$$$	$150+
$$$	$100-$149
$$	$50-$99
$	under $49

Fax: 387-6071.
www.vegasclubcasino.net
Sports-themed hotel at the corner of Main Street. Concierge desk, three restaurants, room service, cable TV. **$**
Main Street Station Casino, Brewery and Hotel
200 North Main Street.
Tel: 387-1896 or 800/713-8933.
Fax: 386-4466.
www.mainstreetcasino.com
Casino with antique woodwork and stained-glass windows. Concierge desk, 3 restaurants, cable TV. **$**
Jackie Gaughan's Plaza Hotel and Casino
1 Main Street.
Tel: 386-2110 or 800/634-6575.
Fax: 382-8281.
www.jackiegaughan.com
A few steps from the Greyhound station. Exercise facilities, swimming pool, wedding chapel airport shuttle, concierge desk, 3 restaurants and cable TV. **$**

NEARBY CHOICES

Howard Johnson
1401 Las Vegas Boulevard.
Tel: 388-0301 or 800/307-7199.
Fax: 388-2506. www.hojo.com
Near the Convention Center on the lower part of the Strip. Olympic-sized pool, wedding chapel and restaurant. **$–$$**
City Center Motel
700 East Fremont.
Tel: 382-4766. Fax: 382-9937.
Pool, sundeck, 58 rooms and restaurant opposite. **$**
Days Inn Downtown
707 East Fremont.
Tel: 388-1400 or 800/325-2344.
Fax: 388-9622.
Slot parlor, elevated pool, sundeck and restaurant. **$**

Off The Strip

There are many properties offering rooms and suites, gaming and other entertainment at lower rates than the huge hotels and mega-resorts. Perimeter hotels in the greater Las Vegas area have become popular with locals and visitors who want to enjoy what the resorts have to offer without having to deal with the traffic and the crowds on the Strip. Some are very upscale and most have similar amenities offered by the Strip resorts.

The Las Vegas Strip

The glamorous Las Vegas Strip is *not* actually in Las Vegas; it's on Clark County land outside the boundaries of the famous neon city.

The city of Las Vegas is only a portion of the population area of the Las Vegas Valley. At approximately 20 square miles (32 square km), Las Vegas sits in the middle of more than a million residents with about half living within the city's official boundaries.

In the late 1940s, developers began to construct small hotel-casinos along the highway that led

from Los Angeles, California, to the small town of Las Vegas around 250 miles (402 km) away. This highway later became Las Vegas Boulevard in the Las Vegas Valley and retains its name today.

For a number of reasons the developers began building south of Sahara Avenue, the southern boundary of the city of Las Vegas. Early successful hotels included the El Rancho Vegas, Last Frontier, Club Bingo and the Flamingo Hotel, the famous casino managed by mobster Benjamin "Bugsy" Siegel.

Other builders continued the trend and the famous neon fantasy

known as the Las Vegas Strip was born. The Strip, that portion of Las Vegas Boulevard South that starts at Sahara Avenue and travels south for about $4\frac{1}{2}$ miles (7 km), is now home to many of the largest hotels in the world. These include the MGM Grand (5,005 rooms); the Luxor (4,467); the Excalibur (4,008); Mandalay Bay (3,276); the Mirage, (3,046); Bellagio (3,005); Caesars Palace (2,471); and the Stardust (2,200).

Despite the fact that these massive hotels are technically outside the city, they still use the address of Las Vegas, Nevada.

St Tropez – All Suite Hotel
455 East Harmon Avenue.
Tel: 369-5400 or 800/666-5400.
Fax: 369-8901.
A luxurious non-gaming all-suites hotel about 1 mile from the airport. Shopping, exercise facilities, business services, pool, motor airport shuttle, concierge desk, a restaurant, cable TV, VCR, data port and coffee hour. **$$$$**

The Carriage House
105 East Harmon Avenue.
Tel: 798-1020 or 800/221-2301.
Fax: 798-1020.
www.carriagehouselasvegas.com
Condominium suite hotel, one block from the Strip near the MGM Grand. This non-gaming hotel has in-room movies, kitchenettes, pool, whirlpool, sports court, airport shuttle, concierge desk, restaurant, room service and cable TV. **$$$**

Convention Center Courtyard by Marriott
3275 Paradise Road.
Tel: 791-3600 or 800/321-2220.
Fax: 796-7981. www.marriott.com
Opposite the Convention Center, this Marriott offers meeting rooms, exercise facilities, business services, pool and spa, concierge desk, cable TV and a restaurant. It has no gaming. **$$$**

Convention Center Marriott Suites
325 Convention Center Drive.
Tel: 650-2000, 800/228-9290.
Fax: 650-9466. www.marriott.com
A comfortable hotel for business travelers and tourists who prefer suites. Three miles (5 km) from the airport, it has exercise facilities, business services, swimming pool, concierge desk, cable TV, restaurant and data port. **$$$**

Crowne Plaza Las Vegas
4255 South Paradise Road.
Tel: 369-4400, 800/227-6963.
Fax: 369-3770.
Just east of the Strip, this non-gaming, all-suites hotel is 3 miles (5 km) from the airport. Exercise facilities, business services and meeting rooms, pool, airport shuttle, concierge desk, restaurant, room service, cable TV and data port. **$$$**

Embassy Suites Convention Center
3600 Paradise Road.

Tel: 893-8000 or 800/362-2779.
Fax: 893-0378. www.eslvcc.com
Three blocks from the Convention Center, this non-gaming, all-suites venue has a restaurant, room service, shopping, exercise facilities, swimming pool, cable TV and data port. **$$$**

Residence Inn – Henderson Green Valley
2190 Olympic Avenue, Henderson.
Tel: 434-2700 or 800/331-3131.
Fax: 434-3999. www.marriot.com
All-suites hotel with no gaming 5 miles (8 km) from the airport. Sports court suited for basketball, tennis or volleyball, exercise facilities, pool, airport shuttle, cable TV and VCR, data port. **$$$**

Amerisuites Hotel
4520 Paradise Road.
Tel: 369-3366 or 800/833-1516.
Fax: 369-0009.
www.amerisuites.com

Located half a mile from the airport, amenities here include exercise facilities, business services, pool, airport shuttle, concierge desk, cable TV and VCR, data port. coffeemaker. **$$**

Best Western Mardi Gras Inn
3500 Paradise Road.
Tel: 731-2020, 800/634-6501. Fax: 733-6994. www.mardigrasinn.com
About 3 miles (4 km) from the airport, the hotel has a casino, salon, business service, swimming pool, airport shuttle, concierge desk, cable TV and data port. **$$**

Boardwalk Hotel and Casino
3750 Las Vegas Boulevard South.
Tel: 735 2400 or 800-635-4581.
Fax: 739-8152.
www.boardwalklv.com
Located on the Strip Boardwalk between Bellagio and the Monte Carlo. Wedding chapel, shopping, exercise facilities, swimming pool,

The Strip's Hotels on the Web

Algiers
www.algiershotel.com
Aladdin Resort and Casino
www.aladdincasino.com
Bally's Las Vegas
www.ballyslv.com
Barbary Coast Hotel and Casino
www.barbarycoastcasino.com
Bellagio
www.bellagioresort.com
Boardwalk Casino – Holiday Inn
www.hiboaradwalk.com
Caesars Palace
www.caesars.com
Circus Circus Hotel Casino
www.circuscircus.com
Excalibur
www.excaliburcasino.com
Flamingo Las Vegas
www.flamingolv.com
Four Seasons Hotel Las Vegas
www.fourseasons.com
Hard Rock
www.hardrockhotel.com
Imperial Palace Hotel and Casino
www.imperialpalace.com
Las Vegas Hilton
www.lv-hilton.com
Luxor
www.luxor.com

Mandalay Bay Resort and Casino
www.mandalaybay.com
MGM Grand Hotel Casino and Theme Park
www.mgmgrand.com
The Mirage
www.mirage.com
Monte Carlo Resort and Casino
www.monte-carlo.com
The New Frontier Hotel and Casino
www.frontierlv.com
New York-New York Hotel Casino
www.nynyhotelcasino.com
Paris Las Vegas
www.paris-lv.com
Polo Towers
www.polotowers.com
Riviera Hotel and Casino
www.theriviera.com
Stardust Hotel and Casino
www.stardustlv.com
Stratosphere Tower Hotel and Casino
www.stratlv.com
Treasure Island
www.treasureisland.com
Tropicana Resort and Casino
www.tropicanalv.com
The Venetian Resort-Hotel-Casino
www.venetian.com

concierge desk, three restaurants, buffet and room service. **$$**

Boulder Station Hotel Casino
4111 Boulder Highway.
www.boulderstation.com
Tel: 432-7777 or 800/638-7777.
Fax: 432-7744.
Boulder Station is about 15 miles (25 km) from the airport. It has movie theaters, childcare, business services, swimming pool, airport shuttle, concierge desk, 12 restaurants, buffet, room service and cable TV. **$$**

Club de Soleil
5499 West Tropicana Avenue.
Tel: 221-0200 or 877/476-5345.
Fax: 579-9120.
www.clubdesoleil.com
Non-gaming hotel with a French-Mediterranean theme. Pool, tennis courts, exercise facilities, a masseuse, concierge desk, cable TV and VCR, Jacuzzi. About 5 miles (8 km) west of the airport. **$$**

Desert Paradise Resort
5165 South Decatur Boulevard.
www.desertparaadiseresort.com
Tel: 579-3600 or 877/257-0900.
Fax: 579-3673.
Located about 1 mile (1.5 km) west of the Strip, Desert Paradise is an all-suites non-gaming hotel. Located 5 miles (8 km) from the airport, it has exercise facilities, business services, swimming pool, spa, fitness center, concierge desk and cable TV. **$$**

Emerald Springs – Holiday Inn
325 East Flamingo Road.
Tel: 732-9100 or 800/732-889.
Fax: 731-9784.
www.holidayinnlasvegas.com
Attractive boutique non-gaming hotel, 2 miles (3 km) from the airport; with exercise facilities, business services, pool, airport shuttle, restaurant, room service, cable TV and data port. **$$**

Greek Isles Hotel and Casino
305 Convention Center Drive.
Tel: 952-8000 or 800/633-1777.
Fax: 952-8100.
Attractive Greek decor with taverna. Showroom and comedy lounge wedding chapel, exercise facilities, business services, pool, airport shuttle, restaurant, cable TV and data port. **$$**

Price Categories

Rates are for a hotel room, using the lowest standard rate.
Suites start at a higher rate.

$$$$	$150+
$$$	$100-$149
$$	$50-$99
$	under $49

Hampton Inn
7100 Cascade Valley Court.
Tel: 360-5700 or 800/426-7866.
Fax: 360-5757.
Tucked away in the northwest portion of Las Vegas, about 15 miles (8 km) from the airport. A non-gaming venue, it has business services, pool and cable TV. **$$**

Hard Rock
4455 Paradise Road.
Tel: 693-5000 or 800/693-7625.
Fax: 693-5010.
www.hardrockhotel.com
Three blocks from the Strip. Large beach club, spa, some luxury suites, music memorabilia. **$$**

Hotel San Remo
115 East Tropicana Avenue.
Tel: 739-9000 or 800/522-7366.
Fax: 736-1120.
www.sanremolasvegas.com
Within walking distance of the Strip (but too hot to walk in summer) with showroom, wedding chapel, business services, pool, concierge desk, four restaurants, room service, buffet, Jacuzzi and data port. **$$**

Key Largo Casino and Hotel
377 East Flamingo Road.
Tel: 733-7777 or 800/634-6617.
Fax: 734-5071.
www.keylargocasino.com
Casino, wedding gazebo, shopping, pool, motor coach parking, airport shuttle, restaurant, cable TV and data port. **$$**

The Orleans Hotel and Casino
4500 West Tropicana Avenue.
Tel: 365-7111 or 800/675-3267.
www.orleanscasino.com
Mardi Gras-themed hotel, 1 mile west of the Strip, offering New Orleans style with salon, exercise facilities, business services, pool, Jacuzzi, concierge desk, eight

restaurants and buffet, room service, cable TV and data port. **$$**

Sam's Town Hotel and Gambling Hall
5111 Boulder Highway.
Tel: 456-7777, 800/634-6371.
Fax: 454-8107. www.samstown.com
On Boulder Highway 7 miles (11 km) east of the airport, enroute to Boulder City, Hoover Dam and Arizona. A beautiful and huge atrium offers patio dining, waterfalls and nightly laser show. Pool, eight restaurants and buffet, cable TV, and childcare. **$$**

Sunset Station Hotel Casino
1301 West Sunset Road, Henderson.
Tel: 547-7777 or 888/786-7389.
Fax: 547-7879.
www.sunsetstation.com
Mediterranean-style architecture and a bar based on the style of Spanish architect Antonio Gaudi. Eight miles (13 km) from the airport, this hotel has a microbrewery, multi-screen movie theater and an outdoor amphitheater. It also offers business services, pool, airport shuttle and 15 restaurants. **$$**

Terrible's Hotel and Casino
4100 Paradise Road.
Tel: 733-7737 or 800/640-9777.
www.terribleherbst.com
Only 1 mile from the airport and a few blocks east of the Strip, Terrible's has bingo, business services, pool, concierge desk, three restaurants and buffet, room service, Jacuzzi and cable TV. **$$**

Doubletree Club
7250 Pollock Drive.
Tel: 948-4000, 800/222-TREE.
Fax: 948-4100.
www.doubletree.com
Non-gaming hotel with free shuttle to the Strip and airport. Fitness center, pool, bakery, cafe. **$–$$**

Westward Ho Hotel and Casino
2900 Las Vegas Boulevard South.
Tel: 731-2900 or 800/634-6803.
Fax: 731-6154.
www.westwardho.com
Five miles (8 km) from the airport, with suites big enough for six guests, seven pools and

Jacuzzis, concierge desk, two restaurants, a buffet and cable TV. **$–$$**

Arizona Charlie's East Hotel and Casino
4575 Boulder Highway.
Tel: 951-5900, 800/362-4040. Fax: 731-2347. www.azcharlies.com
East of town, part way to Boulder City, to Hoover Dam. About 6 miles (4 km) from the airport, amenities include a casino, airport shuttle, five restaurants, buffet and cable TV. **$**

Arizona Charlie's Hotel and Casino
740 South Decatur Boulevard.
Tel: 258-5200 or 800/342-2695. Fax: 258-5192. www.azcharlies.com
The original Arizona Charlie's, located almost one mile west of the Strip and about 11 miles (18 km) from the airport. Wedding chapel, swimming pool, airport shuttle, five restaurants, buffet and cable TV. **$**

Cancun Resort
8335 Las Vegas Boulevard South.
Tel: 614-6200. Fax: 614-6206.
A non-gaming property located 5 miles (8 km) from the airport south of the Strip, Cancun Resort has a penthouse suite and villas with private balconies. Services include exercise facilities, swimming pool, concierge desk, cable TV, VCR, Jacuzzi and data port. Call for rates.

Fiesta Henderson Casino Hotel
777 West Lake Mead Drive, Henderson.
Tel: 558-7000 or 800/899-7770. Fax: 567-7373.
South-of-the-border theme hotel 10 miles (16 km) from the airport with pool, Jacuzzi, three bar/lounges, restaurants and buffet, cable TV and data port. **$**

Silverton Hotel and Casino
3333 Blue Diamond Road.
Tel: 263-7777 or 800/588-7711. Fax: 896-5635.
www.silvertoncasino.com
Two miles (3 km) south of the airport, a Western-themed hotel with cocktail lounge and nightly entertainment. Pool, three restaurants and buffet, room service and cable TV. Pool, kitchenettes, laundromat. **$**

Beyond Las Vegas

Boulder City
Southeast of Las Vegas on US 93, Boulder City is 30 miles (48 km) from McCarran Airport.

Boulder Dam Hotel
1305 Arizona Street.
Tel: 293-3510. Fax: 293-3093.
www.boulderdamhotel.com
This small, quaint and centrally located hotel offering bed and breakfast has a restaurant, room service, shop, charming museum, exercise facilities, cable TV and data ports. **$$–$$$**

Hacienda Hotel and Casino
US Highway 93.
Tel: 293-5000 or 800/245-6380. Fax: 293-5608.
www.haciendaonline.com
Three restaurants, 24-hour shop, buffet, swimming pool, theater, Jacuzzi and helicopter rides. **$$**

Primm
Primm is located 43 miles (69 km) southwest of Las Vegas on the California border

Buffalo Bill's Resort and Casino
31700 South Las Vegas Boulevard.
Tel: 386-7867 or 800/386-7867.
www.primmvalleyresorts.com
Restaurants, food court, 90 mph (145 kph) thrill rides, movie theater, video arcade and outdoor amphitheater. **$–$$**

Primm Valley Resort and Casino
31900 South Las Vegas Boulevard.
Tel: 386-7867 or 800/386-7867. Fax: 679-5424.
www.primmvalleyresorts.com
Resembles a clone of San Diego's Hotel del Coronado. Restaurants, two golf courses and nearby, a very good Fashion Outlets shopping mall with a shuttle bus that runs from Las Vegas' Strip. **$–$$**

Whiskey Pete's Hotel and Casino
100 West Primm Boulevard.
Tel: 386-867 or 800/386-7867. Fax: 679-5424.
www.primmvalleyresorts.com
Bonnie and Clyde artifacts on view. **$–$$**

Jean
A small town on I-15 halfway between Las Vegas and the California border at Primm.

Gold Strike Hotel and Gambling Hall
1 Main Street.
Tel: 477-5000 or 800/634-1359. Fax: 671-623.
Shopping, swimming pool, airport shuttle, cable TV, three restaurants and a buffet. **$**

Nevada Landing Hotel and Casino
2 Good Springs Road.
Tel: 387-5000 or 800/628-6682. Fax: 874-1441.
www.nevadalanding.com
Four restaurants, buffet, shopping, business services and pool. **$**

Laughlin
On the Colorado River below Davis Dam and Lake Mojave, across the river from Bullhead City Arizona, Laughlin is 95 miles (153 km) south of Las Vegas.

Riverside Resort Hotel and Casino
1650 Casino Drive.
www.riversideresort.com
Tel: 298 2535 or 800/227-3849.
The original Laughlin resort by Don Laughlin who founded the town, the Riverside has five restaurants and buffet, 34-lane bowling center, wedding chapel, children's play center, multiplex theater, airport shuttle, a pool and Jacuzzi. **$$**

Harrah's Laughlin Casino and Hotel
2900 South Casino Drive.
Tel: 298-4600 or 800/427-7247. Fax: 298-6802. www.harrahs.com
With a soft sand riverside beach, five restaurants and buffet, Harrah's also offers shopping, exercise facilities, business services, pool, concierge desk, cable TV room service. **$$**

Edgewater Hotel and Casino
2020 South Casino Drive.
Tel: 298-2453 or 800/677-4837. Fax: 298-8165.
www.edgewater-casino.com
This casino has four restaurants and buffet, salon, shopping arcade, swimming pool, spa, airport shuttle, concierge desk and cable TV. **$–$$**

Flamingo Laughlin
1900 South Casino Drive.
Tel: 298-5111 or 800/435-8469.
Fax: 298-5042.
www.flamingo-laughlin.com
The largest hotel in Laughlin in terms of number of rooms (1,900), with six restaurants, outdoor and indoor showrooms, a buffet, wedding chapel, shopping, business services, pool, airport shuttle, cable TV and room service. **$-$$**

Ramada Express Hotel Casino
2121 South Casino Drive.
Tel: 298-4200 or 800/872-4605.
Fax: 298-7462.
www.ramadaexpress.com
Ramada is encircled by a model train offering free rides. Houses a Veterans' Museum with daily live shows. Four restaurants and buffet, wedding chapel, business facilities, pool, Jacuzzi, airport shuttle and concierge desk. **$-$$**

Pioneer Hotel and Gambling Hall
2200 South Casino Drive.
Tel: 298-4200 or 800/634-3469.
Fax: 298-7462.
www.pioneerlaughlin.com
Motel-style on river with Olde West motif. The Oatman Ghostriders perform on weekends. Three restaurants and buffet, pool, cable TV and airport shuttle. **$**

Colorado Belle Hotel Casino & Microbrewery
2100 South Casino Drive.
Tel: 298-4000 or 800/477-8437.
Fax: 299-0669.
www.coloradobelle.com
Built to resemble a riverboat. Two swimming pools and a beach, gift shops, six restaurants, airport shuttle and cable TV. **$**

River Palms Resort-Casino
2700 South Casino Drive.
Tel: 298 2242 or 877/787-7256.
Fax: 298-2117. www.rvrpalm.com
Dominated by a 25-story tower. With seven restaurants and buffet, this resort offers exercise facilities, swimming pool, business services, an airport shuttle, cable TV, a data port and room service. **$**

Price Categories

Rates are for a hotel room, using the lowest standard rate. Suites start at a higher rate.

$$$$	$150+
$$$	$100-$149
$$	$50-$99
$	under $49

Mesquite
About 90 miles (145 km) northeast of Las Vegas on I-15.

Casablanca Resort and Casino
950 West Mesquite Boulevard.
Tel: 346-7529 or 800/459-7529.
Fax: 346-6777.
www.casablancaresort.com
In the Virgin Mountains. Three restaurants and buffet, shopping, salon, exercise facilities, business services, pool, concierge desk cable TV and data port. **$**

Virgin River Hotel and Casino
100 Pioneer Boulevard.
Tel: 346-7777, or 800/356-7721.
Fax: 346-7780. www.virginriver.com
Two restaurants and buffet, pool, laundromat, airport shuttle, concierge desk and cable TV. **$**

Excursions
ROUTE 66

Kingman
Hill Top Motel
1901 East Andy Devine Avenue, AZ 86401.
Tel: 928/753-2198.
Pleasant, well-maintained hotel accommodation with pool. **$**

Oatman
Oatman Hotel
HWY 66, AZ 86433.
Tel: 928/768-4408.
Characterful adobe hotel with a history of movie stars. **$$**

Williams
Fray Marcos Hotel
163 Grand Canyon Boulevard, AZ 86046.
Tel: 928/635-4010.
Originally a unit of the once-ubiquitous Harvey House chain, established in the 1880s along the route of the Santa Fe Railroad line. The hotel has now been pleasantly restored. **$$**

El Rancho Motel
617 East Rt 66, AZ 86046.
Tel: 928/635-2552.
Clean rooms with free movies. **$**

GRAND CANYON

For park information: PO Box 129, Grand Canyon, AZ 86023.
Tel: 928/638-7888.
Web: www.thecanyon.com/nps
All lodgings are managed by:
Xanterra Parks and Resorts
14001 E Iliff, No. 600, Aurora, CO 80014.
Tel: 928/638-2631 (same-day reservations: South Rim);
928/628-2611 (North Rim).
Tel: 303/297-2757 (advance).

Bright Angel Lodge
West Rim Drive.
Tel: 928/638-2631.
Old rustic lodge and bungalows with simple accommodation. Restaurant and bar. **$$**

Grand Canyon Lodge
Bright Angel Point.
Tel: 303/297-2757.
Basic accommodations and cabins on the North Rim; open seasonally. With a restaurant and bar. **$$**

DEATH VALLEY

Furnace Creek Inn
PO Box 1, CA 92328.
Tel: 760/786-2423.
Fax: 760/786-2423.
www.furnacecreekresort.com
An elegant resort in the desert with a restaurant, pool, golf, tennis, horseback riding. **$$$**

Furnace Creek Ranch (same address and phone as above).
Under the same management but less expensive.

Stovepipe Wells Village
State Highway 190, CA 92328.
Tel: 619/786-2387.
Fax: 760/786-2389.
Restaurant, pool. **$**

Where to Eat

There are more than 1,200 restaurants in the Las Vegas metropolitan area. This selection features a few restaurants in each major ethnicity, listed by price (starting with the most upscale) and alphabetically.

Reservation and restaurant searches may also be made online at **www.tasteofvegas.com** or at **www.lasvegas.com**

American

Alan Albert's
3763 Las Vegas Boulevard South.
Tel: 795-7133. Daily 5-11.30pm.
Classic steaks, thick veal and lamb chops, live Maine lobsters and roasted prime rib. **$$$$**

Aureole
Mandalay Bay
3950 Las Vegas Boulevard South.
Tel: 632-7401. Daily 6–11pm.
Celebrity chef Charlie Palmer's version of his New York City classic is architecturally amazing (a three-story wine tower in the restaurant and a pond with swans), with an outstanding wine list. **$$$$**

Rosemary's
8125 West Sahara. Tel: 869-2251.
Monday–Friday 11.30am–2.30pm, daily 5.30–10.30pm.
Creatively presented roast lamb, lamb brochettes, salmon tartar, grilled pork chops and more. **$$$$**

Seasons
Bally's, 3645 Las Vegas Boulevard South. Tel: 739-4651
Tuesday–Saturday 6–11pm.
Filet mignon and fresh Maine lobster as well as more exotic delicacies. Extensive menu that changes with the seasons. **$$$$**

The Palm
Caesars Palace, 3500 Las Vegas Boulevard South. Tel: 732-7256.
Daily 11.30am–10.30pm.
Gourmet steak and seafood, plus poultry, veal and pasta. **$$$$**

Bix's Supper Club
4495 South Buffalo Road.
Tel: 889-0800. Daily 11am–6am.
In southwest part of town. Upscale atmosphere and crowd, classy bar and well-decorated tables. Gourmet burgers, *filet mignon*, prawns, and wood grilled pizza. Wine and cigar rooms. Book in advance. **$$$**

Cafe Bellagio
3600 Las Vegas Boulevard South.
Tel: 693-7223. Daily 24 hours.
Located in the Conservatory and Botanical Gardens, light and airy atmosphere with a gorgeous pool and botanical garden views. **$$$**

Gordon Biersch Brewery
3987 Paradise Road.
Tel: 312-5247. Sunday–Thursday 11am–4pm, 4–10pm;
Friday–Saturday 11.30am–11pm.
Bar: 11.30am–late.
American cuisine with international flavors: dough pizzas, pastas, German-style lagers brewed on site. **$$$**

Price Categories

Prices are based on the average cost of dinner with a glass of wine, before tip.

$$$$	$38 and up
$$$	under $38
$$	under $28
$	under $18

Sir Galahad's Prime Rib House
Excalibur, 3850 Las Vegas Boulevard South. Tel: 597-7448.
Sunday–Thursday 5–10pm,
Friday–Saturday till 11pm.
The house specialty is carved tableside and offered with a choice of old-fashioned soups, salads, and traditional Yorkshire pudding. **$$$**

Blue Note Jazz Club
Desert Passage at Aladdin, 3667 Las Vegas Boulevard South.
Tel: 862-8307. Daily dinner 6pm–2am. Cafe 11am–midnight.
Pepper-rubbed rib eye, roasted chicken breast, cornmeal-crusted calamari and more. **$$$**

Top Of The World
Stratosphere, 2000 Las Vegas Boulevard South. Tel: 380-7711.
Sunday–Thursday 6–11pm,
Friday–Saturday till midnight.
Gourmet lunch daily 11am–3pm.
Happy hour 11am–6pm.
Revolves 360 degrees each hour so great views of the Strip. Steaks, fresh fish, lobster and more. **$$$**

Triple 7 Brewpub
Main Street Station, 200 North Main Street. Tel: 387-1896.
Daily 11am–7am.
Five premium beers and sushi and oyster bars. Varied menu includes gourmet pizzas, barbecue ribs and pale-ale battered shrimp. **$$$**

America
New York-New York
3790 Las Vegas Boulevard South.
Tel: 740-6451. Daily 24 hours.
Philly cheese-steak sandwiches from Pennsylvania, buffalo wings from New York and so on. Burgers and country breakfasts are favorites. **$$**

Bay City Diner
Golden Gate Hotel, 1 Fremont Street. Tel: 385-1906. 24 hours.
In the oldest hotel in town, famous for its 99c shrimp cocktails. **$$**

Coffee Pub
2800 West Sahara. Tel: 367-1913.
Monday–Friday 7am–4pm, weekend 7am–3pm.
A favorite breakfast and lunch spot among business people. Delicious soups, salads and sandwiches, deli croissants, quiche of the day, crab soufflé roll, pastries and fresh fruit smoothies. **$$**

Monte Carlo Pub & Brewery
3770 Las Vegas Boulevard South.
Tel: 730-7777. Sunday–Thursday 11am–2am, Friday–Saturday 11am–4am. Food until 10pm; after that, appetizers and pizzas.
Good meals, great brews and music from 9pm in the first microbrewery in a Las Vegas resort. **$$**

Studio Café
MGM Grand, 3799 Las Vegas Boulevard South. Tel: 891-1111.
Daily 24 hours
Upscale casual dining and health-smart choices. Roasted sweet corn crab cakes, California pitta pocket, hamburgers and Chinese. **$$**

Continental

Wolfgang Puck's Cili
Bali Hai Golf Club, 5160 Las Vegas
Boulevard South. Tel: 856-1000.
Daily breakfast 7–11am, lunch
11am–5pm, dinner 5–9pm; Sunday
brunch 10am–2pm.
Puck's features two menus, Eastern
and Western gourmet. It overlooks
the Bali Hai golf course, with water
features and the mountains in the
distance. The service is a perfect
compliment to this splendid dining
experience. **$$$$**

Michael's
Barbary Coast, 3595 Las Vegas
Boulevard South. Tel: 737-7111.
Daily 6pm–midnight.
This Victorian-style gourmet room
features classic continental cuisine
including fresh broiled Maine
lobster and stone crab,
chateaubriand, rack of lamb and
poultry entrees. **$$$$**

The Burgundy Room
Lady Luck, 206 North Third Street.
Tel: 477-3000. Daily 5–10pm.
This lovely room presents
Continental fare at reasonable
prices, including beef Wellington,
fettuccine Alfredo, veal Oscar and
rack of lamb. **$$$$**

Drai's
Barbary Coast, 3595 Las Vegas
Boulevard South.
Tel: 737-7111. Daily 5pm–12am.
Ex-Hollywood producer and
restaurateur to the stars Victor Drai
brings an upscale ambience to this
beautiful room. Dishes include
crispy duck confit in Merlot sauce
and seared jumbo scallops with
citrus ginger sauce. **$$$**

Wolfgang Puck Café
MGM Grand, 3799 Las Vegas
Boulevard South.
Tel: 891-3019. Daily 11am–11pm.
This brightly colored circular
restaurant surrounds an open
kitchenette. Featuring gourmet pizza
and salads, pastas, rotisserie
chicken and much more. **$$**

Magnolia Room
Jerry's Nugget, 1821 Las Vegas
Boulevard North. Tel: 399-3000.
Sunday 2–9pm, Wednesday–
Saturday 4–11pm.
Excellent continental cuisine. **$**

Southern, Cajun, Creole, Barbeque

Commander's Palace
Desert Passage at Aladdin, 3667
Las Vegas Boulevard South.
Tel: 892-8272.
Monday–Sunday 11.30am–2.30pm,
limited menu 2.30–4.30pm, dinner
6–10pm. Sunday Jazz Brunch
($25–35) features a New Orleans
menu at 11.30am–2.30pm.
New Orleans food, including Gulf
seafood flown in fresh daily and
signature Creole dishes. **$$$$**

Price Categories

Price categories based on the
average cost of dinner with a
glass of wine, before tip.

$$$$	$38 and up
$$$	under $38
$$	under $28
$	under $18

Big Al's Oyster Bar
The Orleans, 4500 West Tropicana
Avenue. Tel: 365-7111.
Sunday–Thursday 11am–midnight,
Friday–Saturday 11am–1am.
Creole/Cajun-style freshly shucked
oysters and clams or steamed
clams, voodoo mussels, pan
roasts, shrimp scampi,
bouillabaisse and pasta. **$$$**

House of Blues
Mandalay Bay, 3950 Las Vegas
Boulevard South. Tel: 632-7607.
until midnight or 1am; Friday–
Saturday blues band 10pm–1am;
Gospel Brunch (Southern-inspired
cuisine and Gospel performances)
10am and 1pm.
Creole and Cajun staples such as
jambalaya and gumbo, plus
Southern-style regional cuisine. **$$**

Kathy's Southern Cooking
6407 Mountain Vista Street.
Tel: 433-1005. Daily 11am–9pm.
Kathy Cook comes from Louisiana,
and makes terrific Southern dishes,
such as smothered chicken, baked
ribs, jambalaya, red beans and rice,
and a wonderful chicken gumbo. **$$**

Memphis Championship Barbecue
2250 East Warm Springs Road.
Tel: 260-6909. Sunday–Thursday
11am–10pm, Friday–Saturday
till 11pm.
Mike Mills is a four-time world
champion in barbecue; his specialty
is smoking meats for hours in a
hickory wood pit. Try the dry-rubbed
baby back ribs, or fiery hot links. **$**

French

Andre's
401 South Sixth Street. Tel: 385-
5016. Monday–Saturday 6pm–until
last reservation.
The downtown Andre's is rustic and
friendly, country French with small
rooms for intimate dining. Andre
Rochat proudly serves classics
such as *sole meunière*, rack of
lamb and outstanding soufflés. An
award-winning wine list. **$$$$**

Andre's at the Monte Carlo
3770 Las Vegas Boulevard South.
Tel: 730-7955.
Upscale dining in a formal, elegant
setting, featuring chef Andre
Rochat's extraordinary gourmet
French cuisine and a world-class
wine cellar and spirits list. **$$$$**

Eiffel Tower Restaurant
Paris, 3645 Las Vegas Boulevard
South. Tel: 948-6937
Sunday–Thursday 5.30–10pm,
Friday–Saturday 5.30–10:30pm; bar
5pm–midnight.
Gourmet entrees in an elegant
atmosphere with a view of the Strip
from the 11th floor. **$$$$**

Le Cirque
Bellagio, 3600 Las Vegas Boulevard
South. Tel: 693-8100.
Daily 5.30–10.30pm. Coat and tie
are mandatory for men.
Creative gourmet entrees such as
black-tie scallops (tied with black
truffles), *consommé de boeuf* with
foie gras ravioli, roasted duck with a
honey-spice fig glaze, and roasted
lobster in a port wine sauce. After
these enjoy luscious desserts.
$$$$

Lutèce
Venetian, 3355 Las Vegas
Boulevard South. Tel: 414-2220.
Daily 5.30–10.30pm.
Classic, family-style and newer
French cuisine in an elegantly
modern restaurant. **$$$$**

Josef's Brasserie
Desert Passage at Aladdin, 3667 Las Vegas Boulevard South. Tel: 732-3000. Daily 11:30am–2am. Enjoy contemporary cuisine from a remarkable French brasserie menu in a casual atmosphere. The oyster bar has seafood flown in daily. **$$$**

Italian

al Dente
Bally's, 3645 Las Vegas Boulevard South. Tel: 967-4111. Nightly 5:30–10:30pm. Light Italian dining in a contemporary atmosphere. **$$$**

BICE
Desert Passage at Aladdin, 3667 Las Vegas Boulevard South. Tel: 732-4210. Sunday–Thursday 11.30am–10pm; Friday–Saturday 11.30am–11.30pm. World famous with restaurants in New York, Palm Beach, Miami, Chicago, London, Milan and other European and South American cities. Serves authentic Italian and many other dishes. Fine wine. **$$$**

Stefano's
Golden Nugget, 129 Fremont Street. Tel: 385-7111. Sunday–Thursday 6–11pm, Friday–Saturday 5.30–11pm. Good wines, singing waiters and classic dishes. The *osso buco* is a favorite; the lobster tail Milanese is outstanding. **$$$**

Terrazza
Caesars Palace, 3570 Las Vegas Boulevard South. Tel: 731-7731. Tuesday–Thursday 5.30–10.30pm, Friday–Saturday 5.30–11pm. Lounge open nightly 6pm–midnight. This beautiful restaurant features excellent Italian dining and jazz nightly in the lounge. **$$$**

Battista's Hole In The Wall
4041 Audrie Lane. Tel: 732-1424. Sunday–Thursday 5–10.30pm, Friday–Saturday 5–11pm. This casual Italian has 30 years' worth of celebrity photos and mementos. It offers one-price meals, pasta, seafood or veal, that include all the wine you can drink. The food is great and the wandering accordion player a local legend. **$$**

Olio
MGM Grand, 3799 Las Vegas Boulevard South. Tel: 891-7775. Sunday–Thursday 5–11pm, Friday–Saturday 5pm–2am. Gelato hours: Sunday–Thursday 11am–10pm, Friday–Saturday 11am–1am. A neo-Italian restaurant offering several unforgettable features including the world's largest antipasto table, multi-leveled, multi-layered dining areas, an 8 ft (2.5 m) fireplace and more. The gelato wall is a sweet-lover's delight. **$$**

Onda
The Mirage, 3400 Las Vegas Boulevard South. Tel: 791-7223. Daily 5.30–11pm. Regional and classic Italian with American innovations, featuring homemade pastas, breads, fresh seafood and meats. **$$**

Wolfgang Puck's Trattoria del Lupo
Mandalay Bay, 3950 Las Vegas Boulevard South. Tel: 740-5522. Sunday–Thursday 5.30–9.30pm. Friday–Saturday 5.30–10.30pm. Trattoria del Lupo means Restaurant of the Wolf, and that means celebrity chef Wolfgang Puck with his first Italian restaurant. This trattoria is full of antiques and unique lighting fixtures and includes an exhibition pizza station. Although famous for the pizza, there are delicious classic and contemporary Italian dishes. **$$**

Il Fornaio
New York-New York, 3790 Las Vegas Boulevard South. Tel: 740-6403. Monday–Friday 8.30am–midnight, Saturday–Sunday till 1am. Regional cooking featuring home-made pastas, bakery-fresh breads dipped in virgin Italian olive oil and a variety of entrees including rotisserie meats and Mesquite grilled fish. The Italian coffees, pastries, muffins and scones are unforgettable. **$**

Mexican and Tex-Mex

Coyote Café
MGM Grand, 3799 Las Vegas Boulevard South. Tel: 891-7349. Daily 8.30am–10.30pm, dining room 5.30–10pm. Using blue corn, chilies and spices,

Coyote Café features hot and spicy modern southwestern cuisine. On the dinner menu (**$$$**) nightly are specialties such as buttermilk corn cakes with chipotle shrimp, pumpkin seed-crusted salmon and much more. **$$$** dinner, **$$** lunch

Cozymel's Coastal Mexican Grill
355 Hughes Center Drive. Tel: 732-4833. Sunday–Thursday 11am–10pm, Friday–Saturday 11am–11pm. In a beautiful Mexican setting, this upscale coastal cuisine features predominately seafood. Grilled *Ahi Tuna* in a citrus marinade, and *Camarones al Mojo de Ajo* (shrimp sautéed in garlic lime butter and julienne ancho chilies) are accompanied by specialties such as lamb fajitas and *pollo poblano*. **$$**

Lindo Michoacan
2655 East Desert Inn Road. Tel: 735-6828. Monday–Wednesday 11am–10pm, Thursday–Friday 11am–11pm, Saturday–Sunday 9am–11pm. In a lovely rustic setting off the beaten path, authentic cuisine from the southwestern Pacific region of Mexico; the signature dish is barbecued goat meat with fresh tortillas and lime. **$**

Middle Eastern

Habib's Persian Cuisine
4750 West Sahara Avenue. Tel: 870-0860. Monday–Saturday 11.30am–3pm, 5–10pm. Excellent Persian/Mediterranean cuisine offering generous portions, served in elegant surroundings. **$$**

Marrakech
3900 Paradise Road. Tel: 737-5611. Daily 5.30–11pm. Enjoy feasting on a traditional six-course Moroccan meal while being entertained by beautiful belly dancers. **$$**

Zanzibar Café
Aladdin, 3667 Las Vegas Boulevard South. Tel: 785-9001. Daily 24 hours. Special late-night menu 1am–6am. Specializes in foods from the Middle and Far East, plus some American dishes. **$**

Seafood

Aqua
Bellagio, 3600 Las Vegas Boulevard South. Tel: 693-7223. Daily 5.30–10pm. Aqua is an upscale seafood house from San Francisco where Chef Michael Mina's creations are exquisitely outstanding. **$$$$**

McCormick & Smick's
335 Hughes Center Drive. Tel: 836-9000. Monday–Friday 11am–11pm, Saturday–Sunday 5pm–11pm; bar lounge Monday–Friday till midnight, Saturday 4pm–midnight, Sunday 4pm–11pm. Daily menu, upscale décor and diligent, friendly service in one of the finest seafood restaurants. Over five types of oysters feature daily. **$$$$**

Rosewood Grille
3339 Las Vegas Boulevard South. Daily from 4.30pm. This very successful restaurant serves huge, fresh lobsters that you can choose and weigh. Also fine steaks and fresh fish. The knowledgeable staff make dining a pleasure in an intimate atmosphere. **$$$$**

Hugo's Cellar
Four Queens, 202 Fremont Street. Tel: 385-4011. Daily 5.30–11pm. Outstanding service, fresh seafood and fine beef. **$$$$**

Buzio's Seafood Restaurant
Rio, 3700 West Flamingo Road. Tel: 252-7777. Daily 11am–11pm. The finest of seafood selections, featuring steamers, chowders, pan roasts, seafood pastas, cioppino, and bouillabaisse. **$$$**

Emeril's New Orleans Fish House
MGM Grand, 3799 Las Vegas Boulevard South. Tel: 891-7374. Daily 11.30am–2.30pm, 5.30–10.30pm, oyster bar 11.30am–10.30pm. Featuring celebrity chef Emeril Lagasse's ingeniously prepared seafood, including Creole Cajun cooking, and his mouthwatering BBQ shrimp. All homemade. **$$$**

Lobster House
3763 Las Vegas Boulevard South. Tel: 740 4431. Daily 5–11.30pm. Select superb Maine lobsters from large display tanks; enjoy Alaskan king crab legs, scampi or one of several nightly fresh fish selections. The room is rigged like a yacht. **$$$**

Tenaya Creek Restaurant & Brewery
3101 North Tenaya Way. Tel: 362-7335. Sunday–Thursday 11am–11pm, Friday–Saturday 11am–midnight. Enjoy handcrafted microbrews and brats, gourmet pizzas and seafood. Favorites include the crab cakes, vodka salmon and spinach and four-cheese ravioli in a basil-infused tomato cream sauce. **$$$**

Steakhouses

Charlie Palmer
Four Seasons 3960 Las Vegas Boulevard South. Tel: 362-5000. Daily 5.30–11pm. Offering Palmer's signature cuisine, including fine steak and seafood, as well as family-style side dishes. **$$$$**

Gallagher's Steakhouse
New York-New York, 3790 Las Vegas Boulevard South. Tel: 740-6450. Daily 5–11pm. A duplicate of the original establishment on 52nd Street in Manhattan offering aged steaks and some excellent grilled seafood. All dishes are cooked to perfection and served by efficient staff. **$$$$**

Morton's of Chicago
400 East Flamingo Road. Tel: 893-0703. Monday–Thursday 5.30–11pm, Friday–Saturday 5–11.30pm. Morton's is less than 1 mile east of the Strip. Featuring meat broiled to perfection, and side dishes such as sautéed spinach with mushrooms and delicious hash browns. **$$$$**

Smith & Wollensky Steak House
3767 Las Vegas Boulevard South. Tel: 862-4100. Daily grill 11.30am–3am, dining room 5–11pm. Steaks of all kinds plus pork shank, lamb, seafood and poultry. Side dishes and appetizers, with a light-as-a-feather jumbo crab cake. **$$$$**

Delmonico Steakhouse
Venetian, 3355 Las Vegas Boulevard South. Tel: 414-3737. Monday–Sunday 11.30am–2pm, Sunday–Thursday 5.30–10.30pm, Friday–Saturday till 11pm. Emeril Lagasse offers a Creole flavor to this steakhouse. **$$$**

The Steak House
Circus Circus, 2880 Las Vegas Boulevard South. Tel: 794-3767. Sunday–Friday 5–10pm, Saturday 5–11pm, Sunday champagne brunch 9.30am, 11.30am, 1.30pm. A large display case shows customers ageing beef. Steaks, seafood and chicken cooked over an open grill. **$$**

Caribbean

Ortanique
Paris, 3655 Las Vegas Boulevard South. Tel: 946-3908. Daily 5.30–10.30pm. Award-winning chef Cindy Hutson calls her style "Cuisine of the Sun: an eclectic fusion of different nations and their natural bounties prepared and placed creatively on one plate." So there. **$$$**

Rumjungle
Mandalay Bay, 3950 Las Vegas Boulevard South. Tel: 632-7408. Daily 5.30–11pm, nightclub 11pm–4am, Thursday–Sunday cocktails 1–11pm. An exotic dining experience behind a waterfall and wall of flames. Grilled meat, fish and fowl marinated in rum, fruit and spices are featured in the cuisine of the Caribbean, Brazil and America. **$$**

Black Mountain Grill
11021 South Eastern Avenue, Henderson. Tel: 990-0990. Daily 24 hours. Chef Jay Yamaguchi's Pacific Rim cuisine is delicious. Also features wood-fired pizzas, steaks and wonderful deserts. **$**

Cuba Mia Café
3035 E. Tropicana Avenue. Tel: 435-6797. Monday–Thursday 10.30am–10pm, Friday–Saturday 10.30am–11pm, Sunday 1–9pm. Cuban cuisine famous for its abundant portions of beans, rice, yucca, pork and beef. Featuring Caribbean barbecue-style meats and wonderful side dish like *yucca frita* with garlic sauce or the *platano madur* (ripe-fried plantains). **$**

Asian

Asia
Harrah's, 3475 Las Vegas Boulevard South. Tel: 369-5000. Friday–Tuesday 5.30–10pm.
A mix of Chinese, Japanese and Asian cuisine served in an elegant atmosphere. **$$$**

Chinois
Caesars Palace, 3500 Las Vegas Boulevard South. Tel: 737-9700. Sunday–Thursday 11.30am–9.30pm, Friday–Saturday 11.30am–10pm; sushi bar daily 3–11pm. Almost adjacent to his highly successful Spago, Wolfgang Puck offers Chinese with a Gallic attitude. Specialties include the Shanghai lobster with coconut curry sauce, stir-fried string beans, whole sizzling catfish, Peking duck and much more. **$$$**

Sahara Korean Restaurant
953 East Sahara Avenue. Tel: 893-3423. Daily 10am–10pm. Featuring Korean cuisine. **$$$**

Lotus of Siam
953 East Sahara Avenue. Tel: 735-3033. Monday–Friday 11.30am–2.30pm, daily 5–9.30pm. Chef Saipin Chutima cooks dishes from her native Chiang Mai and the northeast province of Isaan. Thai specialties include Thai beef jerky, raw papaya salad, steamed catfish and char-grilled beef. **$$**

Malibu Chan's
8125 West Sahara Avenue. Tel: 312-4267. Monday–Saturday 5pm–2am, Sunday 5–9.30pm. Gourmet Pacific Rim menu with touches of Hawaii, including Calamari Asia, garlic shrimp pizza, crab cakes, stuffed chicken breast. Also has a sushi bar. **$$**

Thai Spice
4433 West Flamingo Road. Tel: 362-5308. Monday–Thursday 11am–10pm, Friday–Saturday till 11pm. Order your selection of gourmet Thai cuisine and degree of spices on a scale of one to 10. **$$**

Bangkok Boom
3111 South Valley View Boulevard. Tel: 252-0329. Monday–Friday 11am–4am, Saturday–Sunday 4pm–4am.

Price Categories

Price categories based on the average cost of dinner with a glass of wine, before tip.

$$$$ $38 and up
$$$ under $38
$$ under $28
$ under $18

Do not let the big-screen TV and bank of slot machines deter you from the food. It's wonderful. **$**

Dragon Noodle Company
Monte Carlo, 3770 Las Vegas Boulevard South. Tel: 730-7965. Daily 11am–10pm. A tea emporium and restaurant offering a variety of traditional Asian noodle dishes, roasted meats, chicken and fresh seafood. **$**

Saigon
4251 West Sahara Avenue. Tel: 362-9978. Daily 10am–3pm, 3–10pm. This inexpensive Vietnamese's specialty is phô. Light and flavorful entrees include spicy beef with coconut and curry sauce, and spicy fresh shrimp in a clay pot. **$**

The Thai Room
3355 East Tropicana Avenue. Tel: 458-8481. Monday–Friday 11am–10pm, Saturday noon–10pm, Sunday 4–10pm. Reservations preferred. Homemade Thai and Chinese dishes include spicy sour shrimp soup, jelly noodle salad, pad Thai, and pa-nang nuea (sliced beef tenderloin cooked in a curry sauce). **$**

Tsunami Asian Grill
Venetian, 3355 Las Vegas Boulevard South. Tel: 414-4840. Sunday–Thursday 11am–11pm, Friday–Saturday 11am–midnight. This pan-Asian restaurant has multi-levels and a huge mural showing Asian topography and images. Featuring a wonderful fresh sushi bar, many traditional entrees from Japan, China, Korea and Thailand, the Grill also offers a large range of dumpling and noodle dishes. **$**

Vegas Chinese & Thai Restaurant
115 North Fourth Street Tel: 382-1928. Daily 10am–10pm.

Located in downtown Las Vegas, serving some of the best Thai food, including spicy pad Thai, fiery tom ka kai and wonderful hot-and-sour tom yum. The anise-flavored smoked duck is a specialty. **$**

Chinese

Chang of Las Vegas
3055 Las Vegas Boulevard South. Tel: 731-3388. Daily 10am–midnight. Offers excellent Cantonese seafood, Hong Kong-style dishes, a variety of dim sum and much exotic fare. The pot-stickers and dumplings are fabulous. **$$$**

China Grill
Mandalay Bay, 3950 Las Vegas Boulevard South. Tel: 632-7404. Daily 5.30–10.30pm. Large portions intended for sharing. Mouthwatering favorites include the Shanghai lobster served with ginger, curry and crispy spinach, and crispy duck with caramelized black vinegar sauce and scallion pancakes. The architecture and décor are amazing. **$$$**

La Chine
Paris, 3655 Las Vegas Boulevard South. Tel: 946-4663 Sunday–Tuesday 6–11pm, Friday–Saturday 6–11.30pm. La Chine puts a French twist on authentic Hong Kong-style cuisine, in an upscale atmosphere. **$$$**

Lillie Langtry's
Golden Nugget, 129 Fremont St. Tel: 385-7111. Daily 5–10.30pm. Chinese without MSG. Offers appetizers, soups and a number of poultry, beef, pork, seafood and vegetarian dishes. **$$$**

Mayflower Cuisinier
4750 West Sahara Avenue. Tel: 870-8432. Monday–Friday 11am–2.30pm, Monday–Thursday 5–10pm, Friday–Saturday 5–11pm. Executive chef Ming See Woo has created wonderful gourmet Chinese delicacies such as tropical fried rice, spicy Thai shrimp scampi, and Mongolian grilled lamb chops in a creamy cilantro mint sauce. **$$$**

Moongate
The Mirage, 3400 Las Vegas Boulevard South. Tel: 791-7223.

Daily 5.30–11pm.
Fine Chinese food graced by a
classical Chinese courtyard. **$$$**
Cathay House
5300 Spring Mountain Road.
Tel: 876-3838
Daily 10.30am–10pm, dim sum
brunch 11.30am–2.30pm.
Traditional Chinese-style cuisine
with specialties such as walnut
prawns and sizzling black-peppered
filet mignon. **$$**
Chop Chop Chinese Buffet
Plaza, 1 Main Street. Tel: 386-
2110. Daily 4–10pm.
Authentic Chinese dishes prepared
by chef Tang at this casual buffet. **$**
King's Garden Chinese Restaurant
4750 East Tropicana Avenue.
Tel: 898-3833. Monday–Saturday
11.30am–10pm, Sunday 4–10pm.
Large selection of seafood, chicken,
pork, beef, chow mien and lo mien.
The dinners include egg flower
soup, egg roll, fried wonton and
pork-fried or steamed rice. **$**

Japanese

Benihana Village Hibachi
Las Vegas Hilton, 3000 Paradise
Road. Tel: 732-5755.
Daily 5–10.30pm.
The restaurant that made hibachi-grill
table cooking famous. Presented
in a Japanese village are seafood,
steaks and chicken. Robata at
Benihana offers tempura and
sashimi. **$$$$**
Hyakumi Japanese and Sushi Bar
Caesars Palace, 3570 Las Vegas
Boulevard South. Tel: 731-7731.
Sunday–Thursday 5.30–10.30pm,
Friday–Saturday 5.30–11pm.
Noodles and sushi bar 11am–4pm.
The menu has every type of sushi.
$$$$
Mikado
The Mirage, 3400 Las Vegas
Boulevard South. Tel: 791-7223.

Smoking

Smoking is allowed almost
everywhere in Vegas. If you
require a non-smoking
environment, inquire when you
make a table booking.

Buffets

The all-you-can eat buffets of Vegas
are justifiably famous. Where else
can you order the heartiest
breakfast in the world for $7.99, or
champagne and prime rib for under
$10? Expect long waiting lines,
even at midnight, but guests of the
hotel itself usually have priority.

The Buffet
Bellagio, 3600 Las Vegas
Boulevard South. Tel: 693-7223.
Go for lunch.
Carnival World Buffet at the Rio
3700 West Flamingo Road.
Tel: 252-7777. Highly regarded as
just about the best in town.
Coco Palms Buffet
Stardust, 3000 Las Vegas
Boulevard South. Tel: 732-6234.
Emperor's Buffet
Imperial Palace, 3535 Las Vegas
Boulevard. Tel: 731-3311.
Festival Buffet
Fiesta, 2400 North Rancho Drive.
Tel: 631-7000. Children under
three years eat for free.
French Market Buffet
The Orleans, 4500 West Tropicana

Avenue. Tel: 365-7111.
Garden Court Buffet
Main Street Station, 200 North
Main Street. Tel: 387-1896.
Downtown.
Island Buffet
Tropicana, 3801 Las Vegas
Boulevard South. Tel: 739-2222.
Lady Luck Express Buffet
Lady Luck, 206 North Third Street.
Tel: 477-3000. All you can eat and
drink Downtown.
Molly's Buffet
Fitzgerald's, 301 Fremont Street.
Tel: 388-2400. Downtown.
San Brisas Buffet
Castaways, 2800 Fremont Street.
Tel: 385 9177.
Spice Market Buffet
Aladdin, 3667 Las Vegas
Boulevard South. Tel: 785-9005.
Champagne.
Teahouse/Imperial Buffet
Imperial Palace, 3535 Las Vegas
Boulevard South. Tel: 731-3311.
Kids eat for less.
The Village Seafood Buffet
Rio, 3700 West Flamingo Rd.
Tel: 252-7777. Fish flown in daily.

Daily 6–11pm.
Teppan tables and a sushi bar.
Tempura, hibachi lobster, steak,
chicken and shrimp. **$$$$**
Shintaro
Bellagio, 3600 Las Vegas Boulevard
South. Tel: 693-7223.
Daily 5.30–10.30pm.
Teppan tables. Enjoy teppanyaki
dinners as well as tuna tartar, Kobe
beef tataki, sushi and Pacific Rim
dishes. **$$$$**
Mizuno's Japanese Steak House
Tropicana, 3801 Las Vegas
Boulevard South.
Tel: 739-2713. Daily 5–10.45pm.
Teppan-style with specialties such
as tempura and hibachi. **$$$**
Osaka Japanese Restaurant
4205 West Sahara Avenue.
Tel: 876-4988
also at 7511 West Lake Mead
Boulevard. Tel: 869-9494.
Monday–Friday 11.30am–midnight,
weekend 5pm–midnight.
Outstanding sashimi and sushi.

There are also tatami rooms and
hibachi tables. **$$$**
Dragon Sushi
Chinatown Plaza, 4215 West Spring
Mountain Road. Tel: 368-4328.
Sunday–Thursday 11.30am–
10.30pm, Friday–Saturday till 12pm.
Has a large sushi bar, featuring live
seafood delivered daily. **$$**
Nobu
Hard Rock Hotel, 4455 Paradise
Road. Tel: 693-5090. Daily 6–11pm.
One of five Nobu Matsuhisa's
worldwide. The sashimi has South
American flair, and the menu
features Kobe beef carpaccio and
tiradito with chili paste, cilantro and
the yuzu/lemon juices give an
intriguing twist to Japanese fare. **$$**
Sushi House Manda
230 West Sahara Avenue. Tel: 382-
6006. Monday–Friday 11.30am–
1pm, Sunday–Thursday dinner
5–9.30pm, Friday–Saturday till
10.30pm. Offers 51 types of sushi
and all you can eat in one hour. **$$**

Sushi King

Stardust, 3000 Las Vegas Boulevard South. Tel: 732-6111. Daily 6pm–2am. Fresh sashimi and sushi, as well as yaki shitake and tempura. **$$**

Themed Dining

Buccaneer Bay Club
Treasure Island, 3300 Las Vegas Boulevard South. Tel: 894-7223. Daily 5–10pm.
Dine from an American continental menu as a sea battle takes place before your eyes. **$$$**

Caesars Magical Empire
Caesars Palace, 3570 Las Vegas Boulevard South. Tel: 731-7333. Tuesday–Saturday, 4:30–10pm.
An elaborate, multi-chambered castled dining theme that presents mystery, fine dining and fun. **$$$$**

ESPN Zone
New York-New York, 3790 Las Vegas Boulevard South. Tel: 933-3776. Monday–Friday 11am–midnight; Thursday–Friday bar and arena until 2am; Saturday 9am–1am (bar and arena until 2am); Sunday 9am–midnight. 150 screens featuring nothing but sport. Meals and snacks. **$$**

Harley Davidson Café
3725 Las Vegas Boulevard South. Tel: 740-4555. Sunday–Thursday 11am–11pm, Friday–Saturday 11am–12am.
In addition to over 15 custom motorcycles including Elvis Presley's, a conveyor belt displays seven of the latest Harley Davidson models. Serves American road food. **$$**

House of Blues
Mandalay Bay, 3950 Las Vegas Boulevard South. Tel: 632-7607. Sunday–Wednesday 8am–midnight, Friday–Sunday 8am–1am. Weekend blues band 10pm–1am. Gospel Brunch 10am and 1pm.
Southern/blues-themed restaurant, featuring regional cuisine including Creole and Cajun staples such as jambalaya and gumbo. On Sunday it hosts live gospel music and an amazing buffet. **$$$**

Nascar Café
Sahara, 2535 Las Vegas Boulevard South.

Tel: 737-2111. Daily 11am–10pm
Two-level restaurant features NASCAR stock cars, huge screens showing racing and NASCAR merchandise. American food. **$$**

Quark's Bar and Restaurant
Las Vegas Hilton, 3000 Paradise Road. Tel: 697-8725. Daily 11am–11pm.
Part of *Star Trek The Experience*. The Trekkie-inspired environment features futuristic-looking metallic furniture and costumed employees. Snack on gummy worms, or enjoy a *Star Trek*-inspired menu. **$$**

Rainforest Café
MGM Grand, 3799 Las Vegas Boulevard South. Tel: 891–8580. Sunday–Thursday 8am–11pm, Friday–Saturday 8am–midnight.
The restaurant is decorated with jungle trees, flowers and rainforest animals. You'll even hear the sounds of the rainforest, including a tropical storm, while you dine. Menu items include appetizers, pastas, salads, sandwiches and desserts. Visit the Magic Mushroom Bar to find a selection of specialty drinks. **$$**

WB Stage 16
Venetian, 3355 Las Vegas Boulevard South.
Tel: 414-1699. Daily 11am–11pm
Dine "on the set" of *Casablanca*, *Ocean's 11*, *Batman* and *Gold Diggers*, complete with backdrops, stage sets, movable props and other effects. Feast on Mediterranean, Asian, European and traditional American cuisine. House specialties include such delicious fare as barbecued duck spring rolls, lobster strudel, mango-cactus pear jam, and grilled chicken-and-apricot kabobs. **$$$**

Food without Tears

Kids go crazy over Las Vegas' themed eateries, which are probably the most advanced in the world. Buffets are useful for families, too, because there tends to be a smaller all-you-can eat charge for kids; sometimes they even get to dine for free.

Nightlife

Vegas' nightlife is the heartbeat of the city. Aside from gaming and the shows at the hotels and resorts, there are many lounge acts, nightclubs and dance halls. In Las Vegas, you must be 21 or older to frequent nightclubs, casinos and bars. For a select list of gay clubs, see page 326.

Comedy

Catch a Rising Star Comedy Club
Excalibur, 3850 Las Vegas Boulevard South. Tel: 597-7777 or 800/937-7777. Fax: 597-7009. www.excaliburcasino.com
Presenting a new show every week.

Comedy Stop at the Trop
Tropicana Resort and Casino, 3801 Las Vegas Boulevard South. Tel: 739-2222 or 800/634-4000. Fax: 739-2469. www.tropicanalv.com
Nightly. Some of the best comedians in the country.

Crazy Benny's X treme Comedy
Howard Johnson's, 3111 West Tropicana Avenue. Tel: 360-5576. Nightly, reservations required. Crazy Benny puts on an outrageous, unpredictable adult comedy show.

Dr Naughty: X-rated Comedy Hypnotist, Bourbon Street, 120 East Flamingo Road. Tel: 228-7591. Monday–Saturday nights. Not for the faint hearted, an adult show.

Hip Nosis: Playin' with your Head, O'Shea's, 3555 Las Vegas Boulevard South. Tel: 737-1343. Every night hypnotist Justin Tranz has fun presenting an adult act.

I Love Lafong
Bourbon Street, 120 East Flamingo Road. Tel: 228-7591. Nightly. Impersonations of stars, ventriloquist comedy and more.

Improv Comedy Club
Harrah's, 3475 Las Vegas

Boulevard South. Tel: 369-5111 or 800/392-9002. www.harrahs.com Tuesday–Sunday nights. Presenting some of the new faces in comedy.

Riviera Comedy Club
Riviera Hotel and Casino, 2901 Las Vegas Boulevard South. Tel: 794-9433. www.theriviera.com
This is the original comedy showcase in Las Vegas.

The Second City
Flamingo Las Vegas, 3555 Las Vegas Boulevard South. Tel: 733-3111. www.flamingolasvegas.com
Tuesday–Sunday, plus additional shows some evenings. Second City has been a starting point for many American comedy actors, writers and directors including Joan Rivers, Dan Akyroyd, John Candy and John Belushi. Enjoy some of the finest improvisational comedians.

Live Entertainment

The Bar at Times Square
New York-New York, 3790 Las Vegas Boulevard South. Tel: 740-6969. Features dueling pianos.

Blue Note
3663 Las Vegas Boulevard South. Tel: 862-8307. One of New York City's finest jazz clubs has a branch on the Strip, presenting some of the best live acts in town.

Carnival Court
Harrah's, 3475 Las Vegas Boulevard South. Tel: 369-5111. Admission free. Enjoy live bands throughout the day and into the late wee hours.

Club Rio
3700 West Flamingo Road, Tel: 252-7777. Wednesday–Saturday. Live entertainment and celebrity DJs at one of Las Vegas' hottest music, dance and video clubs.

Drink
200 East Harmon. Tel: 796-5519. With numerous dance floors and rooms, music and concerts. There is a small cover charge.

House of Blues
Mandalay Bay, 3950 Las Vegas Boulevard South. Tel: 632-7600. Nightly, live entertainment including high-class performers like the Blues Brothers, Sheryl Crow and Bob Dylan. Book early for big stars.

Tickets

Tickets for big shows can be purchased online at:
www.vegas.com
www.lasvegas.com
www.lasvegasshows.com

The Joint
Hard Rock Hotel, 4475 Paradise Road. Tel: 693-5000.
Big-name entertainment and the Hard Rock Center Bar.

Kickin' Back Lounge
Key Largo Casino and Hotel, 377 East Flamingo Road. Tel: 733-7777. Live entertainment nightly.

La Piazza, Cleopatra's Barge, Caesars Palace, 3570 Las Vegas Boulevard South. Tel: 731-7110. Listen or dance nightly to live acts.

La Playa Lounge
Harrah's, 3475 Las Vegas Boulevard South. Tel: 369-5111. Admission is free for the music of live bands every day and night.

Lagoon Saloon
The Mirage, 3400 Las Vegas Boulevard South. Tel: 791-7111. Nightly. Piano bar and saloon.

Le Cabaret
Paris Las Vegas, 3655 Las Vegas Boulevard South. Tel: 946-7000. Live entertainment show lounge.

Loading Dock Lounge
Palace Station Hotel, 2411 West Sahara. Tel: 367-2411. Varied and often interesting music to listen and to dance to.

Mardi Gras Room
Castaways, 2800 Fremont Street. Tel: 398-9123. Nightly. Live entertainment.

Minstrels Lounge
Excalibur, 3850 Las Vegas Boulevard South. Tel: 597-7777. Two live bands for listening or dancing, and a video poker bar.

Napoleon's
Paris, 3655 Las Vegas Boulevard South. Tel: 946-7000. Enjoy live music as well as the cigar and pipe lounge, with collections of fine cognac and cigars.

Nefertiti's Lounge
Luxor, 3900 Las Vegas Boulevard South. Tel: 262-4000. Live entertainment and dance.

Nightclub at Las Vegas Hilton
3000 Paradise Road. Tel: 732-5755. Wednesday–Sunday 11pm–2am. No cover charge for dancing to some of the city's best bands.

The Railhead
Boulder Station, 4111 Boulder Highway. Tel: 432-7777. Live headline entertainment with free blues on Monday.

Rain
The Palms, 4321 West Flamingo Road. Tel: 942-7777. This impressive, enormous venue is a concert hall, a nightclub and a special-events facility.

Roundtable Showroom
The New Frontier, 3475 Las Vegas Boulevard South. Tel: 794-8200. Two different shows performing at any time.

Nightclubs

Baby's Nightclub
Hard Rock Hotel, 4475 Paradise Road. Tel: 693-5000. Thursday–Saturday. Men pay; women are allowed in free.

The Beach
365 Convention Center Drive. From 10pm. A popular singles party place that occasionally presents live concerts.

C2K Mega Club
The Venetian, 3355 Las Vegas Boulevard South. Tel: 933-4225. Wednesday–Sunday 11pm–dawn. One of Las Vegas' hottest dance clubs. Men pay more in admission than women.

Coyote Ugly Bar and Dance Saloon
New York-New York, 3790 Las Vegas Boulevard South. Tel: 212-8804. Nightly from 4pm. Hot nightspot with bar-top dancing and fire-breathing coyotes.

Gilley's Dance Hall
New Frontier, 3120 Las Vegas Boulevard South. Tel: 794-8200. Nightly from 4pm. Dance to Country & Western music, try to ride a mechanical bull, and participate in crazy contests.

Light
Bellagio, 3600 Las VegasBoulevard South. Tel: 693-7111. Thur through Sun until around 4am.

State-of-the-art sound and lighting, with Top 40 hits and dance music. A sophisticated atmosphere, two bars and two VIP areas.

Ra
Luxor, 3900 Las VegasBoulevard South. Tel: 262-4000.
Outstanding sound and lighting system, two full bars, a dance floor, stage and a live DJ. One of Las Vegas' liveliest nightspots.

Rumjungle
Mandalay Bay, 3950 Las Vegas Boulevard South. Tel: 632-7408. From 11pm. Interactive entertainment and dining, with volcanic mountains of rum rising in the illuminated bar. Various music from salsa to romantic, techno to hip hop. "Tasteful" attire only.

Shadow
Caesars Palace, 3570 Las Vegas Boulevard South. Tel: 731-7110. Afternoons during the week and weekend evenings, enjoy cocktails, appetizers and top-shelf liquor while viewing silhouetted dancers performing behind a sheer screen.

Studio 54
MGM Grand, 3799 Las Vegas Boulevard South. Tel: 891-1111. Tuesday–Saturday until the early mornings, enjoy a two-story dance club blending cutting-edge house music with the latest pop rock. Beautiful women swing over the dance floor releasing a shower of glitter on dancers below. Distinctive acts nightly.

Cocktail Lounges

All the Las Vegas hotel and casino venues have a lounge, as do most of the restaurants. These are a few with different atmospheres.

Bix's
4455 South Buffalo. Tel: 889-0800. Upscale in both atmosphere and crowd, it has a classy bar and well-decorated tables. Bix's also has wine and cigar rooms.

Blue Agave Oyster and Chili Bar
Fiesta Casino Hotel, 2400 Rancho Drive. Tel: 631-7000.
Cantina style, with an oyster and chili bar. Features over 200 tequilas and 300 margaritas for high spirits – in more ways than one.

Ghostbar
The Palms, 4321 West Flamingo. Tel: 942-7777.
An indoor and outdoor lounge on the 55th floor with tremendous views attracting a stylish crowd.

J.C. Woolooughan
JW Marriott, 221 North Rampart. Tel: 869-7725. Irish pub open all day Saturday and Sunday as well as each evening.

Hideaway Lounge
Treasure Island, 3300 Las Vegas Boulevard South. Tel: 894-7111. Daily. Call for times.

Velvet Lounge
Warner Bros. Stage 16, The Venetian, 3355 Las Vegas Boulevard South. Tel: 414-1699. Daily Wednesday–Saturday from 3pm, live music 6–10pm. Fantastic view of the Strip in a candlelit atmosphere. Food available.

Gambling Terms

- **Comp:** complimentary, or free.
- **Whale or high roller:** a customer who has the bankroll to wager large sums of money. A whale may be flown to Las Vegas aboard a private casino jet and given comp food and accommodations.
- **Shooter:** the individual who is rolling the dice at a craps table.
- **Shoe:** the small box on a live casino game table from which the dealer deals the cards. There are generally several decks of cards in a shoe.
- **Drop box:** a box locked on to the bottom of a casino game table where dealers deposit paper money through a slot on top of the table.
- **Toke:** a tip or gratuity.
- **Pit boss:** the person who oversees numerous table games from behind the dealers.
- **Eye in the sky:** mirrors or dark glass protuberances that decorate casino ceilings concealing people or video cameras that are monitoring table games (dealers and gamblers) to prevent cheating.

Shopping

Las Vegas' array of shopping prospects spans the spectrum from the merely affordable to the lavishly expensive. Major casinos try to outdo each other with their shopping arcades, but there are loads of shopping possibilities everywhere. The tax on goods in Clark County is 8.25 percent.

Shopping Malls

Some of the best shopping in Las Vegas can be found in the huge malls, many of which include entertainment and dining facilities. At the time of going to press, all the stores here have premises in the mall or shopping arcade listed, but if you're interested in a specific shop, be sure to call ahead first or check the web to make sure it has not moved.

Belz Factory Outlet World
7400 Las Vegas Boulevard South at Warm Springs Road. Tel: 896-5599. www.belz.com
Burlington Brands, Calvin Klein, Casual Corner, Famous Footwear, Jones New York, Levis, Nike, Osh Kosh B'Gosh Pfaltzgraff, Reebok.

Boulevard Mall
3528 South Maryland Parkway (between Flamingo and Desert Inn roads). Tel: 732-8949. www.malibu.com. 10am-9pm.
Charlotte Russe, Dillards, The Children's Store, Footlocker, Gap, JC Penny, Victoria's Secret, Macy's, Marshalls and Sears.

Desert Passage at the Aladdin
3667 Las Vegas Boulevard South. Tel: 876-0710.
www.desertpassage.com
Ann Taylor Loft, bebe, Build-A-Bear Workshop, Cutter & Buck, Illuminations, North Beach Leather,

Sephoria, Sur la Table, Tommy's Bahama, Z Gallerie.

Fashion Outlets of Las Vegas
Primm, Nevada (around 35 miles/ 56 km south of Las Vegas on Interstate 15). Tel: 702-874-1400. www.fashionoutletlasvegas.com Versace, Banana Republic Factory Store, DKNY, Gap, Burberry, Last Call from Neiman Marcus, Polo Ralph Lauren, Williams Sonoma Marketplace, Tommy Bahama, Coach, Escado.

Fashion Show Mall
3200 Las Vegas Boulevard South (at Spring Mountain Road). Tel. 369-0704. www.thefashionshow.com Ann Taylor, Dillards, Louis Vuitton, Macy's, Neiman Marcus, Robinsons-May, Saks Fifth Avenue, The Sharper Image, Victoria's Secret and Williams-Sonoma.

Forum Shops at Caesars
3500 Las Vegas Boulevard South (adjacent to Caesars Palace). Tel: 893-4800. www.shopsimon.com Armani, Bertolini's, Christian Dior, The Cheesecake Factory, The Disney Store, Estée Lauder, FAO Schwartz, Ferragamo, Bucci, Hugo Bass, Virgin Records Megastore, Fendi, Polo and Guess.

Galleria at Sunset
1300 West Sunset Road (intersection of Sunset/Stephanie Roads, Henderson). Tel. 434-0202. www.galleriaatsunset.com Ann Taylor, bebe, Chevy's, Dillards, Eddie Bauer, JC Penny, Juxtapose, Limited Too, Mervyn's California, Gap and Victoria's Secret.

Grand Canal Shoppes
3355 Las Vegas Boulevard South (in The Venetian Hotel/Casino). Tel: 414-4500. www.venetian.com Canyon Ranch Spa Club, Burberry, Davidoff, Sephora, Ann Tylor, Banana Republic, bebe, Lladro, Movada and the eatery Postrio.

Meadows Mall
4300 Meadows Lane (Valley View Boulevard and Meadows Lane). Tel: 878-4849. American Eagle Outfitters, Bath & Body Works, Charlotte Russe, Dillards, Express, Gap, Children's Place, JC Penny, Macy's, Pac Sun and Sears.

Clothes Chart

The chart listed below gives a comparison of United States, European and United Kingdom clothes sizes. It is always a good idea, however, to try on any article before buying it, as sizes between manufacturers can vary enormously.

● **Women's Dresses/Suits**

US	Continental	UK
6	38/34N	8/30
8	40/36N	10/32
10	42/38N	12/34
12	44/40N	14/36
14	46/42N	16/38
16	48/44N	18/40

● **Women's Shoes**

US	Continental	UK
4½	36	3
5½	37	4
6½	38	5
7½	39	6
8½	40	7
9½	41	8
10½	42	9

● **Men's Suits**

US	Continental	UK
34	44	34
—	46	36
38	48	38
—	50	40
42	52	42
—	54	44
46	56	46

● **Men's Shirts**

US	Continental	UK
14	36	14
14½	37	14½
15	38	15
15½	39	15½
16	40	16
16½	41	16½
17	42	17

● **Men's Shoes**

US	Continental	UK
6½	—	6
7½	40	7
8½	41	8
9½	42	9
10½	43	10
11½	44	11

Resort Shopping

Most the larger resort casinos have shopping areas that provide guests with almost everything they'll need, but a boutique in a hotel other than your own may have the perfect souvenir to remind you of your Las Vegas visit. Most of the shops open at 10am, and close 5pm–10pm.

Appian Way
Caesars Palace, 3570 Las Vegas Boulevard South. Tel: 731-7110. Some of the finest boutiques and shops, including Cartier Jewelry.

Avenue Shoppes
Bally's, 3645 Las Vegas Boulevard South. Tel: 739-4111 www.ballyslv.com Specialty, clothing and jewelry stores.There's also a wedding chapel and three restaurants.

Carnaval Court
Harrah's, 3475 Las Vegas Boulevard South. Tel: 369-5000. www.harrahs.com The Art of Gaming, Carnaval Corner, Jackpot and Ghirardelli Chocolates.

Circus Circus Shops
2880 Las Vegas Boulevard South. Tel: 734-0410. www.circuscircus.com An array of good shopping including Marshall Rousso, and other stores featuring gifts, clothing, ceramics, jewelry and souvenirs.

Excalibur Stores
3850 Las Vegas Boulevard South. Tel: 597-7777. www.excaliburcasino.com Excalibur Shoppe, Castle Souvenirs, Gifts of the Kingdom, Spirit Shoppe, Dragon's Lair and Desert Shoppe.

Las Vegas Hilton Stores
3000 Paradise Road. Tel: 732-5111. www.lvhilton.com Kidz Clubhouse, Candy Mania, Paradise Gift Shop, Landau Jewelers, Charisma Apparel and Footwear, Sports Zone Arcade, Ozone Business and Regis Salon.

Palms Promenade
The Regent Las Vegas, 221 North Rampart Boulevard. Tel: 869-7777. www.regentlasvegas.com Jewelry by Berger and Son, eyewear by Occhiali, the Markman Gallery and Tolstoys.

Shopping le Boulevard
Paris Las Vegas, 3655 Las Vegas Boulevard South. Tel: 967-7000. www.parislasvegas.com
Upscale French retail outlets fronting quaint cobblestone streets.

The Shopping Promenade
Treasure Island, 3300 Las Vegas Boulevard South. Tel: 894-7111. www.treasureisland.com
Toiletries to designer fashions.

Starlane Shops
MGM Grand, 3799 Las Vegas Boulevard South. Tel: 891-7777. www.mgmgrand.com
Emerald City, Houdini Magic, Harley-Davidson, Pearl Factory.

Tower Shops
Stratosphere, 2000 Las Vegas Boulevard South. Tel: 380-7777. Everything from gifts to clothing, souvenirs to novelties.

The Street of Dreams
Monte Carlo, 3400 Las Vegas Boulevard South. Tel: 791-7777. www.montecarlo.com
Fine jewelry, designer clothing, eyewear and souvenir boutiques.

The Street of Shops
Mirage, 3400 Las Vegas Boulevard South. Tel: 791-7111. www.mirage.com
Childrenswear, swimwear, jewelry, casual wear and designer attire.

Via Bellagio
Bellagio, 3600 Las Vegas Boulevard South. Tel: 693-7111. www.bellagio.com .
Chanel, Armani, Prada, Tiffany, Moschino, Hermes, Gucci.

Specialist Shops

The Attic
1018 South Main Street. Tel: 388-4088. Massive collection of vintage clothes and knick-knacks.

Gamblers General Store
800 South Main Street. Tel: 382-9903. Slot machines, gaming videos. etc.

Gamblers Book Shop
630 South 11th Street. Tel: 382-7555.

Tower/Good Guys WOW! Store
4580 West Sahara Tel: 364-2500. Huge electronics and CD emporium.

Sport

Las Vegas is a sports enthusiast's playground. Lake Mead's deep blue waters and 550 miles (885 km) of shoreline provide a recreation center for all types of outdoor activities including scuba diving, swimming, boating, water skiing and fishing.

Golf

Golf is almost as much a part of Las Vegas history as is gaming. There are enough challenging courses to make the sport the main reason to visit. Here is a selection of those open to the public:

Angel Park
100 South Rampart Boulevard. Tel: 254-4653 or 888/851-4114 www.angelpark.com
Two 18-hole Arnold Palmer courses and one par-3 course featuring holes with similar shot values as at the world's most famous par 3s.

Badlands
9119 Alta Drive. Tel: 382-4653, 800/468-7918. www.americangolf.com
Two-time PGA winner Johnny Miller designed Badlands in consultation with Chi Chi Rodriguez, with three nine-hole courses.

Bali Hai
3220 East Flamingo Road. Tel: 450-8000 or 888/397-2499 www.waltersgolf.com
Located near the south end of the Las Vegas Strip, the course has numerous water features, towering palms and tropical plants.

Bear's Best
1635 Village Circle. Tel: 385-8500 Jack Nicklaus recreated 18 of his most famous holes worldwide.

Black Mountain
500 Greenway Road, Henderson. Tel: 565-7933.

www.golfblackmountain.com
In the shadow of Black Mountain, this par-72 course is one of the oldest in the city.

Callaway
6730 Las Vegas Boulevard South. Tel: 896-4100. www.callawaygolfcenter.com
This facility features a 113-stall driving range, Callaway performance center, St Andrews golf shop and a lit par-3 golf course.

Craig Ranch
628 West Craig Road, North Las Vegas. Tel: 642-9700. With thousands of trees, this 72-par course is a local favorite.

Desert Pines
3415 East Bonanza Road. Tel: 450-8000 or 888/397-2499. www.waltersgolf.com
Just 15 minutes from the Strip, Desert Pines offers a country club experience with more than 4,000 pines and white-sand bunkers.

Desert Rose
5483 Club House Drive. Tel: 431-4653. www.americangolf.com
A county facility with narrow fairways and smooth greens.

Eagle Crest
2203 Thomas Ryan Boulevard. Tel: 240-1320. www.suncitygolf.com
Perfect for quick rounds in under three hours, the Summerlin course has an executive layout.

Las Vegas Golf Club
4300 W. Washington Avenue. Tel: 646-3000. www.americangolf.com
There are several reachable par-5s on this par-72 layout. The oldest in Las Vegas, it's one of the busiest.

Las Vegas National
1911 East Desert Inn Road. Tel: 796-0013. www.americangolf.com
This par-71 has hosted several LPGA and PGA Tour events. It is a traditional-style course with a lit range and lessons available.

Las Vegas Paiute Resort
10325 Nu-Wav Kaiv Boulevard. Tel: 658 1400 or 888/921-2833 www.lvpaiutegolf.com
Owned and operated by Southern Paiute Indians at the base of Mount Charleston, three challenging nationally acclaimed courses.

Legacy
130 Par Excellence Drive, Henderson. Tel: 897-2187 or 888/851-4114.
www.thelegacygolf.com
The Devil's Triangle, a three-hole series on the back nine, can make or break the round on this par-72.

Painted Desert
5555 Painted Mirage Road. Tel: 546-2570. www.americangolf.com
A rugged and arid 18-hole desert-style course.

Reflection Bay
75 Montelago Boulevard, Henderson. Tel: 740-4653.
www.lakelasvegas.com
A Jack Nicklaus-designed par-72 course on the shore of the man-made Lake Las Vegas.

Revere at Anthem
2600 Hampton Road, Henderson
Tel: 259-4653.
Designed by Billy Casper and Greg Nash, the Revere flows down a natural desert canyon.

Rio Secco
2851 Grand Hills Drive.
Tel: 889-2400. www.playrio.com
Said to be one of the world's top golf resorts, the 7,000-yard (6,700-meter) course is frequented by Tiger Woods and is home to the Butch Harmon School of Golf.

TPC at The Canyons
9851 Canyon Run Drive.
Tel: 256-2000. www.pgatour.com
This beautiful desert course is host to the Invensys Classic at Las Vegas, the first professional PGA tournament won by Tiger Woods.

Tennis

There are hundreds of tennis courts in Las Vegas. Andre Agassi, who was born and raised here, learned how to play in the desert heat of Southern Nevada. Many casinos have courts and offer lessons, while numerous courts throughout the metropolitan area are free.

CASINO COURTS

Bally's/Paris
3645 Las Vegas Boulevard South.
Tel: 739-4111. Ten outdoor courts,
seven of which are lit. Non guests pay slightly more than guests.

Flamingo Las Vegas
3555 Las Vegas Boulevard South.
Tel: 733-3444. Four lit outdoor courts on the northeast of the hotel. Reasonable fees considering it's the Strip.

Las Vegas Hilton
3000 Paradise Road. Tel: 732-5648. Six courts with four lit on the pool deck area. For guests only.

Monte Carlo
3770 Las Vegas Boulevard South.
Tel: 730-7777. Four lit courts, all open to the public. The fee is fairly reasonable.

Jackie Gaughan's Plaza
No. 1 Main Street. Tel: 386-2110.
Four lit courts Downtown. Call for reservations and fees.

Riviera Hotel
2901 Las Vegas Boulevard South.
Tel: 734-5110. Lit courts. Guests of the hotel play for free; non guests allowed for a fee.

PUBLIC COURTS

There are numerous public parks around the metropolitan area that have tennis courts available to the public. Many are free of charge when the park is open (generally 7am–11pm daily). They are usually on a first-come first-serve basis, and players simply drive around and look for an open court.

Lorenzi Park Courts
3075 West Washington Avenue.
Tel: 229-4867. Reservations are recommended for these eight lit courts. There is a fee charged.

Paradise Park
4770 South Harrison. Tel: 455-7777. Two free lit courts on Tropicana Avenue just east of Eastern Avenue.

Sunset Park
2601 East Sunset Road. Tel: 260-9803. Located east of Las Vegas Boulevard South, there are eight lit courts. call for opening hours, reservations and cheap prices.

YMCA
4141 Meadows Lane. Tel: 877-9622. Lessons are available at this
public facility which has five lit courts at a small fee.

Paul Meyer Park and Community Center 4525 New Forest Drive.
Tel: 455-7723.

Sunrise Park/Community Center
2240 Linn Lane. Tel: 455-7600.

Whitney Park, Community and Senior Center 5700 Missouri Street. Tel: 455-7573.

Winchester Park and Community Center 3130 South McLeod Street.
Tel: 455-7340.

Skiing

Las Vegas Ski & Snowboard Resort
Office: 3620 North Rancho Drive Suite 103. Resort: Highway 156 Lee Canyon, Mount Charleston.
Tel: 645-2754; Fax: 645-3391.
Snow report: 593-9500.
www.skilasvegas.com
Around 35 miles (56 km) northeast of Vegas off Highway 95, this resort is open from around Thanksgiving to Easter. Fees and hours vary.

Cedar Breaks Lodge
P.O. Box 190248, Brian Head, Utah 84719. Tel: 888-282-3327.
www.cedarbreakslodge.com
A major ski resort in southern Utah around four hours' drive north of Las Vegas on Interstate 15. Several lifts, resort area and rooms.

Elk Meadows
P.O. Box 511, Beaver, Utah 84713.
Tel: 435-438-5433.
www.elkmeadows.com
Around five hours north of Las Vegas on Interstate 15, a small resort famous for its powder.

Water Skiing/Sailing

In winter it is possible to ski in the morning on Mount Charleston, then water ski in the afternoon on Lake Mead. Most, however, would prefer to leave water skiing until the water warms up to 85°F (30°C), which is generally around the first of June.

Forever Resorts
Callville Bay, Lake Mead
Cottonwood Cove, Lake Mohave
Tel: 800/255-5561.
These two marinas rent everything from luxurious houseboats to

Hiking and Camping

Hiking and camping are a wonderful way to experience Southern Nevada outside the dark gaming dens of Sin City.

Some of the larger casinos in Las Vegas maintain RV parking lots in town where visitors driving RVs are encouraged to stay, but there are also some spectacular camping areas around Las Vegas

that highlight the desert side of the city. Most of the marinas at Lake Mead also operate camping areas for a nominal fee.

The US Forest Service on Mount Charleston maintains some outstanding camping areas and trails that can take adventurous guests up to heights of 11,819 ft (36,000 meters). The temperature

on Mount Charleston is generally much, much cooler than in Las Vegas and so can be a welcome retreat from the heat. The mountain is home to unique vegetation and animal life. During a stay on the mountain, it's not uncommon for campers to spot deer, elk, coyote, squirrels or a number of different types of birds.

---

powerboats. Prices very greatly based on the time of year, availability and size of the boat.

Las Vegas Bay Marina
Las Vegas Bay, Lake Mead Drive. Tel: 565-9111. Houseboats, tracker patio boats, Bayliner ski boats and personal watercraft can be rented. There is a restaurant and lounge.

Seven Crown Resorts
Tel: 800/752-9669. Two resorts specialize in luxury houseboats, but also offer a marina, restaurant and lounge and banquet/meeting facilities. The small, quaint hotel at Echo Bay Marina is on the shore of Lake Mead.

Echo Bay Resort
North Shore Road at Lake Mead. Marina and RV Park. Tel: 394-4000.

Lake Mead Resort and Marina
322 Lakeshore Rd., Boulder City. Tel: 293-3484.

Skydiving

Skydive Las Vegas
1401 Airport Road, Suite 4, Boulder City. Tel: 759-3483 or 800/875-934. Fax: 293-5684.
www.skydivelasvegas.com
You can see the Strip, Lake Mead and the Colorado River as you jump. Specializes in first-time jumpers and tandem jumps with a 46-second freefall at 200 mph (322 kph).

Las Vegas Gravity Zone
Tel: 456-3802.
A family-owned school for first-time jumpers. Member of the U. Parachute Association.

Flyaway Indoor Skydiving
200 Convention Center Drive. Tel: 731-4768.
www.flyawayindoorskydiving.com

Cycling

Downhill Bicycling Tours
7943 Cadenza Lane. Tel: 897-8287. A bus drives riders up to the 8,000 ft (2,438 m) mark on Mount Charleston, and you ride 18 miles back down the mountain through several different layers of desert and mountain environments.

Escape Adventures Mountain Bike and Hiking Tours
8221 West Charleston Suite 101. Tel: 596-2953 or 800/596-2953. www.escapeadventures.com
Providing rental bikes and guides, the company conducts tours to Mt Charleston and Red Rock Canyon.

Red Rock Downhill Bicycle Tours
1250 American Pacific Drive Suite 1711, Henderson. Tel: 278-7617. Fax: 947-215. Experienced guides lead safaris down Red Rock Canyon on 21-speed mountain bikes.

Horseback Riding

Bonnie Springs Old Nevada
1 Gunfighter Lane, Blue Diamond. Tel: 875-4191. Red Rock riding stables with desert tours available.

Silver State Old West Tours
Tel: 798-7788. Scenic trail including daily guided rides, sunset and sunrise tours, and Western BBQs.

Cowboy Trail Rides
800 North Rainbow Suite 204. Tel: 387-8778. Fax: 248-9336. www.cowboytrailrides.com
Singles to large groups guided on horseback to breathtaking views.

Car Racing

600 Racing Inc
6825 Speedway Boulevard Suite B 102. Tel: 642-4386.

Richard Petty Driving Experience
6975 Speedway Boulevard. Tel: 643-4343.

Derek Daly Academy
7055 Speedway Boulevard. Tel: 643-2126.

Freddie Spencer's High Performance Driving School
7055 Speedway Boulevard. Tel: 643-1099.

Bungee Jumping

A.J. Hackett Bungy
810 Circus Circus Drive. Tel: 385-4321.
www.ajhackett.com.au.

Hot Air Ballooning

Adventure Balloon Tours
P.O. Box 97. Tel: 800-346-6444.
www.smilerides.com

D and R Balloons
3275 Rosanna St. Tel: 248-7609.
www.lasvegasballoonrides.com

The Ultimate Balloon Adventure
2013 Clover Path Street. Tel: 800/793-9278. www.lvhd.com

Rafting

Black Canyon River Raft Tours
1297 Nevada Highway, Boulder City. Tel: 800/696-7238. www.rafts.com

Western River Expeditions
7258 Racquet Club Drive, Salt Lake City, Utah, 84121. Tel: 800/453-7450.
www.westernriver.com

Further Reading

American Billionaire by Richard Hack. Millennium Press, 2001.
The Anza Borrego Desert Region by Lowell and Diana Lindsay. Wilderness Press, 1978.
Behind the Tables by Barney Vinson. Gollehon, Grand Rapids, 1986.
Casino Holiday by Jacques Noir. Oxford Press, Berkeley, 1970.
Chip-Wrecked in Las Vegas by Barney Vinson. Mead Publishing, 1994.
The Dirt Beneath the Glitter: Tales from Real Life Las Vegas edited by Hal K. Rothman and Mike Davis. University of California Press, 2002.
The First 100, edited by A.D. Hopkins & K.J. Evans. Huntington Press, 1999.
Hiking Southern Nevada by Bruce Whitney. Huntington Press, 2000.
Hometown Living Las Vegas Style by Jack Sheehan. Pioneer Publishers, 1992.
How to Win at Gambling by Avery Cardoza. Cardoza Publishing, 1993.
The Las Vegas Pauites: A Short History by John Alley. Las Vegas Tribe of Pauite Indians, 1977.
Loaded Dice by John Soares. Taylor Publishing, 1985.
The Man Who Invented Las Vegas by W.R. Wilkerson III. Ciro's Books, 2000.
The Money and the Power: the Making of Las Vegas and its Hold on America by Sally Dention and Roger Morris. Vintage Books, 2002.
The Mysterious Lands by Ann Haymond Zwinger. Truman Talley Books, 1989.
The New Gambler's Bible by Arthur S. Reber. Three Rivers Press, 1996.
The Players: The Men Who Made Las Vegas edited by Jack Sheehan. University of Nevada Press, 1997.
Resort City in the Sunbelt by Eugene P. Moehring. University of Nevada Press, 2000.
Saints in Babylon: Mormons in Las Vegas by Kenric F. Ward, 2002.

Searchlight: The Camp That Didn't Fail by Harry Reid. University of Nevada Press, 1998.
Smart Casino Gambling by Olaf Vancura. Index Publishing, San Diego, 1996.
Why Shouldn't a Woman Wear Red in a Casino (the 101 Most Asked Questions about Las Vegas and Casino Gambling) by George Joseph. G&E Enterprises, 2001.
Wilderness Emergency by Gene Fear. Survival Education Association, 1972.

Other Insight Guides

IG: California
An in-depth look in words and pictures at America's most fascinating state.

IG: Southern California
The missions, the movie stars and the people of Southern California.

IG: Los Angeles
Captures the energy and glamour of America's movie capital.

IG: New Orleans
Spectacular photographs and local writers document the food, culture, music and fun of The Big Easy.

Compact Guides are mini-encyclopedias for visitors in a hurry.

Pocket Guides offer tailor-made tours and personal recommendations by a local host.

Flexi-maps provide key sites and a laminated finish.

ART & PHOTO CREDITS

Cartographic Editor Zoë Goodwin
Cover Design Tanvir Virdee
Production Linton Donaldson
Picture Research Hilary Genin,
Natasha Babaian, Corrie Wingate

Index

Insight Guides Website
www.insightguides.com

Don't travel the planet alone. Keep in step with Insight Guides' walking eye, just a click away

Insight Guides Website

Insight Guide
South Africa

This 370-page book includes a section detailing South Africa's history, 22 features covering aspects of the country's life and culture, ranging from living without Apartheid to spectacular wildlife, a region by region visitor's guide to the sights, and a comprehensive Travel Tips section packed with essential contact addresses and numbers. Plus many quality photographs and 15 maps.

UK: £16.99 ISBN: 981-234-223-0
US: $22.95 ISBN: 0-88729-445-6

(Note: cover shown may differ in some markets.)

Close Window

INSIGHT GUIDES

The classic series that puts you in the picture

Alaska	Dominican Rep. & Haiti	London	Rio de Janeiro
Amazon Wildlife	Dublin	Los Angeles	Rome
American Southwest	East African Wildlife	Madeira	Russia
Amsterdam	Eastern Europe	Madrid	St Petersburg
Argentina	Ecuador	Malaysia	San Francisco
Arizona & Grand Canyon	Edinburgh	Mallorca & Ibiza	Sardinia
Asia, East	Egypt	Malta	Scandinavia
Asia, Southeast	England	Mauritius Réunion	Scotland
Australia	Finland	& Seychelles	Seattle
Austria	Florence	Melbourne	Sicily
Bahamas	Florida	Mexico	Singapore
Bali	France	Miami	South Africa
Baltic States	France, Southwest	Montreal	South America
Bangkok	French Riviera	Morocco	Spain
Barbados	Gambia & Senegal	Moscow	Spain, Northern
Barcelona	Germany	Namibia	Spain, Southern
Beijing	Glasgow	Nepal	Sri Lanka
Belgium	Gran Canaria	Netherlands	Sweden
Belize	Great Britain	New England	Switzerland
Berlin	Great Railway Journeys	New Orleans	Sydney
Bermuda	of Europe	New York City	Syria & Lebanon
Boston	Greece	New York State	Taiwan
Brazil	Greek Islands	New Zealand	Tenerife
Brittany	Guatemala, Belize	Nile	Texas
Brussels	& Yucatán	Normandy	Thailand
Buenos Aires	Hawaii	Norway	Tokyo
Burgundy	Hong Kong	Oman & The UAE	Trinidad & Tobago
Burma (Myanmar)	Hungary	Oxford	Tunisia
Cairo	Iceland	Pacific Northwest	Turkey
California	India	Pakistan	Tuscany
California, Southern	India, South	Paris	Umbria
Canada	Indonesia	Peru	USA: On The Road
Caribbean	Ireland	Philadelphia	USA: Western States
Caribbean Cruises	Israel	Philippines	US National Parks: West
Channel Islands	Istanbul	Poland	Venezuela
Chicago	Italy	Portugal	Venice
Chile	Italy, Northern	Prague	Vienna
China	Italy, Southern	Provence	Vietnam
Continental Europe	Jamaica	Puerto Rico	Wales
Corsica	Japan	Rajasthan	Walt Disney World/Orlando
Costa Rica	Jerusalem		
Crete	Jordan		
Cuba	Kenya		
Cyprus	Korea		
Czech & Slovak Republic	Laos & Cambodia		
Delhi, Jaipur & Agra	Las Vegas		
Denmark	Lisbon		

The world's largest collection of visual travel guides & maps